T0338225

"This second edition handbook by Dr. Kirby Rosplock is a true gift to our family wealth community. Before her first edition, there was hardly any book we could recommend to those searching for answers. With the advent of this new benchmark, private families and their advisors searching for an integrated guide on family offices need look no further. I continue to highly recommend this thoughtful resource, as private families deserve more clarity and guidance."

—*Thomas R. Livergood,* CEO, *The Family Wealth Alliance;*
Founder, Bespoke Advocate

"Few institutions are changing as fast as family offices. As the global community is transformed and as enterprising families want to do more than shelter their wealth, their concerns for the future lead them to gather and define multiple financial and non-financial activities they want to pursue. The first edition was a treasure of information but in response to the vast changes taking place every day, a second edition adds even greater value by sniffing out the vast shifts that are occurring. This new edition is actually a new piece of work that should take its place beside the first edition as a more current view of practices that are more than just reactions to global change; they are defining the nature of the new global community that is continually being remade."

—*Dennis Jaffe,* PhD, *consultant; advisor; author,* Borrowed from Your Grandchildren: The Evolution of 100-Year Family Enterprises; Cross Cultures: How Global Families Negotiate Change Across Generations; Stewardship in Your Family Enterprise: Developing Responsible Family Leadership Across Generations; and Working with the Ones You Love: Conflict Resolution & Problem Solving Strategies for a Successful Business

"*The Complete Family Office Handbook* provides readers with tactical guidance, serving as a 'how-to' both for families looking into creating an office as well as those evaluating the wealth management structures they have in place. Kirby's willingness to go into detail and her use of case examples demonstrate that while every family office is unique, the factors that go into operational decisions tend to have similarities across different families."

—*Rebekah L. Kohmescher,* CFP®, CPA, CEO, Altair Advisers, LLC

"If you are one of the many executives and family members who bought *The Complete Family Office Handbook* upon my insistence, head back out and get this second edition, as it is probably time to reexamine how your office has (or hasn't) evolved with the family. For those looking to build a new office, this second edition is even more powerful than the first. With expanded content, sharper insights, and more robust examples, it sets the nuanced context, which family members and executives alike need, to make wise decisions capable of aligning the office and the family."

—*Jim Coutré, family office and philanthropy professional*

"Kirby Rosplock has written a book that will become an essential reference for families wishing to establish a long-term strategy for building an enduring legacy across generations. It helps to unwrap the mysteries of the family office and provides an invaluable guide, containing a wealth of cutting-edge information and insights. It is a comprehensive toolkit for any family embarking on the journey of establishing a family office and for executives who operate—or aspire to operate—within a family office."

—**Dominic Samuelson,** CEO, *Campden Wealth*

"With thoughtfulness and clarity, Kirby Rosplock has brought to life the important questions to ask and steps to follow in creating and effectively governing a family office. Wealth owners, and their advisors, will gain insight into why long-term success depends on the ability to clarify shared values, vision, and purpose, at each generation, and how to dive into those challenging conversations."

—**Anne Hargrave,** *consultant and coach to organizations, family businesses, and families of wealth*

"A comprehensive body of work that serves as an immediately useful tool to help families through the uncharted waters of family office formation and operation. As families struggle to find meaning beyond financial wealth, Dr. Rosplock's book addresses the business, family, and philanthropic legacy that family offices can provide. The second edition of *The Complete Family Office Handbook* will be an indispensable tool sitting on the top shelf of your desk. Immensely helpful. "

—**Preston Root,** *Root Glass Company*

"My 2014 copy is full of Post-it notes. *The Complete Family Office Handbook* is current, independent, comprehensive, and compelling. Rosplock's second edition has distilled the wisdom and guidance of all the major experts in the family office world and made it easy to read. I feel comfortable handing this book to CIOs and nonfinancial people alike. She summarizes big issues with great aplomb and catches the important details. A definitive handbook."

—*Joseph Reilly, family office consultant*

THE COMPLETE FAMILY OFFICE HANDBOOK

THE COMPLETE FAMILY OFFICE HANDBOOK

A Guide for Affluent Families
and the Advisors Who Serve Them

SECOND EDITION

Kirby Rosplock, PhD

WILEY

Published by John Wiley & Sons, Inc., Hoboken, New Jersey.
Published simultaneously in Canada.

This book is the second edition and presents research and insights of the family office marketplace gleaned from working independently with clients and families. Not all information and experiences herein may apply, and the views and professional opinions and experiences of the authors and contributors, individuals and family office advisors, should use these opinions and experiences as guideposts and not as hard and fast rules. There are many exceptions to the cases and advisement presented in this book, and each family should work with their team of qualified experts, accountants, and legal advisors to determine the best course of action(s) appropriate to their specific situation(s).

For general information on our other products and services or for technical support, please contact our Customer Care Department within the United States at (800) 762-2974, outside the United States at (317) 572-3993, or fax (317) 572-4002.

Wiley publishes in a variety of print and electronic formats and by print-on-demand. Some material included with standard print versions of this book may not be included in e-books or in print-on-demand. If this book refers to media such as a CD or DVD that is not included in the version you purchased, you may download this material at http://booksupport.wiley.com. For more information about Wiley products, visit www.wiley.com.

Library of Congress Cataloging-in-Publication Data is Available:

ISBN 978-1-119-69400-7 (Hardcover)
ISBN 978-1-119-69409-0 (ePDF)
ISBN 978-1-119-69407-6 (ePub)

Cover image: © Alexandre Olive/Shutterstock
Cover design: Wiley

Printed in the United States of America.
SKY10082734_082324

This book is dedicated to my family, the families involved in writing the book, and families who are seeking clarity on how to preserve, promote, and sustain family wealth.

Contents

CHAPTER 3
Comparing Family Office Solutions: Multi- and Single-Family Offices   53
Kirby Rosplock, PhD

CHAPTER 4
Family Values, Mission, and Vision and the Family Office   83
Kirby Rosplock, PhD

CHAPTER 5
Establishing and Structuring of Family Offices 103
Ivan A. Sacks, Esq., Partner, Withers Bergman LLP
William J. Kambas, Esq., Partner, Withers Bergman LLP

CHAPTER 6

Strategic Planning for the Family Office   139
Kirby Rosplock, PhD

CHAPTER 7

Legal and Compliance Standards and Practices for
Family Offices   167
David S. Guin, Esq., Partner and US Commercial Practice Group Leader,
Withers Bergman LLP

CHAPTER 8

Investment Management and the Family Office 197

Kirby Rosplock, PhD

CHAPTER 9
Family Office Operations and Information Technology   231
John Rosplock, COO and CFO, Tamarind Partners, Inc.
Robert Kaufold, President and Chief Risk Officer, Cauldera LLC

CHAPTER 10
Family Office Talent, Compensation, and Recruitment   257
Kirby Rosplock, PhD

CHAPTER 11
Governance Issues for the Family Office   **285**
Barbara Hauser, JD, Independent Family Advisor
Kirby Rosplock, PhD

CHAPTER 12
Family Education and the Family Office   **311**
Kirby Rosplock, PhD

CHAPTER 13
Family Entrepreneurship and the Family Bank   335
Warner King Babcock
Kirby Rosplock, PhD

CHAPTER 14
Legacy, Philanthropy, and Impact Investing   361
Kirby Rosplock, PhD

CHAPTER 15
Private Trust Companies: Creating the Ideal Trustee   389
Miles Padgett, Partner, Kozusko Harris Duncan
Don Kozusko, Partner, Kozusko Harris Duncan

Foreword

A wise woman once told me, "Jay, the only reason to have resources is so I can have services."

Kirby Rosplock has provided us with a handbook that comprehensively describes the services, both qualitative and quantitative, that family offices of various types can provide to families with resources. A "handbook" is defined by *Webster's Third International Dictionary* as "a concise reference book covering a particular subject of field of knowledge—a manual." Kirby's book is just such a concise reference manual to the field of family office services.

What is the purpose of services provided to families by family offices, regardless of whether the family office is a single-family or multi-family office? The purpose is the removal of obstacles to an individual family member's ability to integrate and use resources normally created by a previous generation of his or her family, toward that individual's greater freedom, thriving, and flourishing. These obstacles, if not removed, may not only lead to the failure to flourish of those individuals, but to the risk of entropy—entropy as entitlement, dependence, and remittance addiction—that leads to the entire families' system failing. These obstacles then become a detriment not only to the dynamic preservation of the individual's and the entire families' financial capital, but, much more importantly, obstacles to the growth of their human, intellectual, social, and spiritual capital.

As Kirby describes, these four capitals require services that are qualitative and substantially more complex to provide than those that serve families' quantitative needs. She makes clear that distinctions between service providers frequently lie along the divide between services that are purely quantitative and those single-family and multi-family offices that offer qualitative services as well.

In my opinion, this distinction is of great importance to a family's success in obtaining the family office services it needs to overcome the obstacles or, one may say, the "risks" to their family that entropy poses.

All of us who serve families seeking to avoid the suffering decreed for a family by the universal cultural proverb "shirt sleeves to shirt sleeves in three generations," in its many iterations, are in Kirby's debt for giving us a concise understanding of the services available to us and to the families we serve. This understanding will assist us to help these families avoid the proverb's sad forecast and the suffering it represents as the bonds of family rupture. How much better to find and use the quantitative and, more importantly, qualitative services a family office offers to help families flourish for many generations through the enhancing of each family member's journey of happiness!

Thanks, Kirby.

James (Jay) E. Hughes, Jr.

Preface

If you are reading this book, you are likely in one of three camps: you are an individual considering the possibility of building or joining a family office, you're an individual with an existing family office and looking for ideas of how to enhance or transform it, or you may be a professional working in wealth management or advising enterprising families who is looking for leading-edge resources to better serve your clients. Whichever category you find yourself in, this second edition book provides you with current knowledge, research, and cutting-edge approaches from thought leaders in the family office industry and gives you real-life examples and experiences to guide you as you envision, plan, and develop your family office. But, before you turn further in the book, you may find it helpful to understand that this book is geared to the *family owners and their offspring*, first and foremost; however, wealth advisors and other professionals may find the commentary and recommendations useful to apply with their families as well.

The first edition of *The Complete Family Office Handbook* was released by Wiley in 2014. Jay Hughes, Jr., who provided the Foreword, and I had conversations to the lack of practical information about how a family office operates, the services it provides, how it is managed, and why they exist in the first place. I never thought I would be the one to try and codify such a massive body of knowledge, but perhaps my curiosity or my hope to solve for similar issues in my own family was the catalyst. Thankfully, the support and wisdom from so many exceptional family office executives and families inspired my drive and determination to see this through to fruition. Our family office consulting firm, Tamarind Partners, Inc. (www.TamarindPartners.com), has been working closely with many notable family offices to carry on the research, knowledge, and advice provided in the first edition.

Fast-forward to 2020, a year that will be forever marked by the worldwide pandemic. Revising the book during a global crisis provides a lot of perspective to consider the permanency of the family office construct as well as how to make it disruption-ready. Yet, this journey to write this second edition book is also deeply personal. As a family member, owner, board member, and a co-trustee of a family foundation, much of the content in this book is germane to me and my family. Since writing the first edition, I experienced a lot of change and witnessed how quickly the family office landscape adapts with new technology, AI, better security, cybersecurity, and new policies and procedures. The second edition also reveals new insights gleaned from working to bridge generational knowledge gaps on the family education front. Tamarind Learning (www.TamarindLearning.com), an education learning solution for families, their offspring, and advisors, was launched in 2019 to solve the learning gap and provide learning paths that are flexible and customizable.

Spending nearly two decades researching and writing in the family business and family office universe, the second edition that follows is a combination of more than 80 interviews with family office executives, family office owners, industry leaders, and family members. Additionally, I reviewed hundreds of articles, books, and research reports and collected data from families in the United States, to Europe, the United Kingdom, the Middle East, Asia, and Australia. Yet, the more I learned along this journey, the more I realized how much there is to learn. As a result, I collaborated with leading attorneys, from Withers Bergman LLP and Kozusko Harris Duncan LLP, independent advisors around governance, family banks, entrepreneurship, family office operations, and information technology. This book provides their wisdom, many years of experience, and thoughtfulness to the important and distinguishable needs of the family office client.

The *Handbook* is laid out in a chronological order. Chapter 1 introduces the family office concept, its purpose and definition, as well as key roles of the family office; Chapter 2 overviews the family office evolution from inception and highlights key archetypes; Chapter 3 compares the multi- and single-family office solutions; Chapter 4 discusses a family's values and how to create a family office mission and vision statement. Chapters 5 and 7 are written by prominent attorneys at Withers Bergman LLP. Chapter 5 provides guidance on family office formation and the legal structuring of a family office. Chapter 6 shares strategic planning considerations, capital sufficiency analysis, and the importance of reviewing the family office fact pattern on topics including estate, financial, wealth transfer, and insurance planning. Chapter 7 clarifies the legal, fiduciary, and compliance requirements for a successful family office today. Chapter 8 reviews the investment management approach of the family office. This chapter discusses investment concentration, measuring success, time horizon, and the investment governance including investment objectives, policies, and committees. Chapter 9, co-authored by two family office experts, discusses family office IT and operations considerations. This chapter offers advancements and best practices in information technology, operations, and risk management to enhance your family office's performance. Chapter 10 expands on family office talent management, best practices with hiring talent, incentivizing, managing, and retaining key employees, compensation, and performance management. Chapter 11, which is co-authored with a leading family office governance expert, discusses family governance, succession planning, and the role of boards, hallmarks of good governance, and applications and process to set up governance. Chapters 12 sheds light on new thinking for family education and the family office, stewardship, psychology of wealth and developing an education plan. Chapter 13, which is co-authored with a leading family bank expert, provides insights to the setup, structuring, and planning to create a family bank and the use of intra-family loans to inspire the next generation wealth holder. Chapter 14 expands and includes discussion on legacy, philanthropy, and impact investing and the family office. Finally, Chapter 15 of the book concludes with a new chapter from leading attorneys from the law firm Kozusko Harris Duncan. The book provides fresh new cases with updated insights to the various attributes of the family office and gives research to the inner workings of some leading family offices. To learn more about Tamarind Partners, Inc. or Tamarind Learning, please visit our websites www.TamarindPartners.com or www.TamarindLearning.com.

Acknowledgments

This book took a village to write and there are many to thank for their support, wisdom, time, introductions, and professional experiences. First to the families and family offices who shared their personal stories—this book is only possible because of your trust. Thank you to my family and especially my husband, John, who provided constant support and encouragement and contributed to Chapter 9. Thank you to Jay Hughes for giving me the courage to take on this task and being an inspiration, advocate, and mentor.

My deepest appreciation for the wisdom and knowledge shared by (in first-name alphabetical order) Abby Raphael, Alex Scott, Allan Zachariah, Amy Braden, Angelo Robles, Ann Kinkade, Anna Nichols, Anne Ethridge, Annette Rahael, Barb Quasius, Barbara Hauser, Benjamin Kinnard, Bill Thomas, Bill Woodson, Bob Casey, Bruce Arella, Carolyn Friend and Jamie Weiner, Carly Doshi, Chad Harbeck, Charles F. Kettering, III, Charlotte Beyer, Chelsea Cannon, Chelsea Toler-Hoffmann, Chris Battifarano, Chris Cincera, Cricket Harbeck, Christin McClave, Christina Burroughs, Claudia Sangster, Clay Mathile, Dan Berg, Daniel Goldstein, Daniel Gottlieb, David Friedman, David Toth, Daisy Medici, David Friedman, David Guin, David Martin, David Lincoln, Dennis Jaffe, Dennis Kessler, Denny Charad, Dianne H.B. Welsh, Dirk Junge, Dominic Samuelson, Don Kozusko, Doug Borths, Doug Dubiel, Drew Mendoza, Ellen Miley Perry, Edouard Thijssen, Edward Marshall, Elizabeth Minkin, Euclid Walker, Fran Lotery, Fredda Herz Brown, Grant Kettering, Greg Curtis, Gregory T. Rogers, Gunther Weil, Hania Hammoud, Hartley Goldstone, Howard Cooper, Ian D'Souza, Iñigo Susaeta Córdoba, Iris Wagner, Ivan Sacks, Jack Parham, Jason Born, James A. Grubman, James E. Hughes, Jr., Jane Flanagan, Jay Totten, Jean Brunel, Jean Case, Jean B. Harbeck, Jennifer Barber, Jennifer Kenning, Jesus Casado, Jim Coutré, Jim Greer, Joanie Bronfman, Joe Calabrese, John A. Warnick, John Benevides, John Carroll, John Davis, John and Eileen Gallo, John Rau, Joline Godfrey, Josh Kanter, Joe Lonsdale, Joni Fedders, Juan Luis Segurado, Juan Meyer, Juan Roure, Judy Green, Julie Zorn, Justin Zamparelli, Karen Neal, Kathryn McCarthy, Kay Berglund, Keith Lender, Keith Whitaker, Kelly

Atkins, Kent Lawson, Kevin Morrissey, Kit Johnson, Laurent Roux, Lee
Hausner, Linda Bourn, Liesel Pritzker Simmons and Ian Simmons, Linda
Mack, Lisa Niemeier, Lisa Ryan, Lyat Eyal, Maria Elena Lagomasino, Mark
Haynes Daniell, Martin Whittaker, Mark Tice, Matt DaCosta, Matt Walker,
Maya Imberg, Michael Black, Michael Sallas, Miles Padgett, Mindy
Kalinowski Earley, Mindy Rosenthal, MJ Rankin, Mykolas Rambus, Nava
Michael Tsabaris, Nazneen Kanga, Norman Smorgon, Olivia Dell, Olivier
Richoufftz, Patricia Angus, Patricia Cole, Paul Cameron, Paul McKibben,
Paul Westall, Peter Carney, Phil Strassler, Preston Root, Preston Tsao, Rachel
Gerrol, Ralph Wyman, Ray Maas, Rebecca Gooch, Rebecca Oertell, Reuben
Vardanyan, Richard Arzania, Rino Schena, Richard Milroy, Richard Sauer,
Rick Fogg, Rick Stone, Robert Kaufold, Robert Danzig, Robin Satyshur, Ron
and Marty Cordes, Ryan Eisenman, Santiago Ulloa, Sara Hamilton, Sean
Davis, Sebastian Lyle, Stephanie and Eric Stephenson, Stephen Campbell,
Stephen Prostano, Steven Hoch, Steve Legler, Steven Weinstein, Steven
Hirth, Susan Massenzio, Susan Remmer Ryzewic, Tayyab Mohamed, Thomas
J. Handler, Esq., Thomas Mahoney, Tom Livergood, Tom McCullough,
Thayer Willis, Tim Brown, Trish Botoff, Ulrich Burkhard, Victoria Vysotina,
Vahe Vartanian, Warner King Babcock, Wayne Osborne, Wendy Spires,
Wendy Craft, Will Froelich, William Kambas, and Zipi Shperling.

CHAPTER 1

Introduction to the Family Office

Kirby Rosplock, PhD

Family offices serve a vast array of functions for a family and their wealth. Those family office functions are commonly bespoke to the needs of the specific family for whom they were designed; therefore, when asked about the definition of what a *family office* is, the answers often vary from person to person. Generally speaking, family offices are designed to prepare family members to collectively manage, sustain, and grow their wealth across multiple generations. Family offices can aid families in managing the numerous risks that accompany affluence. In addition to offering a potentially wide array of services, such as tax, fiduciary, and compliance needs; investment management, risk management, estate planning, and trust administration; philanthropic advisement, financial education programs for family members; and family governance and wealth-transfer planning, the family office ideally has a higher purpose to bridge generations in order to create continuity and cohesion for families around their wealth.

The last decade has featured disruptive turbulence in financial markets, impressive technological and medical advancements, and dramatic shifts in the global landscape. Family offices need to respond to these changes with equally dramatic adaptations if they are to remain relevant and effective. For example, in 1918, the average human life expectancy was roughly 39 years.[1] One hundred years later, the average expectancy was 80.3,[2] and current statistics indicate that approximately 500,000 people around the globe are aged 100 or older. Moreover, the 100-plus population is predicted to almost double with each coming decade.[3] Increases in human longevity mean that family

1

offices, which once operated on the assumption of needing to survive 100 years, now need to plan on surviving 500 years and manage the multiple inter-generational wealth transfers and leadership transitions associated with this kind of longevity. Low-return financial market environments inject additional complexities, requiring that family offices and their staff members develop additional strategies, competencies, and skill sets to support the achievement of the family's multiple objectives. Thus, the aim of this volume is to construct a futurist lens of the family office: Rather than focusing primarily on concerns of luxury, buying, and traditional investing, we propose the 500-year view of the family office and introduce the leading-edge perspectives and practices for how family offices and their staff members can support the coming ultra-lifespan of the families they serve.

This second edition updates the first book that demystified the concept of the family office and clarified who should consider starting their own single-family office or joining a multi-family office. The second edition provides context, updates, and improvements to inform family office setup, structure, and design as owners more clearly define their family office's over-arching purpose and vision. This book provides expanded coverage regarding the types of family offices in existence, along with who owns them and pays for them, and what services may be rendered by the offices. This guide is designed to be a useful tool for affluent families, individuals, and philan-thropists, as well as for practitioners and industry professionals, as it outlines the important functions family offices may render today and for the genera-tions of family members yet to be born.

In this chapter, we review the macro futurist trends in global wealth to pro-vide context for understanding the basis, purpose, and definition of the family office. We then consider the family office's historical roots in Western econo-mies, which is grounded in the growth and proliferation of family enterprise. The roles the family office plays regarding its client families are then discussed.

A Macro View of Global Wealth

Given that family offices exist to help families sustain and grow their wealth and successfully navigate the various risks that come with that endeavor, measuring affluence and understanding affluent families are important first steps. Yet, there is an art and a science to assess affluence, which begins with defining how much you must have to be considered wealthy. While we all have our own definitions, most industry research firms classify individuals with a minimum of $1 million net worth as high net worth (HNW) and individuals with at least $30 million net worth as ultra high net worth

(UNHW). Due to the associated costs and complexities, family offices generally do not become a realistic wealth management solution until families enter the UHNW category. To provide some context, the total population of individuals reporting a net worth exceeding $1 million is currently 22.8 million, with these individuals collectively having a combined net worth of $94.1 trillion.[4] This wealth tends to be concentrated among the upper strata of ultra-wealthy individuals. For example, the world's top 10 wealthiest individuals retain a combined fortune of more than $743.8 billion (all amounts are in US dollars).[5] More telling, the UHNW population collectively holds more than $32 trillion in wealth (34 percent of the total wealth held by individuals with $1 million-plus net worth). This is particularly noteworthy considering that the UHNW population consists of only 265,490 individuals—just 1 percent of all individuals reporting net worth above $1 million.[6] Table 1.1 provides the growth of the UHNW population.

Examining the global distribution of the UNHW population reveals that these individuals predominantly live in the US (accounting for 31 percent of UHNW individuals), followed by China (9 percent) and Japan (nearly 7 percent). In 2018, all seven major world regions recorded declines in ultra-wealth, albeit with regional variation. For example, while the Middle East UNHW population grew 6.8 percent, its wealth fell 0.1 percent. Meanwhile, ultra-wealth in Latin America and the Caribbean dropped by 7.1 percent, and its UNHW population fell by 6 percent. Net worth in Asia fell at a faster rate than in both North America and Europe, with Hong Kong dropping by 11 percent. Moreover, plunging stock markets resulted in Asia's high net worth (HNW) population—individuals with net worth of $1 million to $30 million—growing only 0.6 percent in 2018.[7]

Prominent research firm Wealth-X concentrates solely on understanding the demographics and wealth profile of HNW and UNHW populations. According to Wealth-X, men comprise 86 percent of the UNHW population and retain 90 percent of the wealth, although the proportion of women has trended modestly upward in recent years, to 14.6 percent in 2018. Furthermore, women accounted for nearly 20 percent of the under-50 global ultra-wealthy class, suggesting that shifts in global wealth distribution and intergenerational wealth transfer, cultural attitudes, and tech-driven entrepreneurship have expanded women's opportunities to create wealth.

Asset allocations in 2018 reflected investor caution in the wake of the global financial crisis, tighter monetary policies in some major economies, and slowed growth and tumultuous stock performance around the globe. Specifically, ultra-wealthy portfolios reflected more than one third (36.5 percent) in liquid assets (cash, income, and dividends) as well as an increase in cash-equivalent holdings. Overall shares of private holdings dropped slightly

TABLE 1.1 World by Wealth Tier

World UHNW	2018	2018	2017	2017	Population Change	Total Wealth Change
Net Worth	UHNW Population	Total Wealth (US$ Billion)	UHNW Population	Total Wealth (US$ Billion)		
$1 billion +	2,604	8,562	2,754	9,205	-5.4%	-7.0%
$500 million to $1 billion	4,616	3,755	4,326	3,080	6.7%	21.9%
$250 million to $500 million	10,680	3,656	10,250	3,504	4.2%	4.3%
$100 million to $250 million	39,610	5,938	38,050	5,701	4.1%	4.2%
$50 million to $100 million	81,030	5,558	77,960	5,348	3.9%	3.9%
$30 million to $50 million	126,950	4,836	122,470	4,663	3.7%	3.7%
Total	**265,490**	**32,305**	**255,810**	**31,501**	**3.8%**	**2.6%**

Source: Wealth-X, World Ultra Wealth Report 2018–2019

to less than a third (32.1 percent) in recent years, likely due to regional and country variations in entrepreneurship rates, access to finance, economic development, cultural trends, and attitudes to wealth preservation. Meanwhile, public holdings remained steady at one quarter (25.3 percent) of total assets, although a slight dip was noted due to volatile capital markets and fewer IPOs and M&As in 2018. Alternative assets (e.g., real estate, luxury goods, fine art, yachts, private jets) accounted for the remaining 6.2 percent of UHNW portfolios. Wealth-X credits another shift—the increased population of those with a combination of inherited and self-created wealth—to several factors: (a) the rapid increase of UHNW individuals (and subsequent focus on self-made fortune) across Asia and the Middle East, (b) the rise of UHNW women involvement in business and entrepreneurism, and (c) one of the largest-ever intergenerational transfers of wealth, including significant handovers in China. The scale of intergenerational wealth transfer underway emphasizes the need to assure that family offices are established when required and that those in existence are high functioning.

The primary sectors for the UHNW population are banking and finance (22.9 percent), indicating the key role financial services has played in creating wealth according to a wealth management survey. This was particularly true in liberalized capital markets of the US, Europe, Japan, and Hong Kong. Although revenue growth continues to face challenges in the wake of the global financial crisis, this industry remains a dominant force for both dynamic wealth creation and wealth preservation. Furthermore, the ultra-low interest rate environment has aided wealth gains in consumer and business services as well as in real estate, the next most significant industry among the ultra-wealthy. Specifically, growth of the middle class across the emerging world, given rising incomes, urbanization, and digitization, are driving growth in consumerism and residential investment within these regions. Moreover, tech-driven innovation and the growth in the population of luxury-minded wealthy millennials in Asia and the Middle East create new channels for wealth creation in consumer and business services.

With regard to the 22.4 million individuals comprising the HNW population, three sectors were particularly noteworthy: wealth management, luxury, and philanthropy.[8] In wealth management, significant changes have occurred in recent years, sparked by regulatory changes and concerns for profitability in low-return markets. Moreover, shifts in the global HNW demographics, given the rapidly expanding population of HNWs in Asia, have caused a significant effort to develop or import HNW services locally. China has been a particular focus for the professionalization and development of wealth management services. Asian Private Banker reports that although the five largest wealth managers in the region have seen a 25 percent increase in assets under management, the population of new advisors has grown by only 7 percent,[9] spawning an intense war for talent and more sophisticated talent management programs. One key focus is developing automated financial advisory software and portals, along with other tech-based and hybrid human-tech wealth management offerings in the effort to increase more effective, efficient, and inexpensive solutions. Providers in this arena include such contenders as SigFig, Betterment LLC, and Scalable Capital.

The luxury industry has been subject to ongoing self-examination and reinvention as its players adjust to various imperatives, such as the needs to develop genuinely holistic global brands and build international growth beyond the mushrooming and now highly competitive China market, appeal to "next generation" luxury consumers, and compete effectively in online luxury sales. Notable recent developments include a proliferation of online luxury products, growth of luxury experiences, expansion of multichannel content marketing by luxury brands, and ongoing product and brand innovation.[10]

Although a strong global economy, healthy stock market returns, and rise of digital donation platforms sustained philanthropic giving over most of the previous decade, economic factors such as escalating economic uncertainty and stock market volatility slowed donors' momentum and shifted how nonprofits engage with the HNW population. Thus, although annual charitable giving in the US rose from $340 billion in 2013 to $410 billion in 2017, giving slowed in 2018 to $390–$397 billion (a 3 to 5 percent decline).[11] Regulatory factors fueling the slowdown included tax-related legislation that increased the standard deduction on federal tax returns (and significantly reduced the number of households itemizing deductions for charitable gifts), reduced corporate tax rates, and included exemptions for estates.[12] Nevertheless, HNW individuals' motivations to give (e.g., personal fulfillment, concern for the less fortunate, belief in the cause) remain strong, and donor-advised funds have surpassed private foundations as the fastest-growing charitable giving vehicle, expanding HNW donors' creative options for charitable giving.[13] Wealth-X notes that despite the attention mega donors like Jeff Bezos and Michael Bloomberg receive, HNW donors continue to play key roles in driving philanthropy.[14]

Another notable trend among UHNW individuals is their use of multiple service providers rather than one individual private banking firm, and the proliferation of providers makes the effects of their behavior even more powerful. While UHNW individuals are confident in allocating and managing their own risk capital, they are relying on wealth advisors for managing risks related to their liquid capital. UHNW individuals seek less volatility, for example, how the bond markets have tended to perform, with the return benefits of the equity markets. Private banking professionals and organizations must respond by seeking deep understanding of their clients' needs and the needs of potential clients. For example, new wealthy entrepreneurs tend to want flexible, customizable investment platforms. While this often does not make economic sense for investors with wealth in the $50 to $100 million range, it can be viable if reasonable platforms are identified, and if the family itself can operate it. Such requests demonstrate the growing market for financial advisors who can provide family office–like service at this level.

Related trends, especially notable among self-made UHNW individuals in Asia, are their proactive participation in their wealth management coupled with their expectation of higher returns. Among this population, there is a confidence in wealth creation and a greater appetite for risk. Currently there is a large amount of private wealth in privately owned and family-owned businesses, and an avoidance of public markets. Single-family offices are thus looking for such enterprises for investment opportunities, and those enterprises are seeking entrepreneurs and families that have had success in building businesses to invest in them. They prefer this investment to private equity or venture capital. Wealth-X predicts an increase in liquidity in privately owned businesses, not from IPOs or private equity fund investments but from family to family.

Billionaire Update

Although the billionaire segment showed dramatic gains in 2017, these gains were not sustained in 2018 due to challenges such as slowed growth, pervasive trade tensions, and slumping equity markets. Ultimately, both the global billionaire population and billionaire wealth dropped (5.4 percent and 7 percent, respectively),[15] although regional variations were evident. North America showed a population increase of 3 percent, with a smaller increase of 1 percent across all of the Americas. Nonetheless, billionaire wealth in the Americas still dropped by 6 percent. Of all regions, Asia-Pacific sustained the biggest losses, with a 13 percent reduction in its billionaire population and 9 percent drop in billionaire wealth. The Europe, Middle East, and Africa (EMEA) region registered more moderate declines, with a 5 percent drop in the billionaire population and 7 percent drop in billionaire wealth.

Given regional differences, it is helpful to consider the three archetypes Wealth-X highlights in the billionaire population: 1) philanthropy-focused US billionaires, 2) young, and 3) self-made Chinese billionaires, and family business–focused German billionaires.[16] The US billionaire population is the largest and richest (average net worth of $4.3 billion) of any region, thanks to the nation's robust technology sector, number of large companies, widespread business opportunities, and mature financial services sector. Nearly two thirds (63 percent) of US billionaires are self-made, although a sizable group (18 percent) also inherited their wealth—usually through well-established family-owned businesses. These individuals also are notable for their extensive involvement in nonprofit and social organizations.

The Chinese billionaire population is second largest in the world and younger than any other group: On average, Chinese billionaires are 56 years old (versus 66 years old globally) and nearly a quarter (22 percent) are under 50 (compared to only 10 percent globally). Given the relatively short history of Chinese economic liberalization, private ownership and family-owned businesses, 95 percent of its billionaires are self-made (compared to only 56 percent globally). Key industries for these billionaires include real estate, industrial conglomerates, manufacturing, and technology.

Germany is home to the most billionaires in the EMEA region, and most of this wealth has been created through billionaire-run, family-owned businesses. Of further note, roughly 20 percent of German billionaires are female (compared to only 11.7 percent globally). The long-standing success of these family businesses is evident in that more than 60 percent of German billionaires made their fortunes through a combination of inheritance and self-creation. Figures 1.1 and 1.2 present data on growth of the billionaire population.

FIGURE 1.1 World by Wealth Tier

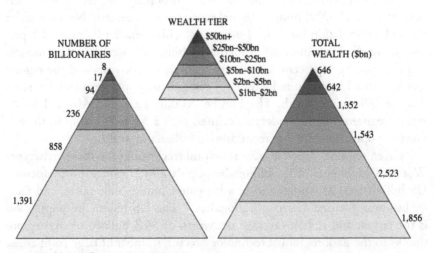

Source: Wealth-X, Billionaire Census 2019

FIGURE 1.2 Percentage of Change of Billionaires by Wealth Tier

Percentage of change 2017–2018		WEALTH TIER	Absolute change 2017–2018	
Number of billionaires	Total wealth ($bn)		Number of billionaires	Total wealth ($bn)
▼ −15.4%	▼ −2.5%	$50bn+	▼ −2	▼ −17
▼ −19.5%	▼ −14.7%	$25bn–$50bn	▼ −4	▼ −110
▼ −13.0%	▼ −10.0%	$10bn–$25bn	▼ −14	▼ −150
▼ −14.2%	▼ −12.0%	$5bn–$10bn	▼ −39	▼ −210
▼ −10.3%	▼ −8.0%	$2bn–$5bn	▼ −98	▼ −220
▲ 0.5%	▲ 3.6%	$1bn–$2bn	▲ 7	▲ 65

Source: Wealth-X, Billionaire Census 2019

While these profiles help generate some insights about the general population of those wealthy enough to possibly have a family office, the question remains: How many affluent families are utilizing the services of a family office? The short answer is that we do not know precisely, primarily due to privacy, anonymity, and exclusivity requirements of the family office, and how and if a family identifies as having a family office. I estimate there are at least 5,000 family offices in the US alone, while EY estimates the global population of family offices to be at least 10,000.[17] I further contend that these numbers would double if you include embedded family offices (those housed within operating companies). Moreover, a sizable proportion of families disdain the term *family office*, and I often hear families sheepishly deny they do have one, even when they actually have all the services, structures, and goals of what a family office provides. This reveals the difficulty in accurately tallying the number of family offices: It relies on families to self-identify as one!

In the wake of the global financial crisis of 2008 and pandemic of 2020, there has been higher scrutiny for Wall Street, as regulatory bodies such as the Securities and Exchange Commission (SEC) are developing clearer definitions of the family office to monitor these organizations' advisory practices and activities. The Family Office Rule defines a single-family office as "any type of qualifying entity that provides investment advice to a single family including traditional family offices and private trust companies."[18] While this definition remains broad, the implication is that the proverbial kimono for many family office outfits has been shredded, requiring many families to carefully determine whether they need to legally register as such. Doing so will aid consumers and the industry in distinguishing single-family offices from registered investment advisors (RIA), those who advise on investments beyond the immediate family members.

How Much Do I Really Need to Fund a Family Office?

One of the greatest ongoing debates in the family office space is the "How much does it take?" discussion to warrant starting a single-family office. Decades ago, experts in the field might have said anywhere from $50 to $250 million. Today, experts such as Kathryn McCarthy, a seasoned advisor who has spent more than two decades working for families including the Rockefeller family, states that current operating costs to build out a fully functioning family office typically begin in the range of $500 million to $1 billion. Why has the number increased so significantly? One reason is the new reality of uncertainty, coupled with low-return markets, which can cause investment returns to stall or drop while overhead remains the same or increases due to regulatory and compliance costs. McCarthy further cautions that deciding whether to create and maintain a single-family office requires more consideration than simply the size of the family's assets. For example, does the family want employees, and does it want to govern and operate a family office?[19]

As further evidence of McCarthy's point, family office sizes vary considerably. In a series of five reports on single-family offices commencing in 2009, the Family Wealth Alliance, a professional organization that serves the family office community, found that of the 34 family offices it surveyed, the offices' financial size ranged from $42 million to well over $1.5 billion, with a median of $275 million assets under supervision and a mean of $516 million.[20] Tom Livergood, founder and CEO of the Family Wealth Alliance, currently estimates that the average single-family office size is approximately $600 million, although some Unicorn offices (on the rise in recent years) number in the multiple billions in net worth served.[21] These statistics indicate, as the old adage goes, "If you have seen one family office, you have seen one family office." Like snowflakes, no two family offices are alike.

Moreover, many family offices do serve families with far fewer than $500 million—perhaps in the range of $50 to $200 million or more of investable assets. McCarthy coins most of these family offices as "coordinator family offices," where most of the family office services are outsourced and perhaps one or more family members runs the family office operations with the support of a bookkeeper or accountant. Most of these families with smaller family offices also tend to identify with the concept of being a family office, underscoring the point that the scale of a family's wealth does not necessarily correlate with classification as a legally established family office.

Furthermore, the key question may not be how much the family has today, but how they anticipate investing, spending, and organizing around that wealth or operating business. I have seen families with several billions who decide to not establish a fully built out family office. Therefore, remember that the ranges presented in this section are general rules of thumb rather than strict guidelines. Ultimately, starting a family office or joining an existing multi-family office represents an individual decision that extends beyond questions of net worth and instead depends on the family's overarching objectives, time, and energy.

Purpose and Definition of the Family Office

The wealth management industry generally defines a family office as "an organization dedicated to serving wealthy individuals and/or families on a diverse range of financial, estate, tax, accounting, and personal family needs."[22] Thus, the purpose of the family office is to manage and oversee the wealth management affairs of highly affluent individuals and their families in regard to such issues as tax, wealth transfer, investment management, governance, estate planning, risk management, compliance, education, communication, financial education, and more. Primary areas of family office services include:[23]

1. *Advisory:* risk management, insurance, compliance and regulatory assistance, tax, and legal advisory
2. *Financial planning:* investment management services, philanthropic management, life management, and budgeting
3. *Strategy:* business and financial advisory, estate and wealth transfer, training, and education
4. *Governance:* reporting and record keeping, continuity and succession planning, administrative services

Because the family office "has a deep understanding of the planning, generational, and tax issues so important to wealthy investors,"[24] it truly plays a key role as integrator and coordinator of all the wealth affairs of the family. These characteristics distinguish the family office from other financial institutions because it is uniquely positioned to execute long-term strategic planning on multiple fronts. Putting the family office in the context of a football team, it becomes the quarterback and "coach" for the management of the family's financial and wealth affairs, providing a centralized point for the family to unify around their wealth. The office can collaborate with the family's professional team members (lawyers, accountants, tax advisors, family business advisors, among others) to decide when to move forward and execute on certain goals (pass or rush, in football speak) and when to refrain from following through on certain objectives (to kneel down, as it may be in football terms). Further, the family office is not only about ongoing maintenance and monitoring of wealth, it is about deriving the strategy to sustain and grow the wealth across generations for a family yet to be born—like enacting day-to-day strategies focused on winning the season championship, rather than winning just a single game. Like the football coach, the family office coordinates, organizes, and aids the many players in implementing a plan for achieving the family's wealth management goals.

The family office also is uniquely positioned to help individuals understand the context of their family wealth, a progressive point of interest adopted by leading wealth experts such as Jay Hughes, Dennis Jaffe, and Sam Lane among others. Such authors have outlined the many forms of capital the family possesses and how these should be managed. Specifically, in addition to basic financial capital, families also need to manage their human capital, the individual family members and what they do; intellectual capital, what the individual family members know and how they learn, communicate, and make decisions together; and social capital, how they engage with their larger societies.[25] Jay Hughes further asserts that managing the family's human and intellectual capital should be of higher priority even than managing its financial capital.[26]

Although each wealth expert has a slight variation on how they define family wealth, the concept of wealth consisting of both the material and immaterial has significant implications for intergenerational wealth transfer, which is rapidly expanding on a global scale. Family wealth is as old as time and is a significant driving force in perpetuating the need and ongoing interest to the creation of family offices.

Historical Background of the Family Office

Although the exact origin of the first family offices is not well documented, the literature suggests that the first family offices emerged in Europe after large, land-owning families liquidated their assets.[27] European family offices were often embedded in the estate offices of French, British, and German nobility in the nineteenth century or earlier and land ownership played a much greater role in wealth preservation in the United Kingdom and Europe than in the United States.[28] While the roots of the family office began in Europe following the Crusades approximately in the 1400s to 1500s, the US family office originated shortly after the Industrial Revolution (1712–1942) and the incredible fortunes that were generated during this booming era.[29] In North America, the family enterprise is the bedrock that supports the domestic economy, contributing approximately 59 percent of the gross domestic product in the United States[30] and 45 percent in Canada.[31] As a result, much of the wealth in North America is the direct result of the success of the family enterprise. The impact of the family enterprise as it relates to private equity transactions is significant: In 2018, there were 164 private-equity deals involving a vehicle that manages the assets of a wealthy family—a 36 percent increase on the previous year.[32] Thus, the vast majority of concentrated wealth in families is linked to the family enterprise and the ways in which their resources are managed.[33]

Family Office from the Industrial Age to Current

The Rockefellers, perhaps the most well-known ultra-wealthy American family, created one of the first—if not the first—family offices in the United States. John D. Rockefeller amassed an enormous fortune as a result of the success of his Standard Oil Trust Company. By 1900, Standard Oil dominated the domestic oil refinery business and controlled 80 percent of all oil refinery capacity in the United States.[34] After a number of years of litigation, the Supreme Court ruled that Standard Oil was a monopoly that had to be dissolved. Standard Oil was dissolved into six sub-oil companies, and John D. Rockefeller became the largest single stockholder in these companies—the predecessors of Exxon, Mobil, Amoco, and Chevron.[35] By 1913, it was estimated that Rockefeller's holdings in these companies were valued at $900 million.

In 1882, prior to the dissolution of Standard Oil Trust, John D. Rockefeller started the Rockefeller family office, which over 138 years has evolved from a small office managing JDR Sr.'s personal business and family matters to a multi-family asset management and wealth advisory firm known as Rockefeller Capital Management headquartered at 45 Rockefeller Plaza. Rockefeller Capital Management and its subsidiary, the Rockefeller Trust Companies, manages assets for members of the Rockefeller Family and other high-net-worth families, as well as for institutions that include foundations, endowments, and corporations. Rockefeller Capital Management has approximately 400 employees[1] in New York, Washington D.C., and other locations.

Recognized as one of the greatest philanthropists of his era, Rockefeller donated an estimated $530 million to various charities during his lifetime. In addition to his generosity to the public good, Rockefeller understood the opportunity that centralizing his family's wealth afforded his immediate family and generations to come. Although John D. Rockefeller, Sr. had three daughters and one son, he passed the vast majority of his wealth ($250 million of $274 million in oil stock) to his son, John D. Rockefeller, Jr., leaving just $24 million to be divided among his remaining daughters.[36] This application of primogenitor, or the passing of the wealth to the oldest male in the family, was a common practice in the early twentieth century. The goal was to keep the wealth aligned with the bloodline and family namesake.

Continuing his father's wealth transfer intentions and planning, John Rockefeller, Jr. was able to protect the vast amount of the family wealth prior to President Roosevelt's 1934 proposed tax wealth increase—the gift tax. Through elaborate estate planning and gifting, Rockefeller, Jr. created a number of substantial generational-skipping trusts, each worth $20 million for his wife and six children.[37] In this manner, the Rockefeller clan was able to perpetuate their family's tremendous fortune from generation to generation. Through John Rockefeller Sr.'s and Jr.'s keen insights into aggregating and leveraging the amassed fortune, and their strategic planning of transferring wealth to future generations, the Rockefeller family established the model for transgenerational wealth transfer.

The wealth of other legendary affluent families, such as the Mellons, Scripps, Phipps, Lairds, Nortons, Pitcairns, and DuPonts, became the foundation for many of the larger US private investment companies, family offices and/or trust companies.[38] Some of the families' wealth was converted into private investment companies that are known today as Bank of America Private Bank, Fiduciary Trust, Glenmede Trust Co., Laird Norton Wealth Management, Whittier Trust Company, Northern Trust, Wilmington Trust, CIBC National Trust (formerly Atlantic Trust), Bessemer Trust, and Pitcairn Trust Company. Again, the aggregation and concentration of these families' wealth gave them an enormous advantage and opportunity to grow and perpetuate their family wealth for generations to come. This is another strategic advantage of the family office that continues to be an important advantage for families today.

The story of the creation of Bessemer Trust provides another example of an historic, renowned family who understood the value of aggregating their collective wealth. Henry Phipps, a partner of Andrew Carnegie, established Bessemer Trust Company in 1907 as a family office.[39] Phipps requested that

$50 million, a portion of the amount he received from the sale of Carnegie Steel to J.P. Morgan, be invested by the family office.[40] Managed by the family office, the initial $50 million investment grew to an estimated $1 billion that was divided among 100 of Phipps' descendants in 2004.[41]

In the early 1970s, with a staff of 200, Bessemer struggled to remain cost-efficient as a single-family office, paying out an estimated 2 percent of assets under management annually.[42] In 1975, Phipps family members hired new management and opened their doors to other affluent individuals and families to become a multi-client family office. As of 2019, Bessemer Trust had more than $100 billion of assets under supervision, more than 2,500 client relationships served from 19 offices, and fiduciary responsibility for 10,000 trusts.[43] The Phipps family recognized that, in order to grow and maintain the success of their family's wealth, they needed to shift their model of wealth management. At the time, the concept of bringing in outside clients was a novel and progressive idea.

The Pitcairn family started another well-conceived family office. John Pitcairn (1841–1916) was a Scottish immigrant who became one of the 1883 co-founders of Pittsburgh Plate Glass Company, known today as PPG Industries (PPG). The company was quite successful; by the twentieth century, the company manufactured 65 percent of all plate glass made in the United States.[44] Following the death of John Pitcairn, his three sons formed the Pitcairn Company, a family holding office that managed the financial and estate planning affairs and maintained the family's voting control of PPG. The three sons, Raymond, Theodore, and Harold, had a total of nine children, and by 1951, there were 61 descendants of John Pitcairn. The success of PPG is evidenced by its incredible dividend payout as, "between 1938 and 1985 alone, the [PPG] corporation paid over $320 million in dividends to their holding company."[45]

In 1973, Pitcairn Company celebrated its fiftieth anniversary as a family office and had grown to more than $200 million in assets under management, after paying over $750 million in dividends.[46] In the late 1980s, the Pitcairn family decided to liquidate their personal holding company by selling nearly all their assets, including their PPG stock. In 1987, the family reconstituted the family office as a private trust company, Pitcairn Trust Company, located in Jenkintown, Pennsylvania, and began a new chapter as a multi-client family office.[47] Pitcairn's departure from a single-family office model was similar to other large family offices, such as Bessemer Trust and Rockefeller Family Office, which made the transition to a multi-family office. As of 2019, Pitcairn had $5.8 billion under management. In speaking with Dirk Jungé, the great grandson of John Pitcairn, and retired chairman of Pitcairn Trust Company, Dirk shared the weight of his family's powerful heritage and their tremendous pride, but also his deep sense of stewardship to the wealth generated over a hundred years prior. Dirk has dedicated most of his entire professional career to leading the family enterprise and has invested tremendously in the family capital to fortify generations to come.

Pitcairn's successful family office is due in part to the intention and effort the family has made in establishing a strong governance structure with their growing number of family members. The Pitcairn family maintains an advisory council that is comprised of family members. In addition, they have codified several generational rituals, such as family meetings and retreats, which help build community and strengthen familial bonds. Giving members of the family a free choice to participate in the affairs of the family and the family office strengthens overall cohesiveness, as they typically choose to participate. Further, these rituals and governance practices provide clear guidelines and expectations for family members as they grow up in the family system. They also foster increased and open communication, clarity of family member roles and responsibilities, and greater family harmony. A more detailed discussion of the Pitcairn Family Office will be shared in Chapter 4 on the family's mission, vision, and evolution.

Key Roles of the Family Office

Although the family office tends to wear many hats for the family, if we were to condense down the key roles that the family office may serve a family, we would find there are typically three core functional areas: executor and trusted advisor, guardian and watchman, and librarian and guru. See Figure 1.3, which outlines the various hats of the family office.

The Executor and Trusted Advisor

For many families, the family office is the primary keeper and executor of transactions and legal documents. Although the families make the final decisions, there is a critical function that the family office plays in implementing and executing transactions based on those decisions, monitoring and complying with the industry rules and regulations, housing and storing critical documents related to strategy, and planning and building continuity and context to the wealth management efforts by the family. Thus, the family office may have to manage or oversee a variety of different tasks and transactions such as:

- Liquidity of family units and various entities.
- Diligence, risk considerations, and time horizon planning for entities.

- Process, method, and steps for transaction approval.
- Assessing the impact that a transaction may have on legal structures.
- Understanding the impact a transaction may have on tax expense or savings.
- Overseeing administrative tasks to be completed once the transaction is complete.
- Documenting and archiving relevant legal, compliance, estate planning, business planning, and/or tax documents.

FIGURE 1.3 The Many Hats of the Family Office

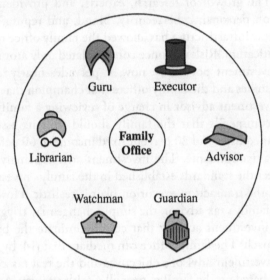

Source: © Tamarind Partners, Inc.

The trusted advisor is a critical function of the family office regardless of the type of family office (discussed in the next section) or the stage of the family office. With the responsibility of being a person of confidence and trust to the family, these advisors are devising the processes enacted for the management of the family's wealth and business affairs.

The Guardian and Watchman

"Are you going to protect the family, Michael?" asks Sandra Bullock, who plays Leigh Anne Tuohy, Michael's adopted mother in the movie *The Blind Side*. Tuohy, who takes in the homeless Michael Oher, uses the analogy for Oher's need to protect his teammates and his quarterback's blind side the way he would protect his own family. The family office adopts Oher's same passion, dedication, loyalty, and heart to guard the family for whom the family office was created—just like Oher understood his responsibility to protect his football team as if they were his family. The roles of guardian and watchman are the family office's greatest duty. There is no doubt that families of tremendous wealth have much vulnerability—more so today than ever before. The family office often functions as a protector and defender to the family when it comes to shoring up potential exposure. Like a watchman, they put in place systems, warning systems, and alerts to apprise family if privacy, confidentiality and/or cybersecurity may have been hacked. The growth of research, experts, and providers to support family offices on personal, cybersecurity, brand, and reputation management and systems infrastructure has allowed the family office to leapfrog in terms of sophistication. Risk was once contemplated only around insurance brokers and investment portfolios; now, it pervades nearly all aspects of planning for families and the family offices that champion that strategy. For example, an investment advisor in charge of reviewing a family's asset allocation plan recommends that the family should shift its asset allocation from 80 percent equities and 20 percent fixed income to 60 percent equities and 40 percent fixed income. The investment advisor's analysis is sound, risk metrics meet the standards established in the family's investment policy statement, and the transaction execution plan is realistic. However, by not consulting the family's tax advisor, the simple change may trigger an unwelcomed tax on investment activity that could eliminate the benefit of the change in approach. The family office can mediate that risk by understanding both the investment advisor's objectives and the real tax consequences that may result based on the families over all wealth strategy. As the integrator and overseer, the family office can best mitigate critical risks that would jeopardize the well-being of the family.

For example, one risk not often discussed is the risk of isolation that often comes with amassing a tremendous fortune. Although wealth can open many exciting new doorways, yet it can also be incredibly isolating. No one really prepares most individuals for the isolation of having extraordinary wealth. Wealth can make you a target of the interest and affections of long-lost relatives, charities, alma maters, old schoolmates, or neighbors from long ago. Further, wealth can create a whole new dynamic among the relationships in your family. These are deeply personal and sometimes challenge even the most levelheaded of individuals. Thus, members of the family office may also act as sounding boards and trusted confidants to the family as they navigate a whole host of issues. As confidant, they provide objective, unbiased advice that helps develop and empower the family members to be their best with their wealth. The family office takes on the role of guardian by saying "no" to inquiries from friends and relatives, as well as others, in a way that protects the family's financial assets while preserving these personal relationships. The role of confidant or consigliore is perhaps one of the most critical functions of the family office. In many respects it is akin to have a second set of eyes that can always see what you are seeing and help to validate or clarify the course at hand.

The Librarian and Guru

Jay Hughes once told a story at an investment conference that best describes the family office as the "Brain Trust" of the family, and today it functions more like a digital repository or "guru." Jay proceeded to ask the crowd whether anyone remembered anything about their dreams from the previous evening. Many raised their hands. He then asked if anyone remembered their dreams from a week ago. Far fewer hands were raised. He then asked about dreams from a month ago. Just a few hands were now raised. He then asked, for those who remembered their dreams from a month ago, how many of those dreams turned into tangible ideas. And, of those ideas, how many of them were successfully implemented such that they resulted in significant financial wealth. No hands were raised at this point from the audience.

And then Hughes reminded the audience, who consisted primarily of advisors, that we have the privilege to serve the few whose creativity and bright ideas have led to major business and financial success. Family offices can be a repository and a thinking partner to foster these seedling ideas and help launch family members into new careers, passions, and interests. Inspiring and fostering a collaborative dialogue between the family and the family office on "what could be" is perhaps one of the richest and most rewarding aspects of the profession. Chapters 12 more deeply explore how to support, educate, and advise future generation family members as they engage in an informed and purposeful life with wealth.

Family Office Orientation to Family, Strategy, and Operations

As we discussed earlier, no two family offices are alike. Why? Because no two families are alike. Accordingly, a critical first step for any family office is to orient (and regularly reorient) itself with the family's long-term strategic goals with respect to their wealth and investments, ownership interests, operating entities and businesses, cash and liquid investments, collectibles, lifestyle needs and more. Together, these variables indicate the operational intensity of the family and their assets, which in turn exert strong implications on the family office's structure and day-to-day operations. For example, a family that indulges in regular luxuries or is aggressively focused on serial entrepreneurship has very different service needs and preferences than a family who lives conservatively and is heavily focused on preserving and building wealth.

Effectively aligning with the family's needs requires family office staff to possess extensive knowledge, skill, and experience related to wealth and investment planning, technologies and software platforms to support the family's needs, and the ability to scale to support the client family as they progress toward their goals.[48] Further adding to these challenges is the rapidly mounting complexity and ambiguity in the field created by forces such as globalization, technological advancement, the creation of increasingly esoteric investment strategies, introduction of more onerous tax laws, and extension in human longevity. These conditions require family offices to retain highly qualified talent, outline and negotiate complex planning and wealth transfer scenarios, and be able to offer diverse wealth management options as required by the family. Similar to defining the family firm by behavior, one can then begin to understand the role of the family office based upon how it operates in relation to affluent families.

Given the foundational understanding that families and their needs from one to another, family office functions can be classified according to three core issues, as shown in Figure 1.4:

1. *Strategic wealth management:* wealth and investment management, taxation and asset protection, family advisory board
2. *Operational management:* operations and compliance, stakeholder reporting, front and back office administration
3. *Family management:* governance and communication, financial planning, trust and estate planning, philanthropic management

Strategic wealth management involves long-term strategic planning that considers the family's wealth objectives for current and successive generations. This intergenerational wealth planning also encompasses building a governance strategy, such as developing family boards and family councils, along with governance protocols to guide the family (e.g., family constitution, family mission statement, family investment policy statement). It also may include the coordination of multiple family members' assets that facilitates group purchasing power and access to alternative investment strategies. Investment planning is another core service offered by family offices and may be conducted in-house or outsourced through an investment provider, such as an outsourced chief investment officer.

FIGURE 1.4　Family Office Functions

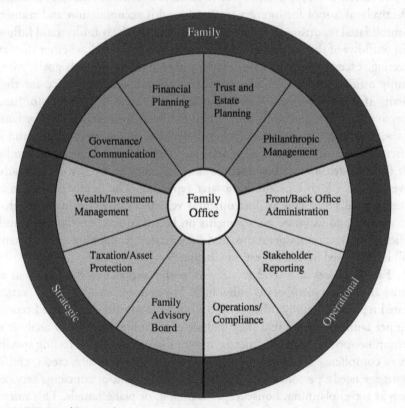

Source: © Tamarind Partners, Inc.

As part of investment advisory services, a family office may oversee asset allocation, portfolio construction, investment and manager due diligence, investment policy creation, and ongoing performance and reporting. The investment advisory function may also conduct money manager selection, as well as performance analytics and constant monitoring, reviewing, and rebalancing of portfolios.

A significant appeal of family offices is the operational management they offer, such as investment recordkeeping and financial reporting. Because the centralization of assets gives many family offices a unique perspective, it also gives them the opportunity to report in aggregate on family assets. Many family offices offer consolidated financial reporting, allowing individuals to see their asset holdings across various accounts and by various asset classes. This allows families to be more fluid and strategic in the coordination of their pooled assets. The Phipps and Pitcairn families utilized pooled asset strategies effectively as a tool for intergenerational wealth accumulation and transfer. Consolidated reporting also allows families to collectively understand inflows and outflows of the combined families' wealth, and to track whether they are meeting, exceeding, and/or not meeting their families' wealth goals. Many family offices, but not all, also provide a tax preparation service for their clients. If it is not performed in-house, tax preparation is an important function to manage by the family office. This can be a monumental task for families whose wealth is spread across hundreds of accounts, asset classes, and in different types of investments or vehicles. Most, if not all, affluent families file for an extension of their income tax as a result of the use of alternative investments, which typically have later reporting. The family office can be a centralized point and an instrumental vehicle to organize incoming K-1 documents and facilitate tax payments on behalf of its client family. Family office administration, operations, and information technology advancements will be discussed in more detail in Chapter 9.

Family offices also tend to offer extensive support to the family as an entity and family members as individuals. For example, in addition to consolidated reporting, family offices will drill down and offer customized reporting per family member that may include performing a cash flow analysis to determine specific budgeting needs. It may also constitute addressing specific tax or compliance issues; risk management strategies; banking, credit, and/or mortgage needs; personal security; and bill paying and/or concierge services, such as travel planning, housekeeper sourcing, or plane rentals. This microperspective of individual family members also creates greater clarity of how individual family members are contributing to, maintaining, or draining the family's collective wealth.

Family offices also frequently have fiduciary responsibilities and provide oversight and diligence on trusts held by their clients. As the trustees in many instances, they are cognizant that investment strategies are in line with the terms of the trust. From aiding in the administration of the trust to overseeing all tax, compliance, and recordkeeping, fiduciary oversight is an important component to successful intergenerational wealth transfer. Chapter 7 discusses the legal, structural, and ownership considerations that a family needs to explore in the context of setting up a family office.

This type of advice-giving that family offices provide creates a transparent and conflict-free relationship with the clients, allowing the clients to know that their wealth advisors are working solely in the families' best interest and are not selling or pushing products for the interests of their employers. Investment policy creation helps the clients to anchor underlying objectives and goals for their portfolios and can ultimately help to create perspective on the long-term intentions for the wealth. In addition to investment management, family offices will provide governance advice to help families build a framework to enhance how family decisions are made.

Family governance is a term more commonly associated with managing the family business; however, it has become increasingly instrumental in organizing families around their wealth.[49] Governance involves the decision-making in the family and how policies, agreements, boards, and councils are formed as related to the family wealth. The family office can be an effective facilitator to aid families as they devise a governance framework that suits their family's needs. A more expansive discussion of family governance practices is shared in Chapter 11. Other strategy issues are whether to build or create a family office; the differences between starting a single-family office and joining a multi-family office (Chapter 3); a strategic planning approach to assess the estate, investment, financial, wealth transfer, and governance planning you have completed to date in your family (Chapter 6); and the legal and fiduciary requirements of setting up your family office (Chapter 7). Chapter 8 highlights investment management considerations for your family office, while Chapter 9 overviews the advancements in information technology and operations; the talent management and human resource requirements of successful family offices are covered in Chapter 10. Chapters 12 discusses the importance of family education in preparing succeeding generations, and Chapter 13 shares the role of legacy, philanthropy, foundations, and impact investing and building engagement and involvement of family. Chapter 14 shares more on the entrepreneurship and the family bank; the book closes with a current discussion of the role of a private trust company, how to establish one, and when it is most valued, and broader insights on fiduciary oversight (Chapter 15).

Conclusion and Final Thoughts

Now that we have established a family office foundation, including its definition, purpose, historical context, and overview of services of a family office, Chapter 2 moves us into a broader discussion of the evolution and inception of the family office. The next chapter shares common experiences and paths to the origination of a family office, what may trigger the need to set up a family office, and different archetypes of family offices from a Founder Family Office, to an Administration/Compliance Family Office, to a Family Business Focused Family Office, to an Investment Family Office or Multigenerational Family Office. Chapter 2 closes with insights from the Mathile Case Study on the inception, setup, and evolution of their family office.

Notes

1. Life expectancy in the USA, 1900-98. Retrieved from https://u.demog.berkeley .edu/~andrew/1918/figure2.html.
2. Grace Donnelly, "Here's Why Life Expectancy in the U.S. Dropped Again This Year," *Fortune*, February 9, 2018. Retrieved from https://fortune .com/2018/02/09/us-life-expectancy-dropped-again/.
3. Elie Dolgin, "There's No Limit to Longevity, Says Study Reviving Human Life Span Debate," *Nature*, July 1, 2018. Retrieved from https://www.scientific american.com/article/theres-no-limit-to-longevity-says-study-reviving-human-life-span-debate/.
4. Wealth-X, World Ultra Wealth Report 2019.
5. "Billionaires 2019," *Forbes*, March 5, 2019. https://www.forbes.com/billion aires/list/;#version:static. Retrieved March 13, 2019.
6. Wealth-X, World Ultra Wealth Report 2019.
7. Wealth-X, High Net Worth Handbook 2019.
8. Wealth-X, High Net Worth Handbook 2019.
9. https://asianprivatebanker.com/asia-2017-aum-league-table/.
10. Wealth-X, High Net Worth Handbook 2019.
11. https://www.usatoday.com/story/news/2018/12/26/giving-charitable-groups-bracing-drop-dontions-year/2352327002/.
12. https://www.taxpolicycenter.org/taxvox/21-million-taxpayers-will-stop-taking-charitable-deduction-under-tcja.
13. https://www.nptrust.org/philanthropic-resources/philanthropist/trends-in-donor-advised-funds/.
14. Wealth-X, High Net Worth Handbook 2019.
15. Wealth-X, Billionaire Census 2019.
16. Wealth-X, Billionaire Census 2019.

17. EY Family Guide, 2017.
18. Federal Register/ Vol. 76, No. 125 / Wednesday, June 29, 2011 / Rules and Regulations § 275.202(a)(11)(G)-1 Family offices.
19. Correspondence with Kathryn McCarthy, November 2019.
20. Family Wealth Alliance LLC, Single Family Office Study, 2010.
21. Correspondence with Tom Livergood, November 2019.
22. John J. Bowen, Jr., "In the Family Way: Do You Have What It Takes to Manage the Complex Affairs of the Ultra-Wealthy?" *Financial Planning* (August 1, 2004): 1–33.
23. EY Family Guide, 2017.
24. Charles Grace, "The Multiple Client Family Office," *Trusts & Estates* 139, no. 2 (2000): 54–55.
25. Charles W. Collier, *Wealth in Families* (Cambridge, MA: Harvard Press, 2002), 6.
26. James E. Hughes, *Family Wealth: Keeping It in the Family* (Princeton: Bloomberg Press, 2004), xv.
27. Sara Hamilton, "Wealth Management: Keeping It in the Family," *Trusts & Estates* 136, no. 9 (1997): 28–34; M. Rankin, "Wealth Management: A Brief History and Evolution of Family Offices," unpublished white paper, presented at the Family Firm Institute Pre-Conference Wealth Advising Seminar, October 5, 2004; Helen Avery, "Keeping It in the Family," *Euromoney* (2004): 1–246.
28. Ibid.
29. H. Shapiro, "Family Matters," *Worth* xx (2002): 109–114.
30. Joseph Astrachan, professor emeritus, Kennesaw State University, based on his earlier study (Astrachan & Shanker, 2003) using updated 2017 US Census data. This figure refers only to the non-government, for-profit entities' contribution to GDP.
31. Joseph H. Astrachan and Melissa Carey Shanker, "Family Businesses' Contribution to the U.S. Economy: A Closer Look," *Family Business Review* 16 (2003): 211–219.
32. Carol Ryan, "Private Equity Gets Family Friendly," *Wall Street Journal*, July 2, 2019, https://www.wsj.com/articles/private-equity-gets-family-friendly-11562065479.
33. James J. Chrisman, Jess H. Chua, and Shaker A. Zahra, "Creating Wealth in Family Firms Through Managing Resources: Comments and Extensions," *Entrepreneurship Theory and Practice* 27, no. 4 (2003): 359–365.
34. Michael P. Allen, *The Founding Fortunes: A New Anatomy of the Super-Rich Families in America* (New York: Truman Talley Books, 1987), 34.
35. Ibid., 35.
36. Michael P. Allen, *The Founding Fortunes: A New Anatomy of the Super-Rich Families in America* (New York: Truman Talley Books, 1987).
37. Ibid.
38. Sara Hamilton, "Wealth Management: Keeping It in the Family," *Trusts & Estates* 136, no. 9 (1997): 28–34.
39. H. Shapiro, "Family Matters," *Worth* xx (2002): 109–114.

40. Helen Avery, "Keeping It in the Family," *Euromoney* (2004): 1–246; H. Shapiro, "Family Matters," *Worth* xx (2002): 109–114; Michael P. Allen, *The Founding Fortunes: A New Anatomy of the Super-Rich Families in America* (New York: Truman Talley Books, 1987).
41. Helen Avery, "Keeping It in the Family," *Euromoney* (2004): 1–246.
42. Ibid.
43. See further information from Bessemer Trust at https://www.bessemertrust.com/what-makes-us-different/key-facts.
44. Dennis T. Jaffe and Sam H. Lane, "Sustaining a Family Dynasty: Key Issues Facing Complex Multigenerational Business- and Investment-Owning Families," *Family Business Review* 17, no. 1 (2004): 81–98.
45. Michael P. Allen, *The Founding Fortunes: A New Anatomy of the Super-Rich Families in America* (New York: Truman Talley Books, 1987), 71.
46. Dennis T. Jaffe and Sam H. Lane, "Sustaining a Family Dynasty: Key Issues Facing Complex Multigenerational Business- and Investment-Owning Families," *Family Business Review* 17, no. 1 (2004): 81–98.
47. Ibid.
48. Robert Casey, "State of the Industry Report—Single Family Offices Take Their Turn on Centre Stage," *The International Family Offices Journal*, December 2018.
49. Patricia M. Angus, "The Family Governance Pyramid: From Principles to Practice," *The Journal of Wealth Management* 8, no. 1 (2005): 7–13; Barbara R. Hauser, "Family Governance: Who, What, and How," *The Journal of Wealth Management* 5, no. 2 (2002): 10–16; Lisa P. Gray, "The Three Forms of Governance: A New Approach to Family Wealth Transfer and Asset Protection, Part II," *The Journal of Wealth Management* 11, no. 2 (2008): 7-18; Charles W. Collier, *Wealth in Families* (Cambridge, MA: Harvard Press, 2002); James E. Hughes Jr., *Family Wealth: Keeping It in the Family* (Princeton, NJ: Bloomberg Press, 2004).

CHAPTER 2

Family Office Evolution: Inceptions and Archetypes

Kirby Rosplock, PhD

In order to understand what a family may need or desire when it comes to a family office solution, it is helpful to step back and review some of the different paths that lead families to build or create a family office. Why are some paths more turbulent than others? What prompts a family to separate the management of its wealth from its operating business? Why do the pathways to a family office have an important link to a family's vision for their family office? What are some of the embedded qualities and characteristics of a family that enhance their chances of creating a unified family office? These questions will be addressed in this chapter. This chapter also presents a short case study of one family's experience, the Mathile Family, as it determined the goals and needs of the family wealth to conceive of an appropriate family office structure and vision. Finally, the chapter will close by synthesizing different goals and potential outcomes that a family office might encompass and will lead into a broader discussion of the family office options in the following chapter.

Inception of a Family Office

The beauty and challenge of the family office is that if you have heard one family office creation story, you have heard one family office creation story. No two stories are exactly alike; however, there are a number of general themes that are consistent. In this chapter, wisdom from Barbara Hauser is shared. She has outlined three typical scenarios of how the family office originates, explaining that it largely has to do with the nature of the liquidity event and the source of wealth.[1] Two other widely observed phenomena of family office creation are also discussed—when families "back into a family office" and when entrepreneurs establish investment offices. Family offices through the back door occur not by intention, but often out of necessity. It isn't until further down the line that a light bulb goes off that they have in fact created a family office. Another pathway to create an investment office is typically strategic and by design.

In the first scenario, the family office is born out of an entrepreneur's operating business.[2] Initially, the financial affairs of the family are managed internally by employees of the business, but as the family's assets grow, the family's financial, tax, estate planning, and investment requirements grow in complexity. Furthermore, as the family's personal financial affairs become more complex, their interest in privacy increases. Hauser notes that employees become increasingly compromised and feel a conflict of interest as they become more involved and responsible for managing the personal and financial affairs of family members while also maintaining their operational duties to the family.

For many families, they may not even be aware of the conflicts of interest of tasking their employees with family office responsibilities. Thus, in many cases, the family office is informally housed within the family business. The embedded responsibilities of the wealth often overlay responsibilities for key employees in the family business. From the accountant to the executive secretary, the chief financial officer to the bookkeeper, there may be numerous employees in the family business involved in serving two masters.

Scale: How Much Is Enough?

The question on everyone's mind is: How much do I really need to fund a family office? How (or does) the scope of wealth and holdings impact the goals and intentions outlined by the wealth holder? "How much is enough?" is the central question in Lee Eisenberg's book, *The Number: What Do You Need for the Rest of Your Life and What Will It Cost?* Written to a broader audience than just the ultra-high net worth, the book probes deeply into perceptions of wealth and how they influence how much is enough to live comfortably. Eisenberg writes a compelling social, emotional, and investment treatise discerning just how big your nest egg must be in order to live comfortably to the end of your days. But don't assume getting to the answer is quick and simple. The catch for the mass affluent is: What is the connection of what you have financially and your level spend to build out an office? Do you live in fear that you will not have enough? Are you overconfident regarding your financial security and the risks of losing it all? Are you comfortable with what you spend and are you living off portfolio income or eroding principal? George Kinder, financial guru and author of *The Seven Stages of Money Maturity: Understanding the Spirit and Value of Money in Your Life and Lighting the Torch,* provides a very rough estimate of how to determine if you have enough by totaling your investable assets,[3] multiply this number by 0.04[4] to roughly calculate how much investment income you can generate, and then add up additional potential sources of income, such as social security, inheritance, expected annual pension benefits, home equity, and any additional sources of income.[5] This is a quick and dirty assessment, as Eisenberg notes, to get to a ballpark estimate of what you can generate to manage your lifestyle needs during your lifetime. Chapter 6, in the capital sufficiency discussion, provides a more detailed analysis for determining whether you have enough to achieve your goals. Yet, for individuals and families of wealth in the tens and hundreds of millions, this analysis can often result in an awareness that their financial abundance provides much more opportunity to invest differently than the average middle-class person who is scraping every nickel together to get to his or her retirement number. When it comes to designing the appropriate strategy and approach to the broader design of the family office, there must first be an understanding of how and if the scale and scope of wealth matches the style of office they desire.

Investment professionals utilize asset/liability matching, or the popular investment approach that endeavors to time the sale of assets and resulting incoming streams to offset expected future expenses. Although more widely accepted by larger institutions, such as pension funds, this strategy attempts to mitigate liquidation risk by anticipating the income needs to be generated in order to match the cash needs of its underlying investors. If the underlying assets are not sufficient to meet the goals of the family on the lifestyle and/or legacy objectives, the family may have to realign, redefine, or reassess goals of the family office. One other item of note that resonates with families is the idea of putting certain goals and aspirations at more risk than others. Routinely revisiting goals and capital sufficiency allows you to continue to put the right goals at great risk, while immunizing (through asset/liability matching) those that are most crucial to the family's well-being.

If the scope of wealth is more than the requirements and goals of the family on their lifestyle and legacy objectives, there may be greater flexibility and freedom in the asset allocation and investment strategy. If there is not enough to achieve the lifestyle and legacy goals with the amount of wealth, then there are choices that must be made:

1. Do the wealth objectives need to be adjusted or scaled back?
2. Should the priority of the goals be modified or changed?
3. What level of confidence must I have to move forward and what level of risk am I willing to take?

In Chapter 6, an in-depth discussion of capital sufficiency planning provides more insight and a case example of this process to help one determine their financial plan and strategy for a family office.

Impact of the Family Business on the Family Office

Being heavily concentrated in a single area and/or business is often the backstory to the creation of wealth in many family instances. U.S. Trust and Campden Research conducted a longitudinal study on family office investing and found that more than 70 percent of their sample identified that the source of the family wealth originated from the core family business, with 60 percent having an ongoing operating business.[6] Forty-six percent of the family offices surveyed had between $100 and $500 million in assets under management, and 57 percent were under 10 years of age. The study found that there appears to be an "operating company effect" whereby those families with operating companies are larger when it comes to assets under management and number of staff, tend to be younger in age, serve fewer family members, direct their investing from in-house, and tend to be more aggressive investors.[7] Further, those family offices connected to families with an operating company have lower family office cost structures, with high expectations that the office be profitable.[8] There may be something to be said regarding how a privately held business may establish an influence and expectation regarding the performance, management, and function of a family office and its investment performance that outperforms its peers. Similar to the impact of an operating business on the family office, there is a paradigm when the investments become the new business (in the case of the investment office).

Attractions and Challenges with Embedded Family Offices

It is simple to see why it would be convenient to have family business and family wealth affairs managed within the family business. First, typically, you have long-tenured, trusted employees who have demonstrated responsibility, loyalty, good judgment, and professionalism on behalf of the family business. Second, the business structure and cash flow may be interconnected with the estate planning structures of individual family members. Family business accountants and financial officers may have a strong understanding of these relationships. Third, the family business may house the records and legal documents involved, so confidential family information may be readily accessible. Fourth, the family may not feel that a full-time staffer is required to handle mainly administrative, organizational, and investment tasks related to the family. These tend to be the main motivators initially for keeping the wealth management affairs managed internally in the family business. However, there are significant risks and reasons why extensive research by Family Office Exchange (FOX) has been done on the benefits of separating the family business from the management of the financial affairs of the family.[9]

In particular, the need for bifurcation of the business from the family wealth grows as the challenges of strapping family business employees with expanding responsibilities of the wealth put them in an increasingly compromised and conflicted position.[10] First, an employee's role may evolve and change to include responsibilities that present them with opportunities to know personal information such as social security numbers, account codes, and balances among other highly sensitive information like security codes to residences and passwords to safety deposit boxes. Access to this private data becomes of heightened concern, should an employee overstep their bounds and utilize the information to breach security of the family's assets. Further, this information could be used maliciously in such a way that could jeopardize a family's reputation, create jealousy, and/or worse yet, present blackmail possibilities for employees who are of a criminal persuasion.

The risks increase dramatically when scope creep occurs for family business employees now tasked with handling family office affairs; especially, when a family business employee is asked to also manage personal financial affairs of one or more family members. During a closed-door gathering of advisors and family office executives on risk management best practices for the family business and family office, an advisor shared an example where a family business employee, who was transitioned over to the family office, had so much access and extensive knowledge of the personal affairs of the family that he blackmailed that family upon his retirement so that he could remain on the payroll. This instance, albeit shocking, is rarely discussed or shared by families, but happens more frequently than families may want to admit.

Further, when families task employees with management of financial and investment responsibilities, they may be in direct conflict with goals and objectives of the family business. This scenario happens quite frequently, as family members may develop a rapport or connection with their accountant, financial office, and/or administrative staff in the family business and may at first make small, seemingly insignificant requests and then increasingly make requests to handle personal affairs such as record keeping, accounting, bill pay, filing and administration, and dividend disbursements, among other common tasks. This can lead to employees feeling pulled in opposite directions when or if the objectives of an individual family branch are not aligned with the family business objectives. This is the quintessential example of when the family business employee becomes triangulated and faced with serving two equally important masters—the family business and the individual family members. This is an eventual "lose–lose proposition" for the employee. The risks are that they fail to fulfill their role within the organization to meet expected performance benchmarks and, equally dismal, they are unable to meet the family member's expectation for support that is beyond their job description.

The family owners are conflicting with their employees who may have personal ties and deep respect for the family member, and consequently do not know how to say politely and respectfully, "I am unable to perform this function for you under my current job description and requirements." And, truth be told, the personal needs and requests from a family member may appear minor and insignificant at first to the employee. However, compounded across years and increasing numbers of family members making those requests, before the employee knows it, she or he may be using 10 to 30 percent or more of his or her time on these extraneous tasks.

Separating the Family Office from the Family Business

There are also families with successful operating businesses, who intentionally create a separate entity, such as a single-family office, to manage the wealth. They may task key employees to shift functions from the day-to-day family business operations to oversee or manage the family office function. It is important to differentiate the evolution of this style of family office, as a family clearly views the need to bifurcate the responsibilities in a separate fashion from the management of the business. The decision to establish a separate home for the wealth to be managed and organized often is motivated by specific drivers, such as diversification of the assets beyond the concentrated scope of the family business, tax efficiencies, or asset protection measures, for example.

In the instance of one family enterprise, there was a holding company with a myriad of sub-companies underneath. The family was in the process of culling some of the underlying limited liability corporations in order to exit from certain marketplaces and to strategically focus on other core lines of business. Although the family could have redeployed those assets back into the operating businesses, they determined that their businesses did not need additional capitalization. Further, the more senior members of the family were looking for ways to garner liquidity for retirement, gifting, and legacy planning. By redeploying the assets into a family office structure, individual shareholders were able to access capital, additional financial stability could be created for more senior family members, and the core family business holding could be diversified. Further, they were able to reduce their risk exposure of being completely captive in illiquid, privately held securities. They were additionally able to create a wealth management process and mechanism for future liquidity events, so the planning, implementation, and execution of wealth management solutions for the family were less cumbersome.

Challenges establishing a family office separate from the family business also abound and not all families may be up for the task. First, families with a weak sense of family cohesion or affinity may have greater difficulties enticing family members, who are or were shareholders of the family business to "double down" on their "familiness," or their sense of family belonging and togetherness, by managing their wealth together under a family office umbrella. Second, families with varying levels of financial wealth may also be at odds to strike a balance for establishing a family office. One family I have come to know over the years faced this exact challenge when a portion of their business was sold, leaving them with several hundred million dollars of liquidity. They had certain branches of the family well-endowed through concentration of ownership over the decades, leaving two-thirds of the wealth concentrated in one branch and the remainder split among several other branches. Compounding the gap of means, the wealth in the "have-nots" branch was further fractionalized through dynasty trusts. As a result, the scale of wealth from the "haves" branch provided opportunities for more complex investment structures and investment planning that simply was not of interest to the other branches. This divide of investment strategy, coupled with very different lifestyle and legacy planning, made the notion of forming a single-family office to meet the needs of the broader family a pariah.

Sudden Wealth

Similar to a windfall from the sale of a family business, a sudden liquidity from an IPO or other significant wealth transfer event such as a large settlement or golden parachute may trigger the desire to establish a family office. The dot-com boom of the late 1990s and tech surge of the early 2000s generated a number of mega-millionaires, from Michael Dell (Dell Computers), Pierre Omidyar (eBay), and Steve Jobs (Apple), to Mark Zuckerberg (Facebook), Larry Page and Sergey Brin (co-founders of Google), and Jack Dorsey (co-founder of Twitter and Square), just to name a few. Many of these individuals have gone on to invest their wealth through a private family office. In rarer incidences, a sudden windfall such as through a lottery winning or mega-divorce proceeding generates significant enough liquidity for the formation of a family office. Although rare, it does happen, and I have personally witnessed what happens when the material trappings of sudden wealth take over a modest-means family. It tends to rock the foundation of the family, and a new status can be associated with the family's means, making them vulnerable to distant relatives, past neighbors, and random acquaintances in their local community. This pressure, combined with an often-predatory mind-set by providers, tends to make it more challenging for these families to cohesively bond together to start or join a family office. Does it happen? Certainly—and it has been my experience that those families who are able to keep the persistent calls for handouts and curiosity from the media at bay are those who navigate a path to set up or join a family office.

The Investment-Focused Family Office

What happens in the case of the successful, first-generation wealth creator and/or entrepreneur who identifies less as a family business and sees his/her wealth as a new business opportunity? They may consider establishing an investment office, which is not to be confused with a family office. The investment office has a fairly rigorous mandate to grow wealth from wealth; it is purely a business pursuit. Often these operations engage the wealth creator in day-to-day capacity leading, running, directing, and strategically managing the corpus of wealth through an efficient and streamlined investment process. These organizations may deploy capital in a number of manners: real estate, private equity, direct investing, alternatives and traditional equities and bonds, and one or more operating businesses. They often have sophisticated investment professionals on staff with many years of direct investing and/or experience managing and running large portfolios for individuals or institutions. Because their purpose is to focus purely on the investments and portfolio management, they tend not to focus as much on legacy and multigenerational issues. Rather, they tend to be more opportunistic and flexible in seeking investment opportunities that align with their risk tolerance, their liquidity needs, and their investment mandate.

I interviewed a number of family office professionals in New York City as to whether the opportunity to create wealth from wealth in an investment office is a common and resounding theme. Phil Strassler, founder and CEO of Strassler LLC, who has advised a number of families and individuals with the creation of their family offices, notes that the individual compelled to establish a purely investment-driven office is typically a "do-it-yourselfer" (DIY) who has a passion for the business and wants to be directly engaged in the investment process of the office on a day-to-day basis.[11] These individuals may be former investment managers, institutional investors, or from the venture capital or private equity space. They make the transition from typically managing others' wealth to having enough personal wealth to solely manage it on a full-time basis. Because of the highly concentrated number of tremendously financially successful professionals, particularly in the investment world, it is not uncommon to discover an investment office with ownership of a hedge fund, for example, as one of its underlying assets. As a result of the high acumen and sophistication of the owner(s) and how the wealth was largely created as a function of prior investment ventures, these types of entities tend to be less focused on multigenerational planning, legacy, and/ or family constraints, and are more focused on the underlying assets and how they may be leveraged, grown, and capitalized. The key nuance between an investment office and a family office is the role and emphasis on family. This is typically rooted to the source of wealth by a successful entrepreneur or business individual, where the wealth creation story was disconnected to the family. The motives for managing the liquid wealth are retained primarily by the wealth creator and tend not to be viewed towards building continuity and cohesion among family members around the wealth. Of course, family members may be owners/beneficiaries to the wealth, but the management of the wealth tends to be an independent function to the family dynamic by design. For families who determine that their wealth is to be managed and directed with wealth objectives directly connected to family, there is a simple maxim to consider.

Family Offices Through the Back Door

One pathway to a family office that is not adequately discussed is what I will refer to as the unintended family office, or the "family office through the back door." Frequently in my interviews with single family offices, I noticed a theme emerging of families who went through some liquidity event or wealth transfer event and had begun the due diligence and rigor to identify wealth management solutions for their circumstance. These families typically were merely setting out to solve for immediate solutions for their ongoing tax complexities, accounting, reporting, and investment needs among other services. Unbeknownst to them, what they were orchestrating and bringing together were many of the services typically wrapped in a family office platform.

One individual I interviewed, who I will call James, shared the story of the evolution of his family office. He currently runs the back office and operations and also wears the hat of general counsel. James and his brother, who I will call Mark, assumed the roles of co-leaders of their family's wealth after the sudden passing of their father, who was a very successful estate planning attorney. Ironically, James shared that his father helped to set up family offices for his larger families, but never really considered the wealth they were building to be of scale to warrant a formal family office. James and his brother, Mark, who heads up the investment function in their family office, shared that their father really did not have a family office intention; but, after his passing, the brothers realized that his financial legacy actually required it. Today they function more as a virtual family office, with each brother and support staff being located in different cities in the United States.

Family Business Exit and Liquidity Event

The transition following the sale of a family business is often a major catalyst for the start of a family office.[12] Some speculate that as much as 80% of wealth is created from a concentrated position in a company or family business. Particularly in families where the tie that binds is not equity in the company, but familial bonds and family cohesiveness, a family office is likely to result. Sometimes it is a first-generation wealth holder and other times it is a multigenerational family enterprise that results in the cash flow to warrant the conception of a family office. These large infusions of capital into a family can be a major disruption and surface a host of issues that may have lain dormant under the veil of family harmony. And wealth has an unusual way of complicating family dynamics, particularly in business-owning families. A serial entrepreneur and wealth creator once shared "the magnifier effect" that wealth can amplify underlying dynamics in a family—be they harmonious or harmful. And when a family is not in clear alignment with their core values and beliefs around wealth, conflict can easily arise.

Similarly, Jay Hughes, family wealth expert, discusses in his book, *Family: The Compact among Generations*, what makes a family of affinity: "Families of affinity, not families of blood, will be those who flourish five generations into the future, and can imagine going on from there in an unending upward spiral of new flourishing generations."[13] When families are bound through privately held stock and a liquidity event that finally occurs to provide substantial freedom and autonomy, the family cohesiveness in the family and the underlying bonds are truly tested. The irony is that wealth and opportunity provide tremendous opportunities for a family to engage one another in a manner that creates synergy and economies of scale—in perhaps another vein than the family's operating business could provide.

Depending on the source of wealth, the type of family office archetype created may vary. The following section provides insights to the different styles of offices and their level of complexity by age and stage.

Family Office Archetypes

Although each family office is unique, there are general models or frameworks that might be useful to consider as you conceive and/or enhance your family office. To follow are six different archetypes of a single-family office that range in complexity and scale depending on the age and stage of the family it serves. (See Figure 2.1.)

The Founder's Family Office

The founder's office is typically born out of the financial success of an entrepreneur. The family office operations tend to be guided and driven by the business founder who may or may not have divested the original operating business(es). Because it tends to focus its efforts on wealth created from the first generation, the emphasis of the founder's family office tends to concentrate on establishing the right family office architecture, legal structures, and financial management of wealth outside of the founder's business(es). The founder's family office tends to be the founder's second stage of the founding family business, with him or her at the control seat. Challenges for the founder's family office tend to surface when the founder is looking to transition the ownership, operations, and/or oversight of the family office to the next generation of family; the founder may struggle with garnering buy-in and support by family owners to continue the office. Founders who successfully empower key non-family leaders and/or engage qualified, experienced, and educated family members into the management of the family office tend to be more successful in transitioning the ownership and management of the family office.

FIGURE 2.1   Family Office Archetypes

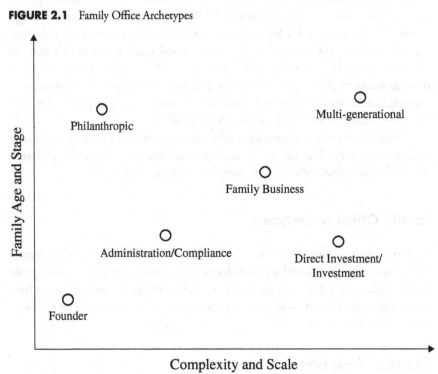

Source: © Tamarind Partners, Inc.

The Virtual, Administrative, and Compliance Family Office

The virtual, administrative, and compliance family office emphasizes the coordination and record keeping of the family's assets and wealth planning needs. This style of family office operates typically in a virtual location today, as the central repository for critical documentation and information of family members' legal, tax, and accounting documents is managed online and in the cloud. However, in days of old, physical files were housed in metal filing cabinets and paper files under lock and key. Family offices have a more robust array of secure, affordable virtual document storage options that may have custom portals. With built-in governance to partition content from administrators and end-users, files are meta-tagged and organized in a logical manner, allowing easier access but also allowing users to see when it was last accessed, updated, and/or downloaded. Because of increased scrutiny to meet compliance regulations, this type of family office is often geared toward mitigating risks and being proactive with the organizational and cost control measures.

These offices may be administrative- and compliance-oriented, but they also typically oversee tax returns, manage banking, insurance, and outside service-provider relationships, and function as a gatekeeper to the family. The investment function of the family office may not, however, be included and might rather be outsourced. Consolidated, tax, investment, and performance reporting are core functions of the administrative and compliance family office. Other services such as bill pay, lifestyle management, tax payments, estate planning, and document management may also be offered. Concierge services such as property management, travel services, jet acquisitions, overseeing private collections, coordinating gifting and insurance, hiring household staff, and/or jet maintenance are some of the amenities that may be offered.

The Philanthropic Family Office

The philanthropic family office has a strong focus on charitable intentions, impact investing, giving, and engaging heirs and beneficiaries of the wealth for the transition of wealth. This style of family office tends to focus on philanthropic, estate, financial, and family education and governance planning. The family foundation and/or family philanthropic fund/trust tend to be an important asset managed by this style of family office. Foundation management, impact investing, and charitable giving oversight, and advisement are central services typically offered by this type of family office, and it may also be an important place for family member education, involvement, and leadership development. Some of these types of family offices may have a very sophisticated grant-making process, while others may be less formal. Families who create a philanthropic family office tend to be bonded by common purpose and values for the wealth and aspire to make a difference with their wealth in an impact investing or philanthropic manner. Investment management tends not to be the focus and is commonly outsourced in this type of family office.

The Direct Investment and Investment Offices

The rise of the investment office and, specifically, the direct investment office has perhaps been the greatest of all the types. Investment offices traditionally handle the financial, accounting, and investment affairs of the family, centrally managed and executed on behalf of the family. Families who determine they desire purely to invest together through an investment-style family office may invest in public equity and private equity markets or may prefer one or the other. The goals of the investment office are to provide a coordinated, managed, and consistent investment process that is efficient, effective, and streamlined for family owners. This advisement translates into a strategic approach to the investment process as well as a tactical view to the asset allocation strategy. The investment office often provides consolidated investment reporting that illustrates attribution of investment performance based on underlying investments. Some offices are solely focused on doing direct investment deals, notes Euclid Walker, Partner and Founder at Parkway Investment Management. Walker, a contributing author to *The Complete Direct Investing Handbook*, shares that "the direct investment offices operate like boutique private equity shops or venture capital firms. They may syndicate deals as lead general partner or co-invest with funds or other families."[14]

Other offices may have more of an emphasis on tax aware and efficient investing, and an interest in asset location as well as integrating in estate planning decisions to inform the investment approach. Investment offices are often focused on managing liquidity needs with short- and long-term wealth objectives. Investment offices may organize some of their investments through investment partnerships, whereby they may pool a portion of an individual family member's capital to invest in select asset classes and/ or direct investments. It is also common for investment offices to have large holdings in real estate or private equity. Finally, many former hedge fund legends from investment icons such as George Soros, Carl Icahn, and Stanley Druckenmiller transformed their hedge funds into investment offices. With the continued scrutiny and regulation requirements for hedge funds, some hedge funds opted for more favorable disclosures and the investor protections of a family office, which became far less onerous under the Dodd-Frank Wall Street Reform and Consumer Protection Act.

The Family Business—Focused Family Office

The family office centered around a family business typically originates and is embedded within the family business itself. As the operating business(es) grow and additional liquidity is created, the family business owners reach a crossroads to separate the management of the wealth from the business. The family has a choice to invest as a collective or to have individual family members manage their wealth affairs independently, and when all or a significant portion of the family decides to pool the management of its wealth, the family business–centered family office is conceived. The family business–centered family office is a separate legal entity that tends to be located in a separate location to the operating business for privacy, security, and risk management reasons among others. The focus of this type of family office is to manage the wealth management needs of owners of the business in a manner that addresses wealth transfer, tax, and provides diversification to the operating business. The family business–centered family office may provide strategy and guidance on ownership control strategies, stock repurchase, buy/sell agreements, managing debt and credit effectively, and generating liquidity. The family business–centered family office may advise and be part of the strategic advisors in regard to family business restructuring or partial or full sale of the business. The family business–centered family office tends to provide financial planning, cash flow, and/or capital sufficiency analysis to its clients and is keenly interested to its client's holdings in terms of legal structures, ownership interests, and income tax planning. This type of family office tends to have a multigenerational perspective and will aid in estate and gift tax planning, fiduciary planning, asset protection, as well as family governance needs.

The Multigenerational-Focused Family Office

The multigenerational-focused family office manages the affairs for a growing, complex group of family owners who typically represent various family branches. This office may provide a variety of services including lifestyle planning, investment advice and management, tax compliance and preparation, estate planning oversight, wealth transfer planning, fiduciary management, document storage and management, risk management, governance, financial education, and philanthropic services. There can be significant challenges to operating this type of family office because of the differing needs and services requested by family members, as well as to expanding administrative functions. In certain cases, families may opt to outsource all or a portion of their services to a multi-family office that may be able to provide certain services in a more efficient manner for less cost than in-house. The multigenerational-focused family office is proactive when it comes to wealth transfer and preparing, educating, and communicating wealth transfer intentions. As a result, this type of office typically has a more sophisticated governance system with articulated family policies such as a family mission or values statement and/or a family constitution. Various governance committees—such as a family board, family council, or foundation board—may be instrumental in the family decision-making process. Strong family continuity, cohesion, and buy-in tend to be important attributes of this style of family office.

The Mathile Case Study that follows provides the inception, evolution, and triggering events that initiated different strategic planning cycles of a multigenerational family office. The case reveals the important early events that spawned the need for planning at different ages and stages of the family office.

Mathile Case Study

From inception to a family office evolution, strategic planning is a critical function to effectively setup, manage, and evolve a family office serving multiple generations. The Mathile Case Study reveals the planning cycles of a family and its office over several cycles and generations. Attention to the triggering events, alignment considerations of family client needs, and operational efficiencies are all important factors to consider when it comes to strategic planning and the family office. The following case provides an example of such attunement and responsiveness in the Mathile family office.

Background: Inception

The Mathiles' story begins 50 years ago in 1970, when Clay Mathile accepted a leadership role at Iams Food Company, a small Ohio-based pet food manufacturer. Over the next several years, he initiated several strategic initiatives and oversaw the company's rapid growth, becoming its sole owner and CEO by 1982. By 1999, Iams commanded a 5.7% share of the US pet food market and sold 100 different products in 75 countries. At that point, they sold the company to Procter & Gamble for $2.3 billion, producing windfall wealth for Clay, his wife, Mary, and his five children, who also were shareholders.

The sale of an operating company and the sudden wealth it creates often is a trigger to create a family office. In the Mathiles' case, they had actually created their family office in 1997 and engaged in some initial wealth planning. Nevertheless, the first 18 months after the sale were consumed with immediately necessary steps such as simply investing the sale proceeds. But after this initial period, the family office group took an important step to pause, reflect, and ask, "Who do we really want to be?" this signaled the official start of outlining the vision and goals for the family office. The patriarch challenged all the family office executives to develop a vision and a five-year goal for the family office. The team considered critical questions such as: What do we want to do? Why are we here? Why do we exist? What are our services? In other words, as Jill Barber, current Mathile family office head, stated, "The first strategic endeavor was really to create a plan for services to manage the family's liquidity, and to provide ways to address the first generation's philanthropic interests and other needs."[15] The outcome of these activities was a full-service family office, primarily focused on the first generation (e.g., concierge services, initial plans for two operating foundations).

Evolution of the Family Office: Strategic Planning Cycles

Not long after the establishment of the first strategic plan for the family office, due to the sale of Iams, did another trigger emerge signaling the need for another strategic planning cycle. Specifically, the family office realized that its culture post sale of Iams now needed to reflect its new reality as a family office truly focused on family member needs and the goals of two adult generations of the Mathile family. The office had to evolve its services by understanding the needs of the first generation may not be the exact needs of the second generation of owners. Allowing second-generation family members more voice in the service model, this strategic planning cycle also focused on evolving the family's governance and approach to engaging family, changing from first-generation parents determining the needs of their second-generation adult children to engaging them in the process. Through organized family meetings just for the second generation, this younger generation of family members discussed what they wanted and could afford for themselves and their children. Clay Mathile understands the importance of involving the family in the broader planning sharing: "I believe it is imperative to invest as much care in the business of the family as you do in the family business. What does that mean? I think it means acknowledging that your business has an impact on your family and purposefully managing that impact, proactively determining how the family will be involved."[16] The need to align and involve members of the second generation and the departure from Iams were the triggering events to prompt this cycle of strategic planning, the results of which included improving family office efficiencies and risk management protocols and scoping appropriate services to different generations of the family.

Change in leadership or management is another triggering event that often prompts the need for key stakeholders to convene and strategically plan. In 2009, the need for yet another strategic planning cycle was evident when the patriarch stepped down as chair of the board and the founding family office president retired, signaling a transfer of leadership from the first generation to the second generation. The resulting strategic plan led to sweeping leadership changes, including designation of a new family office president, hiring of a CIO, establishment of a senior leadership team (i.e., President, CIO, COO, chief client services officer [CCSO]), and moving a second generation family member into the role of family office board chair. Ancillary services were adapted for the family's evolving needs. The global financial crisis also forced the family to review how investing was being done and to dramatically increase the overall professionalism of the office. Changes included the creation of an internal investment function and a dedicated client service group, which allowed customized planning for each family branch. The revenue model was revised, with the new billing structure involving fees based on agreed categories of AUM/AUA. Navigating these changes has kept the family office quite busy until the most recent trigger for change occurred in 2019.

A Multigenerational Perspective

As of 2020, roughly half of the family's third-generation family members have come of age, meaning the Mathile assets are becoming far more dispersed across now three generations. With this dispersion comes the realization that the family office is no longer serving one or even two types of clients. Instead, the office now serves a collection of three highly diverse client types, each with a unique set of needs, preferences, and abilities (including abilities to pay). This client diversity requires equally diverse and nimble service offerings. Moreover, the rapid technological innovation and advancement fundamentally disrupting every area of life also has shifted how the family office delivers services and what third-generation family members, in particular, have come to expect. As Jill Barber observed, "Whereas the first and second generation are very similar, how this third generation thinks about the world and how they perceive value is so different. It is requiring us to take another look at what we're doing and why we're doing it, and what that value is to the family."[17] Accordingly, this fourth strategic planning cycle is focused on three main aims:

1. *Developing a flexible wealth advisory platform to meet its ever-diversifying client base:* Barber emphasized that "one-size-fits-all services or ways of reaching our clients isn't going to work for us, as it had for the last 20 years."[18]
2. *Providing family with visibility about family office activities:* Barber explained, "As a service business, we need to understand what we do and what it takes to do it in order to explain the value and time spent to the family members."[19] Such insights are crucial for demonstrating that, although the tasks for one generation versus another may vary, the attention the office dedicates to each family branch is roughly equal.
3. *Engaging the third generation:* As the youngest family members continue to reach adulthood, they want to be heard and have influence over the family office. The older generations and the family office are unified in supporting the third generation in doing just that and have created

opportunities for the younger Mathiles to experience a progressive string of successes so that they earn their leadership roles and acquire vital confidence as they do so.

Alignment, Urgency, and Action

Strategic planning shifts in the family office will continue to occur as new information, triggers, and changes are incorporated allowing the office to remain nimble and responsive to the current plan and path. Upon reflection of the Mathile family office, four critical takeaways to its strategic planning success surface. Those takeaways include the need for: (1) action, (2) alignment, (3) fluidity and order, and (4) help from time to time from outside experts and facilitators to stay the course.

The need for action becomes clear with the realization that there is never a good time to start strategic planning. But as many family office executives sheepishly admit, getting family owners, stakeholders, and executives to the table to focus on planning is a challenging task to say the least. Why? Because there is never a natural lull or break in activities when the family office staff will magically have the time to begin the process or a good time for family to often see an urgency to feel they need to be involved.

Reflecting on the first strategic planning cycle for the Mathile family office, it was initiated when just enough "firefighting" had subsided for planning to begin. It was then through Mathile's mandate to create a vision and accompanying plan, along with the office's subsequent activities, that strategic planning became part of the office's DNA. Often what holds families and their offices back from engaging in the planning exercise is lacking a sense of urgency or a consequence of not completing a strategic plan. This resistance may be reduced by viewing the family office as an operating business that provides services to its customers (the family members). If customers do not want or like the services, they will go elsewhere. This points both to the need for engaging families in planning process and the need to develop relevant metrics (e.g., costs as a percentage of AUM, expense ratios, investment performance after fees and taxes, client satisfaction, employee satisfaction, financial peace of mind) and accountability that guide planning and subsequent activities. Helpful questions include: What are the metrics the family holds you accountable to? How do you measure the success of the plan and the effectiveness of the plan? Simply identifying these metrics can trigger a planning process if it is revealed that performance against these metrics (or metrics themselves) are lacking. Moreover, a firm believer that "structure follows strategy," Mathile has always emphasized that strategy informs mission and vision, and that subsequent plans must be created and implemented to achieve the growth and change central to organizational success—and, in this case, achieving the family's goals.[20]

Strategic planning is continuous and informed by the reality of new information triggering the need to reassess the steps along the path. New data forces the family office to evaluate and confront if the current plan is still valid and accurate, or if the family office may need to pivot. Each of the four strategic planning cycles in the Mathile family office was triggered by a fundamental misalignment between the family's needs and the office's services: first was the need for vision-guided wealth management; second was the rise and emergent needs of the second generation of owners; third was the stepping down of the first generation of leaders and need to transition leadership to the second generation; and fourth was the rise of third-generation owners and need for diversified multigenerational services. Misalignments can be detected using simple feedback tools like surveys, follow-up with family members or committees, or input from family office employees (e.g., assessing their perspectives about the family office vision and services). Because the main purpose of strategic planning is aligning the family's needs with the family office's resources, dissonance across these constituents' viewpoints indicate that a strategic planning cycle may be needed. (See Figure 2.2.)

FIGURE 2.2 Strategic Planning Cycle

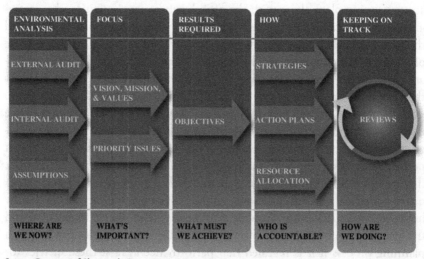

ENVIRONMENTAL ANALYSIS	FOCUS	RESULTS REQUIRED	HOW	KEEPING ON TRACK
EXTERNAL AUDIT	VISION, MISSION, & VALUES		STRATEGIES	
INTERNAL AUDIT		OBJECTIVES	ACTION PLANS	REVIEWS
ASSUMPTIONS	PRIORITY ISSUES		RESOURCE ALLOCATION	
WHERE ARE WE NOW?	WHAT'S IMPORTANT?	WHAT MUST WE ACHIEVE?	WHO IS ACCOUNTABLE?	HOW ARE WE DOING?

Source: Courtesy of Shamrock Group

Discovery and Steps

In the Mathile family office, the planning process for all but the first plan started with discovery. By surveying family members, the board, and staff members, the family office gauged the needs and desires of all stakeholders as well as gaps in knowledge about what the family office can and cannot provide. Surveying other family offices that are further along in the family's lifecycle also can be helpful for identifying best practices and possible service trajectories. For example, the Mathile family office surveyed and discovered what many other family offices that had transitioned to the third generation of family and beyond had done well, what they would avoid if they were to do over, and best practices to streamline their efforts. They concluded from this assessment that the family office had to become more of a quarterback or wealth advisor for the youngest generation, while continuing the high touch service offering for the senior family members (e.g., offer concierge services). In other words, they realized that their services needed to align with each generation to address the diverse needs present throughout the family. Furthermore, maintaining alignment requires ongoing, extensive communication, time, and involvement from all family stakeholders as well as family office staff (and not just the leadership team). If trust exists among the family members, the Board chair and family board members can usually act as the ambassadors to assure adequate communication and appropriate execution of the strategy. Nevertheless, employee engagement throughout the office is critical to identify issues and actionable solutions, efficiently execute the plan, and create sustainable change. Although it may be tempting to drive top-down change in the interests of time, keeping the employees engaged and informed ultimately saves time, promotes cohesion and commitment to the vision, and dissuades reversion to old habits.

Although strategic planning, in a traditional sense, is a formal event lasting 12 to 18 months and occurring every 5 to 10 years, the Mathile case demonstrates that contemporary strategic planning approaches need to embrace both fluidity and order. This shift is due to the overall accelerated pace of change and technological development that affect both the services that need to be delivered and how those services are delivered. At the inception of the Mathile family office, for example, there was no need for social media policies or online security, nor were automated web-based governance solutions available. These innovations act as external misaligning forces that trigger the need for strategic planning. The composition of the family, such as the ages, life stages, and other needs of family members, similarly impose internal forces that trigger change. Other factors that prompt change include regulatory changes, market shifts, and inputs from advisors. These conditions mean that strategic planning has evolved from being a static, multi-year design and implementation effort to a far more dynamic and agile endeavor. Jill Barber described it as a process of maintaining a dual heads-down (task-focused) and heads-up (vision-focused) approach. She explained, "You're maybe 80 percent heads-up while doing the intense strategic planning, and only 30 percent up when you're in a maintenance or working phase. But you're still watching for those changes and progressions to happen, and when an inflection point hits, you call a timeout for more involved strategic planning.[21]

She added that although the pace and some details of strategic planning has changed over the years, the process and steps have fundamentally remained the same, consisting of:

1. Defining and surveying the stakeholders to get feedback on issues and assess the current operating environment.
2. Reviewing family's mission, vision, values, and beliefs.
3. Revisiting the family office mission, vision, values, and beliefs in parallel with the plan, assessing the alignment of each with the family.
4. Performing a Strengths, Weaknesses, Opportunities, Threats (SWOT) analysis on the family office.
5. Reviewing the business model, including key partners, activities, resources, overall value added, cost structure, and revenue sources.
6. Identifying core issues, developing those key priority issues by studying their impact and desired change.
7. Defining goals and desired outcomes.
8. Prioritizing and developing action plans with metrics, steps, and owners.

Based on this process, the strategic planning team then navigates toward the "flag on the hill," as Barber describes, and constantly evaluates what the next right step is.

Involving Outside Experts

Clay Mathile has always been a firm believer in strategic planning. He credits such planning as a key contributor to the success of Iams. He also subsequently established Aileron, a public charity to foster better professional management among other organizations.[22] Perhaps for this reason, the final takeaway from this case is the need for help. Jill Barber emphasized that even within their office, "We always use outside help because you can get into a lot of blind spots when planning. You can miss a lot of things without a facilitator to help you see those blind spots."[23] While facilitators should not be given control over the plan, they can bring sophisticated content and process perspective based on extensive experience with other family offices. Moreover, they generally bring less bias because don't have a vested stake in the outcome and can play important roles in holding family members accountable—often a difficult thing for family members to do for each other. Outside help also can help families navigate one of the biggest challenges in a multigenerational family office: privacy. What the family office knows about individual family members or branches needs to remain confidential. Even family board members may not know the special needs or wealth of other family members or what is going on with a specific family branch project. Outsiders can aid in providing vital input while keeping sensitive information private.

The Mathile family office, now twenty years old, is exemplar of the power of embracing strategic planning as an efficient and effective process to managing change. Through several transitions—from a founder-focused office run by an ex–Arthur Andersen partner to a second-generation, family-led office focused on the diverse needs of multiple generations—the office has embraced a vigilant and responsive approach to strategic change. "We expect that this nimble approach will serve the family office far into the future as the family and its wealth continue to change, grow, and diversify," shares Barber as she looks forward to the family office's future.[24]

Conclusion and Final Thoughts

Pathways to a family office are all unique. Some will arrive at the need to set up a family office after one generation's success, while others may have a business entity for two, three, or more generations before a sale necessitates the interest for a family office. Other family members may not even realize that they are operating or functioning as a family office and may later in their evolution discover there are benefits to identifying as a family office. Other wealth creators and entrepreneurs will prefer to keep the family separate from the management of the wealth and may determine establishing an investment family office is more appropriate. Time also plays an important role in the development of a family office. Differences between a radical wealth event versus a slow, gradual, incremental need to create a family office impact the nature of the planning as does the complexity and number of generations involved. The history behind a family office's creation can be an important connection to the vision for wealth and the ongoing management and operations of the family office. The Mathile Case Study illuminates the best practices to set up, strategically plan, and iterate a family office over generations. A special thank you to Jill Barber, Kathryn McCarthy, Clay Mathile, Joni Fedders, and the entire Mathile family for sharing their story.

Notes

1. Barbara R. Hauser, "The Family Office: Insights into Their Development in the US, a Proposed Prototype, and Advice for Adaptation in Other Countries," *Journal of Wealth Management* 4 (2001): 15–22.
2. Ibid.
3. Assuming a diversified portfolio such as 60/40 stocks-to-bonds ratio.
4. A more exact approach is to take your total spending and liabilities annually and divide them by your total base of investable assets to come up with more of an exact percentage of required investment income.
5. Lee Eisenberg, *The Number* (New York: Simon & Schuster, 2008), 251.
6. "The U.S. Trust/Campden Research North America Family Office Study," presented to the Institute for Private Investors Winter Forum 2013, San Francisco, California.
7. Ibid.
8. Ibid.
9. Family Office Exchange, "Boundaries That Matter: Managing Family Assets Separately from the Family Business," 2008; and "Taking Care of Business: Case Example of Separating Personal Wealth Management from the Family Business," 2011.
10. Ibid.; FOX study, 2011.
11. Interview with Phil Strassler, CEO of Strassler LLC.
12. Barbara R. Hauser, "The Family Office: Insights into Their Development in the US, a Proposed Prototype, and Advice for Adaptation in Other Countries," *Journal of Wealth Management* 4 (2001): 15–22.
13. Jay Hughes, *Family: The Compact Among Generations* (New York: Bloomberg, 2007).
14. Correspondence with Euclid Walker, Founder and Partner, Parkway Investment Management, February 2020.
15. Interview with Jill Barber, President of the family office for the Mathile Family, January 2020.

16. Clay Mathile, *Run Your Business, Don't Let It Run You* (Berrett-Koehler Publishers, Inc., 2013).
17. Ibid.
18. Ibid.
19. Ibid.
20. Ibid.
21. Ibid.
22. To learn more about Aileron visit their website, https://www.aileron.org/.
23. Interview with Jill Barber, President of the family office for the Mathile Family, January 2020.
24. Ibid.

CHAPTER 3

Comparing Family Office Solutions: Multi- and Single-Family Offices

Kirby Rosplock, PhD

> If you don't know where you are going, any road will lead you there.
> —Lewis Carroll, author of *Alice in Wonderland*

The ever-changing landscape of wealth management makes it challenging to determine which solution is right for you and your family. If you do not have a guide or a map to get you to your destination, how will you know when or if you arrive? Knowing where to begin the journey, who to trust in the process, and how to systematically evaluate options are critical to the result. But in order to know what you may need for a wealth management solution, one must first evaluate family wealth needs to identify which of them are acute to the family—these are deemed the "must haves." The wealth needs that are not as imperative are the "nice to haves" when it comes to serving the family's wealth objectives. Finally, there are a few myths that are debunked in this chapter as I share some insights about how the family office world truly operates. A SWOT analysis explores the Strengths, Weaknesses, Opportunities, and Threats for the single-family office (SFO) and the multi-family office (MFO).

Trends in the Family Office Landscape

Family offices traditionally have been a cloistered, ultra-private segment of the wealth management industry, affordable only by the very rich. When quizzed in 1930 about how much it would cost to operate his massive new trans-Atlantic yacht *Corsair*, legendary financier and banker, J. P. Morgan, Sr., famously remarked: "Sir, if you have to ask that question, you can't afford it."[1] Such has also been the case traditionally with family offices. For those who can afford one, the value derived from a single-family office—including total privacy and control, continuity of staff, and custom services available 24/7—outweighs concerns over what might seem to others as outlandish operating expenses.

Today, change is sweeping this very private world and upsetting the traditional calculus for determining who needs a family office, what structure to use, what array of services to offer, and how much the whole thing should cost. On the one hand, surging wealth creation is bringing forth new fortunes, with family offices popping up in their wake. Every new billionaire has to have one, and semi-billionaires as well. On the other hand, many established family offices are being downsized, restructured, or dissolved because they can't sustain themselves in the transition to the second or third generation of family control. Some may simply run out of financial capital as the process of generational decay takes hold and the ranks of heirs grow faster than the corpus of family assets. Yet quite often it is human capital that runs out first, and the effect is just as fatal. The family's cohesion and amity, its consensus over governance, the alignment of goals and values among kin, its ability to develop and inspire a new generation of leadership—when they are lost, the financial capital will soon be gone as well.

Stiff crosswinds are buffeting the family office world. The challenges it faces have never been greater. Here are ten noteworthy trends in the family office environment:

1. *Grappling with complexity:* Life, it seems, has been getting vastly more complex for many of us in recent years, and that goes tenfold for family offices. Complexity presents growing challenges in almost every aspect of family office operations and management. New investment strategies are often driven by an esoteric approach to the markets. They force family offices to raise their games in terms of evaluating and monitoring the results of such strategies. Direct private equity investments may require complex ownership structures and sophisticated reporting systems

to integrate them onto the family office's books. Taxes on investment income have grown more complex, making tax compliance more of a challenge, particularly where large numbers of ownership entities or non-US business activities are involved. Wealth transfer strategies that may take months or years to implement can be voided by a change in the tax law, and thus require a do-over on short notice. Dealing with complexity requires expertise, and experts are expensive, whether hired in-house or from an outside source.

2. *Updating structure and strategy:* What is our mission, and what is the optimal structure and strategy to accomplish it? Many family offices are asking those questions and finding themselves dissatisfied with the answers. Thomas J. Handler, J.D., P.C. Partner at Handler Thayer, LLP, a leading law firm for family offices, spends considerable time focused on restructuring and reorganizing family offices to bring them current and make them more efficient, effective, and secure. "Most existing family office entities are out of date, not integrated, inefficient, and attended by income tax and estate tax leakage compared with modern best-in-class standards."[2] Also, up for review—the practice of using operating business employees and resources to handle personal financial matters for the owner's family, an arrangement known as an embedded family office, often co-located within operating businesses. Handler shares that "such offices will become increasingly disfavored by families and attorneys due to unnecessary tax, business, and compliance risks."[3]

3. *Paying new heed to risk management:* Old-fashioned, low-tech embezzlement by internal employees was once a leading risk facing family offices. Now it's way down on the list, overshadowed by more modern perils. Today, family offices are prime targets for internet scams and abuses. Identity theft, computer hijacking, ransom ware attacks, wire transfer scams, security lapses by family members using social media—these have all taken a heavy toll on family offices, earning them a reputation among fraudsters as easy marks. The UBS/Campden Wealth Global Family Office Report 2019 found that 20 percent of family offices admitted they have experienced a cyber security attack. What are the most common forms of attack? They are cyber-attacks including phishing (76 percent), malware (33 percent), and social engineering (33 percent).[4] Simple but effective financial controls can foil most low-tech embezzlement. It takes much more effort and expense, however, to safeguard the family office against cyber-attacks. Thankfully, family offices have got the message and are paying attention to cyber risks. In doing so, many have had their eyes opened to the broader importance of addressing the whole array of risk

management issues, not just as risk relates to cyber vulnerabilities, and are benefitting from their new across-the-board awareness.

4. *Pushing multigenerational governance and empowerment:* As noted, a key to family office sustainability in the long-term is the family's ability to develop new generations of leadership and transition them into the governance and management of the family's affairs. Autocratic leadership by the senior generation—once almost universally practiced—is giving way to new forms of governance such as family councils that give voice and responsibility to younger generations, helping them to develop and gain experience. There is new emphasis on family education, starting at early ages, and getting young people involved in decision-making. One favored approach gives younger family members responsibility for some of the family's charitable activities, including development of philanthropic strategy, participation in the family foundation's affairs, and approving charitable grants. It's a step toward meaningful involvement and inclusion for the next generation, and that is the order of the day for family offices that want to sustain themselves long-term.

5. *Sorting through the impact of longevity:* Increased longevity affects family offices in a variety of surprisingly important ways. It has added an extra living generation to many families. Where there were three or four living generations, now there are four or five living generations. Financial plans may need to be rewritten to account for the substantial living expenses of the 100-year-old who was expected to die by age 90. Elaborate multigenerational trusts may have to be scrapped and redone. Life insurance policies can cause tax or other problems if the insured lives to the point where policy "endows" and is distributed in the form of cash value instead of a death benefit. The family office may suddenly need to develop expertise in such areas as eldercare arrangements or legal competency of the elderly. Whereas the Grim Reaper was once in charge of family leadership succession decisions, it's now often up to the family: If grandpa is developing dementia and still has control of family assets, what do we do? Increasingly, family offices are asking those kinds of questions.

6. *Enjoying (or maybe not) a higher public profile:* Family offices have always been publicity shy and certainly remain so. Yet despite their individual best efforts to stay offstage, family offices as a group are finding they have acquired a much higher public profile. Several factors are fueling this trend. One is the growth of private financial markets, where family offices have become key players since the financial crisis of 2008. To attract deal flow and gain market clout, family offices have found themselves taking a much more visible role, thus drawing public attention. Another factor

putting them in the spotlight: Since the Dodd-Frank financial reform legislation, which crimped hedge fund activities, several dozen hedge funds have converted themselves to family offices and now manage money just for their owners and key employees, thus avoiding the need to register with the Securities and Exchange commission as advisors. Many of the individuals involved are leading Wall Street figures and their actions now draw added attention to the family office world.

7. *Integrating core values with investments:* In just a few years, impact investing has become widely accepted among family offices. This approach also goes by the names of ESG (environmental, social, and governance) investing, purpose-driven investing, ethical investing, and, originally as known in the 1970s, socially responsible investing. Whichever the label, impact investing strategies are now ubiquitous in the family office world. Families increasingly want to invest responsibly according to their own values and will want impact investments tailored for their needs. A wide variety of strategies is available using both public market securities and direct private equity investments. Jennifer Kenning, CEO of Align Impact, explains that the number of families who are aligning their investment practices with their values, including concerns for the environment, health, wellness, and education, among others, has ramped up quickly. She shares, "The overall trend among families is finding opportunities to not just make more with their wealth but to make the world better. My clients are investing in new directions to seed a brighter future for their offspring."[5]

8. *Blurring lines between single-family offices and multi-family offices:* Single-family offices and multi-family offices once lived in largely separate worlds. True, many leading multi-family offices were formed when single-family offices opened their doors to nonfamily clients. Their intent was to build economic scale and use revenues from outside families to help cover fixed costs of the family office's operations. But once they opened their doors, these single-family offices became commercial enterprises and drifted away to some extent or other from the single-family office world. Today, a new dynamic is emerging as form and function of single-family offices and multi-family offices become more flexible. For example, multi-family offices now provide platforms used by single-family offices to augment their service menus on an outsourced basis. A single-family office might contract with a multi-family office to provide family education to the younger generation or serve as investment consultant for specialized asset classes. Or a single-family office might make advance arrangements to fold its entire operations into a multi-family

office when the current control generation is ready to retire. All signs point toward this trend continuing to flourish.

9. *Dealing with suboptimal scale:* To be viable, businesses need to reach a critical mass in terms of asset size and operating revenue. Most family offices function as investment advisors, albeit for one family. It's a business that depends for success on scale, and family offices are not immune from the economics of that business. Research by the Family Wealth Alliance has found that small single-family offices (under $100 million in assets) pay three to four times as much in operating expenses for each $1 supervised than do big ones ($1 billion plus). It's no wonder that the minimum asset size considered feasible for starting a single-family office has escalated well above $100 million today. Scale is essential if the family office is to afford experienced professional management and obtain essential information technology. Indeed, suboptimal scale is typically behind decisions by family offices to outsource key services.

10. *Braving the new world of technology:* More and more family offices are concluding that they need an up-to-date, comprehensive information technology solution. The old jury-rigged set of Excel spreadsheets often used to keep the books is labor-intensive, error-prone, lacking in functionality, and not able to deliver data via mobile devices favored by younger family members. While it may be clear that the old system isn't working, it's rarely clear what to do about it. The essence of the problem is that family office information needs are exceedingly complex as compared, for example, to the requirements of a typical business of similar economic size. Such a business is likely to do just fine with a general ledger accounting system. The family office needs general ledger accounting, but it also needs portfolio accounting, trust accounting, specialized tax accounting—and some means of consolidating their various outputs. The good news: There are plenty of technology vendors, and outsourcing will likely be the best choice.

Determining Family Wealth Management Needs

The first step to determining your family wealth management needs is to review the types of family office services and the family office archetypes described in the prior section. Consider which of these services and family office archetypes most apply to your family's circumstance. Next step is to explore more deeply the relationship of how these services are performed, their importance to all family members versus individual households, and the costs to administer these services in-house versus outsourcing them. To follow is a discussion of the appropriateness of a family office as compared to the merits of joining a multi-family office structure.

Why the Single-Family Office Solution?

Once you have identified the priority activities needed by the family, the next logical step is to determine which type of family office structure may apply. Why do individuals and families establish their own family office? In this section we explore the Strengths, Weaknesses, Opportunities, and Threats (SWOT) analysis of the family office. There are several key drivers for creating a family office; however, the greatest two drivers are control and privacy. The interest for total control is not at all surprising, as the wealth is created by one or more families through perseverance, calculated risk-taking, and concentration. The source of wealth of the vast majority of family offices was a result of a sale of a business, a partial liquidity event from an operating business, a major executive compensation package, or other windfall event as described in Chapter 2. In nearly all cases, the first-generation wealth creator was or is at the helm of the wealth creation and is comfortable leading and directing wealth management decisions. Further, these individuals are typically shrewd, savvy business leaders who have realized that their wealth is in fact a new business and they are attracted by this opportunity. They appreciate the opportunity to customize the services desired in their family office and often have more complex underlying assets that may include various legal structures, control, and variyng levels of governance oversight. Thus, being able to customize and direct the design is an attractor for those interested in establishing a family office.

Other drivers for creating a family office are privacy, anonymity, and confidentiality. Families do not create a family office to be seen or known; rather most are attracted by its low-brow, discreet profile. More often than not, families select a family office name that is obscure and unidentifiable to the family. They typically are not looking to attract commercial visibility, so they operate quietly under the wealth management radar, their family office often acting as a gatekeeper to the outside provider world. Where once there may have been "Keep Out" signs to providers, many family offices view institutions who provide family office services as now part of their "team" in areas where they lack bench strength or want to learn from others' mistakes prior to setup.

Instead, a family office no longer just relies on friendly help from other colleagues and family office peers; rather, they are augmenting with specialists like Carly Doshi, Head of Philanthropy and Family Governance at HSBC Private Bank. Doshi sees that families often seek best practices from other families before they get started building a family office, and banks can provide a first point-of-contact for learning about the landscape and formulating a plan. "Because we work with a large number of families around the world, we can offer a unique perspective on what other families are doing, and what practices are trending." This guidance may be particularly useful in early stages since most families are not always familiar with the range of options available. Doshi's philanthropy and family governance group is an expert resource within HSBC Private Bank, and, because they are a neutral and available exclusively to the bank's clients, they can be more objective. Doshi notes, "I have seen instances where the advice we provide is later embedded into the family office structure. I've also seen that the introductions we've made between family offices lead to information sharing and collaboration between those entities, even resulting in co-investing and shared philanthropy initiatives."[6]

Family offices are also communing more and more in free or private membership forums. Shared family office membership organizations, such as the Global Family Office Community (GFOC), provide a private global community for family offices and the family members they serve. GFOC is approximately 1,000 family offices of international members with 60 percent based in Europe and approximately 30 percent in North America. Providing conferences, seminars, education, and the *GFOC Journal*, GFOC also supports international recruitment.[7]

The Forge Community (FORGE), backed by Fidelity Labs, is a self-governing, peer-to-peer network of family offices sharing best practices and "lessons learned" to help them along their journey. FORGE started organically from 295 family offices and has grown to more than 1,245 in its eight years of existence.[8] Other leading private membership organizations that convene are the Family Office Exchange (FOX), Family Office Association (FOA), and Family Office Network (FON).

The networking and sharing among family offices allows for the cross pollination of ideas, best practices, and shortcuts. One family office even described the in-house reporting system they built at significant cost and time to themselves, adding that they offered to share this system with other family offices. This type of behavior displays the more collegial versus competitive nature of single-family offices. Another example of collegiality and trust surfaced around succession. Because some family offices implicitly trust each other and there is typically far less competition among them, they recognize that they have each other's best interests in mind. One interesting development in a peer group of Chicago-based family offices was the creation of a contingency plan when an executive-level family office professional becomes incapacitated. If a key executive in a family office was suddenly not able to work, professionals from the other family offices would step in and fill in for the short-term while the family and its remaining family office executives identified the successor. The peer group would also act as strategic advisors to the family and the family office professionals in the search process to replace the key leader. Although this case was unusual, it illustrates the level of trust, confidence, and solidarity that some family offices have with one another.

Another important strength is the ability to have total alignment with the family's values, beliefs, goals, and business practices. Because the family office is created with the family's best interest at hand, conflicts of interest and the typical challenges other financial services models face are rare. The simplest examples are firms that provide products and the compensation for selling them, whereby the advisor may be influenced to sell one product over another because the compensation from the sale benefits them or the firm better than the other product. With the family office, the family office can clearly define a business model that establishes clear rules of engagement with providers to mitigate such risks. The level of dedicated service coupled with the integration of knowledge can be worth the premium.

Finally, family offices tend to operate under a different time horizon than the traditional individual investors, who contemplate managing financial means for their lifetime. Because family offices are considering how to manage wealth for decades, they tend to operate with a patient capital point of view. Patient capital denotes an ability to plan and allocate investment with varying degrees of risk and over a longer time horizon. Patient capital also refers to the mind-set that the family typically brings to investing—stay rich versus get rich. In other words, families with a family office are more often focused on wealth preservation than on wealth accumulation or get-rich-quick schemes to building wealth. See Figure 3.1 for a short list of family offices' top strengths.

Family offices, like all wealth management models, have blind spots or weaknesses that can be challenging to their existence. Attracting and retaining key employees can be a weakness of a family office as described in Chapter 10 on talent management, compensation, and recruitment. Because family offices have grown in interest significantly in the last decade, the number of individuals trained to work in a family office is relatively low. The competition to hire top talent with the experience, credentials, and chemistry fit can be difficult. Further, because the career path in an SFO is typically nonexistent, professionals interested in advancing up the traditional corporate ladder may be disappointed.

In addition to recruiting, retaining, and incentivizing talent, family offices may also be challenged by the growing costs to operate as their assets may dwindle in scale from one generation to the next. Costs may vary with the scope of services rendered in-house versus outsourced, the number of individuals working in the family office and the compensation they command, coupled with basic overhead business operating expenses. One family office interviewed calculates a Family Office Expense Ratio (FOER), which is the partnership expenses divided by the average net assets of the partnership. To make this calculation each month, the family office annualizes the result to compensate for beta, the inherent risk-free rate in the market. For instance, if looking at January through June,

> FOER^9 = year – to – date total partnership expenses
> (including manager fees) / partnership net assets at the end
> of the month divided by 6 to get the average balance

For this family office, FOER has become an important metric to evaluate the sustainability and viability of their family office. Other family offices may have slight variations of how they calculate their FOER.[10]

There are direct expenses associated with the family office, which encompasses costs such as talent, operations, infrastructure, investments, technology, reporting, administration, and risk management, among other services. There are variable costs that include the fees associated with managing the assets, custodial fees, and outside expenses associated with services rendered from accountants, attorneys, and other professionals. Although there are no hard and fast rules around the operating costs of a family office, operating expenses generally range from 60 to 150 basis points, or approximately .6 to 1.5 percent of assets under management. For smaller family offices, those with assets of $250 million or less, the cost to operate can be slightly more expensive. For example, a global study of family offices with $250M or less had an operating cost of 114 basis points compared to offices with $250M to $1B at 114 basis points and 118 basis points for family offices of $1B or more.[11]

This brings into question the cost-to-scale tradeoff and what scale is required for operational efficiencies. For families who are very cost sensitive, the complexity coupled with the cost associated with operating a family office may deter this option for wealth management. There are a number of

FIGURE 3.1 SWOT Analysis for the Single-Family Office

Strengths	Weaknesses
Control	Attracting and Retaining Talent
Customized, Dedicated Service	Cost Controls
Privacy and Anonymity	Access to Products and Services
Alignment and Integration	Operational Efficiencies
No SFO Competition	Service Level Inadequacies
Patient Capital	Bridging Family Continuity
Wealth Preservation	Urgency Toward Strategic Planning
Family First	
Opportunities	**Threats**
Open Architecture	Managing Scope
Co-Investments	Controlling Costs
First-Class Service	Compensation Challenges
Collaboration	Generational Mathematics
Sharing/Streamlining Costs	Family Conflict
Peer-to-Peer Exchange	Succession Planning
SFO Best Practices Information	Keeping Family on Board
and Research	

Source: © Tamarind Partners, Inc.

headwinds to maintaining the scale of the wealth, including taxes, inflation, increased cost of living, and investment fees among other expenses, as will be discussed in Chapter 8 on investment management. However, other families may be comfortable paying a premium for the benefits of control, privacy, customization, and objective advice.

There are several opportunities and threats to the very existence of the family office. Opportunities for the family office include the ever-expanding pool of family offices, which in turn translates into a growing underground network of family offices. At first, many of these families connected with one another through professional organizations; however, an increasing number are creating smaller, informal networks for peer exchange and to share best practices. In fact, one family office interviewed shared that their family office had an emergency plan that involved other family office peer executives advising on replacing key leadership if one or more family office executives unexpectedly became incapacitated. Because they had created such a high level of trust and confidence with one another, managing through such a crisis would be enhanced by the objectivity, aligned values, and wisdom of peer family office leaders who could advise independently. In addition to emergency and continuity planning, family offices are finding solace investing with one another in co-investment structures. This topic is covered in greater depth in Chapter 8 that focuses on the investment process in the family office. Because family offices are not in competition with one another, the opportunities to collaborate extend far beyond investing together. From sharing best practices and real case experiences, to exchanging research and manager due diligence, there are multiple ways that family offices can enhance one another's existence. In certain cases, family offices will defray or share costs through engaging a consultant or advisor across a series of offices. There is power in collaboration and partnering with like-minded family office peers who operate from a similar base of values, goals, and family objectives.

Some of the greatest threats to a family office are managing expenses, managing family expectations, and scope creep. Scope creep refers to ever-expanding expectations and services rendered by the family office that may be:

- More costly to perform in-house than to outsource.
- Added on incrementally and not monitored in terms of the scope of services rendered.
- Reflected as an imbalance of the level of services provided to one family or household than another.
- Keeping up with rapid technology changes.
- Managing data and timely, aggregated reporting.
- Retaining, incenting, and recruiting talent.

Other threats to the long-term viability of the family office include keeping the family engaged, onboard, and supportive of the family office concept, managing family conflicts, and building continuity of the ownership and leadership succession in a family office. Figure 3.1 provides a SWOT analysis of the single-family office model.

Why the Multi-Family Office Solution?

A FOX survey indicates that MFOs have an average of 131 client relationships amounting to $5.1 billion in Assets under Management (AUM), which would indicate a median of investable assets per client of $39 million.[12] The fee structure for MFOs varies from:

* A fee on assets under management.
* A project or hourly based fee structure.
* A retainer for family office services and a fee for assets under management, creating a blended fee structure.
* Fee structures will vary depending on the number of accounts, complexity of the legal structures, number of households, complexity of the reporting structure, number of custodians, number of advisors required to serve the family, number of transactions, number of households in more than one country, number of beneficiaries among other criteria.[13]

The primary services provided by most multi-family offices include cash flow planning and analysis, estate planning, tax planning, financial planning, investment management, family member education, philanthropic administration and advisement, and family meeting facilitation. Other services often provided may include fiduciary services, life insurance, credit and lending, tax preparation, banking services, trust administration, expense management or bill pay, concierge services, and lifestyle management such as property management, managing art and collectables, among other services.

The growth of the multi-family offices model is driven by three areas—the interest to buy family office services versus building a single-family office, the desire to delegate and centralize the management of wealth management needs, and the relative cost savings associated with being a multi-family office client versus the costs associated to build out a full-service family office. If we consider the strengths, weaknesses, opportunities, and threats of the multi-family office model, we begin to see that there are many of the same perceived benefits of the family office within the multi-family office model, which may explain their increased interest and adoption of this approach for affluent families and individuals.

There are several strengths of the multi-family office model, including its ability to scale expertise and provide a number of services at a reduced expense, as compared to what might be rendered in a single-family office. For example, most family offices will not opt to hire a full-time expert on family dynamics, meeting facilitation, family governance, or family education; however, larger, established multi-family offices are likely to have one or more on staff. Additionally, multi-family offices with a dedicated investment team may have multiple analysts, researchers, economists, and investment professionals conducting a wide array of investment due diligence. The breadth of talent that may be afforded by a multi-family office tends to trump the type of talent that the smaller single-family office can attract.

Multi-family offices tend to have more sophisticated compensation packages for its top-tier talent that may include base salary with bonus or long-term equity, for example. Multi-family offices may be willing to pay slightly more, but also require more from their employees who may be serving greater volumes of clients. Further, multi-family offices tend to have client service teams with anywhere from two to five or more advisors serving the family. The make of this team is typically a mix of more experienced, seasoned subject matter experts, coupled with one or more relationship managers and junior staff who assist with the administration of the relationship.

An additional strength of multi-family office is their ability to invest in infrastructure and build business processes that streamline and make the operating model of the business more effective. This can translate into lower fees for the client. From more comprehensive reporting, to sophisticated and secure document management services, to offering secure family website services, there are many "nice to have" elements that a multi-family office may be able to provide for families that a single family office may not.

Another benefit of the multi-family office model is the breadth of experiences that the advisors learn from the variety of families that are served. Because of the greater volume of similar situations, multi-family offices tend to have devised strategies for different fact patterns that families are trying to solve. This is a tremendous advantage for a family that is less experienced to wealth and investment management and who would rather not have to pay a consultant or outside advisor to gain this knowledge.

It is important to acknowledge, however, that with the multi-family offices' strengths also come weaknesses. Multi-family offices are for-profit entities and as such have profit-seeking motivations. Understanding the client-to-advisor ratio is critical, so a client does not begin to feel like just another number. Second, it must be recognized that the availability of their advisors may not be as high touch as having the direct attention of a dedicated family office employee. Third, more institutionalized multi-family offices may have a more limited scope of available products and services depending on their profitability. Thus, these types of multi-family offices may outsource underlying services or products, which may mean you are paying the multi-family office as a middleman for these types of services as opposed to buying direct. Finally, there are additional embedded costs, such as marketing and business development, which do not typically exist in a family office. I have yet to meet a family office with a marketing department.

The opportunities of multi-family offices are plenty. First, there is more bang for your buck as an individual or family; thus, you can typically get a lot more services relative to the expense. Second, being a client of a multi-family office can be a wonderful learning ground for families to examine if the family office concept is of interest and if they desire to really pursue building out a family office of their own. Coming up the family office learning curve under the guidance of a multi-family office can be a superior training ground to understand the level and sophistication of services desired versus required. Third, more extensive multi-family offices can have a one-stop shop appeal, as you can have a wide array of wealth and investment management services all centrally coordinated through one provider. With greater access to a variety of managers, products, and services, families can streamline their time to get the services and advice that they are seeking. Finally, multi-family offices tend to invest more in research and development, which means innovation is typically engrained in their business strategy.

One of the greatest threats to the multi-family office model is the desire to grow too quickly. Although growth is critical to sustainability of the multi-family office model in the long term, firms that have grown quickly though acquisition, mergers, and/or rapid expansion may find it challenging to bring everything onboard and integrate it into the multi-family office. When multi-family offices grow too fast, tremendous pressure may be placed on the multi-family office's infrastructure, meaning that the advisory teams must serve more families. This can translate into lower-touch service. Other threats include multi-family offices overpromising on how and what they can deliver. Sometimes it is a function of access to resources, other times it is a function of how timely tasks can be executed. Multi-family offices are owned in several different fashions and, increasingly, institutional owners such as banks, trust companies, and investment companies (among others) may have a controlling interest in the multi-family offices. This may become a conflict of interest depending on how and if certain products or services are being pushed from the parent company to the multi-family office's client. Further, when there is a corporate parent company, there can be challenges with the culture of the firm. What follows in Figure 3.2 is a SWOT analysis for the multi-family office model.

FIGURE 3.2   SWOT Analysis for a Multi-Family Office

Strengths	Weaknesses
Scale	Client/Advisor Load (+/−)
Comprehensive Services	Institutionalize Service Offering
Streamlined and Efficient	Access to Product/Services
Integration	Group Think
Breadth of Resources	Customization and Personalization
Top Talent and Retention	Bureaucracy
Centralized Data Management	

Opportunities	Threats
More for Less	Getting Too Big Too Fast
Learning Curve	Maintaining Close Relationships
Open Architecture	Overpromising
One-Stop Shop	Talent Retention and Turnover
Sharing Costs for Specialty Services	Ownership and Leadership Alignment
Access to Investment Managers,	Corporate Culture
Products, and Research	
Thought Leadership and Innovation	
Corporate Culture	

Source: © Tamarind Partners, Inc.

Now that we have reviewed the family office trends, services, archetypes, and SWOT analysis for the family office and multi-family office models, what are the questions an individual or family should inquire to become an informed consumer? To follow is a comprehensive section reviewing leading questions to pose to potential service providers.

Questions to Ask During the Evaluation Process

When evaluating wealth advisory firms and multi-family office providers, there are key questions to ask. The following list of categories will provide an understanding of who they are, what they offer, and how they rank themselves against their peers.

What Is the Scope of the Firm's Services?

Websites and brochures provide a compelling presentation of services rendered, but ask specifics on what the firm would recommend for your family. Drill down to how these specific services are delivered and ask to see a sample letter of engagement. Not all firms can provide the services in-house and may contract out portions of their service offering. If services are rendered by a third party, request to interview them and understand the business relationship between the firm and the third party. Finally, ask them to compare themselves to their peer group and what makes them different and better than other firms.

With Whom Will You Be Working Directly?

Sending in the cavalry of the C-suite is a common first introduction of a firm to a prospect family. Yet, in nearly all wealth advisory and multi-family offices, the most senior leadership is not working day-in and day-out on the front lines; rather, they are the face of the firm. If you feel a connection in your first meeting to the firm's senior leadership team and are curious to explore the relationship further, make sure to request a face-to-face meeting and interview with the advisor(s) who will be your primary relationship manager(s). Also, understand who else is on the team and what level of access you have to subject matter experts within the firm. Request to see resumes that illustrate their experience, credentials, and sophistication. Conducting background checks on those individuals and the key leadership in a firm is a prudent step. Finally, understand how many clients the relationship manager currently services and what is considered capacity. Many wealth advisory and multi-family office providers have a limit to the number of relationships that an advisor manages. If there is no limit shared, consider this a red flag and inquire, "Why not?"

What Is the Firm's History?

Registered investment advisors are annually required to disclose to the SEC ownership, management, and any conflicts of interest among other pertinent information in its Form ADV. For more information and access to ADV forms, please see the SEC's Investment Adviser Public Disclosure website at www.adviserinfo.sec.gov.

Further marketing materials can provide insights to the history, founding, and how the firm is owned. Is the firm affiliated or owned by another firm, and if so, what do these other firms provide for services or products? Inquiring about the organizational chart and reporting and ownership structure is also useful. Be sure to ascertain whether the firm is in an early stage, started within the last five years, mid-stage, five to fifteen years of age, or an established firm, more than fifteen years of age. Do not be fooled that just because a firm has been around for decades means it is the best fit for you. Many larger firms have gone through various metamorphoses over the years with transitions of leadership, ownership, business affiliations, and inflows and outflows of talent. Also, inquire how the firm has grown and what the growth plan is for the next 5, 10, and 25 years. Has the firm grown organically through client referrals or through acquisitions or mergers? What percentage of the firm's budget is dedicated toward public relations, marketing, and business development? How the firm perceives growth provides important insight into the motivations and aspirations of the firm's owners and stakeholders as opposed to the interests of the clients whom they serve. Conduct a check to see if there are pending lawsuits or arbitration cases against the firm. Finally, ask about the professional liability coverage that the firm carries and ask if you can have a copy of the coverage.

Who Do You Serve, How Many, and How Do You Know If Your Clients Are Satisfied?

Inquiring about the background and typical client profiles of the firm's client base will provide insights if your circumstances and wealth advisory needs are comparable and similar to their existing client base. Demographic data, such as the typical age, net worth, occupation, number of accounts, and types of client wealth objectives are helpful criteria to discern if you are like their existing client base or an outlier.

Scale is a major point to consider in finding the right fit. You may prefer a smaller, boutique firm with a dozen or so clients, or you may be interested in a medium-sized firm that has some economies of scale but is not totally institutionalized, or you may be inclined to go to a larger firm with hundreds of clients because they have elevated their service offerings from their integration and knowledge of so many families. Finally, ask about the increase or decrease in assets under management versus the number of new clients added or lost in the last year and to what do they attribute the growth or decline of their client base. This can be a powerful indicator to the direction of the firm. For the firms that submit to rankings in publications such as *Barron's*, *Forbes*, and *Financial Advisor Magazine*, families can see many of these lists online.

Satisfaction is an important metric to gauge whether a firm's client base is positive about the services they are receiving. Ask about how they gather client satisfaction data from their families. Do they survey or randomly interview in-house; do they contract through a third provider? How do clients rate their level of satisfaction, the perceived value proposition, and how willing they are to refer this firm to other families?

What Are the Critical Wealth Advisory Issues Your Firm Solves?

Earlier in the chapter, we discussed the differences of "must have" needs, those that are critical to your family's success in managing its wealth, and those that are "nice to have," but which are not critical services required by the family. During the interview process, provide the top three "must haves" that you need the firm to resolve and ask them to provide examples of how they have handled similar advice to families, what they have recommended, and what was the result. Also ask them to share experiences of families where the solution may not have worked out well and understand what went wrong. No firm is perfect; if you perceive their responses as disingenuous or not authentic about challenges in resolving complex family wealth issues, consider their responses a red flag. Ask to see references of clients who have a similar profile as you and request families who have been with the firm for more than a honeymoon period (more than three to five years). It takes this much time to see how their services and advice is panning out.

What Is Your Practice Around Client Privacy and Confidentiality?

Anticipate that every firm will provide compliance-approved language around their stringent privacy and confidentiality measures; however, a scan of credible news sources can reveal quickly which firms have a track record of violating client confidentiality or breaches within their systems. When evaluating firms around their client privacy and confidentiality practices, ask them to provide a list of measures and how/if they routinely implement these measures. How often are internal audits conducted to ensure that the firm is following these measures? How many employees will have access to your personal information and have they all signed a nondisclosure and confidentiality agreement? What happens to personal client information following the termination of a client relationship?

What Security Measures Are in Place in Your Firm?

Security has many facets in wealth advisory and multi-family office firms today. At a brick-and-mortar level, inquire about the security practices for physical client documents, archived family information, and client files. Where is this information housed? Who has access to it? How is the firm's physical security? For documents maintained off-site through a third party, what are their security measures? Consider the firm's physical location when it comes to security. Are they in a flood, hurricane, or tornado zone or in a geography prone to brown- or black-outs that could disrupt their services?

At a virtual level, inquire about information systems security and the firm's disaster recovery plan. How often is the firm's online security tested? Firms typically will go through a disaster recovery exercise annually, where they switch over to backup servers. The drill is no joke. All employees should have test scripts to follow. If the firm does not have a comprehensive approach and track record of backing up systems, securing pertinent physical and virtual data, and having employees who abide by these measures, these are red flags.

What Potential Conflicts Exist That May Impact How I Work with the Firm?

Compensation is the number one area where conflicts typically arise. Specifically, ask about how the firm is compensated for the services rendered. If the firm indicates there is more than one stream of revenue, such as an advisory fee as well as a commission on products sold, be sure to probe more deeply to determine if they follow the Suitability Standard or the Fiduciary Standard discussed later in this chapter.

Other potential conflicts may occur with referral sources. Does the firm have affiliates or alliances with firms where they routinely refer and receive compensation from those firms for bringing them business? There are several ways that a firm's fee structure can create conflicts of interest, so pay close attention to various types of revenue streams and how they are managed to help reveal if those conflicts are putting you at risk.

How Does the Firm Distribute and Communicate Information to Its Clients?

Once the firm has engaged you as a client, how will the firm demonstrate and communicate the progress that is being made on your behalf? Are the firm's strengths in its reporting capabilities or does the firm have better capabilities in its face-to-face interactions or firm-wide correspondence? How frequently will you be visited or connect with your advisor? Request to see a sample client report package and learn the degree to which the package can be customized to your specifications. Finally, different wealth holders—specifically those of upcoming generations—may have a preference to access reports and documents as well as correspond online. How much of the information may be exchanged virtually?

What Government or Industry Organizations Must You Comply with and What Is Your Track Record?

Virtually all organizations providing wealth advisory services or selling financial products are subject to some type of government or regulatory oversight. If they are providing investment advice, they would be registered with the SEC and likely the states where they operate. US banks are primarily regulated by the Federal Deposit Insurance Corporation (FDIC), the Federal Reserve Board (FRB), or the Office of the Comptroller of Currency. Request to see the policies and procedures in place established for these governing agencies. You may also request to receive verification of the balances and transactions from custodians whom you may elect to choose. Finally, see if there is an opportunity to do a personal, unannounced audit of how the offices work to check that client information is being protected and to verify that the practices the firm does are in accordance with your policies and procedures manual. More on the topic of compliance, regulatory requirements, and practices is covered in Chapter 7.

Which Standard of Care Are You Required to Comply with When It Comes to Advising Clients—the Fiduciary Standard or the Suitability Standard?

The Fiduciary Standard applies to investment advisors and registered investment advisors. It requires that they always put the interests of their clients first. It also requires that the advisor acts with care and prudence and exercises good judgment that is aligned with the interests of the client. The Fiduciary Standard is about transparency and providing full and fair disclosure on all relevant facts. Finally, the Fiduciary Standard desires advisors to avoid conflicts of interest and requires that the advisor fully disclose any if they exist. Further, the advisor is expected to manage those conflicts in a manner that is favorable to the client if unavoidable. The Fiduciary Standard is about leading with the client's best interests in mind in a way that intends not to do any harm.[14]

The Suitability Standard provides that brokers and advisors give advice at an "arm's length" and does not require that recommendations be in the best interest of the client. Instead, products or services may be recommended that may be in the best interest of the firm over the client's needs. If misdoing is determined by the advisor, in the case of the Suitability Standard, it is up to the investor to find the wrongdoing with the advisor. Conversely, with the Fiduciary Standard, if wrongdoing is determined, it is on the advisor to prove that they behaved in the client's best interest. Clearly, the Suitability Standard does not protect or inform the investor in the same fashion as the Fiduciary Standard. Further, the Fiduciary Standard has a duty to disclose fees and control expenses; maintain, follow, and document the due diligence process; and diversify investments in the best interest of the client. A typical broker who meets the minimum requirements has no such obligation to watch out for the client.

Pathways to Selecting a Multi-Family Office

Many families will work in concert with a consultant or directly with the firms they are evaluating to garner answers to the questions provided above. The reason families may choose to hire a third-party consultant is typically to help with the search and evaluation process, as well as to aid in deciphering the responses from firms under consideration. Families typically are not experts in evaluating the structure, organization, talent, and investment process, so an expert consultant can work for the family as an agent to identify the best potential fits for the client. They may also act as a moderator (mediator), when or if family members may not all be aligned and need a third party to weigh in on best-in-breed after careful consideration of prioritized family office needs.

Evaluation of multi-family office providers has evolved from the Request for a Proposal (RFP) days. Today, the process may be informal, automated, and even truncated as technology, and systems may allow families to gather a first cut of data about a firm relatively quickly (under a week). In years past, a long laundry list of questions from a family to twenty or thirty firms may take two, four, or even eight weeks to receive feedback—sometimes longer if the data to be gathered is more comprehensive or broad spectrum. After the firm sends the information back to the family to review and consider, the family makes a first "cut" and then typically decides which of the remaining firms to meet through video conference initially or in face-to-face meetings with key stakeholders and family leaders.

The courting begins, as the firms in consideration present their top executive leadership, subject matter experts, and/or technical experts to display their talent, as well as the advisors who would potentially serve the family. Depending on the family's deep dive and review, courting process may take several weeks or months, and it is not uncommon that there are fits and starts in the process, whereby families are in and out for extended periods of time.

One family who requested to remain anonymous described the transition and process of unwinding their single-family office and moving on to find a new home with the guidance of a family office consultant.

Godspeed Case Study

Introduction

Dana was in her early 40s and charged with managing the Godspeed Family Office. She wore multiple hats as CEO, CIO, and expert generalist. Additionally, she engaged in many of the family's investment discussions and supported how the family's holdings were managed, but ultimate authority resided with her grandfather. Many of the family's interests were held in a series of limited partnerships that were the result of the sale of an investment business by Dana's grandfather—a serial entrepreneur and a larger than life character. Dana had always looked up to him. Her grandfather tapped Dana, a stand-out student and investment protégé, as she was the only one in her family with any interest in the family office and investments. The Godspeed family office managed an active investment portfolio with investment consultants involved, but they were advisory. Beyond portfolio management, other key tasks were liquidity management and tax preparation for all of the limited partners, managing the family foundation, and concierge services for the senior family member. In one sense, it was a full-service office for the grandfather, taking care of his bills and household staff, investing, administration, concierge services, for example, and simply an investment/tax office for all the other beneficiaries of the grandfather. The office had small staff with an accountant plus a bookkeeper and Dana as head of office and CIO.

Although her grandfather had stepped back from day-to-day management, Dana described, "He was always holding an ace in his hand so to speak so that if things were going in a direction that he didn't like he could always reverse it." For Dana this was on one hand reassuring, and at the same time gave her an impression that she had tremendous responsibility, but clearly ultimate control and authority still resided solely with her grandfather.

Background of the Family and Family Office

The family office served three generations of family members who were not close, as the limited partnership interests were the primary tie that bound the family together, allowing the grandfather to control the family's collective interests. A long-time accountant, loyal to the grandfather, who also served as a trustee, provided accounting advice and services and all the financial controls and prepared the tax returns.

Dana mainly interfaced with the investment managers and the investment consultants, and there were limited family office services provided to the family. Inspired to bring more family cohesion, she attempted bringing the family together through family meetings, but became frustrated with the lack of participation and the lack of engagement among family members.

The siblings of the second generation were geographically dispersed and shared few common interests, and spouses were not encouraged to participate in the family office. If there was no engagement that was often positive, as when the siblings were involved, they tended not to get along and had difficulties making decisions together. The members of the third generation were mostly absent and due to the lack of connection at their parent's generation, the cousins were even further disconnected and indifferent.

A Trigger and Decision for a New Direction

Dana got the news that the CFO was going to finally retire. He was her right-hand man, trusted mentor, and thinking partner. She shared, "The hard catalyst was him [the CFO] retiring and me coming to the conclusion that being an office with only me as chief investment officer, no CFO, and an administrative assistant was pretty lonely . . . then contemplating the notion of it being maybe me and an admin indefinitely into the future was just deeply unappealing." Ultimately, a family office consultant was vetted and engaged to be an objective third party to help the family consider their options for their family office. The family had determined that the current state of the family office was not sustainable, and specifically Dana had advised that she was considering a different career path. She recognized that while her grandfather was alive, she would be in a very challenging situation to carry out his wishes while also holding an isolated and lonely post within an office that would not grow in staff or resources. To evolve the office was not her grandfather's master plan. By bringing in a consultant, Dana felt relief that, with their expertise and experience running a family office coupled with their keen knowledge of the wealth management industry including multi-family offices and small independent investment firms (RIAs), the family would have greater confidence that their individual interests were each being represented.

Journey to Find What Is Next

Embarking on the multi-family office search was what Dana coined, the "journey to find what is next." She also described the experience at times to be "lumpy" before engaging a consultant, realizing that there was limited family governance as the grandfather up until that point had ultimate authority and control for the family office. The experience to create a process, steps, and how to engage the family owners to consider, evaluate, and review candidates were all new. This was where the family office consultant was invaluable. Without this third-party expert, the process may have, as Dana shared, "dissolved into conflict." Happy that she was taking the steps to "fire herself," she also recognized that the family was embarking on a process they had never done.

The first step was to start a dialogue among major stakeholders and establish the leadership team for the search. The second step was to educate family members about the family office and its current investment program to appreciate what they may seek in a multi-family office provider. This included a review of its services, for whom, and what the future needs of family may be. The third step was to survey family members on the services they currently used, valued, and wanted to continue to use. This helped to determine the list of most requested services, which the consultant matched to best in breed multi-family offices, boutique RIAs and commercial trust companies offering multi-family office services. (See Figure 3.3, Checklist of MFO Criteria.)

A Request for Information (RFI) was sent to several firms by the consultant on behalf of the client, who reviewed the forty firms for which Dana had initially already conducted diligence prior to engaging the consultant. Then the responses to the RFIs were graded with an A=exceeds criteria, B=acceptable, C=meets minimum in five main categories—The Firm and its Services, Client Servicing, Client Account Management, Investment Approach, and Fees. (See Figure 3.3, Checklist of MFO Criteria.) It was interesting to note that fees were all within a narrow range.

Decision-Making Process

It was challenging to engage the second generation and bring them up the learning curve, so the education process took a long time. A framework to understand the issues had to be developed for them. (See Figure 3.5.) Due to the lack of consensus, expecting that there would be a unanimous vote was not feasible. Thus, the second-generation family owners knew that a governance process where a majority vote ruled would be most effective to keep the process moving. The reality was that the family office was not a major priority for them. It had always been their father's domain. Trading their personal, philanthropic, business, and family lives to focus considerable effort on what was next for the family office seemed like work with not a lot of immediate gratification. Ultimately, they bought into the process to work together to accomplish the task at hand. (See Figure 3.4.)

FIGURE 3.3 Checklist of MFO Criteria

☐ MFO location

☐ Minimal acceptable AUM or AUA

☐ Independence/ownership

☐ Length of time in wealth management business

☐ Primary focus: investments

☐ Client base: focus on taxable investors generally or focus on multi-generational wealth

☐ Investment services: open architecture required

☐ Accounting and tax compliance: in house vs outsource

☐ Accounting and compliance: partnership accounting

☐ Trust: trust company or outsourced fiduciary service

☐ Other services: financial planning

☐ Other services: family meeting and governance

☐ Other services: philanthropic

☐ Other services: bill pay and lifestyle services

☐ Fees: menu of services and fees/asset based only

Once the leadership team reviewed the documentation that came in from the RFI, they prioritized and scored each provider. Step four was to bring family together to educate them about the family office search—current activities of the office and complexity and the services available to review the top candidates—and garner initial feedback from the family group. (See Figure 3.5 for the family meeting agenda.)

Final Cut

The final cut was made by assessing the relative strengths and weaknesses of each using a slightly different set of criteria. The family ultimately prioritized small to mid-sized firms, considering geography, culture fit, employee owned, full-service, the ability to take over a sophisticated investment portfolio, and to take over the leadership and service capabilities of their office. They specifically sought a team who had the following:

• Experience in taking over a single-family office
• Ability to manage and transition an alternative investment portfolio

- Ability to provide seamless co-ordination of all services
- Client services team with quality and compatibility
- Investment process and ability to implement
- Accounting and tax compliance experience
- Experience/expertise in financial planning/other services

At a family meeting, the three finalists were reviewed with the second-generation owners in detail. The third generation was invited but did not attend and received verbal updates along the way from Dana, representing their branch's interests. The final step was for the family to have in-person

FIGURE 3.4 MFO Search Process

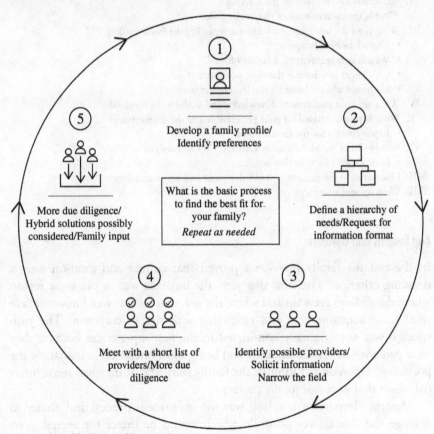

1 Develop a family profile/Identify preferences	
2 Define a hierarchy of needs/Request for information format	
3 Identify possible providers/Solicit information/Narrow the field	
4 Meet with a short list of providers/More due diligence	
5 More due diligence/Hybrid solutions possibly considered/Family input	

What is the basic process to find the best fit for your family?
Repeat as needed

Source: Adapted by Tamarind Partners, Inc.

interviews with each of the top three finalists who represented three very different styles of offices:

1. A small boutique RIA firm offering a full suite of services, and excelled at managing alternatives, custom portfolios, and family enterprise clients.
2. A larger commercial trust company that had a prominent founding family at its origins and a full suite of fiduciary, trust, investment, tax, legal, estate planning, investing and multigenerational planning.
3. An investment-oriented RIA who was a recognized leader in the investment space and provided broader family office services.

FIGURE 3.5   Family Meeting Agenda

AGENDA

    I. Introduction—Purpose of the meeting
   II. What is the current state of the family office?
  III. What does the landscape look like for replacing the family office?
- The advisor landscape
- Wealth management vs. a family office
- Challenges to selecting the right advisor(s)
- Common advisor business models/challenges

  IV. What are your preferences? Knowledge and desire to be involved
   V. What is possible based on your preferences and the marketplace?
- Replacements for the family office

  VI. Family Office vs. Multi-Family Office – SWOT Analysis
- Basic process for selecting advisors

 VII. Discussion of the process to make decisions and vet alternatives
VIII. Wrap up and next steps

Key Insights and Outcomes

In the end the family interviews proved that culture and location were a deciding criterion. The firm that won the business was in the same region where the siblings grew up and where the grandfather was well known. There were some acquaintances and charitable activities in common. The firm selected was not originally considered in the first top-tier cut because they were perceived as investment only and being most interested in managing the portfolios. Upon deeper inquiry, the family learned that they had some internal biases that were not totally correct.

Another important criterion was the investment process and ability to manage the alternatives portfolio which would be intact for several years because of redemption restrictions or private equity commitments. One firm was disqualified because they would effectively outsource the decisions on the alternative investments to a third-party consultant. The ability to handle the alternatives portfolio was ultimately key in winning the business.

The final family decision was to bifurcate the grandfather's investment interests from his children and grandchildren who sought together the multi-family office provider. Dana was disappointed that a unanimous vote was not achieved but satisfied that the family did reach a majority vote, and the minority conceded that the process was fair. They negotiated their contract with the provider as a unified block to negotiate more favorable terms.

Fast-forward a few years later, and to Dana's surprise, her grandfather decided he was in favor of the multi-family office model. He ended up following his children and grandchildren to the same provider. Happily, the family has now been clients for more than five years and learned that the firm has maintained a 98 percent client retention for the same time that they have been clients. Their extra due diligence and hard work has paid off in the end, and the family has perhaps grown closer with the privacy, service, and customization that the multi-family office provider has allowed. Dana too has thrived, moving on to a larger institution and rising on the corporate ladder.

Conclusion and Final Thoughts

The journey to identify the appropriate family office solution is complex and evolving. There is no one perfect solution; however, this chapter explored some existing trends in the family office space and identified the variety of services that may be provided by family offices. It then reviewed family office archetypes and asked the reader to consider which services are top priorities to their family. Next the chapter highlighted, using a SWOT analysis, the leading characteristics of family offices versus multi-family offices. Then the chapter identified critical questions families should ask providers whom they are evaluating along with ideas for the RFI process, concluding with a family office who decided to wind down and identify a multi-family office provider instead. Determining family wealth needs is perhaps one of the most challenging aspects of the journey; however, families who embark on the voyage with an open mind; who seek wisdom and advice from experienced, objective family office advisors; and who understand the process is evolving are more likely to identify a result best suited to them. A special thank you to Bob Casey and Kathryn McCarthy for their involvement in developing the trends and Godspeed case for Chapter 3.

Notes

1. J.P. Morgan as quoted in an article from Michael Grace, *The Tragic Life of the Corsair IV*, featured in the New York Social Diaries at https://www.newyork socialdiary.com/the-tragic-life-of-the-corsair-iv/.
2. Correspondence with Thomas J. Handler, J.D., P.C. Partner, Handler Thayer, LLP, February 2020.
3. For more information, see Family Office Outlook 2020 by Thomas J. Handler, J.D., P.C. Partner, Handler Thayer LLP (January 2020).
4. The UBS/Campden Wealth Global Family Office Report 2019.
5. Correspondence with Jennifer Kenning, Founder of Align Impact, March 2020.
6. Correspondence with Carly Doshi, Head of Philanthropy and Family Governance, HSBC Private Bank, March 2020.
7. Correspondence with Vahe Vartanian, Founder and CEO, Global Family Office Community, January 2020. See the GFOC website at https://www.globalfamily officecommunity.com/ to learn more.
8. See the FORGE website at https://forgecommunity.com to learn more.
9. To get an annualized family office expense ratio, this family office would divide this number by 6 and then multiply by 12.
10. Operating expense ratio of a family office is not to be confused with the operating expense ratio (OER), which is also commonly used to assess a mutual fund's cost of doing business. The mutual fund's prospectus will disclose the percentage of assets, or its OER. OER includes management and advisory fees, overhead costs, distribution, and advertising (12b-1) fee, but not brokerage fees for trading the portfolio.
11. This range for operating costs ascertained by looking at multiple studies including: The UBS/Campden Wealth Global Family Office Report 2019, Fidelity Family Office Investment Study 2019 and Family Office Exchange, Family Office Benchmarking Study 2019.
12. Family Office Exchange, "2019 FOX Multi-Family Office and Wealth Advisor Benchmarking Study," Chicago, Illinois, 2019.
13. Fees on assets under management to vary on scale of wealth. Smaller accounts ($10 million or less) will have a higher fee whereas large accounts may be able to negotiate down the fee. Fee schedules vary, but generally range from 25 to 100 basis points depending on the scale of the wealth.
14. To read more about the Fiduciary Standard go to www.thefiduciarystandard .org/about-us.

CHAPTER 4

Family Values, Mission, and Vision and the Family Office

Kirby Rosplock, PhD

Understanding a family's base of values, clarifying a family's mission, and articulating a clear vision are perhaps the major differentiators among the families whose family offices exist longer than the tenure of one generation of owners. A reoccurring theme described by family-office executives and their owners is the need for a clear direction, purpose, and vision from the family that provides leadership and a destination to where the family desires to be well into the future. This chapter introduces the concept of values and how a family's identity is closely linked to its shared values. Next, it discusses how values inform and influence a family's mission and influence their vision for both the family and its family office. The concept of vision is explored through a process of engaging family in the visioning retreat. Further, I discuss the role and purpose of a family office and the process to craft a family mission statement.

Introduction to Values

Values are the governing principles, beliefs, and behavioral guidelines that inform our actions and perceptions. Values have been defined as the "ideals that give significance to our lives that are reflected through the priorities that we choose, and that we act on consistently and repeatedly."[1] In his definition of values, Brian Hall emphasized that there is a hierarchy of our values developed based on how we prioritize them. Values have also been described as being connected to our belief system, personal experiences, and significant keepsakes, and as a guide to how we live and what we most treasure.[2] Informing our choices, how we behave, and the decisions we make, the presence of wealth in a family informs and shapes their collective principles, family norms, and shared views. Just like net worth cannot replace our self-worth, values are a constant in our lives. Our financial means may shift, pushing us up or down the economic ladder depending on our income, expenses, and lifestyle; however, many individuals retain some of the core values from their formative childhood through their young adulthood.

For families who venture down a path to explore their values, the opportunity is to discover deeper connections and even greater potential within the family system. For many this is breaking ground into some new, unfamiliar, and somewhat daunting territory. The idea of discussing values may be off-putting, so some families shy away from this exploration stating that the "soft stuff" is not for them. Mark Haynes Daniel, an accomplished family office executive and writer reveals that many of these "soft issues" are the most challenging issues a family may confront. In his book, Daniel recalls an observer stating: "These people issues, these so-called soft issues, aren't 'soft' issues at all. Maybe we should call them the 'even harder' issues."[3] The reality is engaging in a conversation around our values can feel like stepping off the high dive for the first time. You have an idea of what to expect, but the sensation of free-falling into the pool of water below can still come as quite a shock. It is not as if you can dip your toe in from the high diving board to check the temperature. Similarly, talking about values can feel a little strange and perhaps uncomfortable at first and some families need practice jumping off the "values springboard" before it will not seem so awkward. Ellen Miley Perry writes in her book *A Wealth of Possibilities* about the importance of fostering these types of conversations that engender trust and connections with one another. She writes, "To earn trust, one must be vulnerable. It is the only path to real intimacy."[4] For some individuals and families, the act of being vulnerable about how they feel, experience, or think about the wealth in their family places them outside of their comfort zone.

Values are unconscious to most individuals, and the processes of becoming self-aware to these guideposts makes them feel less in control, not just vulnerable. Yet, when one allows themselves to be open with their values to those they care about, like their family, there is an opportunity to break down old constructs, behaviors, and feedback loops that may have thwarted fostering family cohesiveness. A values discussion can be a springboard to foster connectivity and openness that may bridge generations.

The Process of Exploring Values

The process of exploring values may occur in many ways. Some families prefer to identify their values privately and amongst only family, while others may hire an outside consultant or facilitator to guide them through the process. Having a structured approach to having the conversation is key. Some prefer to utilize aids such as values cards, values games, or techniques learned from books. The experience of sharing the insights and views of family around their collective values is as meaningful as identifying them. The Values Edge Process, developed by Dennis Jaffe, author and advisor, employs a series of cards to aid families to prioritize values into a hierarchy.[5] Similarly, 21/64, an independent nonprofit practice that provides multigenerational advising, facilitation, and training primarily with a philanthropic focus, also has developed various card decks to foster values-driven discussions on wealth, giving legacy, and values.[6] Through open dialogue, families can create a safe and comfortable environment to freely and openly share their individual values and also have a deeper discussion as a family of the values that overlap. Where the values intersect, the family identifies these as the family's values that are critical to the family's identity and culture. Jaffe shared that "in order to keep the family connected as they cross generations, they need a shared purpose that will motivate the next generation to stay together. By working together on family values, they can combine the legacy of the founding generation and what they stand for with the concerns and ideas of the newer generations. Working on values is a dynamic process, whereby two or more generations of a family talk about what they stand for, and what they want to create in the future. It involves stating the principles that form the family legacy and balancing them with the new conditions that the family finds itself within as they move across generations."[7]

Values also have been described as "cultural currency" that help underpin relationships and meaning among family members.[8] Values conversations are increasingly becoming more common in the commercial family office space. Some firms train their advisors to conduct personal mentoring and values conversations with each family member that may culminate in a family meeting discussion about the family's shared values. Following the individual values work, documenting the family values and articulating how they support common goals are the first steps towards crafting a values-driven mission statement. Mission statements are discussed later in this chapter. Imagine bringing together 20 or 30 family members from different geographies, age groups, and educational backgrounds who may or may not be close in their relationship and helping them find their commonalities? A values discussion of this scope is impactful and helps families to connect on not just shared experiences but the values they ascribe to them.

Nuclear families may also enjoy going through the process as parents and children explore the ties that bind to bridge generational differences. Understanding the shared values are the bedrock of the family and allows the hot spots, or the proverbial potential problem areas, to be less polarizing among family members. A misnomer about values exploration is that you must be a large family to benefit from having one. Families of any size and scale can go through this experience.

Can families explore their values on their own? Of course, however, most families interviewed prefer to work with an outside expert to go on this journey. If you are a family of "do-it-yourselfers" approach the exercise by asking each family member to consider what values are most important to them and their meaning. Ask them to provide an experience or memory where that personal value was demonstrated or tested. Then have them share their greatest lesson learned from the experience or memory and where it fits in priority of the family's shared values. This exercise may give you a head start. See Figure 4.1 as an aid to support this shared values exercise.

FIGURE 4.1   Family Values Discussion Aid

Value	Importance	Experience/ Memory	Individual/ Shared	Lesson Learned	Priority

Source: © Tamarind Partners, Inc.

Values Statement

Once a family has had a series of discussions related to their family values, the output of their work is reflected in a values statement. A values statement is typically a short summary of the key values that matter most to the family or where their family values overlap. These values become the proverbial pillars that inform the family's actions, beliefs, and ultimately their behaviors. Selecting the most critical values to be a part of the family's values statement is an important element of the process. Only the shared values the family believes are important to the family's identity and culture need to be included. Figure 4.2 is a sample values statement.

FIGURE 4.2 Sample Values Statement

James Family Values Statement

Our values are the bedrock of our family and are the fabric of our family binding each generation to its family ancestry. We are committed to uphold, honor, and adhere to the following values:

- *Integrity and Honesty:* Truth and transparency are important values for each and every family member to uphold. The family values consistency, character, and loyalty to its fellow family members and community.
- *Humbleness and Kindness:* Family is encouraged to be modest and reverent both with the financial success as well as their personal and professional accomplishments. Being respectful, kind, and humble are enduring qualities of the James family.
- *Strength and Perseverance:* The James family values hard work and tenacity. Being strong and overcoming obstacles with a positive outlook have helped to sustain the family for generations.
- *Family Belonging and Unity:* The James family honors the importance of family togetherness and unity and encourages a culture of inclusivity. We believe our greatest assets are the shared knowledge, wisdom, and connections that our family continuity provides one generation to the next.
- *Social Responsibility and Stewardship:* The James family has a moral obligation to be responsible to one another as a family, but also to be good stewards of our communities. We believe in supporting the communities where we live, the employees that are an extension of our family, and being engaged through volunteer work, philanthropy, and outreach to live these values.

Mission Statement

The mission statement provides the intention and purpose for keeping the family connected with the wealth and/or the enterprise. A family's mission answers the questions: *Why are we together and what are we going to achieve as a family? What are our views about the family wealth that need to be memorialized?* The mission is typically grounded by the governing values or principles the family wants all members to live by. Thus, the family's values statement often is embedded in the mission statement. Figure 4.3 is an example of the Smith Family Office's mission statement.[9]

Missions are like an individual's signature: Each is special and unique, yet they share consistent features with other statements. The mission *becomes* the family signature to ground and align family interests towards a common purpose.

FIGURE 4.3 The Smith Sample Family Office Mission Statement

The Smith Family Mission

The purpose of the Smith Family is to foster a caring, nurturing, and supportive family culture in pursuit of family happiness through love, hard work, and purposefulness. We commit to better ourselves and the world through:

- Demonstrating our shared values, generosity, honor, education, empathy, integrity, and responsibility.
- Leading from behind and by example.
- Cherishing, promoting, and sharing our family values, heritage, and legacy.
- Safeguarding all family members from harm or peril.
- Preparing our family to be good stewards.
- Fostering family to pursue a healthy, happy, and productive life through hard work, positive behaviors, and good attitudes.

Values, Mission, and the Family Office

There is no one way to explore a family's values or to craft a mission statement. Some families may have a trained facilitator on staff who can provide advice regarding the values and mission process; however, most families will choose to outsource to an outside consultant or advisor. If outsourcing, then it is critical for the family office leadership and advisors to the family to be looped in with the values and mission work completed by the family. The values and mission discussion provide principles to guide the operations and advisement of the family office to the family. Further, some families will determine that they desire to know the values of the individuals serving in their family office to validate that their values are in alignment. Some consultants provide values assessments with key employees, particularly those in a leadership and an advisory capacity to the family. That can be helpful in understanding the working relationships. Other tools such as the Dominance, Inducement, Submission, and Compliance (DISC) assessment and Myers-Briggs Type Indicator (MBTI) may be used in the pre-hire phase in order to confirm that values match prior to hiring key family office executives.

Although the exercise and process to develop a shared values and a mission of a family may take anywhere from several weeks to several months, the family and the family office should hold these core documents front and center in how they operate on a day-to-day basis. Similarly, family often use their values and mission statement as a guide to orient new family who marry in along with stepchildren as a means to demonstrate the family's core beliefs and family norms. Additionally, creating rituals and opportunities to share and celebrate the family's values and mission can provide greater significance and meaning to the family's shared values and purpose.

Why is it so critical for the family office to be apprised of the shared values and mission of the family? First, the family's values and mission become the grounding principles and directives for how the family office should work in alignment with the family. Second, it helps advisors in the family office to validate and reinforce to younger family members the purpose of the wealth. Third, the family office typically exists as a function of a family's commitment to one another and the cohesion that exists among family members. If the family office holds different values or operates under a mission in conflict with that of the family, conflicts are likely to arise.

The Importance of Vision

The basic question is what vision do you aspire to?

—Abraham Maslow

Imagine that you and your family were able to catapult yourself 10, 20, 50, even 200 years into the future: What would be the state of your family in this perfect future world? How are you working with one another? What is the culture and enterprise of the family? Would there be a strong sense of connection and family togetherness? What is the sense of health, intellectual, and financial well-being of each individual family member and collectively? If you were to walk into your futuristic family office, what would it be like? What aspects of the family office would have stayed essentially the same? What elements of your family office would have changed? These questions get to the heart of visioning—the process of establishing an inspired futuristic view of where your family and your family office would like to be. The process of developing a family vision as well as a family office vision is an exciting journey; nevertheless, some families may think it is not all that important or does not apply to them.

A key responsibility is setting the long-term strategy of the office, rooted in the family's mission and vision—not just one year or five years in the future, but two or three generations hence. Chapter 6 explores more deeply the strategic planning process for a family office, but what sets a vision in motion? Clay Mathile, the successful businessman and executive at Iams prior to selling the pet food company to Procter & Gamble for $2.3 billion in 1999, was also the founder of Aileron, a professional management nonprofit consultancy dedicated to strategic planning. Mathile in his book, *Run Your Business, Don't Let It Run You* describes vision as one's "dream with a plan."[10] Mathile suggested that vision should emerge from questions such as:

What do you want to achieve in your life? What are your personal, long-term goals? What meaning would you like your life to have? What contribution would you like to make? Where do you see yourself down the road? What does your vision of the future look and feel like?

After clarifying the family's vision, the family office strategy should then begin from the family's current state and aspirations for the future.

If yours is one of those families that think a vision does not apply, consider a study that examined visionary firms in the same industries with similar attributes and compared them to similar firms without a vision.[11] In his paper "Demystifying the Development of Organizational Vision," Mark Lipton writes, "The study found that a dollar invested in a general stock market fund in 1926, with all dividends reinvested, would have yielded $415 by 1990. The dollar invested in the comparison firms [no vision] on the same date, with adjustments made for when the firms became available on their respective stock exchanges, would have grown to $995, more than twice the general market. But this same dollar invested in the group of visionary companies would have returned $6,356, more than 6 times the comparison group and 15 times the general market. Not surprisingly, in a study by Shareholders Survey Inc., long-term vision was most important to shareholders for selecting companies in which they would invest."[12] What this is telling us is the notable difference between the value enhancements for a visionary firm versus a firm without a vision. But why should having a vision only apply to business enterprises? It shouldn't. At their core, a family office is simply a business enterprise. Why then are professionals not writing more about visionary family offices? Creating visionary family offices will enable the family to better weather the "Shirtsleeves to Shirtsleeves" phenomenon but will also help families to prepare and manage through the most unlikely scenarios or "Black Swan"-type events. Visionary family offices will connect the dots between their aspirations and their ability to execute as it relates to leadership, strategy, execution, and change management in traditional enterprises.

There are three main components of a vision. First, a vision lays out an intention and expectation of the preferred future for the family. Second, it articulates and/or refers to the underlying values of the family. Third, it inspires the stakeholders of the organization—family members in the case of the family and employees and executives in the case of the family office—to be their best to achieve this vision. Like an anchor thrown far into the future, visions are intended to create energy, momentum, and excitement for the road ahead while firmly pulling its constituents towards a positive future. A vision can be broken down into the following components:

$$Vision = Mission + Strategy + Culture^{13}$$

The process of articulating a family's vision is one aspect of building continuity and the bridges that will endure through generational wealth and business transfers. Researchers, who conducted a study on values identified eight best practices that help families manage their wealth successfully over the long-term. The eight proactive practices are:

1. Articulate a clear and powerful vision.
2. Cultivate entrepreneurial strengths.
3. Plan strategically to mitigate risks and capture opportunity.
4. Build unifying structures to connect family, assets, and environment.
5. Clarify roles and responsibilities.
6. Communicate, communicate, communicate.
7. Help members develop competencies.
8. Provide independence, including exit options.[14]

These best practices, acted upon in concert, give families more likelihood of cultivating stronger family governance, which then enables families to manage their wealth in a forward-thinking, generative manner. At the top of the list of best practices is the act of "articulating a clear and powerful vision." What are the critical elements that should be in place to enhance a family's ability to execute their vision? Three key elements enhance a family's likelihood of success when creating a vision. They include:

1. *Family engagement and committing to the collective shared good:* In other words, get family members to the table to create an atmosphere of inclusivity.
2. *The notion of stewardship:* Establish a sense of responsibilities around the wealth that looks to future generations in addition to the needs of the current generation.
3. *The principle of "hastening slowly":* To move quickly, taking the time to methodically consider ramifications of each decision point will move the process along faster than moving too fast.

Elements for Successful Family Office Visioning

Embarking on a path to create and/or enhance your family office can be an exciting and empowering journey for a family. However, the process can be more challenging when certain underlying characteristics do not exist in the family. During an interview with Jay Hughes, he shared three core criteria that he has observed in families that make them more likely to succeed in the development, ownership, and management of a family office. First, Hughes shared the importance that family cohesion plays into the co-creation of a family office and creating a sense of commitment to the family's vision. Specifically, Jay discussed the trade-off that individual family members must make when they sacrifice their autonomy and independence in exchange for being a part of the family collective. Following is an excerpt from that interview with Jay Hughes.

> When the family's vision is to exist a hundred and fifty years from now, the family makes the choice to be together. We then have a common vision that we believe together we will be more successful than as individuals being apart.
>
> But the family office vision must be dependent upon the family's vision. It must be hanging down from it because its purpose is to implement the family's vision just like anyone else that works for that family or helps that family. So, the family's vision has to be grounded in a belief or the idea that joining together is better than going one's own way. Is there a family of affinity here? Do we have a common sense of vision?
>
> A family's vision has to be guided by the principle that through a common journey in which the individuals give up some freedom, they will become freer. That's the only reason to go on that journey. . . . You're taking on obligations because, in turn, you believe that the action of those obligations to help everyone else will, in fact, increase your freedom.[15]

Hughes conveys that greater freedom may come at the expense of personal autonomy and independence; however, being a member of a family clan has advantages and benefits that provide greater potential for freedom. These freedoms or opportunities may manifest in access to investment managers, aggregative vehicles for investors, lower costs associated with family office services, greater transparency and information exchange, more free flow of information, and greater understanding of family wealth planning of extended family members that may or will impact individual household planning. Not to mention the qualitative benefits to the family of fostering strong familial ties among siblings, cousins, and distant relatives: the support network when crises and challenges arise in the family; the deeper pool of human, social, and intellectual capital of the family; and the broader sense of community that family can experience with a clan approach.

One may ask how exactly does committing to the family clan take form? For many, it is implicit and occurs almost unconsciously, as if it is an expectation woven into their family culture through examples set by leaders in the family over generations. The commitment and value of being part of the family tribe is imbibed through rituals such as family gatherings, experiences working together in the context of the family or business, or even through social occasions. Other rites of passage, such as joyous events like the birth of a child, wedding, or anniversary; attaining accomplishments such as an advanced degree or promotion; experiencing losses through death, divorce, demotion, or termination of a position; or loss of health are critical experiences that allow individuals to develop a sense of self while affirming the family's values, beliefs, and guiding life principles transferred from one generation of the family to the next.[16] Thus, coupling individual experiences that overlap with a broader family context begins to inform the social relationships that individual family members have to the broader clan. Transparency is a key element to creating and fostering strong family bonds. How information is shared, how families engage its members to be part of the decision-making process, results in family members feeling respected and their voices heard. For newer wealth creators, leading by example to foster inclusion, involvement in decision making, and commitment to the family goals and vision is paramount. Further, a challenge for the founder generation is how to encourage not only family members, but their trusted advisors, including fiduciaries, to see the opportunity created by committing to a shared vision.

Shared ownership of assets does not connote strong connections and cohesion among family members; however, continuity can be fostered through the visioning process. A common oversight by business-owning families is, in fact, not recognizing the importance of "familiness,"[17] or their sense of family belonging and togetherness. Hughes, Massenzio, and Whitaker also identify familiness as evolving into a "family of affinity,"[18] which requires an investment of time, energy, and personal commitment to fortify the bonds among family members. Making regular deposits in the family's human capital to strengthen these relationships is critical for these connections to span generations.

Through family meetings, shared family experiences, retreats, mentoring, family gatherings to celebrate family member accomplishments, anniversaries, and history are just some of the ways that families fortify their familiness. These types of activities play a vital role in building trust among a family as well as provide an opportunity to really get to know family members, particularly distant relatives, whose interactions may not be as frequent. Thus, family members have a choice to engage in the whole, which can yield greater freedoms and resources because of familiness and committing to the family group.

The second profound point that Hughes noted about families who are successful at co-creating a family vision is related to how they govern—specifically, how they are able to make joint decisions. A broader discussion of governance is in Chapter 11, which focuses on governance and succession in the family office. As it relates to crafting a family's shared vision, families who truly can collaborate and co-create tend to have a family dynamic that fosters inclusion and a willingness to see the other person's point-of-view, even when it differs from their own. Families with a strong set of social norms that celebrate its differences and who are willing to work through conflict will be more generative in creating their vision than a family where one individual's views or ideas carry all the weight.

Building Your Family Office Vision

The process of crafting your family office vision is based on the family's anticipation of where the family wants to be as a collective unit in the future. Thus, the family office vision is directly a function of the family's personal vision. If there is not a strong sense of guidance and intention of the family around its wealth and collective well-being, it is difficult for the family office vision to take shape. With that said, this exercise does not have to be daunting and overwhelming. Rather, it can be an engaging exercise to bring family members into the fold and bring clarity for your family regarding what makes it a family of affinity. One family office executive interviewed who has served in an advisory role to a SFO for the better part of three decades shared a critical insight: "Families are not responsible for creating the strategic plan for the family office. . . . No, that is my job as the Chief Executive Officer of the family office. Rather, the family is responsible for creating the vision for their family and the family office."[19] What this executive brings to light is the importance of differentiating vision from the strategic plan. The vision is what the family office will help our family to do more, better, or differently. The strategic plan maps out the steps and process of *how* to achieve the vision. Brian reveals that the family may not know the tactical steps of how to execute on their vision, but they certainly have a clear idea—once they discuss and come to consensus—of where they want their wealth to take them and how they want their wealth to enhance opportunities for the family.

This may appear to be an obvious and overly simplistic discussion on the merits of deriving a vision, but the reality is most families never take the time to have the vision discussion. Organizational experts, such as Peter Drucker, recognize the power of involvement of stakeholders in the vision-creation process. Drucker once said, "If you want to know what the future is, be part of its development."[20] If the family office is the metaphoric bridge that helps span generation to generation in the family, then involvement from the family to develop the vision for the future of the family office is instrumental in crafting the ideal future. The next section describes the Pitcairn Family Case Study, including how they engaged their family in the development of their values, vision, and mission statement.

Pitcairn Family Case Study

Vision, mission, and core values serve as the bedrock for successful affluent families. As the longevity and success of the Pitcairn family demonstrates, family values constantly evolve—impacted by external and family events alike. Understanding that it takes commitment, energy, and insight to manage core values over the long term is the key to unlocking multigenerational accomplishment.

John Pitcairn, a Scottish immigrant and entrepreneur, co-founded Pittsburgh Plate Glass Company (now PPG Industries) in 1883. His new company transformed plate glass manufacturing in the United States, and its success made John Pitcairn one of the wealthiest individuals of his time. Yet with all the financial and business success, Pitcairn continued to hold certain core values above all others: family, faith, honesty, and integrity.

He remained incredibly dedicated to his family, as well as upholding his respected reputation as an honest, fair-dealing, and hardworking businessman. These core values exhibited by the founding father of the Pitcairn family are manifested in many of the shared values held by the broader family today, five generations later.

At the time of the Pitcairn family values meeting, the family was still engaged in running a variety of operating businesses in 1986. These included a single-family office (SFO) as well as advising on multiple trusts established over the years. Led by Dirk Jungé, a fourth-generation family member and his cousin, Feodor Pitcairn, a third-generation family member and chairman at the time, the family engaged its various family members, who wore one or more hats from owner, to shareholder, to employee, to family member, to trustee, and to beneficiary. Although the process was not high-tech or sophisticated, it encouraged participation from all family members to share which values were important to them as individuals and as a family. Exploring the family roots, history, and heritage, the family identified the following values statement during this initial process designed to inform and guide how they operated as a family. Following are highlights from the first values and mission statement created by the family members in 1986. Their mission was compact, yet powerful, and reflected the values and principles of the family.

Mission: to provide quality financial products and services and achieve superior investment returns.

Principles in Brief

- Concern for Pitcairn Family Values
- High Standards of Ethics and Integrity
- Client Oriented
- Professionally Managed Team with Entrepreneurial Spirit

With a new mission and principles in place, Pitcairn formed a private trust company in 1987 and became a multi-family office (MFO), serving additional multigenerational families and single-family offices.

In 2013, the Pitcairn family came together at its annual shareholder meeting to celebrate two significant milestones—90 years as a family office and 25 years as an MFO. The family had experienced several changes, including selling the core operating business, transitioning from an SFO to an MFO office, and divesting its investment product offering in order to execute a pioneering open-architecture investment platform.

This time, the process to evaluate the family's values had broader participation, including over 100 of some 120+ family members representing three generations. Again, they wore the multiple hats of owners, board members, employees, family, trustees, and beneficiaries. The family used a series of values cards and broke into smaller groups of eight to 10 individuals—first to assess the individual family values and then to discuss shared values. Using technology this time around to provide real-time results, the responses were imported into a program that sorted and prioritized the family's shared values.

Family office employees and independent board members, joined by key partners and client families, conducted a similar values process. They discussed individual values reports and linked these to the business mission of the family office and its relationships with clients.

That set the stage for combining the individual values from each of the groups into a single set of values, and then evaluating the results to determine if the values from 1986 were still appropriate. Following is the values, mission, and vision statement created from the values meeting in 2012–2013:

Pitcairn is committed to:

Building strategic partnerships with multigenerational families and family offices.

Delivering unparalleled advice and service leading to long-term relationships and successful generational transitions.

Being recognized as a thought leader by clients, peers, and centers of influence.

Serving families as an independent, prosperous family office boutique.

By continuing to develop and practice:

Integrity and trust.
Mastery and excellence.
Collaborative partnerships.
Continuous learning.
Entrepreneurial spirit.

Fast forward to today. In addition to the Pitcairn family, the MFO serves 100 multigenerational families along with 15 single-family offices. As the family office prepares to celebrate its 100th anniversary, the firm continues to seize additional opportunities to build on its legacy and realize further innovations in the family office space.

Dirk's unwavering focus on the future evolution of the business drove him to develop a vision for the next chapter of growth for the family enterprise. He saw tremendous potential in Leslie Voth, a longtime Pitcairn employee. Under Dirk's guidance, she assumed a key role as a leader at the firm and a trusted voice for family members and clients. In 2012, she became President and CEO and took her leadership role to the next level.

As Dirk prepared for his own transition away from day-to-day leadership of the firm, he worked closely with the board to develop a strategic framework for selecting his replacement. This selection criteria were directly connected to the strong mission and values the family had developed, and those standards guided the firm's search. In 2019, Leslie was named Chairman of Pitcairn.

As the first non-family and first female board chair, Leslie is ushering in a new era for Pitcairn focused on redefining family office services. Under her leadership, Pitcairn has formalized an approach that manages the family and financial dynamics impacting families over generations. She has defined and formalized the Pitcairn culture and client experience to meet the evolving demands of families and rising generations. The result has been a true family office that's well positioned to serve the needs of client families for generations into the future.

Leslie recognizes the power of evolution: "Change is constant in the family office industry. New generations enter the fold, needs change, and businesses evolve. Navigating that change demands a focus on the future while staying true to the principles that define the business and the families it serves. At Pitcairn, transparency and open communication remain at the center of our business, even as we develop new innovations and pursue new ways to transform our industry and the ultimate value we deliver to our clients."

The Pitcairn story reveals what's possible when a family undergoes the hard work of developing a meaningful, cohesive vision and commits to staying true to those values as it reimagines the possibilities for its family enterprise and the evolution of its business.

Now that you have learned from the Pitcairn family, the next section provides a sample exercise of how you may engage your family to create a family vision.

Disclaimer: Families may have a number of ways to achieve a family vision. The sample exercise provided is just one approach to crafting a vision statement for the family.

Five Steps to Creating a Family Vision

The process of creating a family vision requires bringing the family together for anywhere from a one- to three-day period depending on the scope, complexity, and the size (number of households and individuals). There may be a series of pre-planning discussions in advance of the retreat, often led by a committee or family council who spearhead the development of the vision process. Although this process can be organized by a family through its family council and/or a subcommittee, many families find it constructive to engage a consultant or family office advisor to guide this process. When identifying who will lead the retreat, it is helpful to have a well-respected family leader or family wealth advisor who can manage the logistics as well as facilitate the dialogue. Thus, it is helpful to begin the planning three to six months in advance at a minimum in order to apprise family members well before the event about the date, location, and time commitment and to engage a consultant or advisor.

Step 1: Clarifying the Process and Expectations

For some family members, an invitation to come to a family retreat may be unexpected and foreign. Providing clear instructions and information as to why their presence is requested and what they will experience is advised. All families operate uniquely, so it is critical to recognize that family leadership in this initial engagement process is important. Once you have identified the date, time, and location, follow-up communication from the family leadership by phone, video conference, or e-mail to answer the following questions is advised; you may customize this list as needed for your family's unique situation and answer some or all of the following questions:

- What is a family office?
- What is the vision retreat's purpose for the family?
- Why am I asked to come?
- What will I be expected to do?
- What if I have had little or no involvement with the financial affairs of the family?
- What do I need to bring?
- What will be the anticipated outcomes of this process?
- What will the family do with the information sourced from the meeting?

Step 2: Vision Retreat Pre-Planning

What preparations are involved with the pre-planning for a vision retreat? Providing family members with questions to consider two to three weeks prior to the retreat will help them to prepare and articulate their ideas more effectively during the retreat. Following is a list of possible questions to consider sharing with the family in advance of the retreat:

- As a family, why do we need a family office?
- How will we work together towards creating a family office?
- What are the family's values that should influence the mission and vision of the family and family office?
- What are our collective objectives for the family office?
- How will vision contribute to our strategic plan?
- How will family members be involved with the management of the family office, if at all?
- What roles and responsibilities belong to the owners versus the office executives?

- How will we govern the family office?
- How will we measure the success of the family office?
- How will we keep the family office accountable?

Step 3: Staging a Vision Retreat

Some families prefer to host the retreat at a family property, while others prefer to host it at a neutral place such as a hotel or resort. A central location that has easy access to an airport is recommended. If an outside facilitator or consultant is conducting the retreat, any number of methodologies may be employed as most consultants have a preferred approach to this process.

For the family office executive who is embarking on this process for the first time, be advised that there are a number of logistics for a smooth-running vision retreat. First, make sure family leadership is involved and on board, and can clearly articulate the value to the other family members. Second, engage a member of each generation to be on a committee to help with the planning. Some family members may have a natural gift to help with different aspects of the retreat, such as catering, planning, facilitating, educating, and so on. Harnessing the raw talent in the family will help to facilitate buy-in and engagement. A site visit ahead of time to meet with hotel catering and staff well sets expectations for the vendor. Draft up an agenda with the flow of the day and defined breaks. At the start of the meeting, consider starting with some type of icebreaker that will bring family members together in an unexpected and entertaining way. From exercises that help foster teamwork, trust, awareness, and knowledge, an icebreaker helps set the tone of the experience to follow and gets family members excited for the work ahead.

Step 4: Timing for a Vision Retreat

Allow for a half-day to multi-day process, depending on the scale and scope of the visioning exercise. The timing requirements will vary on a number of different factors, such as how many individuals are involved (10, 20, 50+), how much has already been identified (family's shared values, purpose statement, etc.) and the level of harmony, engagement, and buy-in for the process. Further, the visioning experience largely depends on who is leading the process—an outside facilitator or family office executives or family members.

Step 5: Aligning Vision and the Strategic Plan

The final step in the process is to align the vision of the family and the strategic plan for the family office. The tactical elements of the management and operations of the family office are responsibilities of the key executives, board, and owners of the family office, who take direction from the family owners they serve. The broader family group is likely less to be involved with discerning the steps and actions required to align the strategy and planning of the family office with that of the vision.

Assuming the family office has a board of directors, the board coupled with family leadership will play an instrumental role in the planning and advisement of the management team on how to devise and execute a plan that identifies short-term goals as well as long-term objectives. The board leadership may ask questions such as:

- How do the operating objectives of the family office meet the goals of the family's vision?
- What gaps exist between how the family office is operating today and what the family envisions the office addressing?
- Is the family office providing services that are not in alignment with the family's vision?

The family office management team will be tasked with identifying a strategic plan that aligns the values of the family and its mission and vision with that of the family office. The iterative process may take several weeks or months to finalize the strategic goals and action steps associated with the family office the correlate to the family's vision.

Conclusion and Final Thoughts

> Personal leadership is the process of keeping your vision and values before you and aligning your life to be congruent with them.
>
> —Stephen Covey

Values, mission, and vision provide the backbone of stability, organization, and unity for a family and its family office. Without defining these components, a family may have greater difficulty inspiring commitment, creating continuity, and building cohesion across branches and different generations of the family. For the family office to help guide the family to its preferred future, the family must be clear on who they are, what the purpose of staying together is, and where they are headed. If the family is not clear of their family vision, assigning a vision to the family office becomes challenging and less productive. However, the power of aligning the family's vision to that of the family office and its overarching strategic plan is empowering, may foster alignment and commitment, and also help mitigate conflict by resolving differences and providing inspiration to guide the family.

Notes

1. Brian P. Hall, *Values Shift: A Guide to Personal and Organizational Transformation* (Rockport, MA: Twin Lights Publishers, 1994), 21.
2. Brian P. Hall, *Exploring Religion in Schools: a National Priority* (Adelaide: Open Book Publishers, 2004), 63.
3. Mark H. Daniell and Sara Hamilton, *Strategy for the Wealthy Family: Seven Principles to Assure Riches to Riches Across Generations* (Singapore: John Wiley & Sons, 2008).
4. Ellen M. Perry, *A Wealth of Possibilities: Navigating Family, Money, and Legacy* (Egremont Press, 2012).
5. Dennis Jaffe, The Values Edge Cards, to learn more visit https://dennisjaffe.com/publications/.
6. To learn more about 21/64 and their tools visit https://2164.net/shop/.
7. Correspondence with Dennis Jaffe, March 2020.
8. ValueMentors LLC, "Dr. Gunther Weil," 2012, http://valuementors.com/about-us-2/gunther-weil/.
9. This anonymous sample mission was provided by Tamarind Partners, Inc.
10. Clay Mathile, *Run Your Business, Don't Let it Run You* (San Francisco: Berrett-Koehler Publishers, 2013), 64.
11. Collins and Porras, as cited in Mark Lipton, "Demystifying the Development of an Organizational Vision," *Sloan Management Review* 37, no. 4 (1994): 83–92.
12. Mark Lipton, "Demystifying the Development of an Organizational Vision," *Sloan Management Review* 37, no. 4 (1994).
13. Collins and Porras, as cited in Mark Lipton, "Demystifying the Development of an Organizational Vision," *Sloan Management Review* 37, no. 4 (1994): 83–92.
14. Amy Braden and Dennis Jaffe, *The Eight Proactive Principles of Wealthy Families* (New York: JP Morgan, 2003), 80–82.
15. Interview conducted with James E. Hughes, August 21, 2012.
16. James E. Hughes, *Family Wealth: Keeping It in the Family*, Second Edition (New York: Bloomberg Press, 2010).
17. Timothy G. Habbershon, Mary Williams, and Ian C. MacMillan, "A Unified Systems Perspective of Family Firm Performance," *Journal of Business Venturing* 18, no. 4 (2003): 451.
18. James E. Hughes, Jr., Susan E. Massenzio, and Keith Whitaker, *Complete Family Wealth* (New York: Wiley | Bloomberg Press, 2018).
19. Family office executive who requested remain anonymous, 2020.
20. "Inspirational Quotations." Appreciative inquiry commons. http://appreciative inquiry.case.edu/.

CHAPTER 5

Establishing and Structuring of Family Offices

Ivan A. Sacks, Esq.
Partner, Withers Bergman LLP

William J. Kambas, Esq.
Partner, Withers Bergman LLP

While there have been important developments since the first edition of this book, the starting point remains the same: Family offices are as unique as the families they serve. Establishing and structuring one is a bespoke process. The architecture depends on the family and its goals. What might be right for one family might not be right for another.

That being said, families often have similar questions when beginning the process. Moving through those questions helps give shape to the structure most suitable for a newly formed or reorganized family office. The questioning process helps to organically build an efficient yet effective family office structure. Therefore, to describe the formation of a family office and the structuring process, we will proceed by exploring the following questions and integrating the learning through a fictitious case:

Question 1: What legal form should the family office take?
Question 2: Who should pay for establishing and operating the family office?

Question 3: Who should own the family office and how?
Question 4: Who should manage the family office and how?
Question 5: How are family offices structured to optimize tax efficiency?
Question 6: How should a family office be structured to manage risk?
Question 7: What is the process of establishing and structuring a family office?

Ultimately, family governance that integrates a family office will become a way of life for the family. Family members, particularly in senior generations, must understand their overall structure, including the roles and responsibilities of each respective component.

Case in Point

The most effective family offices are designed to meet the specific needs of the family served. The breadth of services (and by consequence the level of staffing and capabilities) will depend on the family.

In order to illustrate the decision-making process to design a family office, consider this hypothetical case. The grandparents established a successful business. As it grew, they put their equity into a complex trust for estate planning purposes. Keeping ownership of the business in the family trust, the grandparents' daughter, Mom, ran the business, increasing its success exponentially. Mom and Dad have four children, each of whom graduated from reputable colleges and established families of their own. The business has regularly paid out substantial dividends, allowing the family to establish an investment program that is fast approaching the net value of the business itself. These investments, too, are held in the family trust. Mom, Dad, and the four children all agree that they require assistance with certain aspects of business management as well as making and monitoring investments. They also agree on institutionalizing their long-term commitment to philanthropy, through a private foundation. Finally, with the growth of grandchildren, there is a recognized need to preserve and share the family's rich history in building their business and philanthropic activities.

To meet these goals and transfer the family business, investment, and philanthropic enterprise to the next generations, our hypothetical "Family" would like to establish a family office.

The Family's initial asset structure is illustrated in Figure 5.1.

FIGURE 5.1 A Family Enterprise

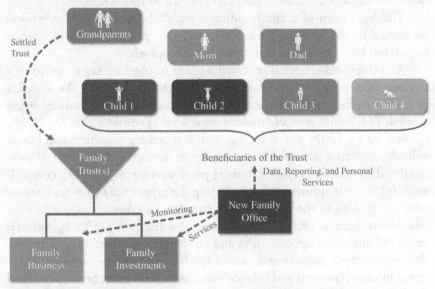

Source: Withers Bergman LLP

The Family also considered that it might be possible to integrate their cousins or others into the family office in order to eventually make the family office itself a viable business that could be grown or sold to a third-party buyer, such as an MFO.

To begin with, the Family must consider a series of questions relating to the architecture, infrastructure, and operability of the family office arrangement.

Question 1: What Legal Form Should the Family Office Take?

Since a family office is but one aspect of a family enterprise, a typical starting point is to identify the breadth of the enterprise itself so as to best integrate the services that could be provided through the family office. The emphasis should be similar to that of starting a new business. After all, the family office is a captive services business within the family enterprise. In our hypothetical, the Family's goal is to create a structure through which they could share costs and services in a centralized and cohesive manner. The four children have many common needs, but they also have unique preferences. Therefore, their goal is to create a family office integrated into their overall asset management structure, for investment entities and business entities, so that each person can benefit and be allocated costs proportionate to their usage.

The legal form of a family office is greatly influenced by the services performed by the family office as discussed in the prior chapter and, equally important, how profits and losses should be allocated.

As a threshold matter, one is well advised to consider key elements of a business plan as they might relate to a SFO. Like any business, the founders of a family office should have a reasonable forecast for the business being created. This would typically include some level of consideration on: (1) the mission for the family office, such as what it is seeking to achieve and how it will effectuate that mission; (2) the specific services to be offered; (3) why the family office would be superior to third-party service providers (i.e., competitors); (4) the management team, including the experience of key team members; (5) analysis of the family office's strengths, weaknesses, opportunities, and threats (because this will help illustrate that the family office operation is being realistic about opportunities and challenges); (6) development of cash flow expectations (sources and uses of funds); and (7) development of projected income statement and balance sheet, as this will affect both operational flexibility as well as tax liability.

These seven points common to any business plan can be distilled into four points that take on greater significance in the family office context:

1. In-house capability versus outsourcing: What expertise resides within your family office? What services may be better provided or less expensive to outsource? What are fixed versus variable costs associated with various services, such as bill paying (that could be a flat rate or based on the volume of bills over a monthly rolling average) or tax compliance (that could be based on number of entities or groups of entities for various family branches)?
2. The particular structuring requirements for your family's mix of venture capital, private equity, non-US investments, real estate, financial instruments, marketable securities, and special assets.
3. Relationship with other family governance structures, such as trusts and private trust companies: Are these structures to be separate and complementary or are they integrated in the family office as owners, governors, and/or clients of the family office? For example, the family office might be staffed and operated separate from existing private trust companies or for some purposes integrated with them (such as, with a shared investment

committee). For example, a private trust company might handle fiduciary services and investment discretion but a family office provide staff to facilitate reporting and consolidation services with the family's non-fiduciary investors and help find access to select investment opportunities.

4. The taxation of income and deductions for expenses might also play an influential role in the setup and structure of the family office, including whether and to what extent income or losses can best be used by a family office entity itself, or allocated to the owners.

Choice of Entity

It is important to differentiate between the family office entity itself and those entities that the family office will serve, as the decision variables will be different. The family office entity is the focus of this chapter, but the integrated nature of the family office operation and the other entities within a family enterprise will influence the ultimate impact. In any case, the family office should be an entity separate and distinct from its owners and those it serves

Family offices can be established in any number of legal forms. Types of entities often seen include a partnership, a limited liability company (LLC), an S corporation, or a C corporation.[1] Without dismissing the sometime utility of LLPs and S-corps for certain historic, international, and special situations, we will focus on LLCs because of potential liability risk or complexity of partnerships and potential restrictions in flexibility of income and expenses in S corporations. Today many family offices are established as either an LLC or as a C corporation.

Deciding Between an LLC and a C Corporation

Although the driving force in decisions about choice of entity is usually tax-driven, there are differences in state law legal formalities and governance requirements that apply to C corporations and LLCs. An LLC can be managed by its members or by one or more managers. Directors and officers are typically not included, as they are not required, but LLCs have the virtue of flexibility to adopt bylaws, officers, and titles similar to a corporation, if so desired. A C Corporation, on the other hand, is required to adhere to certain formalities of having both directors and shareholders, usually certain officers, to hold at least one annual meeting, and at times to document its decisions through resolutions or votes.

By default, LLCs are taxed as pass-through entities or partnerships and thus are not subject to annual Federal taxes, but they are required to file annual federal and state information returns and may be subject to State-level taxes and/or fees. However, an LLC established in the US can also elect to be characterized as a C corporation for US tax purposes, exemplifying both its management and tax flexibility. A C corporation, by contrast, is a separate tax-able entity by default (although it can elect to be treated as an S-corporation provided it and its shareholders meet certain requirements). One advantage of a corporation (or an LLC that elects to be taxed as a corporation) is often, but not always, that it is presumed to be engaged in a trade or business (see, for example, Rev. Rul. 78-195, 1978-1 CB 39), and corporations should not be subject to a series of tax attribute limitations, such as passive activity limita-tions, basis limitations, at-risk limitations, and excess business loss limitations that otherwise apply to partnerships and S corporations under Sections 469, 704, and 1366 and 461(l), respectively.

There may be international governance or tax concerns in the choice of entity. If there were family members with a management interest resident in certain non-US jurisdictions, such as the United Kingdom, then man-agement and control issues must be addressed. For example, if a family was considering establishing a family office through an LLC structure, it might be preferable to use a limited partnership, since an LLC with a UK resident man-ager would likely be characterized as a domestic UK corporation for UK tax purposes under their entity classification and management and control rules.

Formation of a C Corporation

C corporations are formed under applicable state law. Articles of Incorporation must be filed with a Secretary of State and a nominal registration fee paid. State law and the provisions in the Articles of Incorporation govern C corpo-rations. C corporations also operate through detailed bylaws, which memori-alize the corporation's governance requirements. Though it varies by state, corporations (through their articles and bylaws) must generally comply with a variety of legal requirements including: electing directors and officers; hold-ing an organizational meeting; adopting bylaws; holding annual meetings of the directors and owners; documenting decision making; keeping minutes of meetings; filing an annual tax return; and filing reports required by the state.

Formation of an LLC

LLCs are formed by filing Articles of Formation (sometimes referred to as Articles of Organization) with a state and payment of a designated flat fee. The heart of the LLC is the Operating Agreement, which is generally drafted concurrently with the formation of the LLC and may be amended and/or restated multiple times over the life of the LLC. There are far fewer state law requirements for operating LLCs than for operating C corporations.

The Governing Instrument

Regardless of whether the family office is established as a corporation or LLC, the entity will have a primary governing instrument. In the case of a corporation, this is usually the bylaws. In the case of the LLC, this is the Operating Agreement. Either document provides an opportunity to protect the family from internal and external threats.

The governing instrument establishes the structure and operating procedures of the business and should address family office services; formulate leadership, management, and compensation provisions; allocate the shareholders' or members' (i.e., owners') interests in the office; divide voting power; define the owners' and managers' relative rights and responsibilities; assign profits and losses according to class of shares or interests; and establish rules for holding meetings and taking notes. More specifically, the governing instrument should be drafted with sensitivity toward protecting the ownership of the family's (or its enterprise's) intellectual property rights; providing for non-competition agreements; resolving conflicts among managers and members to prevent litigation; providing liability protection to directors, officers, and managers; and, to the extent possible, protecting the business in the case of the failure of business partners. A governing instrument could also contain a plan for a transition in ownership, such as shareholder rights or buy-sell provisions. Ultimately, the governing instrument establishes a system of governance and memorializes the rules and procedures for decision-making and, as such, the general operation and management of the family office.

Family office governance should also reflect family values and complement a family's overall mission. It should be developed in accordance with a family's constitution and/or mission statement, if the family has one. Additionally, if a family has established teams of family members and/or outside advisors to serve on committees and/or counsels, then areas of input from these groups might also be memorialized in the family office's governing instrument.

Multi-Entity Structures

Where a family office performs multiple types of services, it might be prudent to establish different types of affiliated entities within an overall legal structure for tax efficiency and/or to insulate one service area from possible creditors of another service area. Similarly, multinational families might employ family office services differently in different jurisdictions (such as for real property oversight and management) and therefore find it useful to decentralize the overall structure through multiple entities.

Simple Family Office (Investment and Portfolio Management)

We discuss more broadly the investment function in the family office in Chapter 8; however, it is relevant to consider the type of investment function the family requires or desires as it relates to the appropriate family office structure. Where the family office is structured to assist a family with its investments, it might serve as an intermediary consolidating investment performance, reporting, and exchange of ideas among the family and its bankers. A basic family office structure might be a single entity, as illustrated in Figure 5.1.

The Investor Family Office

In some families, there is a strong desire to employ family assets in furtherance of start-ups, entrepreneurship, and/or private equity investing, whereby the family associates take a board seat in an underlying business. Similarly, a family may wish to establish its own fund-of-funds.

Two important cases provided guidance on what is required for a family office to qualify as a bona fide trade or business for tax purposes, thereby allowing it to charge deductible profit shares from its family investor clients. First and most notably, the US Tax Court issued an opinion in the case of Lender Management, LLC v. Commissioner ("Lender").[2] Shortly thereafter, a similar case was settled but after parties had submitted petitions and statements of their position to the US Tax Court. This second case was Hellmann v. Commissioner ("Hellmann").[3] In both cases, family members established an investment management business to serve their family enterprise. In Lender, the Court sided with the taxpayer affirming that multigenerational, centralized management and control structures can be organized and operated in a manner that rises to the level of a bona fide trade or business, especially where the extended family can demonstrate that the various family branches are not acting with a "single mindset." In Hellmann, the taxpayers asserted they met the same standard, but the IRS disagreed, focusing on the fact that the family office was co-owned by the same four family members who were also the named (and therefore primary) beneficiaries of the trusts which own the managed investments. Both Lender and Hellmann were investor-oriented family offices, the structure of which could be illustrated as shown in Figure 5.2.

FIGURE 5.2 Investor Family Office Structure

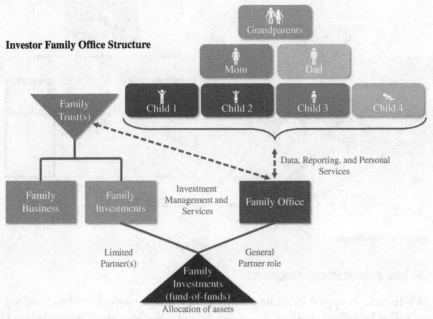

Source: Withers Bergman LLP

Complex (Multi-Entity) Family Office

Family offices originating from or including operating business wealth might be best served with a family office that resembles a multinational corporate structure. This will allow for effective tax rate management among the different wealth sources as well as isolation of assets and/or services for privacy, liability, and/or staffing efficiency.

In such situations, the top tier would be a headquarters or holding company with one or more wholly owned subsidiaries. A subsidiary might be tasked solely with management of a family's intellectual property, finances (such as a family bank, to be discussed further in a later chapter), data reporting, and/or specific technology or back office services. A tiered family office structure might look like the one displayed in Figure 5.3.

FIGURE 5.3   Corporate Style Family Office Structure

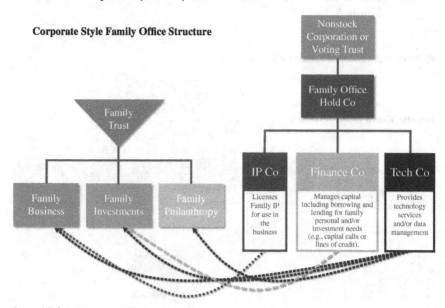

Source: Withers Bergman LLP

The Value of Overall Structure Management

While there is appeal in adding entities, services, personnel, and technology to a family office, there is also value in reducing structural complexity. A complex multi-member entity or group with broad and diverse responsibilities adds costs and is potentially difficult to operate and manage over time. In other words, an overly complex structure decreases overall productivity. Ultimately, it can detract from the value of having a family office and its long-term success. Creating a structure that allows for flexibility often means beginning with an entity (or entities) that can be restructured in an easy and tax-free manner, should the structure need to evolve over time as the family's needs and goals change.

The management structure must fit the family decision-making practice. The worst scenario from a compliance, risk management, and efficiency standpoint is one where the members do not follow the structure that has been adopted.

From an estate tax perspective, an overly complex structure also may lead to compliance risks, or difficulty transitioning control to succeeding generations.

The Lender and Hellmann cases, which are described further below, illustrate the benefits of delegating management to those with relevant skills, time, and dedication. In fact, in most cases, while some family members may be well positioned to own or manage the family office, all family members usually are not.

All told, we recommend that the structure be as simple as possible, but no more simple. Ultimately, it should be one that:

- Formalizes a legal structure for management that memorializes an optimal decision-making hierarchy, including, but not limited to ensuring that the family's legal structure complements its actual decision-making practice.
- Has an appropriate number and organization of entities and is therefore cost effective for staff to operate. For example, a real estate family might have tens or hundreds of entities for each respective investment, development, and/or project, which might not be complex for a family with those interests. Similarly, a family that has remained unified through many generations might have a large number of trusts.
- Minimizes income tax liability.
- Is designed with the family's estate planning goals in mind.

Case in Point

Turning to our hypothetical family, we know that Mom ran the business and had significant expertise with its technical operations. We might learn that she had developed customized technology to run the operations and manage sales. Whether the technology was developed for the family business or as an independent endeavor, planning for this intellectual property would be prudent.

Next, we may find that one or more members of the family have been active in venture capital or private equity. In this case, they participate in the general partnership that manages a family fund-of-funds and may provide a family liaison between the family office and the fund manager.

Finally, we may learn that one or more of the children has a particular interest in the family's philanthropic efforts and is willing to lead those efforts. If a private foundation was established, that child could serve as the liaison between the family office and the foundation.

Question 2: Who Should Pay for Establishing and Operating the Family Office?

The majority of start-up and operational costs of a family office (such as employees, technology, and infrastructure) are generally borne by those to whom the family office provides services. The costs are part of overhead that is incorporated into the fees charged for family office services. These fees would be paid by either individuals or family entities within the family structure.

The costs can be material. Proper planning for the ownership, operation, and client expectations often expose variables that require navigation by multiple parties. The set-up process is not dissimilar to architecture and engineering where all interested parties need to evaluate their expectations as well as the realities of existing (surviving and thriving, ideally) within the family office ecosystem (or not). Once the architecture is agreed, implementation costs come into play. Simple entity formation is not necessarily a material cost, but drafting of bespoke, legal, and tax efficient and compliant documents can create anticipatable costs. Proper architecture and document drafting should go a long way to protecting the parties involved and also preserving flexibility for the parties (and family) to grow. During the establishment phase, the family office should be funded in a manner where, directly or indirectly, it would not be characterized as owning the assets under management and therefore should not be characterized as an investor itself, but, rather, as an entity that serves investors to the extent that investment management services are offered.

For example, where a family office is tasked with management and oversight of a family's investments, the net profits of those investment activities might be partly used to pay for the services provided by the family office. The family office fees can be structured in a variety of ways as described below.

Initial capital for the establishment of the family office can be provided as a contribution for equity, as debt, or as a mix of debt and equity. In any case, contributions of capital for an equity interest in the family office would cause the contributor to be (at least) a part owner of the family office. Debt, by contrast, would not result in an equity stake.

Equity ownership is particularly important in the context of a family office established as an LLC and taxed as a partnership because flow-through entities, such as LLCs or partnerships, allow for expenses to flow through to the ultimate owners, who might be able to use such expenses as deductions for income tax purposes. By contrast, a family office established as a corporation will retain those expenses and any net operating losses for future use on its own tax return, limiting the ability to use any expenses or losses by specific family members or family trusts.

Ultimately, the costs associated with setting up and operating the family office, as well as payment of fees for family office services, must be structured so that each generation understands and accepts the cost structure as being fair and impartial. Understanding and acceptance are important because the operations could be substantial. The Global Family Office Report 2019, published by Campden Wealth Limited and UBS, illustrates that in 2019 family offices' total average spend on services included $6.8 million in operational costs and $5.1 million in external investment management administration and performance fees. Expanding on these operational expenditure, the report in Section 5.1 (Family Office Costs) found that services that are most often provided through a balance of both in-house and outside resources include tax planning, estate planning, and investment banking functions (e.g., deal sourcing, due diligence, capital structuring, etc.)

The final result often also incorporates the family philosophy with respect to generational planning. For example, among first generation wealth founders, there might be a desire to bear the costs of establishing a family office or pay for its use, as a subsidy to subsequent generations. In others, particularly families in the second generation and beyond, it may be more important that each user pay their fair share.

Following are examples of how fees and costs might be structured:

1. *Pure billable hours:* The family office maintains records for the time spent serving each entity and invoices accordingly. This requires invoicing and multiple service agreements, but can be very precise.
2. *Service-by-service charges:* Each entity and/or person pays for those services it requires and hires the family office to provide such services. This is similar to the above, but allows the family office to establish set prices for standardized activities, which should minimize the recordkeeping and administration costs.
3. *Set service fee with hourly rates:* Each entity and/or person pays a set fee for family office services. Time spent can be recorded to monitor use. Once an agreed threshold is reached, charges can be on an hourly basis. This can be simple to administer.
4. *Assets under management:* The family office allocates its costs ratably (plus a small margin) to each entity and/or person based on its respective value of assets under management within the entire structure.
5. *Profits allocation:* The family investment partnership(s) allocate a "profits interest" to the family office and/or key employees that is attractive for

incentive compensation arrangements, for which no capital contribution is required. For the family, this can be a tax-efficient approach as it may render the payment of family office expenses essentially tax deductible subject to the issues discussed later in this chapter relating to tax considerations associated with the profits allocation. For the single-family office itself as well as its key employees, it can be an effective incentive compensation arrangement to align their interests with the family.

6. *Management fee:* Investment management businesses, such as similarly tasked family offices, may charge an annual management fee. This could be calculated using one of the approaches above. In the alternative investment fund industry, the management fee is often 2 percent of committed capital or assets under management, but can actually range from 1 to 3 percent or more in many cases, depending on how active the manager is and how high the annual operating expenses.[4]

Question 3: Who Should Own the Family Office and How?

Ownership of a family office has two facets:

1. The legal owner of record
2. The beneficial owner

In some cases, these two are the same, but in others they might be separate. For example, in a multigenerational setting, the family office could be owned by one or more trusts. This splits the ownership because the trustee would have legal ownership and vote and/or make ownership level decisions, subject to fiduciary obligations, while the family members would retain the beneficial ownership so that any profits or assets would be for their benefit.

Ownership also calls into question whether the family office is intended to be a profitable enterprise or operate on a break-even basis. If the operation is intended to run a profit, for example, a family might consider sharing that profit with family office managers as incentive compensation and would need to structure the family office entity accordingly.

In all cases, equity ownership in a family office is allocated based on their capital contributions. Thus owners need to provide proportionate funding sufficient to meet organizational and start-up expenses, and therefore it is important in choosing owners that are able and willing to fund start-up costs and any shortfalls in income sufficient for expenses thereafter.

Legal Ownership

Legal ownership is a concept relating to an owner of record; that is, the legal owner of the property (such as a trustee, in the context of a trust) has the right to possess, use, and/or convey the rights and privileges associated with the property held in trust. The legal owner, therefore, typically appears to outside parties as the owner of the property, even though the trustee might only be holding the property in order to maximize benefits for the beneficial owner(s).

Beneficial Ownership

Beneficial ownership (sometimes referred to as equitable ownership) is a concept where the benefits related to property, rather than in the property itself, is allocated to an individual. In the context of a trust, a beneficiary of a trust may receive distributions of principal or income from the trust if a distribution is made. However, they would not have decision-making authority with respect to the underlying property or the income itself. Similarly, a person could have beneficial ownership of stock or other securities without actually having that stock held in that person's name.

Models of Ownership

Today, we find that ownership of a family office and facets of the family enterprise can take a variety of forms. Addressing the options available to a family is part of the overall structuring process. Some options include ownership by or through:

- Individual members of the family
- A combination of family members and non-family managers and/or advisors
- A complex family trust (within the existing estate planning structure)
- A private trust company (as part of the family fiduciary system)
- A standard stock corporation (similar to a standard active business)
- A non-stock corporation or membership company (with an infrastructure similar to standard corporations but with limitations on activities)
- Certain types of limited companies used outside of the United States (assuming the family is best suited with an international structure)
- Statutory Foundation (New Hampshire and Wyoming)
- A voting trust (allowing the family members to retain voting on matters relating to family office affairs)

Analysis of each of these options involves questions relating to:

- Models of governance where the owners are primarily involved
- Models of governance where family caretakers are involved in a representative capacity for family branches or generations
- The role of family fiduciaries pursuant to trusts, a constitution, and/or family council
- Whether outside directors or managers are involved
- Generational input: whether by voting or in an advisory capacity

In considering who should own and/or govern a family office, some families have developed family mission statements and/or family constitutions to establish a baseline mission with respect to the multigenerational management of the family and those services necessary for the success of the family.

A family council is often integral to a successful constitution, similar to a Congress or Parliament. The family council can serve as a collective voice for the family, the value of which increases as wealth structures become more diverse and the number of family members increases. In larger, more complex family structures, a family council might be employed to formalize governance and be a representative body for minority family stakeholders. It can serve as the family's institutional memory and as a governance enforcer. It can also oversee risk areas such as:

- Investment in liquid and family business interests
- Legal matters
- Tax matters
- Reputational risk and media management
- Information technology and security

Family governance and succession are more broadly discussed in Chapter 11 and understanding these concepts is critical to the formation phase of a family office because they inform the education of succeeding generations to achieve both buy-in and understanding of the family's overall goals.

Case in Point

Larger families may find it useful to stagger boards of the family business and a family council and maintain a balance between family members and non-family members.

In one example, a family business created a seven-member board of directors, three of which were non-family members and the remaining four were members of the extended family. All were competent and well versed in the family business and industry. After a change in the market, there was some disagreement as to the future direction of the family business. After many board meetings with no conclusion, the family members went to the family council to confirm the goals and intentions of the family at large. This gave the four family board members guidance to speak for all family owners and eventually resulted in a majority vote and resolution of the board's disagreement in favor of the family goals. It also resulted in a vote of no confidence concerning a couple of non-family board members and ultimately their replacement with other non-family members who shared the family's vision and brought new expertise to the board so that the enterprise could navigate the evolving marketplace in a manner consistent with the family values.

Question 4: Who Should Manage the Family Office and How?

A family office's governing documents must address the management and day-to-day operations of the family office. This should be established with consideration of a variety of questions which are outlined below. In considering these questions, one must keep in mind the requirement that a family office providing investment advice should generally be "exclusively controlled" by family members or family entities in order to qualify for the SEC's family office exemption from registration under Federal securities laws. Otherwise, SEC registration may be required. This can be satisfied as long as decisions are made by a majority of family members. Additionally, the family office should operate in a professional manner, with regular and continuous operations and a consistent profit earning motive if it is seeking either the tax qualities of a bona fide trade or business, or simply the discipline and efficiency that a business exemplifies. For example, if employing an investor style family office, one is advised to consider and incorporate applicable division of labor and costs and profits allocation rules not inconsistent with those typical in real estate, private equity, or venture capital structures.

When developing the family office management structure, two areas for consideration are:

1. The legal formalities
2. The scope of services needed and people performing those services

Ultimately, these two areas need to be integrated. A broader discussion of talent management is provided in Chapter 10.

Structuring the Legal Formalities

With respect to the legal formalities, the ownership and management of a corporation is made up of three components: stockholders, directors, and officers. While this is the strict case for corporations, LLCs have greater flexibility. LLCs typically only have members and managers (which in some cases may be the same person or people). That being said, LLCs can be structured to mimic the governance formalities of corporations. In some cases, this allows for a level of clarity on the division of labor. As such, for purposes of this section we will describe the building blocks for structuring corporate management.

Stockholders (or members in the case of an LLC) are the owners of the entity. Directors are appointed by vote of the stockholders. The directors, in turn, are responsible for appointing the officers. In an LLC, the manager(s) fulfill the role of both director and officer. Typical officer positions include a President (and perhaps a Chief Executive Officer), one or more Vice President(s), a Secretary, and a Treasurer (and perhaps a Chief Financial Officer). Although stockholders own the corporation, they generally do not engage directly in the day-to-day operation and management of the corporation. Rather, on an annual or other regular basis, they elect a board of directors, which is responsible for the strategic direction and most major decisions, pertaining to the corporation's business. The board delegates the day-to-day operation and management of the corporation to the officers. However, stockholder consent is generally required by statute or if desired, by the corporation's articles of incorporation for certain major decisions, such as the dissolution of the corporation.

The Board of Directors

The board has the ultimate responsibility for managing and supervising the corporation's business, and must answer to the corporation's shareholders. The board is generally held to a standard of care that requires the directors to perform all duties and responsibilities in good faith, with a degree of care that an ordinarily prudent person in a similar position would use under similar circumstances, and in a manner reasonably believed to be in the best interests of the company.

The board must meet from time to time to transact business and fulfill its responsibilities. It is typically best practice for the board to meet at least annually, and it may also meet at such other times as may be necessary. Duties and responsibilities of directors typically include the following:

- Oversee the performance of management, such as:
  - The appointment of officers
  - The review of periodic financial statements (i.e., quarterly, annually)
  - The review of internal policies and controls to ensure they are effective
  - The monitoring of duties delegated to officers and setting officers' salaries
- Determine time and location of stockholder and board meetings, if not set forth in certificate of incorporation or bylaws
- Review terms (and adopt an agreement or plan) of any proposed merger, consolidation, or share exchange and confirm Board approval prior to stockholder vote
- Review and approve terms of any proposed sale or encumbrance of company assets and confirm Board approval prior to stockholder vote
- Ensure that the company maintains a registered office and a registered agent within the state of incorporation and file any changes with the Secretary of State
- Determine whether (and in what amount) the corporation should declare a dividend or distribution
- Maintain books and records of the company (typically delegated to an officer)

The Officers

The officers generally include a President, one or more Vice President(s), a Secretary, and a Treasurer. A Chief Executive Officer and a Chief Financial Officer may augment the President and Treasurer, respectively. Officers are typically appointed by the Board and are given specific authority and responsibilities either by resolution of the Board or by the corporation's bylaws. Like directors, officers are also held to standards of care (e.g., good faith, fair dealing, and loyalty).

Responsibilities of officers typically include:

- Signing contracts and company instruments such as stock certificates)
- Maintaining a stock ledger and list of stockholders

- Performing all day-to-day operation and management of the company delegated by the directors
- Performing all officer duties and responsibilities set forth in the bylaws

In addition to the responsibilities set forth above, the bylaws define specific responsibilities for each officer. For example, the President might be tasked with submitting regular reports to the Board.

Structuring the Scope of Services

With respect to those providing services to the family, policies and procedures should be structured to address:

- Data security and privacy
- Employment policy regarding family vs. non-family members
- Separation of family business and family office information, costs, or services
- Employment incentives for performance
- Outsourcing where that is most efficient
- Expense approval and monitoring

Ownership and control are closely linked, but have distinct attributes. In our hypothetical case, Mom and Dad were interested in transitioning certain aspects of the business and investment to the four children. Therefore, the structure needed to account for the fact that they would each manage a portion of their own money. Mom and Dad wanted to remain active with their philanthropic goals but also seek regular grant-making input from the four children.

The family office should have an employment policy for family members as well as one for non-family professionals. In a commercial setting, businesses often have an employee handbook, as well as specific employment contracts or agreements that protect both the business and the employee and create baseline expectations for the way the enterprise will be operated, including bonuses provided. A family office is no different. In the family office context, however, family members often expect different treatment than do those outside of the family. They also have different expectations. Structuring the family office should address this set of issues appropriately.

Additionally, a family office that serves a single family may be subject to US SEC oversight, as discussed in Chapter 7. Therefore, the formation of the family office must anticipate these regulatory requirements in deciding who shall be involved in management and how.

When structuring the family office, the management responsibilities should be addressed in the context of both internal and external matters.

Internal Operations

There are certain questions that will affect decisions and relations within the family when it comes to establishing a family office. Some critical questions a family should ask include:

- How should power be balanced between and among the members and the managers(s) (or shareholders and directors, as the case may be)? That is, what power (or consultation rights) should separate the "owners" and managers?
- Who should be represented at meetings? Should membership be branch-based with one member per branch? Equal participation is seen as the starting point. What if a branch lacks an eligible adult member? Each parent family member might determine eligibility criteria for children and decide on a regent who can act for a child who does not meet eligibility criteria in case of the parent's death or permanent incapacity. Should non-family members (such as spouses) be capable of acting as regents?
- How will decisions be made: by consensus or by vote? If voting, which system will apply:
  a. A simple majority or greater for most decisions?
  b. A super majority or unanimity for a category of major decisions?
  c. Who will act as a chairman and/or president?
- How should reporting to family and accountability be structured and how will performance be evaluated:
  a. Who does it?
  b. How is it done?
  c. How often?
- Should there be standards of communication (from family office to family and to/from family office to other entities in the structure)? How should the members and/or managers work together? Such issues include:
  a. Meeting frequency: quarterly/monthly/other
  b. Minute-taking/record keeping
  c. Should there be established parameters for internal operations between and among members and/or managers of the family office?
  d. Linkages to other entities
  e. Boards/Members/committees
  f. Key employees
  g. Audit committee(s)

- What other links exist between the family and the family office (such as reporting, officer/board membership, etc.)? How will the separate members/managers of the family office link to the other parts of the overall governance structure:
  a. Other family members (children/spouses)
  b. Directors of business interests
  c. Family wealth holding structures (trusts, foundations, etc.)
- The family office should be involved with fostering the next generation/education/talent building. Should this include fostering inclusion of the next generation at annual meetings? Should there be a next generation advisory committee to develop their input and future leadership? Should the family office encourage and/or manage the family's philanthropic goals? Are there other special areas which the family office should address?

External Operations

Some questions that a family should ask in connection with establishing a family office that will offer services to entities serving the family's investment, business, or philanthropic interests include:

- Should members' or shareholders' voting interests be governed solely in shareholder or LLC operating agreements or should they be held in voting trusts?
- Should family office meetings include a consultative or decision-making forum?
- What information flow is desirable to and from the family office as it relates to affiliated or managed entities and business interests, particularly where those entities include non-family investors or other participants?
- Should the family office address issues such as employment of family members in business?
- How/should the family office provide services to a family's nonbusiness interests, such as an individual family member's residences, personal assets, or hobby activities?
- Should there be areas of individual or branch autonomy for investment (separate shares or tracking interests)?
- Should the family office be tasked with review, monitoring, or separate investment activities of family members?
- Should the family office be responsible for the integrity of investment structures and should there be third-party audit and review?

- Should external advisors have a role (including trustees, investment managers, accountants and legal advisors)?
- Should the family office engage professional facilitators or other consultants?

Family Philanthropy, Legacy, and Social Capital

Family office involvement in a family's philanthropy, legacy, and social capital is often uniquely tied to that family's mission and social objectives. Some questions that every family should ask in connection with establishing a family office that will participate in these services include:

- Should the family office monitor and implement a family foundation's annual contribution requirements (such as the 5 percent per year distribution requirement required to avoid Federal excise tax) or is this lead directly by the family foundation alone?
- Should the family office assist with identifying and/or making recommendations for charitable donations?
- Should the family office monitor charitable activity and/or success of prior recipients?
- Should the family office oversee a family's reputation and standing such as monitoring of newspapers, press, community events, as well as litigation management?

Managing Regulatory and Estate Planning Concerns

Structuring the family office must be undertaken cognizant of both Federal security and tax law and regulatory concerns. This is because both the SEC and the US Treasury Department have created rules that could require informational reporting and/or taxation, in certain circumstances, that can otherwise be minimized or avoided with anticipatory planning.

As detailed in Chapter 7, where a family office provides investment advisory services, care should be taken to qualify for the so-called "family office exemption" from registration by structuring the operations so that designated activities are "exclusively controlled" by family members or family entities. Certain matters that can be provided by the family office (directly or through committees) without triggering regulatory reporting include:

- Investment advisory and monitoring, provided such advice cannot be for or on behalf of any funds that serve non-family clients
- Asset management

- Tax compliance and/or oversight
- Accounting
- Legal (management of outside advisors)
- Risk management

When it comes to safeguarding the success of estate planning vehicles, such as trusts, it is important that family office management services not take over or violate the formalities of those structures in key tax-related aspects. Though not a complete list of every situation, some matters that likely should not be directed by family offices, but should rather be reserved to independent trustees or appropriately appointed fiduciary committees, include:

- Trust distribution decisions
- Trust amendment decisions
- Trustee selection, protector selection, and certain management services to or on behalf of a private trust company

As always, qualified tax advisors should always be consulted before substituting any formal or practical authority over trust and estate-planned vehicles.

Question 5: How Are Family Offices Structured to Optimize Tax Efficiency?

Tax (and cash flow) efficiency requires compliance with all applicable tax rules—income tax, estate tax, gift tax, employment taxes, withholding tax, state and/or local income taxes, state and/or local real estate taxes, and sales and/or use taxes. Typical tax-oriented services that a family office provides or outsources include:

- Careful record and bookkeeping to enable calculating both net ordinary and net capital gain income or losses and maximizing net operating losses, where they might be available.
- Tracking and memorializing costs, such as employee and investment management expenses.
- Meeting tax reporting requirements for the family office as an employer for state and local tax considerations.
- Paying and tracking employee compensation (both size and form of compensation).

- Coordinating consistency of tax services and reporting of common family interests and structures. Where applicable, coordinating joint defense agreements (mutual support of tax positions on audit).

Key issues in evaluating the tax efficiency of a family office structure itself involve the allocation of costs to underlying entities and the classification of services being provided by the family office in such a way as to maximize the appropriate deductibility of expenses, where appropriate, and avoid generating taxable income from intra-family payments so far as practical as well. In this regard, it is important that all services' agreements are considered and carefully drafted.

Tax developments have impacted the economics of family office operations. The enactment of the Tax Cuts and Jobs Act (TCJA) created a reduction of the Federal corporate income tax rate to 21 percent, and the reduction of the tax rate on active business income earned by individuals and trusts through partnerships that qualify for the 20 percent qualified business deduction were two important changes to general income taxation that can have an impact on the choice of entity for family offices and related investment structures today.[5] In addition, the limitations on favorable tax treatment for carried interest where managers receive a profits interest (often called the incentive allocation or carried interest allocation), and the reduction in application of the alternative minimum tax (or full exception, in the case of a corporation) may also affect structuring choices or consequences in some circumstances.

In regard to the tax efficiency of family investment partnerships, the reduction of various income tax deductions, including miscellaneous itemized deductions for state and local taxes, net active business losses, and net interest expense deductions where debt is used, are imposing a potentially very significant net increase in the cost of investment management expenses of all kinds, including the after tax cost of family-office operations unless they qualify to be appropriately covered through the kind of profits interest addressed in the Lender case.

On way of synthesizing the economics of the family enterprise between the family office and those entities through which investments are made (such as family investment partnerships) is to employ the previously mentioned profits interest. Profits interest arrangements require a series of considerations based on the business deal as well as tax regulations.[6] The profits interest is a means of aligning the management with the passive investors (typically the limited partners). While the regulations are fairly complex, as a threshold matter, the arrangement must reflect significant entrepreneurial risk (SER).

Lacking SER is based on the family office's (i.e., the service provider's) risk relative to the overall risk of the partnership. Tax regulations illustrate that certain arrangements are presumed to lack significant entrepreneurial risk (and, therefore, constitute a disguised payment for services) unless facts and circumstances establish otherwise by clear and convincing evidence.

In the international context, families should also consider the possible application of a new withholding tax on dispositions of fund (US partnership) interests by non-US partners and new international tax provisions expanding the immediate taxation of profits and gains derived from non-US activities as well as the increase in the number of entities that are subject to the CFC rules. In addition, the application of income tax treaties, estate and gift tax treaties, and/or bilateral investment treaties (BIT) should be considered. Treaties help establish an agreement between countries as to how certain provisions of law will be applied to citizens of respective countries. This is especially important when family operations cross over contrasting legal traditions, such as the civil law jurisdictions in much of Western Europe and parts of Asia, the common law jurisdictions of the United States, United Kingdom, and other parts of Asia, and Sharia (Islamic law) in the Middle East. This leads to differences in jurisprudence and greatly affects the way legal decisions are made and the way legal transactions are executed and authenticated.

The United States has entered into income tax treaties with over 50 different countries (sometimes referred to as a Convention between the governments of each country "for the avoidance of double taxation" or referred to as Double Tax Avoidance Agreements). These treaties are generally reciprocal, therefore applying to both treaty countries, and potentially benefiting residents of either country, provided residency and limitation on benefits provisions are met. The consequences of receiving tax-treaty benefits are that income may be taxed (and/or withheld) at a reduced rate or could be exempt from US or treaty partner taxes. However, the amounts of reduction or qualifications for exemption vary among countries and specific items of income or asset.

The United States has entered into estate tax treaties (and in some cases estate and gift tax) with almost 20 different countries, far fewer than countries with which the United States has entered into income tax treaties. These treaties are generally broken into two categories—old, which address estate taxation on the basis of the situs of an asset; or new, which addresses estate and gift taxation on the basis of residency but also apply certain situs rules with respect to real estate and business property.

BITs generally provide protection for investment assets where such assets are located outside of the family's country of citizenship or organization of an entity (corporate or otherwise). Specifically, they provide protection from nationalization and expropriation, unfair treatment, confiscation or damage caused by revolution, and interference with enjoyment, and they provide a mechanism for dispute resolution through international arbitration. Taken together, the combined tax and investment treaties could provide valuable protections to a multinational family.

Finally, it is important to consider how the jurisdictional location of a family office and its employees may affect the taxation of a family fiduciary structure (such as trusts or a private family trust company) or related investment structures. When tasked to assist with such management responsibilities, family offices could generate or avoid nexus for state taxation of such structures. In general, states initially base their original jurisdiction to tax the income of a trust based on the location of the trustee or where the grantor was domiciled when the trust became irrevocable. However, it has been ruled by the courts that certain minimum contacts are constitutionally necessary to permit this taxation. This was illustrated in the 2019 US Supreme Court case of North Carolina v. Kimberley Rice Kaestner 1992 Family Trust.[7] In this case, the US Supreme Court evaluated whether a US irrevocable discretionary trust had nexus with the State of North Carolina when the only contact with that state was a resident beneficiary. The State claimed that the residence of a beneficiary was sufficient nexus, but the US Supreme Court disagreed on the grounds that imposing an annual income tax on only such limited contact would violate the Due Process Clause of the US Constitution. The US Supreme court focused on, among other things, how and where trust assets were administered. Because there was no administration (investment or otherwise) in North Carolina, the State did not have sufficient contact. If this case had involved a family office in North Carolina, managing investments of the trust, the result might have been different. The point is the situs and integration of a family office into trust administration could be construed as a point of contact for state income tax nexus purposes. On the other hand, siting a family office location in a jurisdiction where trusts are not taxed, based on administration of the trust in that state, can provide an important advantage to help the family reduce or eliminate state income taxation of their trusts.

Tax Deductibility of Services Provided by the Family Office

The tax deductibility of a family office's operations depends first on the business character of the services provided. Are they an extension of the owner(s) managing their own investments or is the family office owned and operated in a manner that rises to the level of a separate and bona fide business?

There is ample US tax case law that helps define the parameters of the analysis, which collectively help distinguish active from passive investors and focuses on whether the activity is profit-oriented, not personal (which excludes hobby or entertainment activities, and mere managerial attention to one's own investments). These cases illustrate the importance of the family office activity being continuous, regular, and substantial (which is a highly factual analysis). Finally, they illustrate that a shareholder must establish his or her own trade or business, separate from the trade or business of the corporation whose shares are owned (such that there is "compensation other than the normal investor's return, income received directly for his own services rather than indirectly through the corporate enterprise."). While a survey of the cases is beyond the scope of this chapter, the basics are important. The term "trade or business" is famously not defined in the Internal Revenue Code or Treasury Regulations. However, case law and IRS rulings have illustrated that activities for the production of income that are "considerable, continuous and regular" are indicia of a bona fide trade or business.[8]

When considering the tax deductibility of a family office's business activity, certain key considerations are relevant, including:

- Ordinary and necessary expenses paid by individuals in relation to active businesses in which they materially participate should be fully deductible for income tax purposes.
- Passive activity losses (when the individual does not materially participate in the business) can only be deducted when that activity generates a profit.
- While investment expenses were previously partly deductible (i.e., subject to limitation under a 2 percent of adjusted gross income floor and nondeductible for AMT purposes), since January 1, 2017.[9]

Since January 1, 2017, following the adoption of the TCJA, the potential deduction for these investment expenses was suspended along with other miscellaneous itemized deductions through the year 2025. Therefore, tax efficient strategies will put greater focus on the ability of a taxpayer to take deductions for expenses that are ordinary and necessary in the course of the active conduct of a trade or business.

The tax character of services performed by the family office for family trusts include:

- Miscellaneous itemized deductions if attributable to the trusts' businesses, may be active or passive depending on material participation of trustees.

- Investment management fees for trusts had been tax deductible but subject to a 2 percent floor and AMT limits. Following the TCJA's amendments, fees earned by family offices that are organized in corporate form should not be subject to a corporate AMT.
- Expenses in connection with the administration of the trust such as tax and legal advice and trustee fees are generally regarded as not being subject to a 2 percent floor for certain tax deductions because they might be able to be characterized as being in connection with the administration of the trust that would not have otherwise been incurred.
- Trusts may be eligible for a full deduction of expenses paid to the family office if the trust materially participates in an active business.

Services performed by the family office for family-owned corporations include:

- Ordinary and necessary expenses to C corporations should be fully deductible against trade or business income and/or investment income. These services might include money and property management services. However, passive losses rules might also need to be considered.
- It is often most tax advantageous for a family office to maximize services for C corporations in the group.

In all events, family office charges must be at arm's length prices.

State and Local Tax

Going back to our example of the Family, if we were to learn that one of the children, an avid skier and outdoor enthusiast, was contemplating a move and was willing to relocate to California, Wyoming, or Nevada for tax purposes, the child would be strongly advised to favor a move to Wyoming or Nevada (rather than California) for tax purposes because those states do not impose either a state individual income tax or corporate income tax.

This illustrates that the first rule in state and local taxation, like real estate, is: location, location, location. A significant amount of income tax efficiency can be achieved by operating out of one or more states that do not levy an income tax in the first place.

As previously noted, a state only has nexus to tax an enterprise if there is some link or minimum connection between a state and the person, property, or transaction it seeks to tax. As such, a family enterprise will only be taxed in those states that levy an income tax and can prove that such state has a minimum connection with (and jurisdiction over) some portion of the enterprise and/or the potentially taxable activity.

In this regard, the ownership of real or tangible personal property (including an office) in a state is generally sufficient contact to allow a state jurisdiction to tax the income of the owner of such property. Therefore, determination of the location of the family office headquarters should be a key part of the tax planning in the formation process.

Question 6: Can a Family Office Be Structured to Manage Risk?

An important responsibility of a family office is risk management. This is particularly apparent in times of transition for the family. Risk management touches most if not all aspects of family operations associated with a family office:

• Economic and cash flow risk
• Tax and legal compliance risk
• Employee liability and fraud
• Property and casualty risk
• Privacy, identity theft, and loss of confidentiality

Case in Point

Not long ago a family hired an individual to undertake certain investment management and bookkeeping tasks. This individual was successful in his undertakings, progressing up the ranks, and over time was given greater and greater responsibilities within the single-family office, earning the family's trust. Unfortunately, the individual succumbed to the temptation of embezzling funds for his personal use. Eventually, he was caught, but the fraud occurred over the course of seven years and was not detected during this time because the family was provided with fraudulent financial statements.

Incidents of embezzlement like this are not a new area of risk to private enterprises and family offices. However, it appears that it is increasing in frequency, with a number of high profile cases occurring since the 1980s.

Proper fraud mitigation strategies and best practices will help minimize this area of exposure to risk. As a result of the incident described in this case, the family office did a major overhaul of its governance system. Although the fraud was a traumatic experience for the family, their family office has rebounded and proven more resilient as a result.

Risk Management Through Architecture

Some risks can be insured against, but others are best addressed through the design of infrastructure itself, such as divisions of labor and checks and balances. For example, a multimember LLC may offer liability protection in addition to tax efficiency. Additionally, a tiered family office structure isolates risks within each respective subsidiary entity.

Not only entities, but also the management of such entities should be diversified. This could involve oversight of the persons who have authority to write the checks or make withdrawals, and creating redundancy in the team that keeps books and records. Third-party service providers, such as certified public accountants with reputable firms and lawyers in good standing, can also help in the process for review and audit of books, records, tax filings, and corporate governance. Regular or periodic internal audits for and on behalf of the family also are helpful in addition to third-party audits.

People-Oriented Risk Management

A family office is a service enterprise. People are the key asset in providing those services. However, employees inevitably pose a certain amount of risk. It is important to have carefully drafted employment agreements, as well as an employee handbook that clearly establishes the rules relating to and responsibilities of those providing services to the family. A well-drafted employment agreement will include provisions relating to confidentiality of information, data security and privacy protection, as well as nonsolicitation and noncompetition provisions. In addition to individual employment agreements, employee handbooks or manuals establish baseline understandings and prevent unintentional or inadvertent missteps. These would likely include provisions relating to confidentiality, nondisparagement, domestic worker rights, pay notice requirements, and overtime matters, which protect not only the day-to-day business information shared and legal regulations that apply in employee-employer relationships, but also help protect the personal information and reputation of family members and their acquaintances.

Balance Sheet, Cash Flow, and Economic Risk Management

Economic and cash flow risk management is central to the core purpose of most family offices to preserve and protect the wealth that a family has generated. Whether having concentrated stock positions, real estate development, or operating businesses, families usually build their fortunes through taking extensive financial risk. But they create their family offices in no small part to preserve that wealth. Therefore, a family office is commonly tasked with monitoring family's assets and liabilities carefully and bringing a risk diversification and enhanced wealth management perspective to the family table. How this is done for each individual family has unique features but will generally include:

- Enhancing cash and expense management and monitoring; creating safe lending facilities
- Ensuring and managing good estate planning, including liquidity for estate needs
- Monitoring and maintaining life insurance and retirement planning
- Promoting diversification from concentrated risks and monitoring manager performance fees and counter-party risk
- Developing succession and competence for next generation family leaders

Question 7: What Is the Process of Establishing and Structuring a Family Office?

A successful family office is one that:

- Achieves a family's personal and professional strategic goals
- Is accepted (and embraced) by the family who has established and/or engaged the family office, as well as key employees, and any third-party clients/investors that might also participate in family affairs
- Is managed in a professional and cost-efficient manner on a long-term basis
- Is flexible enough to adapt to the inevitable changes in the lives of those involved

A good family office should also function in a manner that promotes unity amongst family and key employees (to the extent either or both are involved). This usually involves a board of directors and/or a family council through which the family members successfully communicate and understand and respect each person's role and responsibilities.

The successful integration of a family office into a family's overall control and management structure is often a time-consuming and carefully calculated process. As such, it is generally created through a series of steps. Each step has a variety of facets and builds on the prior. As an introduction, these steps might be as follows:

Step 1. Develop a mission (strategic plan)

a. What are the founders' (and family's) personal objectives for their role in the family's investments, business, philanthropic and social objectives?
b. What are the family's goals for the office itself and the clients it serves?
c. What are the family's goals for any collective investment program in which there are outside investors that the family might also serve?
d. To what extent should the extended family be involved in the family office, first while the founders are active and second after a complete transition to the next generation (and so on)?

Step 2. Identify when, how, and to whom you would like to transition services of the family office

a. Internally, who should be involved? When and how?
b. Externally, how will the investment program, family business, and family philanthropy be affected by the transition and what steps need to be undertaken to ensure a smooth transition over the short and long term?

Step 3. Choose the structure

a. Evaluate the different legal forms available to achieve your objectives, and determine which legal forms will best address tax, business, and personal concerns.
b. Consider how the various legal forms could impact the ownership, management, control, day-to-day operations, administration, and transitions that will occur over the medium term.
c. Choose the legal structure and corporate governance that best reflects the founder's and founder's family's personal and business strategic plan.

Step 4. Establish governance

a. Outline how the family office should be ideally managed, controlled, and operated in the short and long term.
b. Identify who will have leadership roles in the short term and how succession will be developed in the long term.
c. Communicate with each applicable individual, and agree on annual or periodic meetings.
d. Work with a team (in-house or external accountants, lawyers and/or consultants) to consider and address potential regulatory and compliance requirements.

Step 5. Implementation

a. Draft and execute the documents necessary to memorialize each facet of structuring the family office (that is, the specific services arrangements as well as any ancillary planning such as estate planning modifications that might be necessary).

Step 6. Periodic evaluation and re-evaluation

a. Begin with
   1. A mutually agreed upon action plan
   2. A well-defined scope of review
   3. A reasonable timeline and procedures
   4. Deliverables memorializing the evaluation
b. Review to include one or more disinterested second opinions that can provide a fresh look at purpose and scope of the family office.
c. Examine whether legal structures can be molded to better serve family goals.
d. Address questions such as: Is the structure efficient? Does it protect the family's interests? Does it further its goals? Does the structure encourage the best performance from staff and service providers?

Conclusion and Final Thoughts

The establishment and structuring of a family office is a bespoke process. To be successful, many questions should be addressed ahead of time so that the process can be undertaken in an efficient and meaningful way.

It is often valuable to integrate family members with non-family members in a family office setting. Including family members in positions of leadership and responsibility in the family office, and as directors of the family structure, can help achieve buy-in by family members and help to keep a family enterprise (whether business, investment, or philanthropically oriented) operating consistent with family values.

Families should work with their legal counsel and key advisors in developing a structure and drafting the documents to memorialize that structure for the family, the family office, and its related and associated parties (i.e., staff, employees, consultants, and board members).

Notes

1. Other options exist, including tiered structures, but these are the most common and are therefore the focus of this commentary.
2. Lender Management, LLC v. Comm'r, T.C. Memo. 2017-246 (Dec. 13, 2017).
3. Hellmann v. Comm'r, U.S. Tax Court Docket Numbers 8486-17, 8489-17, 8494-17, and 8497-17.
4. Since January 1, 2017 tax reform, investment management fees subject to the rules of IRC Section 212 ceased to be tax deductible at all. Therefore, even if a family-office operation is structured in a manner to that described in the Lender case, such fees would still not be tax deductible to the individual limited partners (or passive members in the case of an LLC).
5. Tax Cuts and Jobs Act, Public Law 115-97 (131 Stat. 2054) introduced in Congress on November 2, 2017, that amended the Internal Revenue Code of 1986.
6. Generally speaking, four requirements must be met: (1) Upon issuance, the interest must not give the employee a share of the liquidation proceeds if the family-office assets were sold at fair market value and the proceeds were distributed in complete liquidation of the partnership (i.e., the interest cannot be a "capital interest"); (2) The interest must not relate to a substantially certain and predictable stream of income from the family office assets; (3) The family member employee must not dispose of the profits interest within two years of receiving it; and (4) The LLC must not be a publicly traded partnership. A profits interests may compensate the family office in the right situations. This is not suitable to all family-office structures, but in certain cases it will be viable.
7. North Carolina Dept. of Revenue v. Kimberley Rice Kaestner 1992 Family Trust, 588 U. S. (2019)
8. This was most recently illustrated in the Lender and Hellmann cases. These factors have also been explored in Higgins v. Commissioner (1941), Whipple v. Commissioner (1963), Gentile v. Commissioner (1975), and Ditunno v. Commissioner (1983), among other similar tax cases, each of which help inform the analysis relevant to the scope of activities that should be considered when analyzing the substance and materiality of a trade or business.
9. Formerly deductible investment expenses included: a. Costs incurred for the production or collection of income from investments; b. Costs incurred for the management, conservation, or maintenance of property held for the production of income; c. Certain expenses to collect a refund of any tax, which might include financial planning services, tax planning and preparation fees, and certain legal and accounting fees; d. Nondeductible expenses include: personal bill paying, personal travel, expenses associated with tax-exempt income. Generally speaking, these expenses should be minimized or, if possible, capitalized.

CHAPTER 6

Strategic Planning for the Family Office

Kirby Rosplock, PhD

Family offices perform and accomplish various services depending on the nature of the family and their underlying goals for the family office. An office may spend 15 to 30 percent of their time on planning, gathering data, and providing data to the client for strategic planning considerations on an ongoing basis. Having a strategy to approach the strategic planning process contributes greatly to an office's success.

Chapter 4 focuses on the overarching mission, vision, and values of an office, while this chapter emphasizes the strategic and financial planning to efficiently and effectively operationalize the mission or vision of the office. This chapter provides a starting point for the strategic planning process and types of baseline information that may be gathered by a family office to best serve the needs of the family. From estate planning, tax, legal, accounting, insurance, financial, compliance, and family background information, the family office increasingly operates as a repository. This chapter then shares approaches to gather the baseline information and tools to help with the foundational reviews. A capital sufficiency case study emphasizes the importance of financial modeling with the strategic planning process. This chapter omits covering family office investment considerations, as they are covered more extensively in Chapter 8 on investment management approaches within the family office.

Creating a Family Office Strategic Plan

Developing a family office strategic plan is kindred to establishing the blueprint for a home. There is a tremendous amount of information to "spec out" prior to the construction, execution, and implementation of their plan. A family office cannot truly deliver the highest quality integrated service without having a handle on many foundational aspects of the family and its wealth. Instead of a blueprint for a physical home, this chapter discusses planning aspects for the family and maps out both elements of its financial capital (wealth and business), family capital (who the family members are), and its intentions (wealth transfer and/or philanthropic). The strategic plan consists of four main phases:

1. *Discovery:* an environmental scan to establish a baseline for each main functional aspect of the family office
2. *Focus:* a clarity of purpose and mission and objectives for the plan
3. *Execution:* outlining the action plan and steps for implementation
4. *Maintenance:* updating the plan over time

Chapter 2 provides the Mathile Case Study, an in-depth example of the setup, design, and iteration of a family office. And over time, as a function of external and internal triggers, the family office is prompted to update its plan and its corollary action steps. The President of the Mathile Family, Jill Barber, maintains the importance of being heads-down (tasked-focused) as well as heads-up (vision-focused).

For the strategic plan to be current, the strategic planning process is ongoing and iterative. Thus, the family office executives typically aggregate, organize, and integrate with family and the technical advisors routinely. The exchange of information between family owners, family office, and external advisors and providers is fluid and constant. See the Strategic Planning Interface in Figure 6.1.

From accountants and attorneys to bankers and trust officers, there may be a myriad of professionals who touch some aspect of the family in one way, shape, or form, and who may contribute, evaluate, and weigh in on various reviews and the planning process. How efficiently these advisors work together is also critical to the success of the foundational information you are creating and can help streamline the process. A significant amount of knowledge is created in the intersecting areas and overlap from each advisor.

Finally, a common misunderstanding is that the baseline information is solely technical documentation, such as copies of wills, trusts, and account

FIGURE 6.1   Family Office Strategic Planning Interface

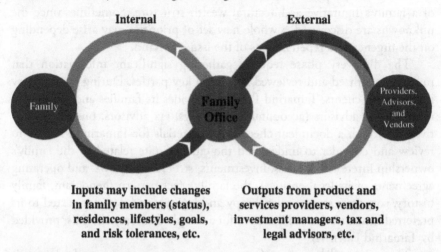

Internal   External

Family   Family Office   Providers, Advisors, and Vendors

Inputs may include changes in family members (status), residences, lifestyles, goals, and risk tolerances, etc.

Outputs from product and services providers, vendors, investment managers, tax and legal advisors, etc.

Source: © Tamarind Partners, Inc.

information. However, the reality is that there are critical qualitative insights that are equally important to ascertain that influence, direct, and/or inform the technical documentation. For example, as you gather more insight about the family and individuals and learn their preferences for information exchange and styles of decision-making, the issue of whether the family is open or closed around how it communicates wealth issues is very important too. Advisors who know their clients can spot when their client's values or intentions may conflict with their underlying legal documents. The family office advisor must know the legal, investment, compliance, financial, philanthropic, and wealth transfer aspects of the client, but also the client's values, intentions, and belief system. What drives them? What motivates them? What are their dreams and aspirations? What are their greatest fears? What do they most desire to achieve with their wealth?

Discovery

The discovery phase maps the current state of a family, the family office, and/or the existing circumstance if the family is establishing a new family office, transitioning an office, or winding an office down. A consultant or advisor may be instrumental to outline the steps, provide guidance on critical issues, and clarify a pathway to the family's office requirements. This is a role in which Tamarind Partners frequently finds itself when a family desires third-party, unbiased expertise to evaluate their desired course of action.

The discovery phase establishes the knowns and identifies the unknowns of a family's figurative architectural wealth structure. Sometimes once the unknowns are discovered, a whole new set of priorities may arise depending on the urgency and repercussions of the issues at hand.

The discovery phase requires gathering significant information that must be organized and reviewed by several key parties. During its discovery process with clients, Tamarind Partners provides its families and often their most trusted advisors (accountants, attorneys, tax advisors, business executives, etc.) with a document checklist of materials for Tamarind Partners to review and consider to understand the current state related to the family's ownership interests (business, investments, structures, bylaws, and operating agreements of its legal entities), the family's fact pattern (genogram, family history, corporate story, philanthropy and legacy), and data connected to its preferred future state. See Figure 6.2 for a sample discovery checklist provided by Tamarind Partners.

Thus, the collaboration of owners, executives, experts, and advisors is imperative for this process to be a success to gather, review, and discern the priority issues and any critical concerns or inflection points that may take precedent to the priority issue. Second, the process of gathering the information is both an art and a science and typically requires time to gather and review. Third, the strategic plan is a snapshot, a picture of the family at one point in time. The information may be up to date (or not) at the time that it is gathered; thus, family office advisors must recognize that updating, monitoring, and reviewing the information periodically is vital. Therefore, having some strategic planning guidelines is so critical to the process. Otherwise, the family office risks creating a plan that has no accountability measures or metrics associated with its success. To follow are the baseline reviews in five major segments that inform the Discovery Process. Those reviews include: (1) the family capital review, (2) the advisor network, (3) the legal review, (4) the insurance review, and (5) the financial review and capital sufficiency analysis.

The Family Capital Review

The greatest asset in the family, no question, is its human capital. Although the wealth management industry has typically focused its attention to the financial assets and measures its stature by its assets under management or assets under advisement, the most invaluable element is the family members themselves. During the process of gathering baseline information, it is important to begin to understand the macro and micro aspects of the family. One useful tool to understand how the family, like a puzzle, fits together is to use a tool called a genogram. A genogram is a way to map the family tree and to see the relationships between family members. It is also a way to understand complicated relationships either due to divorce, death, separation, or tension. There are various genogram programs available online. (See Figure 6.3 Sample Genogram.)

FIGURE 6.2   Discovery Family Office Checklist

- **Family ownership documentation** (including business mission, vision, values or culture statement(s), organizational charts, business performance documentation, line of credit or loan documentation, financials, balance sheet, ownership structure, etc.)
- **Business entities or legal entity structure(s)** (including operating agreements, employment contracts, advisor agreements, direct investment agreements, personnel charts, business documentation, etc.)
- **Family governance documentation** (family mission, constitution, family charter, family policies/procedures, board of directors, or board of advisors, governance documentation, etc.)
- **Trust documentation** (including trust documents, letters of wishes, guidance to beneficiaries and/or trustees, trust summaries, etc.)
- **Estate planning documentation** (including estate planning summary, copies of trusts, estate plan flow chart, wealth transfer outline, letter of wishes, POA, HPOA, advanced directives, etc.)
- **Financial planning documentation** (including financial plan, cash flow statement, personal balance sheet, statement of net worth, etc.)
- **Compliance and risk management documentation** (including insurance coverage, property/casualty, umbrella, private placement life insurance, personal, life, health, errors and omission insurance, etc.)
- **Investment documentation** (including investment reports (quarterly, annual), tax return, asset allocation, investment policy statement(s), list of managers, partnership accounting, record keeping of personal property, list of all privately held assets, list of relevant collectibles, etc.)
- **Charitable structures or foundation information** (including foundation charter, board of directors, mission, form 990, grantmaking summary, officers, key employees, etc.)
- **Summary of any current or projected litigation** and projected damages if applicable

Source: Tamarind Partners, Inc.

The Family Background

Although the process to capture a family's wealth creation story may be formal and include interviews, a family video, or biography, the family story also

FIGURE 6.3 Sample Genogram

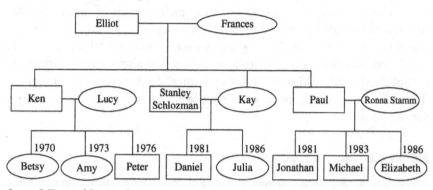

Source: © Tamarind Partners, Inc.

may be shared informally around the dinner table or at family reunions. It is powerful for an advisor to understand the story firsthand and to keep this in mind as a full understanding of the family is crafted. The heritage, behaviors, and values of individual family members are testaments to the character of these individuals and reveal important wisdom on the adversities they have faced and overcome through their involvement and engagement in different communities, organizations, and institutions, and their influence in the family. The wealth creation story can help to anchor a family to its primal roots and underlying values. This information can help advisors appreciate and see the tremendous journey an individual or family has undertaken to arrive at this point.

Gathering an in-depth understanding of each family member can also provide insights to many challenging and difficult realities of wealth. There is no question that wealth impacts relationships, from how wealth may create tensions, resentments, feelings of regret or inadequacy, to family members' feelings about preferential treatment or sense of entitlement because of their financial means. Other inheritors may feel challenged to live up to the expectations of a preceding generation's wealth creator's success or feel as though they are living in the shadow of another family member's success. Some families prefer not to talk about some of these feelings and experiences; but often, they have profound influences on how a family interacts with its wealth. Often, wealth creators may become isolated or insulated by business and financial success, often at the expense of family relationships and those with their peers. Although these facets of wealth may not be easy to discuss for a family, they also can provide greater insights as to why the family behaves differently when it comes to their financial means, their outlook, and their goals.

The Advisor Network Review

Families are often surrounded by several trusted advisors who are critical to the planning, operations, and smooth functioning of the family. A valued practice is to identify those key advisors who are instrumental in advising the family. Following is a list of advisor types who likely are connected and trusted advisors to the family. To better understand the complexity of the relationships, consider identifying who each of the advisors are, their primary role, their family client member, and who their contact is in the family office.

Typical Advisor Types

- Attorney
- Accountant
- Business executives
- Board members
- Family business consultant
- Insurance broker
- Concierge specialist
- Therapist or psychologist

The Estate Plan Review

Estate plans provide the instructions for an individual's wishes and intentions, for how and where they would like their wealth and any personal effects to go upon death. For the family office, the documents that comprise the estate plan—will, power of attorney, trust documents, health care power of attorney, living will, ethical will—are perhaps the most important components of the foundational material to gather. One important consideration the family office needs to address is how the individual and his or her family evolves, and how or if the estate plan should reflect changes over the years. For example, let's imagine a young man, Henry, sets up his estate plan with his estate planning attorney when he is 25. Henry then gets married and has three children and grows a very successful business, which generates more than $20 million in liquid wealth by the time he is 45. Although Henry has an estate plan, it is likely dated and does not reflect significant changes in his personal net worth nor the changes in his marital and family status. The family office can work with Henry's estate planning attorney (or perhaps has a dedicated estate plan attorney in-house) to proactively incorporate changes to his estate plan, such as setting up a marital trust, a trust for his children, and/or updating his intentions regarding heirs for his wealth after death. The family office may not only be a repository to hold on to these documents, but it may also be tasked with making sure they are current and up-to-date on underlying provisions. In addition, the family office can be a resource to educate, mentor, and prepare beneficiaries as well as grantors and trustees to best practices for a smooth wealth transfer when the time comes. There is considerable preparation that is involved to provide a base understanding of what the family owns and what/if some or all those assets may flow to family beneficiaries. Chapter 12 discusses more broadly the perspectives of the next generation and preparing them for beneficial ownership.

Mapping and Summarizing Legal Entities

Another practical exercise that the family office can be helpful in coordinating is mapping and summarizing legal documents and ascertaining the various legal entities and the connections to each family member. One family interviewed for this book had more than 150 legal entities including partnerships, limited liability corporations, and trusts. Other families, who were prior clients, had more than 300, 400, even 500+ separate entities, depending on the size and complexity of the family and its holdings. More does not necessarily mean better planning, but it often does increase administration. It also means more reporting, compliance, and oversight for the family office to maintain the number of entities.

In addition to mapping out the entities, it is helpful to have a clear understanding of the history behind each entity. For each entity, document the answers to following questions:

- Why was this entity created?
- When was it created?
- What purpose does it serve?
- Who set up the entity? Identify family, advisors, attorneys, and other professionals engaged.
- Who is legally connected to this entity (e.g., shareholders, owners, beneficiaries, grantors, trustees, and partners) and what are their roles?
- When/will this entity terminate?
- Where was the entity established?
- What are the tax ramifications of this legal entity?

- Are there any foreseeable issues/concerns associated with the entity?
- What are the "triggers" or specific events, if any, that would require a change or update of the entity?

In addition to answering the questions above, if the entity is a trust, the review should also identify if it is (a) testamentary (a gift upon death) or *inter vivos* (a gift during one's lifetime) and (b) revocable (capable of being revoked by the grantor) or irrevocable (the bequest cannot be taken back). Additionally, the summary may include the distribution provisions, the powers of appointment, and the total return provisions for the trust.

If the family office does not have a trusts and estate planning attorney in-house, working closely with the family's estate planning counsel is recommended. Estate planning attorneys can be instrumental in developing the summaries of the legal entities, and the exercise can be beneficial for the attorney as often provisions or environmental issues may have changed that influence the trust.

Figures 6.4 and 6.5 illustrate a sample trust summary and an estate plan flow chart as points of reference, respectively.

Family Office Stress Tests

Families are constantly managing and coping with a multitude of stressors from family life events to macro events such as market downturns, pandemics, or natural disasters. In addition to understanding who the family members and their trusted advisors are, it is also vital to understand the likelihood that these family office stressors may occur. Personal life events are most common and may encompass issues from birth to death, marriage to divorce, retirement to career change or unemployment, as examples. For a more comprehensive list of life events, see Figure 6.6.

Some of these issues may require urgent attention—for example, when or if a family member loses his or her job and needs to supplement the household income or obtain health insurance coverage. Another urgent example may be a shortfall due to a business closure from a fire or accident, requiring a family member to call capital. Other life events, such as declining health, may change gradually overtime and should be monitored, but may not trigger an immediate response from the family office. They may, however, trigger planning for anticipated future life events. Bonnie Brown Hartley, PhD, and Gwendolyn Griffith highlight the heightened need for families of wealth to

FIGURE 6.4 Sample Trust Summary

Legal Entity Name	1985 Jones Irrevocable Trust
Inception Date	2/3/85
State of Governing Law	FL
Tax Status	Taxable as a Trust
Taxable Year End	12/31
Employer ID or EIN	65-1234567
Investment Authority	Trustee
Corporate Trustee	XYZ Trust Co.
Successor Trustee(s)	James Jones, then Maryann Jones
Trust Protector	Henry Jones

Summary Description

- Trust intent: Transfer wealth to children.
- History: Mary and Mike Jones divested a portion of their business and decided to establish this trust for the benefit of their children.
- Structure: Irrevocable Trust.
- Communication/Authority: Mary and Mike are primary contacts; children will receive trust statements once they reach age of majority.
- Decision limitations: None.
- Unusual provisions of the trust: Only "natural children" will be beneficiaries.
- Total return provisions: Yes.
- Income distributions: Distribution at the discretion of the corporate trustee.
- Principal distributions: No principal distributions until trust termination.
- Trustee succession: Always two individuals and one corporate trustee.
  - Successor individual trustee appointed by surviving trustee.
  - Individual trustee may select another corporate trustee.
- Other: Corporate trustee has right to release and renounce its discretionary right to accumulate or distribute income.
  - Annual $10,000 emergency payments authorized.
  - Decision of two of the trustees have same force/effect as all.

Source: © Tamarind Partners, Inc.

be proactive and forward thinking to the myriad of critical issues that could be devastating to the family continuity, business, and/or wealth.[1] Otherwise, a family may be blindsided by events when the stress, anxiety, and negative effects could have been drastically mitigated with some simple planning. For example, when a family member is in a declining state of health, perhaps after a major accident or fall, understanding their needs when it comes to care, companionship, and/or home maintenance or oversight can often be anticipated by other supportive family members. A family may determine to make sure adequate cash reserves are on hand when and if a family member

FIGURE 6.5 Sample Estate Plan Flow Chart

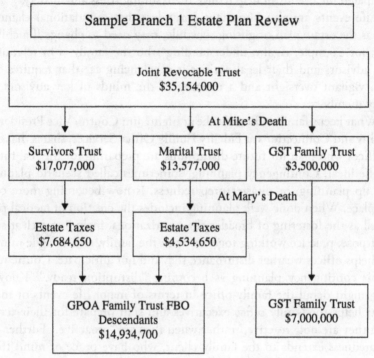

Sample Branch 1 Estate Plan Review

Joint Revocable Trust
$35,154,000

At Mike's Death

Survivors Trust	Marital Trust	GST Family Trust
$17,077,000	$13,577,000	$3,500,000

At Mary's Death

Estate Taxes	Estate Taxes
$7,684,650	$4,534,650

GPOA Family Trust FBO Descendants	GST Family Trust
$14,934,700	$7,000,000

Source: © Tamarind Partners, Inc.

FIGURE 6.6 Major Life Events

Major Life Events		
Birth or adoption	Involvement in a lawsuit	Job change
Death	Accident	Family member
Marriage	Buying/Selling a major asset	Health event
Divorce	Move	Joining a board
Lifestyle change	Separation	Incapacitation
Surgery	Sale of home	Promotion
Starting a business	Unemployment	Windfall
		Retirement

Source: © Tamarind Partners, Inc.

becomes incapacitated and needs more care or may move in with other family members. This is a simple example of when being prepared to deal with an anticipated life event can help reduce the resulting stress and anxiety.

Life events are also important reminders that foundational elements, such as the estate plan or gifting schedule, may need to change if a child is born, for example. Again, understanding who the family is in relation to their advisors and their legal entities is a balancing act that requires constant, vigilant oversight and a meeting of the minds of key advisors and family members.

What keeps family offices awake at night? Jim Coutré, Vice President of Insights and Connections at Fidelity Family Office Services, shares that family offices who plan for future disruptions are preparing for the real future, not the ideal. Contingency planning, sometimes called scenario planning, back up planning, or disaster preparedness, is now becoming more commonplace. When done well, planning includes the creation of tactical plans as well as the fostering of broader characterizations, including a clear sense of purpose, practice working together with the family, and an agile mindset that helps offices weather disturbance they did not anticipate. Coutré refers to this contingency planning as becoming "disruption ready."[2] Knowing what might derail the family office in terms of major life events or macro events helps the family office executives and staff prepare for their actions when they are not "reactive," rather when they are "proactive." Further, this preparedness extends to the family client, who have peace of mind that a contingency action plan may kick in when/if a disaster or unexpected life event occurs.

"Peace of mind" and "happiness" were ranked top priority by older generations (Gen X and Boomers) in a Boston Private study entitled "The Why of Wealth."[3] Being prepared for the unexpected helps them better sleep at night. The study further finds that one of the greatest lessons learned from wealth by all age categories of participants is the importance to "build a plan and to stick to it." See Figure 6.7.

Risk and Insurance Management Considerations

The prevailing theme among families and family office executives is to build resilience through annual planning. Unfortunately, there is not a way to risk proof the family office or family members, given the wide range of the global risk environment such as global pandemics[4] or the ongoing billion-dollar global natural disasters.[5]

FIGURE 6.7 Lessons from Wealth by Generation

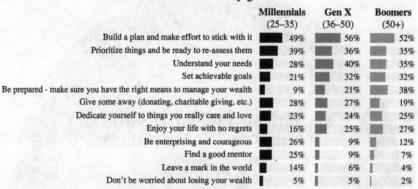

Lessons from wealth by generation

	Millennials (25–35)	Gen X (36–50)	Boomers (50+)
Build a plan and make effort to stick with it	49%	56%	52%
Prioritize things and be ready to re-assess them	39%	36%	35%
Understand your needs	28%	40%	35%
Set achievable goals	21%	32%	32%
Be prepared - make sure you have the right means to manage your wealth	9%	21%	38%
Give some away (donating, charitable giving, etc.)	28%	27%	19%
Dedicate yourself to things you really care and love	23%	24%	25%
Enjoy your life with no regrets	16%	25%	27%
Be enterprising and courageous	26%	9%	12%
Find a good mentor	25%	9%	7%
Leave a mark in the world	14%	6%	4%
Don't be worried about losing your wealth	5%	5%	2%

% Multiple answers allowed

Source: Boston Private, The Why of Wealth Report 2018, Lessons from Wealth by Generation, 2018, p. 37.

To build resilience, Alliant Private Client and their Family Enterprise Risk Practice recommend that family office boards and executives' annual planning include a two-part holistic risk assessment. First, assess the family office operations to ensure that staff can work from home or any location and continuous service can be coordinated as well as delivered across all services including legal, tax, reporting, accounting entities, and insurance. Second, address risk and insurance planning for the family itself.

Family Office Risk Assessment and Insurance Planning

Key questions family offices should consider annually include:[6]

- What are the new risks that we are facing that could have a substantial impact on family office operations and how are we addressing them?
- What plan do we have in place to protect the family office and family members against cyber-crime?
- Do we have an annual review process to identify the risks to family members and is it aligned with an insurance strategy?
- Have we aligned our family office risk exposures with an insurance strategy?

See Figure 6.8, which represents core family office operations risks and corresponding insurance areas.

FIGURE 6.8   Family Office Risks and Insurance Areas

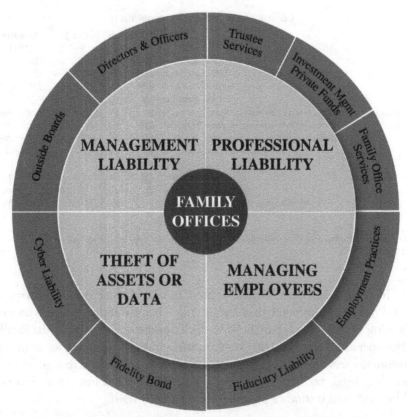

Source: Alliant Private Client, Family Office Risks and Insurance Areas, Family Risk Map, Family Insurance Program, 2020

Family office management and professional liability insurance areas include:

- Directors & Officers and private company liability
- Errors & Omissions: family office services, trust services, investment management and private funds, including vicarious liability
- Employment Practices Liability
- Cyber and Crime
- Social Engineering
- Fiduciary
- Property & Casualty (business office insurance)

FIGURE 6.9 Family Risk Map

	Tangible Assets	Digital Profile	Roles	Travel
Description	· Real estate · Collections · Unique assets: aviation, luxury yachts · Farm, ranch, land ownership	· Devices · Home networks	· Boards · Trustee · Employer	· Adventure travel · Remote locations · International locations
Risk Profile	· Gulf/coastal flooding zones · Hurricane/typhoon areas · Wildfire areas · Operations/location management	· Personal data breach · Cyber financial loss/extortion · Ransomware · System attack or unauthorized access	· Director's & officer's liability · Professional liability · Employment practices liability	· Country/city specific risks (e.g. natural disasters, crime, protests) · Security of accommodations
Risk Management Questions	· What has changed in the last year? · Do you have any plans we should be aware of? (E.g. renovations, loaning artwork, transferring ownership to LLC, Trust, Children moving out of the house on their own) · What property risk mitigation measures are currently in place?	· How are you limiting exposure to Cybercrime? · How do you monitor and detect threats to your identity? · Are mobile device settings securing your devices and protecting data if your phone is lost or stolen?	· Are you a director or officer of any for-profit or not-for-profit organization? · Do you employ any full-time or part-time employees? · Do you serve as a Trustee?	· Do you have an adequate emergency medical and security response plan? · How are you staying aware of what is happening where you travel?

Source: Alliant Private Client, Family Office Risks and Insurance Areas, Family Risk Map, Family Insurance Program, 2020

Family Member Risk and Insurance Planning

Family office professionals generally partner with a firm that is an expert at overseeing the evaluation of risks and complex insurance needs for wealthy families. An insurance review process should include reviewing existing insurance and confirming that it addresses risks unique to the family risk map illustrated below. If there are any changes, the family office and insurance advisor should work together on exploring new policies each year to help keep pace with any new risks or changes that have occurred. (See Figure 6.9.)

In addition to mapping family member risks, there may be additional risk mitigation services available from insurance carriers that can help address natural disaster risks. The chart below illustrates core areas of potential services available from various insurance carriers as part of a family insurance program. (See Figure 6.10.)

Given the family office risk considerations, an annual planning process can help both the family office and families they serve. One of the opportunities that family office professionals have is to create a conversation with their families about risk using current headlines as a backdrop for the importance of annual planning.

FIGURE 6.10   Family Insurance Program

EARTHQUAKE PROTECTION	WILDFIRE PROTECTION	HURRICANE PROTECTION	HOME SECURITY & CONTRUCTION SERVICES	PRIVATE COLLECTIONS SERVICES
• Develop an emergency plan	• At-home wildfire consultation	• Pre-season disaster planning	• Home security assessments	• Consultation to address various vulnerabilities such as fire, water, theft, renovations, etc.
• Home consultation with an earthquake mitigation specialist	• Ongoing monitoring before and during a wildfire	• Home consultation with a hurricane mitigation specialist	• Crisis and liability management assessments	• Installation supervision
• Post-event communication and outreach	• Fire retardant treatment services and various mitigation products	• Post-storm communication and outreach	• Background checks, certified first aid/ CPR training for household staff	• Additional services available for paintings, sculptures, furniture, etc.
			• Pre-build consultation and risk mitigation techniques	

Source: Alliant Private Client, Family Office Risks and Insurance Areas, Family Risk Map, Family Insurance Program, 2020

Overview of Capital Sufficiency Analysis

Increasingly, family offices are asked to model the sufficiency of the capital of a family in relation to their lifestyle spending and legacy aspirations. Do they have enough today to fund their lifestyle and what capital (if any) is left to leave to heirs, charities, or beneficiaries now or upon death? The process of modeling this information is often done with a Monte Carlo simulation, which provides the probability of the family being able to achieve their goals under certain conditions. First the advisor must identify a domain of inputs, such as current net worth, monthly lifestyle expenditures, any other liens or obligations, performance metrics, and distributions. Criteria such as inflation and taxes are embedded into the modeling program itself and are projected based on comparable data; however, software that allows for input override is preferred. Once the data are entered, the algorithmic computation is run providing the likelihood of whether the current spending or gifting goals can be achieved and at what confidence level or likelihood.

Capital sufficiency analysis is a tremendously powerful tool when used in conjunction with the broader fact pattern and planning considerations. It can provide confidence and peace of mind for the family regarding the spending of their wealth. For some, the tool reveals that the family may have to cut back their lifestyle. For others, it may reveal that they may have more of a surplus than they anticipated. In all scenarios, the capital sufficiency analysis with the guidance of their advisor may provide invaluable insight to the family's needs from a planning perspective. Further, capital sufficiency analysis can be an important tool to engage beneficiaries and inheritors regarding their lifestyle and budgeting. For those who may be living beyond their means, it can reveal when financial capital will likely run out and for others it can provide confidence to capital expenditures such as purchasing a home, a car, or making a substantial gift. The software provides the ability to model various scenarios and show the impact that one or more wealth decisions can have. It also provides a dynamic look for families when it comes to their wealth management planning. Finally, it may provide clarity around the prioritization of certain decisions above others and may reveal that certain goals are less important when the likelihood of success decreases. If the results are not what a family anticipated, changing assumptions such as timeline, spending, performance, etc. can be tested. Objectives can be redefined, or reprioritized, and a family can see how those adjustments affect the results.

Simple vs. Sophisticated Approach

A simple approach to capital sufficiency would be to project a portfolio's future value using an annual withdrawal amount and a static assumption for investment returns (e.g., 5 percent per year). A more sophisticated approach to capital sufficiency is to run a Monte Carlo analysis. A Monte Carlo analysis is a process that uses random outcomes, within a statistical framework, for certain variables used in the analysis (usually investment returns). The randomness simulates what actual investment results could look like over a lifetime and what a family's ending financial picture would look like under such a scenario. One lifetime simulation is referred to as a "trial," and a full Monte Carlo analysis involves running many different trials or randomized scenarios. An objective is set at the onset, and the results show how many trials successfully meet or exceed the stated objective. For example, the goal could be having greater than $1 after 30 years. If 1,000 trials are run, and 704 trials show ending assets of greater than $1, the probability of success is 70.4 percent.

Using Capital Sufficiency in the Family Office

Capital sufficiency analysis is an essential tool for strategic planning and should be a cornerstone in every family office. The analysis should not be limited to assigning probabilities to goals but also used to reverse engineer how much capital is required to be set aside for various purposes or projects. For some families, this might mean answering the question: How much capital is needed to sustain desired distributions from a trust? Christina Burroughs, Managing Partner at MRA Associates, has been using the capital sufficiency process in the context of ultra-high net worth families for many years. According to Burroughs, "It can help us answer, if we distribute this fixed percent now, how are the dollar values of distributions affected in the future. It can point to flaws in assumptions that families or advisors have taken for granted or assist in strategically planning for more desirable outcomes."[7] She shared how the use of Monte Carlo simulation informed the trustees of a large, multigenerational "pot trust" that similar per capita distributions would not be possible as the number of eligible beneficiaries grew. Beneficiaries would have to make meaningful lifestyle adjustments if they had no other material sources of income. There wasn't a prudent investment strategy that would overcome this dynamic. An alternative would be to distribute less today to make larger per capita distributions available to future generations. Modeling this was useful for the beneficiaries to see for themselves, demonstrating that it is ideal to engage beneficiaries in the capital sufficiency process to align goals with probable outcomes. When family office executives and fiduciaries can provide confidence in making capital expenditures and/or a distribution strategy, the family can know they are aligned, on track, and working in harmony with their own objectives. It may provide clarity around the prioritization of certain goals above others and may reveal that some goals are less important when the likelihood of success decreases.

The following expanded case study explores a fictionalized family considering whether to establish a single-family office or to utilize a multi-family office to achieve their wealth transfer, planning, and family office goals. Specifically, the family has three main legacy goals, and they want to know how their decision regarding family office structure affects their ability to meet their three objectives. The results illustrate a realistic dilemma and how a capital sufficiency analysis can be used to help a family make an informed decision. For most families there is no right or wrong answer, and tools such as capital sufficiency help families to explore the risks and opportunities involved with their ultimate choices. To follow is a sample case of a multigenerational family considering options to build out a full-service family office versus alternate pathways to solve for family office services with a virtual family office or multi-family office. The case provides various Monte Carlo simulation models depending on various inputs.

Case in Point: Doryman Family

The Dorymans own a regional business and have created material wealth for their family over the past few decades.[8] Mike and Emily Doryman (G1) are the co-founders and remain heavily involved in the day-to-day operations of the business. Mike and Emily have four children (G2), Luke, Samuel, Grace, and Matthew. All four are involved in the management of the business and are not employed or receive any other income outside the business. Both Luke and Samuel have children of their own (G3), and their names are Amara, Gabe, and Alec.

The Doryman Family balance sheet totals to approximately $500MM and consists of the details provided in Figure 6.11.

FIGURE 6.11 Ownership and Net Worth by Generation

Asset	G1	G2	Total
Operating Business	$280,000,000	$70,000,000	**$350,000,000**
Investable Assets (AUM)	$75,000,000	$50,000,000	**$125,000,000**
Primary Residence	$8,750,000	$10,000,000	**$18,750,000**
Vacation Homes	$4,000,000	$2,250,000	**$6,250,000**
Total	**$367,750,000**	**$132,250,000**	**$500,000,000**

Source: Christina Burroughs and Will Froelich, MRA Associates

The operating business distributes approximately $10.5MM per year to the family. The Doryman family's investment assets consist of cash, liquid marketable securities, and illiquid investments. For purposes of this analysis, assumptions for expected return, standard deviation, and life expectancy were made. The expected return assumption for the portfolio is 6.46 percent with a standard deviation assumption of 10.35 percent. Modeled investment returns are gross and do not include investment related expenses. The life span assumption is that Mike and Emily are both 70 years old and have a remaining life expectancy of 25 years.

Additional General Assumptions[9]

Mike and Emily spend approximately $4MM per year, and G2 (as a whole) spends about $2.5MM per year. All family members live in Florida, a no income tax state. For conservative purposes, we will assume the operating business income grows at approximately 3 percent per year. We will assume inflation is 2.5 percent per year, which applies to both spending and the growth of real estate. Monte Carlo will be the method of capital sufficiency analysis, and each simulation will consist of 1,000 trials.

It is important to perform sensitivity analysis on the results of any evaluation. Sensitivity analysis is the process of changing certain assumptions used in the analysis and measuring the updated results against the original results. The process can illustrate how sensitive an analysis is to changes in certain variables. For example, sensitivity analysis can inform if their goals may be achieved under a bear market or changes in lifespan. For purposes of the following analysis, sensitivity analysis will mean decreasing expected investment returns by 15 percent while leaving expected standard deviation unchanged.

Doryman Family's Prioritized Objectives

1. Mike and Emily having sufficient financial assets to last their lifetime.
2. Mike and Emily leaving financial assets of $20MM to each child and $5MM to each grandchild.
3. Mike and Emily leaving financial assets of $100MM to charity.

Scenario Analysis

Scenario 1: Single Family Office (SFO)

Mike and Emily's preferred scenario is one in which they build out a full-service SFO. They plan on hiring approximately three staff, and family members will be heavily involved in the day-to-day operations. Material setup costs will be set aside in addition to ongoing operating expenses. Mike and Emily have committed to the family that if they were to pursue the single-family office option, they would want to immediately endow the annual operation costs for the family office for their remaining lifetime plus 10 years post-death, for a total of 35 years. They have worked with a variety of consultants and estimate the SFO will cost $3MM to set up. It will take approximately one to two years to set up, and they would begin the process immediately. The Dorymans have estimated that the annual operating costs are to be $1.175MM and include everything from administration to general advisory expense. In addition to operating costs, the family anticipates paying external investment management fees of approximately $625,000 per year (50 basis points on assets under management). Based on projected investment returns, approximately $23.6MM is necessary to fund the operating costs for 35 years.

$$PVEndowment = \$1,175,000 \times ((1 - (1/(1 + (6.46\% - 3.00\%))\,\hat{}\,35))/(6.46\% - 3.00\%))$$

Scenario 2: Multi-Family Office (MFO)

The family may choose instead to outsource the family office and save a substantial amount of money on sunk costs to set up their family office coupled with the level of annual operating expenses. Of course, this comes with the tradeoff of family ownership control, direct involvement, and the opportunities for cohesion from day-to-day interaction. The benefit of the MFO is there is no setup cost, the ongoing annual cost is materially less, and there is no transition period while the office is built out (1–2 years in SFO Scenario). Further, there is no human resource management, employee management, or concerns of attracting, retaining, and incenting top talent. G1 will not endow operating costs in the MFO Scenario because it is not their preferred choice. The family will begin a request for proposal (RFP) process immediately and plan on including a variety of potential service providers. Consultants estimate the total annual cost of the MFO to be approximately $1.25MM or 100 basis points on assets under management. Fees include, but are not limited to, investment advisory, investment management, investment performance, tax compliance, tax planning, and other general family office services.

Summary of Results

Scenario 1 Results: Single Family Office (SFO)

Mike and Emily are always successful in reaching their first objective of having sufficient financial assets during their lifetime. More than 80 percent of trials showed financial assets exceeding $150MM in the year 2044, and the lowest single trial had ending financial assets of $66MM. They are comfortably able to spend $4.0MM, in today's dollars, throughout the remainder of their lifetimes and with no risk of asset depletion. However, successfully meeting their legacy objectives was not as successful, and objective three is especially at risk in the SFO scenario. In 548 out of 1,000 trials they were able to amass the necessary $195MM of financial assets to leave $20MM to each child, $5MM to each grandchild, and $100MM to charity in the year 2044. In other words, all three objectives were successfully met 54.8 percent of the time. (See Figure 6.12.)

FIGURE 6.12   Monte Carlo Simulation Results

Scenario	Monte Carlo Ending Median Financial Assets	Monte Carlo Success % Objective #1	Monte Carlo Success % Objective #2	Monte Carlo Success % Objective #3
SFO	$203,461,975	100.0%	99.4%	54.8%
SFO (Bear Market)[1]	$177,086,149	100.0%	97.8%	37.9%
MFO	$261,150,595	100.0%	99.9%	80.6%
MFO (Bear Market)[1]	$220,959,738	100.0%	99.5%	59.0%

[1] Bear Market scenarios decrease expected investment returns by 15%.
Source: Christina Burroughs and Will Froelich, MRA Associates

Sensitivity analysis showed further stress in achieving their legacy objectives. Decreasing expected returns by 15 percent decreased the percentage of successful trials from 54.8 percent to 37.9 percent with regard to the third objective and therefore successfully meeting the $195MM threshold. However, in all trials the first objective was never at risk and not a single trial, in any scenario, showed ending financial assets below $60MM.

Figure 6.13 shows the results of scenario 1 at various confidence levels. The percent confidence is the percentage of trials that showed assets above the stated number. For example, 80 percent of trials (the bottom hashed line) showed ending financial assets of greater than $161,189,609 in the year 2045. The dotted line, second from the top, is the median amount and therefore half of trials showed ending assets above $203,461,975.

FIGURE 6.13 Projected Confidence Levels for 1,000 Trials for the SFO—Standard Investment Assumptions

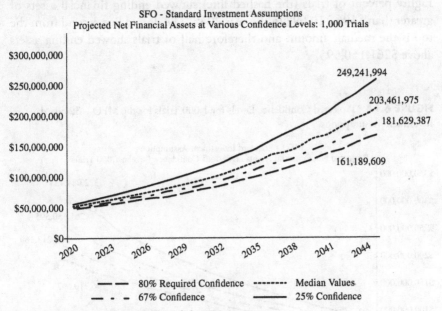

SFO - Standard Investment Assumptions
Projected Net Financial Assets at Various Confidence Levels: 1,000 Trials

- — — 80% Required Confidence   -------- Median Values
- — - — 67% Confidence   ———— 25% Confidence

Source: Christina Burroughs and Will Froelich, MRA Associates

Scenario 2 Results: Multi-Family Office (MFO)

Just like the SFO scenario, Mike and Emily meet their first goal in all 1,000 trials. The MFO scenario does not incur a multi-million expense in year one (setup cost) nor does it require the setting aside of $23.6MM for an SFO endowment. This adds substantial cushion to beginning financial assets, and it is no surprise that the likelihood of success for all objectives (1–3) goes up materially. In 806 out of 1,000 trials they were able to amass the necessary

$195MM of financial assets to leave $20MM to each child, $5MM to each grandchild, and $100MM to charity in the year 2044. All three objectives were successfully met 80.6 percent of the time. (See Figure 6.12.)

Decreasing expected returns by 15 percent decreased the percentage of successful trials from 80.6 percent to 59.0 percent with regard to the third objective and therefore successfully meeting the $195MM threshold. As with scenario 1, the first objective was never at risk and the lowest trial of any simulation showed ending financial assets of $79MM.

Figure 6.14 shows the results of scenario 1 at various confidence levels. Eighty percent of trials (the hashed line) showed ending financial assets of greater than $196,710,697 in the year 2045. The dotted line second from the top is the median amount and therefore half of trials showed ending assets above $261,150,595.

FIGURE 6.14   Projected Confidence Levels for 1,000 Trials for the MFO—Standard Investment Assumptions

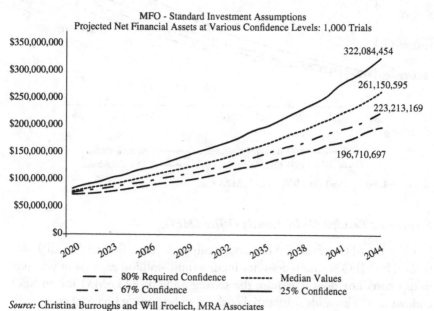

MFO - Standard Investment Assumptions
Projected Net Financial Assets at Various Confidence Levels: 1,000 Trials

— — 80% Required Confidence   ------- Median Values
— · — 67% Confidence   ——— 25% Confidence

Source: Christina Burroughs and Will Froelich, MRA Associates

Interpreting the Results

The Dorymans have a difficult decision to make when it comes to whether to proceed with a family office setup or the multi-family office option. Both options are viable; however, there is no question that the additional expense associated with an SFO causes a substantial difference in financial assets over a 25-year timeline. Prioritization of the importance of control, privacy, convenience, and cost-efficiency needs to be discussed by all interested parties. The family agreed to meet and go over both the analyses, as well as the objectives, with their advisors.

At the meeting, the first topic of discussion was the prioritization of inheritance and philanthropy. Mike and Emily drove the beginning of the conversation, while their children absorbed their intentions. There is a realization by G2 that they are not the wealth creators, and they are respectful of their parents' wishes. They also all appeared content with their current lifestyles. In going through the details of the analysis, G2 was surprised by the amount of additional business cash flow that would go to each of them at their parent's deaths. That additional amount is expected to be more than $2MM each in today's dollars, and that doesn't include any additional income from other marketable securities or private investments. Once G2 had taken grasp of these details, the conversation quickly turned to philanthropy, and they all showed a keen interest in working together. The advisors shifted the conversation to discuss a private foundation and how it might work in the context of the Doryman family. That conversation ultimately came back to the eventual distribution of the estate, and there was unanimous agreement among G2 that a private foundation should be priority with regards to the distribution of financial assets. All appeared content with allocating the first $100MM of financial assets for philanthropic purposes and anything in excess would be divided among the family members.

Mike and Emily were pleasantly surprised to discover how much interest their family had in philanthropy. Emily asked the advisors how to operate a family foundation within the context of either an SFO or MFO. She was advised that one could be operated in either environment but that a family heavily focused on a private foundation might prefer to do so within the framework of an SFO. The privacy and exclusivity that come with an SFO mean that they would always be able to direct their staff to make the foundation their number one priority. It also allows family members the opportunity to work for the foundation itself and be full-time employees of the organization. This comment caught the attention of Grace, who was immediately interested in making philanthropy her full-time job.

The advisors used the moment to summarize the conversation and clarify what decisions needed to be made. First, G2 was comfortable with their expected inheritance of the business, and any additional financial assets would be more than expectations. Second, the family has a strong desire to form a private foundation where they could give as a family and at least one member desired to work within the organization. Pointing to the results of the SFO analysis, it was shown that more than 80 percent of trials showed greater than $160MM of ending financial assets and that the lowest of any trial, sensitivity analysis included, was $60MM. The family began to be comfortable that a more expensive SFO would ultimately affect their inheritances. They also preferred to aggressively fund philanthropy now. Samuel asked whether individual capital sufficiency analysis could be run for him or others so that he can see how decisions made today affect him individually. It was concluded that analyses would be run for each of the G2 families.

The meeting adjourned with everyone leaning toward the SFO option but all wanting to digest the discussion for a few weeks. The advisers recommended allowing the individual capital sufficiency analyses to be run before making a final decision. They didn't want the results to surprise anyone and ultimately change how they felt about their inheritance or what they believed the family should prioritize. The advisers suggested allowing one month to build out the four analyses, discuss individually, and then reconvene as a group to make a final decision on whether to move forward with an SFO.

Key Takeaways

Transparency and Clarity: Capital sufficiency planning can augment the typical strategic planning process by providing financial simulations for forecasted goals and objectives. Without the financial rigor behind a strategic planning process, testing possible scenarios and outcomes under different sensitivity screens, a family may not have the full financial picture to make the best decisions. No one tool or approach will solve such a complex, multidimensional, and consequential issue such as whether to set up and outsource a family office.

Communication and Discussion: Interpreting the findings from a capital sufficiency analysis provides one level of knowledge application; however, it is advised that family owners with their key advisors collectively discuss and communicate the opportunities, challenges, concerns, and possible unknowns that may influence the action planning resulting from the analysis. What is often missed is the chance for owners to be part of the deeper conversation. Processing the findings is a means to arrive at the best path forward. The capital sufficiency process, done collectively with family members, key personnel, and expert involvement, can lead to a better eventual action plan.

Strategic Planning and Governance Are Not the Same: It is important to be explicit that a strategic planning process and capital sufficiency analysis does not equate to authorizing one or more parties to make a final decision. On the contrary, strategic planning should inform key parties and owners to be able to have the appropriate information, tools, and rubric to move forward to govern accordingly. A family should have a clear governance process in place prior to engaging in strategic planning.

Iterative and Evolving: The strategic planning process is iterative and continuous. In the case of the Doryman family, they may desire to re-evaluate their capital sufficiency modeling as well as strategic plan in three to five years to see if they remain on track. A best practice is to monitor and track the plan to actual performance. When there is a major gap perceived by management, ownership, leadership, and/or family, it is a signal to revisit and evolve the strategic plan to align it with the current reality and desired future outcomes.

Conclusion and Final Thoughts

Developing a baseline of information around the family is perhaps the most critical step for a family office. This chapter reviewed a broad array of baseline information that may be gathered to approach the strategic planning process. It then moved through a deeper review of a family's estate plan and examples of mapping out legal entities, summarizing trusts, and constructing an estate plan flow chart. Finally, it then moved into a more comprehensive financial review and explored the concept of capital sufficiency analysis based on differing goals of a family. It then provided a discussion on conducting a risk management assessment and insurance review through a third-party provider. Through a fictionalized case with sample reports, the chapter took a deeper look at the baseline information, a strategic planning crossroads, and application of capital sufficiency analysis. Ultimately, the information gathered in the baseline of the family office informs both the strategic planning and development of the family as well as the direction of the family office. The baseline information is dynamic and evolving and reflects the partnering of advisors and family office employees. This information becomes the cornerstone of what the family owns, who is responsible, and a record of the decisions that have led the family to this point. Tailored for the needs of each family, the baseline, like taking a person's pulse, helps to inform the family office of the overall financial health and well-being of the family. Without this base of information, it is difficult for the family office to discern forward or backward progress towards milestones. Thank you to Christina Burroughs, Will Froelich, and the team at MRA Associates for contributing the Doryman Case Study and to Linda Bourn and Chelsea Cannon at Alliant for their input for the risk management and insurance discussion.

Notes

1. Bonnie Brown Hartley and Gwendolyn Griffith, *Family Wealth Transition Planning* (New York: Bloomberg Press, 2009).
2. Correspondence with Jim Coutré, Fidelity Family Office Services April 2020.
3. Boston Private, Why of Wealth Report, 2018.
4. World Health Organization (WHO), www.who.int, "WHO Characterizes COVID-19 as a Pandemic," March 11, 2020.
5. National Oceanic and Atmospheric Administration NOAA, United States Billion Dollar Natural Disasters Map 2015–2019; *Scientific American* Blog, January 22, 2020, "Earth's 40 Billion-Dollar Weather Disasters of 2019: 4th Most Billion-Dollar Events on Record."
6. Barbara R Hauser, consulting editor, *Family Offices: The STEP Handbook for Advisers,* Second Edition (Globe Law and Business, 2019); Linda Bourn, "Risk and Insurance Management."
7. Correspondence with Christina Burroughs, Managing Partner at MRA Associates (www.mraassociates.com), February 2020.
8. The identifying details of this family have been obscured to protect the privacy of the actual family.
9. These assumptions apply to all the scenarios that are provided in the Doryman Case Study.

CHAPTER 7

Legal and Compliance Standards and Practices for Family Offices

David S. Guin, Esq.

Partner and US Commercial Practice Group Leader, Withers Bergman LLP

In this chapter, we review US regulatory requirements that impact family offices, including compliance issues. Key among these is the Family Office Rule, which exempts single-family offices from SEC investment advisor registration requirements. We also discuss rules governing the reporting of beneficial ownership of public company securities, as well as the reporting of a person's engagement in large transactions in securities. As part of this discussion, we refer to a sample family office structure to demonstrate the application of relevant disclosure rules.

Our discussion of disclosure rules is followed by a discussion of insider trading concerns for families, including snapshots of recent insider trading cases that provide lessons learned from real-life examples. Finally, this chapter closes with an overview of compliance procedures, document retention, and management, as well as insights into the true burden of compliance for family offices.

Regulations Affecting Family Offices: Dodd-Frank Act

Family offices faced potentially closer oversight by the SEC when rules traditionally relied on by family offices to avoid registration as investment advisors were repealed by the Dodd-Frank Wall Street Reform and Consumer Protection Act (the Dodd-Frank Act) in 2010. However, when the Dodd-Frank Act was signed into law, it directed the SEC to implement new rules governing registration exemptions for certain investment advisors.

In response, the SEC adopted the Family Office Rule, which we discuss in greater detail in the sections that follow. The Family Office Rule defines the term family office and other key terms that must be considered for exemptive purposes. A family office that fails to meet the SEC's definition must register with and become regulated by the SEC unless it satisfies another exemption.

We do not discuss regulation by the US Commodity Futures Trading Commission (the CFTC) in this chapter. However, you should note that the CFTC has released a no-action letter providing that any family office that otherwise satisfies the exemption under the SEC's Family Office Rule will not be subject to regulation by the CFTC as a commodity pool operator or a commodity trading advisor.

There are a number of other regulatory matters affecting the family office. For example, the requirement that beneficial owners of significant amounts of a public company's equity securities, as well as directors and officers of such companies, report their ownership of such securities and/or relationship with the company is a requirement that has existed for years.[1] Disclosures of this nature provide the public with knowledge of who may wield influence over the company's activities, directly or indirectly. *Beneficial ownership reporting* is of particular note for family offices in light of their clients' privacy concerns, as the beneficial ownership reporting rules may compel disclosure of individual family members' holdings in publicly reporting companies. We discuss beneficial ownership reporting requirements in greater detail below.

The SEC also continues to require persons who exercise direct or indirect investment discretion over large amounts of securities to file periodic reports for informational purposes only[2]—requirements that affect many family offices, as we explain below. These institutional investment managers who exercise investment discretion over at least $100 million of so-called Section 13(f) securities must report their holdings to the SEC on a regular basis. In other words, if you advise or direct assets of $100 million or more, you may be required to report periodically to the SEC. In addition, large traders who exercise investment discretion over accounts that engage in sizable transactions on a particular day or over the course of a particular month must report such transactions to the SEC.[3] These reports have the sole stated purpose of permitting the SEC to monitor significant holdings and transactions for systemic risks. The SEC may treat many institutional investment manager reports confidentially, and all large trader reports are nonpublic filings. However, family offices often are concerned with the potential privacy implications of these reporting obligations.

In addition, the SEC continues to focus enforcement efforts on insider trading, and, contrary to common understanding, rogue investment bankers are not the only individuals who bear significant risk. As we discuss below, family members of individuals with material, nonpublic information about an issuer may be targeted by the SEC if they discover such information and engage in trades on that basis. Further, the individual who (intentionally or unintentionally) made such material, nonpublic information available to family members may also be held liable in any insider trading inquiry.

Case in Point

In this chapter, we illustrate the application of SEC rules that affect many family offices by referring to a fictional family office structure. Although no two family office structures are exactly the same, the structure we will use as an example is not atypical. The sample structure, although not as complex as many family office structures can be, also provides us with an opportunity to demonstrate the complexities that arise when SEC rules are applied to family offices and their investment activities.

For purposes of our fictional structure, Jennifer Smith is the matriarch of the Smith family. The Smith family office (Family OfficeCo) is a Delaware corporation. Family OfficeCo wholly owns another Delaware corporation (IntermediaryCo), and IntermediaryCo, in turn, is the sole member of each of two Delaware limited liability companies (InvestCo A and InvestCo B). InvestCo A and InvestCo B are each a family investment vehicle.

Jennifer Smith and her husband, Joe Smith, are the directors of Family OfficeCo, and Family OfficeCo is wholly owned by a South Dakota private trust company (TrustCo). TrustCo is wholly owned by the Smith Trust, a revocable trust settled by Jennifer Smith for the benefit of her and her family. The trustee of the Smith Trust is Jennifer's husband, Joe.

A diagram of the Smith Family Office Structure is shown in Figure 7.1.

FIGURE 7.1   Smith Family Office Structure

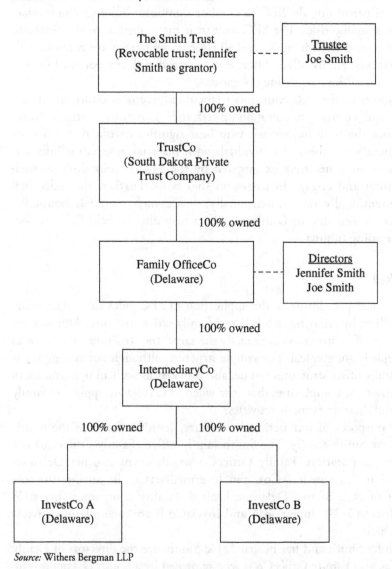

Source: Withers Bergman LLP

The Single-Family Office Exemption

Family control is a critical component of the Family Office Rule, and in order to satisfy the exemption from SEC registration as an investment advisor, a family office must be owned by family clients and exclusively controlled by family members and/or family entities. Family members, for purposes of the

Family Office Rule, are all lineal descendants (including by adoption, step-children, and foster children, among others) of a common ancestor, and their spouses or spousal equivalents, as long as the common ancestor is no more than 10 generations removed from the youngest generation of family members. Family entities include trusts, estates, companies, or other entities set forth in the definition of *family client*, excluding key employees and their trusts from the definition of family client solely for the purpose of determining whether an entity is a *family entity*.

Although the Family Office Rule states that a qualifying family office must be owned by family clients and "exclusively controlled (directly or indirectly) by one or more family members and/or family entities,"[4] the SEC has indicated that any structure in which the family is "in fact" in control of the family office entity will satisfy this requirement. In a response to frequently asked questions about the Family Office Rule,[5] the SEC clarified that the exclusive control requirement may be satisfied if family members or family entities have majority control over the management or policies of the family office.

Where might you fall in the family office spectrum? Figure 7.2 is a flow chart that family offices may use to help them determine whether their investment advisory activities fall within the Family Office Rule's SEC registration exemption.

The SEC exempts from SEC registration family offices which it defines as any company that:

- Provides investment advisory services only to "family clients";
- Is wholly owned by family clients and is exclusively controlled (directly or indirectly) by one or more "family members" and/or family entities; and
- Does not hold itself out to the public as an investment advisor.

Refer to the definitions below of "family client," "family member," "family entity," "key employee," and "affiliated family office."

The SEC determines whether a family office is in compliance with the exclusive control requirement based on a review of the particular facts and circumstances of the family office structure. For example, a family office with a board of directors, a majority of whom are family members, would satisfy the exclusive control requirement as long as there are no other arrangements that would give non-family members or non-family entities control over the family office management or policies.[6] However, a family office with a board of directors entirely comprised of non-family members, but who are all appointed by—and may be replaced by—family members, would not satisfy the exclusive control standard, absent any other arrangement providing that family

FIGURE 7.2 SEC Final Rules on Family Offices—June 2011

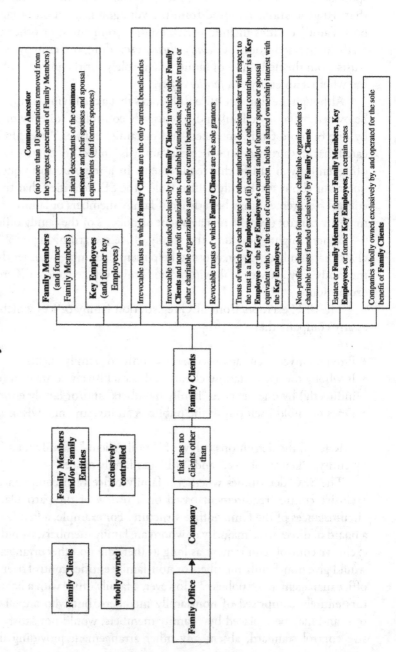

Family Office

A "family client" includes:

• Family members and "former family members";
• "Key employees" (and former key employees, in certain cases);
• Certain non-profit organizations, charitable foundations, charitable trusts (including CLTs and CRTs whose only current beneficiaries are other family clients and charitable or non-profit organizations), or other charitable organizations, in each case funded exclusively by family clients;
• Estates of family members, former family members, key employees, or former key employees, in certain cases;
• Irrevocable trusts in which family clients are the only current beneficiaries;
• Irrevocable trusts funded exclusively by family clients in which other family clients and non-profit organizations or certain charitable entities are the only current beneficiaries;
• Revocable trusts of which family clients are the sole grantors;
• Trusts of which (i) only key employees are trustees or authorized decision-makers, and (ii) each settlor or other trust contributor is a key employee or, in certain cases, the key employee's current and/or former spouse or spousal equivalent; or
• Companies wholly owned (directly or indirectly) exclusively by, and operated for the sole benefit of, family clients.

A "family member" includes:

• All lineal descendants (including by adoption, stepchildren, and foster children, among others) of a common ancestor, and such lineal descendants' spouses or spousal equivalents; provided that the common ancestor is no more than 10 generations removed from the youngest generation of family members.

A "family entity" includes:

• Trusts, estates, companies or other entities, but excluding key employees and their trusts from the definition of family client (solely for the purpose of determining whether an entity is a "family entity").

A "key employee" includes:

• Executive officers, directors, trustees and general partners (or similar individuals) of the family office or its " affiliated family office"; or
• An employee of the family office or its affiliated family office who, in connection with his or her regular duties, has participated in the family office's or the affiliated family office's investment activities for at least 12 months.

An "affiliated family office" includes:

• A family office that (i) is wholly owned by family clients of another family office, (ii) is controlled by family members of such other family office and/or family entities affiliated with such other family office and (iii) has no clients other than family clients of such other family office.

Source: Withers Bergman LLP

member shareholders decide matters relating to the management or policies of the family office.[7] This could be accomplished, for example, by providing in the family office's organizational documents, a list of management and policy decisions that are reserved to the family member owners—even if a majority of the board of directors does not consist of family members. Many family offices are controlled on a day-to- day basis by professional staff, and outside advisors sit on the board of directors. As such, a detailed review by legal counsel of the family office entity's organizational documents is necessary to insure that the family has the requisite control over the family office.

A family office may provide investment advisory services only to individuals or entities that qualify as family clients. However, the definition of a family client under the SEC's Family Office Rule is quite expansive and includes the following:

• A family member or former family member.
• A key employee of the family office or certain former key employees.

- A charitable foundation, charitable trust, or charitable organization established and funded exclusively by family clients.[8]
- Certain, *but not all,* types of trusts settled or funded by family clients or benefitting family clients. You should consult with legal counsel to determine whether a particular trust is a family client for regulatory purposes.
- A trust for which only key employees of the family office are trustees or authorized decision makers, and each settlor or other trust contributor is a key employee (or, in some cases, a current and/or former spouse or spousal equivalent of the key employee).
- An estate of a family member, former family member, key employee of the family office or, in certain cases, former key employee.
- A company that is wholly owned by, and operated for the sole benefit of, family clients.

Entities that believe they are operating as family offices may fail to satisfy the Family Office Rule exemption from SEC registration because they have clients that do not fit the definition of a family client. Some family offices provide investment advisory services to collective investment vehicles that are owned, at least in part, by non-family clients. Others provide such services to family friends or to family members of key employees, who are not deemed family clients. Still others act as multi-family offices that provide investment advisory services to more than one family, which is not permitted under the Family Office Rule. These problems may arise over time as, for example, when a family member dies and transfers interests to a non-qualifying client. In such cases, the Family Office Rule allows a period of twelve months for the family office to come back into compliance.

Finally, in order to satisfy the requirements under the Family Office Rule, a family office cannot hold itself out to the public as an investment adviser, a standard that the SEC interprets very broadly. For example, an investment adviser may be found to be holding itself out to the public simply by including "investment adviser" on business cards and stationery, or by providing information about its US advisory activities on a website or other publicly available electronic medium.[9]

Case in Point

For purposes of determining whether the Smith Family Office Structure qualifies for the family office exemption from registration with the SEC, we will assume that Family OfficeCo provides investment advice to both InvestCo A and InvestCo B.

Family OfficeCo is wholly owned by family clients, since TrustCo, as its sole stockholder, is a company wholly owned exclusively by, and operated for the sole benefit of, The Smith Trust, which is a revocable trust with Jennifer Smith (a family member) as sole grantor (i.e., it is a family client). Family OfficeCo is also controlled by family entities, as Jennifer Smith and her husband Joe are the sole directors.

Following this same line of analysis, InvestCo A and InvestCo B, as wholly owned subsidiaries of IntermediaryCo (which itself is a wholly owned subsidiary of Family OfficeCo), are ultimately owned exclusively by The Smith Trust and are family clients. As such, the Smith Family Office Structure satisfies the family office exemption from SEC registration as an investment adviser.

However, if the circumstances were different, Family OfficeCo might not qualify for exemption. For example, if the directors of Family OfficeCo were Joe Smith and two non-family investment professionals, Family OfficeCo would fail the control requirement, absent provisions in its organizational documents reserving management and policy decisions to its owner, TrustCo. Likewise, if InvestCo A were partially owned by Jennifer Smith's brother-in-law, InvestCo A would no longer qualify as a family client, and the Smith Family Office Structure would fail to satisfy the exemption. In-laws are not included among acceptable family members for purposes of the family office exemption.

Consider also a situation where Family OfficeCo advises a charitable foundation. If the charitable foundation were to receive outside funding—that is, funding from sources other than solely family clients—it would not be deemed a family client, and the Smith Family Office structure would fail to satisfy the family office exemption.

Clients of the Family Office May Need to Report Beneficial Ownership of Securities of Publicly Reporting Companies

What is the beneficial ownership reporting requirement and why is it so important to family offices? Family offices should be aware that publicly reporting companies have an obligation[10] to disclose persons who own or acquire beneficial ownership of more than 5 percent of their equity securities. Although the rationale behind these reporting requirements is to provide the market and other stockholders with information on large acquisitions of stock that may portend potential changes in control, family office clients may have privacy concerns in connection with such disclosure.

A beneficial owner of a security is a person who, directly or indirectly, through any contract or other relationship has (or shares) the power to vote or direct others to vote the security, or the power to dispose of or direct the disposition of the security.[11] Beneficial ownership of equity securities is reported on either Schedule 13D or on the abbreviated Schedule 13G.

How to Report Beneficial Ownership

A beneficial owner must file a beneficial ownership report with the SEC within 10 days of acquiring more than 5 percent of a class of a public company's equity securities. Day number one, for the purposes of the filing window, is the first calendar day after the trade date.[12] The beneficial ownership report allows potential investors to see who holds significant amounts of a public company's securities and, therefore, has the potential to influence or control the company's actions.

The beneficial ownership report on Schedule 13D requires somewhat detailed disclosure as to the reporting person. However, a reporting person may in some cases be eligible to report on the more abbreviated form, known as a Schedule 13G, if he or she satisfies one of the following exemptions:

Ownership of Securities in the Ordinary Course of Business[13]

A beneficial owner of securities may be eligible to report his or her holdings on the shortened Schedule 13G if that beneficial owner acquired the securities:

- In the ordinary course of business;
- Not with the purpose nor with the effect of changing or influencing the control of the issuer; and
- Not in connection with or as a participant in a transaction with the purpose or effect of changing or influencing control of the issuer.[14]

However, this exemption from reporting beneficial ownership on the more detailed Schedule 13D is available only to certain filers.[15] You should consult with legal counsel to determine whether this may include family office clients.

Passive Ownership of Less than 20 Percent of a Class of Securities[16]

A beneficial owner of securities may be eligible to report his or her holdings on the shortened Schedule 13G if that beneficial owner:

- Has not acquired the securities with the purpose or effect of changing or influencing the control of the issuer;
- Has not acquired the securities in connection with or as a participant in a transaction with the purpose or effect of changing or influencing control of the issuer;
- Is not reporting on Schedule 13G under another exemption; and
- Is not the beneficial owner (directly or indirectly) of 20 percent or more of the class of securities.

If a passive investor acquires 20 percent or more of the class of securities or no longer passively holds its shares (i.e., no longer holds shares without the intent to change or influence control of the issuer), then it must begin reporting on the more detailed Schedule 13D.

Other Acquisitions[17]

A beneficial owner who fits within an exemption for reporting to the SEC at the time of his or her acquisition of beneficial ownership may be required to report on the abbreviated Schedule 13G shortly after the end of the year in which he or she reached the 5 percent ownership threshold in a class of equity securities.[18] In order to qualify for this year-end filing requirement, a beneficial owner must otherwise be exempt from reporting on the more detailed Schedule 13D because the acquisition of securities was effected through a registration statement under the US Securities Act of 1933 or because the reportable acquisition, when added together with the beneficial owner's acquisitions of the same class of a company's equity securities in the last 12 months, does not equal more than 2 percent of the class of securities.

Clients of the Family Office May Need to Report Beneficial Ownership as Insiders of Publicly Reporting Companies

Securities regulators, in light of their concern for improper insider trading, also impose reporting obligations on insiders of public companies. This beneficial ownership reporting requirement arises at a higher percentage of beneficial ownership of a public company's equity securities than the 5 percent threshold described above. However, the reporting obligation also applies to officers and directors of the public company—a condition that often applies to at least a handful of family office clients.

This reporting regime requires the following insiders to report initial ownership of a public company's equity securities, and to report thereafter any changes in the amount of securities beneficially owned by:[19]

- Directors
- Executive officers
- Stockholders who directly or indirectly beneficially own more than 10 percent of the company's SEC-registered equity securities

Although clients of family offices may be leery of the privacy implications of this reporting requirement, the rationale behind the requirement is that the foregoing insiders are presumed to be privy to inside information about the public company, and the market and other stockholders should be made aware of the transaction any time the insiders transfer the company's securities.

The definition of beneficial ownership for this purpose is dependent upon the context. When determining whether a person is subject to insider reporting due to ownership of more than 10 percent of a class of the company's equity securities, beneficial ownership is the direct or indirect power to vote or direct others to vote the security, or the power to dispose of or direct the disposition of the security. This is the same standard for determining beneficial ownership under Section 13(d) of the Exchange Act, discussed above.[20]

However, determining whether a person is subject to an insider reporting obligation is only the first step. Next, a person must determine which securities are reportable, using a different standard than the one described above. For this purpose, beneficial ownership is defined as a pecuniary interest in the securities (i.e., the right to receive, directly or indirectly, profits from a transaction in the securities).[21]

Reporting Insider Status on Form 3, Form 4, or Form 5

An insider must disclose his or her insider status by reporting on the applicable Form 3, Form 4, or Form 5. The timing requirements for filing are different for each form, as described below.

- *Form 3:* Generally, an insider must report on a Form 3 within 10 calendar days after becoming an insider.
- *Form 4:* An insider must report on a Form 4 within two business days of the change in beneficial ownership, or within two business days after losing a prior exemption from filing.[22] Beneficial owners should be made aware of the particularly short window for reporting on Form 4.

- *Form 5:* An insider must report on a Form 5 within 45 calendar days after the end of the company's fiscal year, unless the filer did not have any transactions to report during the entire year, or the filer has already reported each relevant transaction on Form 4 reports.

How Do I Determine Beneficial Ownership in a Multi-Tiered Family Holding Structure?

A family holding structure that includes multiple levels of entities and trusts can make it difficult to determine which individuals or entities need to report beneficial ownership of a public company's securities. Broadly, a person or an entity that directly or indirectly controls an entity that itself directly owns a security is deemed to have indirect beneficial ownership of the security.

This standard—direct or indirect control of an entity that owns a security—can be surprisingly difficult to apply to a given family structure. There is no bright-line test to determine whether a person has sufficient control over an entity to be deemed a beneficial owner of shares that such entity owns directly. Evaluating control (at least for beneficial ownership reporting purposes under Section 13(d) of the Exchange Act) is a highly fact-dependent exercise, and family offices should engage counsel to help them determine the extent of their clients' reporting obligations.

Case in Point

Going back to the Smith Family Office Structure, we assume that InvestCo B acquires 12 percent of the issued stock of a public company (the Issuer). Because InvestCo B owns in excess of 5 percent of the stock, a beneficial ownership report must be filed, but what form should be used and who should be filing the report?

Before we begin, it is important to note that determining beneficial ownership obligations in a multi-tiered structure is highly fact-specific. As such, you should seek the advice of counsel when making that determination.

Because InvestCo B owns less than 20 percent of the Issuer's stock, it will qualify for filing the abbreviated Schedule 13G unless it has an intent to change or influence control of the Issuer. We will assume InvestCo B has no such intent, so it will qualify for the passive investor exemption, allowing it to report on the abbreviated Schedule 13G.

In order to determine who must file a beneficial ownership report, you must determine who has the direct or indirect power to vote or dispose of the shares in question. InvestCo B, as the direct owner of the Issuer stock, clearly has the power to vote or dispose of the stock. InvestCo B must be reported on Schedule 13G.

IntermediaryCo, as the sole member of InvestCo B, has the power to direct InvestCo B to vote or dispose of the Issuer stock. Accordingly, IntermediaryCo must also be reported on Schedule 13G.

Similarly, Family OfficeCo, as the sole owner of IntermediaryCo, has indirect power to direct the voting or disposition of the stock. As a result, Family OfficeCo must be reported on Schedule 13G as well.

It is less apparent whether the entities further up the Smith Family Office Structure must be reported. A straightforward analysis suggests that TrustCo, as sole owner of Family OfficeCo, and its sole owner The Smith Trust, each have indirect power to direct the voting or disposition of the Issuer stock.

However, the analysis may not be as straightforward as it seems. For purposes of this example, we will assume that Family OfficeCo provides discretionary investment advice (i.e., that it can make investment decisions and execute investment transactions without any approval from its direct or indirect owners). In this instance, an argument may be made that TrustCo and The Smith Trust, therefore, do not beneficially own the Issuer stock and do not need to be reported.

In addition, entities under common control must aggregate their ownership of stock in the Issuer. For example, if InvestCo A has the power to vote or dispose of 2 percent of the Issuer stock, it does not meet the reporting threshold on its own. However, since InvestCo A is under common control with InvestCo B, InvestCo A's shares in the Issuer must be aggregated with those reported by InvestCo B, for a total ownership of 14 percent of the stock of the Issuer.

Are You an Institutional Investment Manager? (The Answer May Surprise You.)

The SEC is also interested in keeping track of investors, known as institutional investment managers, who control very large amounts of securities. How will a family office know if it is considered to be an institutional investment manager? If a person or entity exercises investment discretion over $100 million or more in so-called Section 13(f) securities, then that person or entity will be deemed an institutional investment manager with an obligation to report those holdings to the SEC. Section 13(f) securities generally include equity securities that trade on an exchange (including the Nasdaq National Market System), certain equity options and warrants; shares of closed-end investment companies, including exchange-traded funds; and certain convertible debt securities. The shares of open-end investment companies (i.e., mutual funds) are not Section 13(f) securities.

What Is an Institutional Investment Manager?

In general, an institutional investment manager is either of the following:

- An entity that invests in, or buys and sells, securities for its own account
- A natural person or an entity that exercises investment discretion over the account of any other natural person or entity

Institutional investment managers can include investment advisers, banks, insurance companies, broker-dealers, pension funds, and corporations. A trustee is an institutional investment manager, but a natural person who exercises investment discretion over his or her own account is not an institutional investment manager. If a family office exercises investment discretion over securities directly or indirectly owned by the family, it will be deemed an institutional investment manager.

You should note that foreign institutional investment managers are required to report to the SEC. Institutional investment managers do not need to be SEC-registered investment managers to be required to file a report.

Reporting on Form 13F

In order to determine what should and should not be included on any institutional investment manager report on Form 13F, institutional investment managers should rely on the official list of Section 13(f) securities that is published quarterly and is available for free on the SEC's website (www.sec .gov/divisions/investment/13flists.htm).

An institutional investment manager must report shares of a foreign issuer only if those shares are traded on a US exchange (e.g., NYSE, AMEX) or are quoted on the NASDAQ National Market System (this excludes pink sheet ADRs). Shares of securities that trade on non-US exchanges (e.g., Toronto Stock Exchange, London's FTSE, Tokyo's Nikkei) should not be reported on an institutional investment manager report.

An institutional investment manager's first institutional investment manager report should be filed for the December quarter of the calendar year during which it first reached the $100 million reporting threshold (i.e., 45 calendar days after the end of the December quarter). The institutional investment manager will then need to submit reports for the March, June, and September quarters of the following calendar year, even if the market value of its Section 13(f) securities falls below the $100 million level.

The institutional investment manager report on Form 13F requires disclosure of the name of the institutional investment manager who files the report, and, with respect to each Section 13(f) security over which it exercises investment discretion, the name and class, the CUSIP number, the number of shares as of the end of the calendar quarter for which the report is made, and the total market value.

Institutional investment managers in complex corporate structures may have difficulty determining which entities in the structure exercise the investment discretion over Section 13(f) securities that triggers a reporting obligation. Institutional investment managers are deemed to exercise investment discretion over the same accounts for which any persons under their control exercise investment discretion. Further, an institutional investment manager is deemed to share investment discretion with its subsidiary, even if the subsidiary exercises investment discretion without interference from its institutional investment manager parent. As such, a parent of a subsidiary that exercises direct investment discretion over Section 13(f) securities may have as much of an obligation to make an institutional investment manager report as its subsidiary.

In addition, each affiliate or subsidiary that an institutional investment manager lists on its Form 13F as an Other Included Manager must make a notice filing indicating which entity in the structure is filing the main institutional investment manager report. For example, if a parent entity files the main institutional investment manager report, the subsidiary (or subsidiaries) with whom the parent entity shares investment discretion for Section 13(f) purposes must make a notice filing.

Consider the following examples:

- If a lower-level subsidiary directly owns more than $100 million in Section 13(f) securities, its immediate parent and ultimate parent also may be deemed to have investment discretion over the Section 13(f) securities. The ultimate parent may file the institutional investment manager report and name the mid-level subsidiary and the lower-level subsidiary as Other Included Managers in the report.
- If additional subsidiaries of the ultimate parent acquire Section 13(f) securities valued at more than $100 million, these subsidiaries must also be included as Other Included Managers in the ultimate parent's institutional investment manager report.

Determining If the $100 Million Threshold Has Been Met

When determining if it exercises investment discretion over $100 million or more of Section 13(f) securities, an institutional investment manager must calculate the fair market value of such Section 13(f) securities as of the last trading day of each calendar month. Note that the trade date, not the settlement date, is the date that controls with respect to determining the date of acquisition of shares.

Case in Point

Consider an example where InvestCo B acquires stock (which constitutes a Section 13(f) security) with a total value of $150 million as of October 31st.

InvestCo B has exceeded the $100 million threshold as of the last trading day of the month. As such, InvestCo B must begin reporting as an institutional investment manager within 45 days after the end of the year.

As with beneficial ownership reporting, we must also consider which other entities in the Smith Family Office Structure must be identified in the report. In the case of institutional investment manager reports, every entity in the structure that is deemed to exercise investment discretion must be identified. The SEC has indicated that control persons will be deemed to exercise investment discretion over securities that are under the management of controlled persons. In this instance, IntermediaryCo controls InvestCo B and, therefore, is deemed to exercise investment discretion over the Issuer stock. IntermediaryCo, as a result, is an institutional investment manager and must be included in the report on Form 13F.

The same principle holds true with respect to Family OfficeCo, which controls IntermediaryCo and, indirectly, InvestCo B. As such, Family OfficeCo is an institutional investment manager and must be included in the report on Form 13F.

Further, like our example above regarding beneficial ownership reporting, we will assume that Family OfficeCo provides discretionary investment advice, and that TrustCo and The Smith Trust have no role in the investment decisions made by Family OfficeCo. Here, as above, an argument may be made that the reporting obligations stop at Family OfficeCo and go no higher in the Smith Family Office Structure.

As with beneficial ownership reporting, entities under common control must aggregate their holdings of Section 13(f) securities for purposes of reporting as institutional investment managers.

Confidential Treatment

Although reports on Form 13F are generally publicly available, in certain circumstances, it may be possible to request confidential treatment of the specific 13(f) security in question. Generally, confidential treatment is available when the Form 13F would identify securities held by a natural person, an estate, or a personal trust.[23] However, the SEC has granted confidential treatment of the specific 13(f) securities on Form 13F filings made by a family office if it can be demonstrated that the filing would identify securities owned by an identifiable family. There are specific procedures for requesting confidential treatment, and you should consult your attorney to determine if confidential treatment may be available and the procedure for making the request for confidential treatment.

Are You a Large Trader?

Some family offices also may be deemed large traders with additional SEC reporting obligations. The nomenclature and threshold reporting requirements are easy to confuse with the institutional investment managers described above. Further, the SEC tracks the investment activity of both for similar reasons—to stay informed of people or entities with control over large amounts of securities.

A large trader is a person who has direct *investment discretion*—or indirect investment discretion through an entity the person *controls*—over at least one account that effects transactions in US exchange-listed stocks and options (so-called NMS securities) in amounts that equal or exceed either of the following:

- 2 million shares or $20 million during any calendar day
- 20 million shares or $200 million during any calendar month[24]

If a person effects transactions at or above this identifying activity level, it must disclose its status as a large trader by filing a large trader report on Form 13H with the SEC. However, it is important to keep in mind that a person, for purposes of the relevant rule (Rule 13h-1 under the Exchange Act), may refer to a natural person, a corporation, a limited liability company, a limited partnership, or another type of entity.

A person exercises investment discretion with respect to an account, for large trader purposes, if such person, directly or indirectly:

- Authorizes to determine what securities or other property will be purchased or sold by or for the account;

- Determines what securities or other property will be purchased or sold by or for the account even though another person may in fact have the responsibility for making such investment decisions; or
- Exercises any other influence that the SEC determines should be subject to regulation in connection with the purchase and sale of securities or other property by or for the account.[25]

As noted above, a person may be a large trader even if that person exercises investment discretion only indirectly, through an entity it controls. For purposes of the large trader rule, a person controls an entity if that person possesses, directly or indirectly, "the power to direct or cause the direction of the management and policies of a person, whether through the ownership of securities, by contract or otherwise." For clarity, the rule further provides that a person will be presumed to control an entity if that person has either of the following:

- The direct or indirect right to vote or direct the voting of 25 percent or more of a class of the entity's voting securities
- The power to sell or direct the sale of 25 percent or more of a class of voting securities of the entity (or, in the case of a partnership, has the right to receive upon dissolution, or has contributed, 25 percent or more of the partnership's capital)[26]

A large trader must aggregate all of the purchases and sales of NMS securities in a calendar day or calendar month, made by or for any account for which the large trader directly or indirectly exercises investment discretion, to determine whether it has reached the identifying activity level. Accordingly, all transactions for or on behalf of affiliated entities must generally be aggregated.

Even so, complex organizations have some flexibility to determine which entities should file a large trader report with the SEC. For example, if a parent entity files with the SEC as a large trader, but one or more of its subsidiaries would independently qualify as a large trader, only the parent entity must comply with the rule. The subsidiaries in that instance do not need to file separately. Likewise, if each entity that a large trader controls (and for which such large trader otherwise exercises investment discretion) complies with the SEC reporting requirements under the large trader rule, then the controlling entity may not need to make a filing with the SEC. In light of the complexity of the large trader reporting requirements, you should consult with legal counsel to determine which entities in your organizational structure may have an SEC filing obligation.

Case in Point

In this example, we assume that InvestCo A executed trades in NMS securities in the amount of $200 million in the month of October, thereby meeting the threshold to be deemed a large trader. We will also assume that InvestCo B executed trades in NMS securities during that month, but only in the amount of $5 million—far below the identifying activity level.

Although InvestCo A could file its own large trader report, we should keep in mind that parent companies of large traders must aggregate all of their subsidiaries' trading activities in NMS securities when determining whether a large trader report is required. If a subsidiary that would not ordinarily qualify as a large trader trades in NMS securities, its activities must be included with the activities of its large trader affiliates with whom it is under common control.

Since InvestCo B (which trades in NMS securities below the identifying activity level) is under common control with InvestCo A (which exceeds the identifying activity level), InvestCo B also has an obligation to report. If InvestCo A were to report on its own, then InvestCo B would also have to file a large trader report. Alternatively, IntermediaryCo, as the controlling parent of InvestCo A and InvestCo B, may file a large trader report on Form 13H for both entities.

The SEC Gets Personal About Insider Trading

Trading shares of a public company on the basis of material, nonpublic information has long been a priority for SEC enforcement actions and may bring to mind high-profile cases of Wall Street traders making millions of dollars based on confidential information gleaned from clients. However, family offices should be wary—and should make their clients aware—of the risks to family members or acquaintances becoming entangled in insider-trading cases as a result of information shared at home. As we demonstrate below, the SEC does not distinguish much in its pursuit of the ill-gotten gains of high-powered traders and family members' profits on a cousin's inadvertent disclosure of confidential information.

What constitutes insider trading? An insider trading enforcement action must prove that the following elements were present in a particular transaction:

- *Element 1—Material nonpublic information:* The information on which an individual trades stock cannot have been in the public domain. For purposes of determining whether information is material, the SEC will always have the benefit of hindsight and will consider whether there was a substantial likelihood that an investor would consider the information important in deciding whether to sell, hold, or buy a particular stock.

- *Element 2—A duty to the company to which the nonpublic information pertains:* In most enforcement actions, the insider possessing material, nonpublic information must have a fiduciary relationship to the company whose stock has been traded. However, a duty to the company may also arise from social or family relations (i.e., a relationship with a fiduciary to the company), where an insider with a fiduciary obligation to the company knowingly or unknowingly acts as a *tipper*, making material, nonpublic information available to a *tippee* who, by extension, develops a duty to the company.
- *Element 3—*Scienter *(acting knowingly or recklessly):* Once a tippee has knowingly or recklessly traded on the basis of material, nonpublic information, the tippee and the tipper can be held liable for insider trading and can be subject to fines and penalties.

The following are three examples of SEC enforcement actions resulting from family members or acquaintances becoming entangled in insider-trading inquiries. *Family offices should note that the cases below demonstrate that even those who do not trade on inside information may be implicated in an SEC investigation.* Further, family offices should caution their clients that no gains are too small to escape SEC enforcement action.

1. SEC versus Goetz (2011)

In this case, Dean Goetz was an attorney in California whose daughter (also an attorney) visited for the holidays. Goetz's daughter brought home documents relating to a transaction for a publicly traded company.

Goetz was alleged to have gained access to his daughter's work documents, and to have made trades in the stock of the company based on material and nonpublic information in those documents. Goetz was forced to disgorge his profits on the trades and pay a penalty equal to the amount of the profits on the trades.

Lesson: In this example, material, nonpublic information about a public company was left unguarded in the family home—presumably a safe space. Family offices should ensure that their clients understand that material, nonpublic information should never be left unguarded, even among family members. Further, family members should never trade based on information that may be material and nonpublic.

2. SEC versus Deskovick and Haig (2011)

In this case, Kim Ann Deskovick was a director in a bank that was considering putting itself up for sale. Deskovick allegedly disclosed information relating to the potential sale to a friend who then allegedly divulged the information to Brian Haig.

Although Haig was alleged to have traded in the bank's stock on the basis of the nonpublic information while Deskovick did not, both Deskovick and Haig were forced to pay penalties in connection with the insider trading charges. In addition, Deskovick was barred from serving as an officer or director of a public company for five years.

Lesson: An individual with a duty to a public company may be sanctioned by the SEC simply for divulging material, nonpublic information that is ultimately used by a third party as the basis for trades. Family offices should warn their clients that any disclosure of material, non-public information may take on a life of its own, resulting in sanctions against the family office client.

3. SEC versus Macdonald and Maresca (2010)

In this case, Bruce Macdonald, whose wife was an officer of a public company, learned nonpublic information about a transaction involving the company. Macdonald allegedly made trades on his own account and for Bruce Bohlander, an acquaintance, based on the information. Macdonald also allegedly tipped Robert Maresca, and Maresca was alleged to have traded based on the information.

Even though the profits on the trades were relatively small—Macdonald made $8,198, Maresca made $12,335, and Bohlander made $25,508—the SEC pursued an enforcement action for the misappropriation of material, nonpublic information for the purpose of trading.

Lesson: In this example, the trading profits that attracted the SEC's attention were relatively small. Family offices should make their clients aware that what is important in insider trading inquiries is *not* the amount of profit gained on an illegal trade, but rather the fact that an illegal trade was made at all.

Compliance Policies

Compliance is a critical function in the day-to-day operations of a family office. If the family office is an SEC-registered investment adviser, it

- Must have implemented certain compliance policies and procedures that are reasonably designed to prevent, detect, and promptly correct violations of the Advisers Act; and

- Must have appointed a chief compliance officer (a CCO) who is responsible for administering such compliance policies and procedures in accordance with the Advisers Act.

Even if it is not SEC-registered, a family office should act to shield its clients against multiple types of risk. Family office professionals with whom we have spoken have cited the benefits of a compliance policy in establishing expectations between the family and its professional advisers. For example, a formal compliance policy can encourage family office personnel to act professionally, legally, and ethically, and can guide the family office in its efforts to address the following areas of risk, among others:

- Fraud and misappropriation of family assets
- Potential personal liability of family office employees
- Reputational risks of the family office
- Satisfaction of directors' duties to the family office and its clients

In addition, family offices can mitigate potential SEC sanctions if they take steps in advance to prevent unethical and illegal conduct. A formal compliance program, including sufficient training for family office personnel, greatly assists in this regard.

What Are the Components of a Good Compliance Policy?

An SEC-registered investment adviser's compliance policy must incorporate the following components, but it is also good practice for unregistered family offices to develop similar policies:

- A code of ethics that
  - Sets out standards of business conduct expected of an investment adviser's partners, officers, directors, managers and employees.
  - Addresses personal trading by these individuals.
- Policies and procedures designed to prevent the misuse of material non-public information.
- Policies to ensure that the investment adviser makes and keeps current, true, accurate, and complete books and records relating to its investment advisory business, including (among others) financial and corporate records, records relating to fees and the adviser's authority to act for accounts, and e-mail correspondence.
- Policies and procedures regarding the investment adviser's ability to continue operating after a disaster or the departure or death of key personnel.

- A privacy policy to safeguard clients' personal data and to inform clients about the investment adviser's privacy policies and practices.
- Anti-money laundering policies and procedures that the investment adviser must strictly adhere to. A registered investment adviser must update such policies and procedures at least annually to take into account new money laundering threats.
- Policies ensuring compliance with Advisers Act regulations restricting the forms of marketing activity that a registered investment adviser may undertake.

Each family office should appoint an individual to be responsible for developing, maintaining, and monitoring adherence with the compliance policy. If the family office is registered, it is required to appoint a CCO for this purpose. If the family office is unregistered, the individual overseeing the compliance policy should be someone senior in the organization, with enough knowledge of the activities of the organization to develop an appropriate policy and with enough authority to enforce the policy.

Document Retention Policies

SEC-registered investment advisers are subject to stringent guidelines for document retention and management. Under the recordkeeping requirements set forth in Section 204 of the Advisers Act, registered investment advisers must maintain specific books and records and make them available to SEC examiners for inspection in the event of a regulatory audit. However, unregistered investment advisers also benefit from having a document retention policy in the event clients request records and in order to comply with tax and other requirements.

Registered investment advisers must maintain accurate books and records on a current basis, including typical corporate and accounting records, and records necessary to demonstrate compliance with the adviser's fiduciary duty to its clients. The required books and records include, but are not limited to, the following:

- Corporate and accounting records (including organizational documents, records of each securities purchase or sale order given by the investment adviser, bank statements, and cancelled checks, among others)

- All written agreements entered into by the investment adviser with any client or relating to the business of the investment adviser, and any powers of attorney
- Communication records (including marketing materials, communications from clients, research reports, and other materials received from third parties)

Books and records required under the Advisers Act generally must be preserved in an appropriate office of the investment adviser for at least two years from the end of the fiscal year during which the last entry was made on the record or during which the adviser last published or otherwise disseminated the regulated information. After that, the books and records must be kept in an easily accessible place for an additional three years. However, articles of incorporation (or partnership articles or certificates), minute books, and stock certificate books of the adviser and of any predecessor must be preserved in the investment adviser's principal office until at least three years after the termination of the enterprise.

If the investment adviser maintains books and records electronically, it must arrange and index the records in a way that permits easy location, access, and retrieval of any particular record. The investment adviser must also separately store, for the time required for preservation of the original record, a duplicate copy of the record on any medium allowed by Rule 204-2 under the Advisers Act (i.e., electronic storage media). When requested by the SEC, the investment adviser promptly—and, in some cases, immediately—must provide any of the following:

- A legible, true, and complete copy of the record in the medium and format in which it is stored
- A legible, true, and complete printout of the record; and means to access, view, and print the records

Some family offices have moved from more traditional methods of storing documents in hard copy and electronic storage on internal hard drives to using cloud-based solutions for document storage. While cloud-based solutions can be convenient and cost-effective, they do pose potential privacy issues. Family offices that have moved to cloud-based storage have told us that they have retained data security professionals to vet potential providers and to perform ongoing data security audits.

What Are the Components of a Good Document Retention Policy?

When developing a document retention policy, a family office should keep in mind the following guiding principles:

- *Include all records in your document retention policy:* Your policy's definition of records must be construed broadly to include not only written or printed documents relating to all activities of the family office, but also data stored in an electronic format (which should be safeguarded from alteration or destruction and protected from use by unauthorized individuals).
- *Appoint a record owner:* One employee should have ultimate responsibility for keeping track of family office records.
- *Promote shared compliance with document retention procedures:* All employees of the family office should follow established protocols regarding the creation, use, maintenance, and destruction of family office records.
- *Safeguard records appropriately for business continuity:* Your records should be stored and kept from harm's way (even in multiple locations, yet easily retrievable) with an eye toward being able to continue the business of the family office in the event of any disaster.
- *Encourage strict adherence to a record destruction policy:* You should have a detailed policy governing the destruction of records that are not necessary to keep for legal reasons, such that records are not destroyed accidentally, without the knowledge of appropriate employees or for any improper reason (such as in connection with an impending audit, investigation, or lawsuit).

A good practice for family offices concerned about document management is to designate someone who will be responsible for maintaining and monitoring adherence to the document retention policy. If the family office is registered, the CCO should serve this purpose. If the family office is unregistered, the document retention policy should be overseen by someone senior in the organization, with enough knowledge of the activities of the organization to develop an appropriate policy and with enough authority to enforce the policy.

The Compliance Function: In-House Versus Outsourced

Although the compliance function technically may be outsourced, it appears from staff remarks on the subject that the SEC is particularly concerned about advisers who designate compliance consultants who are outside the firms they serve to act as CCO for those firms. For example, in public statements, SEC staff has expressed doubts that an agent whose business it is to serve as CCO to multiple firms can carry out his or her compliance responsibilities effectively. Further, SEC staff has suggested that an outsourced CCO who is not within close physical proximity with the firm he or she serves may not have the requisite intimate knowledge of the business to be effective. Finally, SEC staff have emphasized that an investment adviser's CCO must be empowered with the responsibility and authority to develop and enforce appropriate policies and procedures. In some cases, an outsourced CCO simply may not wield the same level of authority among employees that an internal CCO enjoys when carrying out a firm's compliance efforts.

Special Issues for Family Offices When Considering Regulatory Requirements

When adopting the Family Office Rule, the SEC clearly stated that it did not wish to regulate the investment activities of private families. However, this statement has lulled some into a false sense of security. Even though the Family Office Rule is fairly broad, the SEC has indicated that it will require strict compliance with its requirements. There is no *de minimus* exception for noncompliance and even minor deviations can lead to the harsh result of requiring the family office to register with the SEC and comply with rules that were designed to regulate financial professionals offering their services to the public at large.

Further, as we have demonstrated above, even if a family office is able to avoid regulation as an investment adviser, there are a host of other regulatory requirements that apply to the family office's investment activities. For example, even though most family offices would not consider themselves institutional investment managers, they will be subject to the same rules that apply to commercial investment managers if they pass certain ownership or trading thresholds.

It is important that family offices understand these requirements. In the first instance, many family offices operate in a manner specifically designed to avoid reporting obligations. For example, some family offices choose to own mutual fund shares rather than exchange-traded funds because, unlike exchange-traded funds, mutual fund shares are generally not subject to disclosure on institutional investment manager reports. Even when reporting is required, an understanding of the rules can reduce the negative impact. In the case of institutional investment manager reports, it is often possible for a family office to request confidential treatment of their holdings, thereby protecting the family's privacy even when reporting is required.

Conclusion and Final Thoughts

Going forward, family offices must actively balance their clients' wealth planning and privacy goals with regulatory requirements. If history is a guide, the regulatory landscape will continue to change—and it is likely to become more complex. As families continue to adopt structures and practices that mirror those utilized by financial services professionals when offering products and services to the public, they will increasingly find they are subject to regulatory requirements that were not designed to apply to them and, in many cases, are not easily applied to structures designed to hold and manage personal and family wealth. While non-tax regulators may have little interest in regulating the investment activities of private families, they can be expected to remain vigilant in not allowing exceptions that might be used to create regulatory loopholes that can be used by the financial services professionals they do want to monitor, oversee, and regulate.

Notes

1. Beneficial ownership reporting requirements are provided in Section 13(d), Section 13(g), and Section 16 of the US Securities Exchange Act of 1934 (the Exchange Act).
2. See Section 13(f) of the US Securities Exchange Act of 1934.
3. See Section 13(h) of the US Securities Exchange Act of 1934.
4. See Advisers Act Rule 202(a)(11)(G)-1(b)(2).
5. Staff Responses to Questions About the Family Office Rule (updated as of March 23, 2018).
6. Ibid., Question I.1.
7. Ibid., Question I.2.
8. If non-family clients provided funding to a charitable foundation, charitable trust, or charitable organization in the past, the organization could have complied by spending those non-family client funds by December 31, 2013.
9. See R. Bate, 1988 SEC No-Act. LEXIS 847 (June 28, 1988). See also Use of Electronic Media by Broker-Dealers, Transfer Agents, and Investment Advisers for Delivery of Information, Investment Adviser Release No. IA-1562 (May 9, 1996), at Section II.D.

10. See Section 13(d) and Section 13(g) under the US Securities Exchange Act of 1934.
11. See Rule 13d-3(a) under the US Securities Exchange Act of 1934.
12. SEC Compliance and Disclosure Interpretations for Exchange Act Sections 13(d) and 13(g) (Question 103.10).
13. See US Securities Exchange Act of 1934 Rule 13d-1(b).
14. See US Securities Exchange Act of 1934 Rule 13d-1(b)(1).
15. Ibid.
16. See US Securities Exchange Act of 1934 Rule 13d-1(c).
17. See US Securities Exchange Act of 1934 Rule 13d-1(d).
18. See US Securities Exchange Act of 1934 Rule 13d-1(d).
19. See US Securities Exchange Act of 1934 Section 16.
20. See US Securities Exchange Act of 1934 Rule 16(a)-1(a).
21. See US Securities Exchange Act of 1934 Rule 16(a)-1.
22. See US Securities Exchange Act of 1934 Rule 16(a)-6.
23. See US Securities Exchange Act of 1934 Section 13(f)(4).
24. Rule 13h-1 under the US Securities Exchange Act of 1934 defines a large trader as a person who "directly or indirectly, including through other persons controlled by such person, exercises investment discretion over one or more accounts and effects transactions for the purchase or sale of NMS securities for or on behalf of such accounts, by or through one or more US-registered broker- dealers, in an aggregate amount equal to or greater than the identifying activity level."
25. See US Securities Exchange Act of 1934 Rule 13h-1(a)(4), which defines investment discretion by reference to Exchange Act Section 3(a)(35).
26. See US Securities Exchange Act of 1934 Rule 13h-1(a)(3).

CHAPTER 8

Investment Management and the Family Office

Kirby Rosplock, PhD

This chapter is dedicated to a primary function in many established family offices—investment management.[1] When an individual or family has experienced one or more liquidity events justifying the creation of a family office, the wealth creator(s) have to solve for how to manage and invest that wealth. This chapter provides investment guidance and insights for those who have or are considering directing the investment function in-house from their family office. This chapter explores some of the theoretical underpinnings of investing and how family offices are approaching investments, and a simple, yet important foundational principle of how a family office may solve or think about family wealth investments. This chapter then expands on the family office that invests as paradigm to their institutional counterparts and the importance of deriving an investment philosophy. The chapter further discusses how one's investment philosophy provides the guiding principles to create one's investment objectives and investment policy statement. It then shares further about the family office's investment approach and governance, including important structures such as the investment policy statement, investment committee, and investment governance approaches. The latter portion of this chapter discusses the investment process and the option to outsource the CIO function.

Family Office Investment Management

Investing the family's financial capital is traditionally a central *raison d'être* or purpose of the family office. However, the universe of family office types and styles is vast, and when it comes to the investment discipline, I have not identified any two family offices that invest the same way or in the same types of investments. The investment approach is unique in just about every case; however, there are certain consistent themes and/or constraints that are present in nearly all family offices:

1. There are often family, business, fiduciary, and/or estate planning aspects that create a context and may influence the investment approach.
2. There may be certain legal or tax constraints in various estate planning structures such as trusts that provide specific guidelines to how wealth may be invested.
3. There may be relevant family situations, such as varying needs or requirements for dependents. For example, a child with special needs may require care and financial support from birth until death that is different from other children who can earn and provide for themselves.
4. There may be underlying assets, such as concentrated positions in publicly traded securities, family business(es), direct investments, partnerships, and other business structures that generate cash flow and/or may require capital that influence the investment approach.
5. There may be fiduciary aspects that may influence and/or guide aspects of how certain assets, particularly those in trust, are invested and managed.

The reality for multigenerational, wealth-owning families in the United States is that most assets (90 percent) are held in trust by the time those assets reach the third generation of a family.[2] This reality has considerable influence on the investment approach. If there is one truism, the investment approach should have guiding values and principles that are foundational; however, the process of investing is one that is dynamic and always evolving. To follow is a simple maxim to keep in mind in developing one's family office investment approach.

Concentration

> The way to become rich is to put all your eggs in one basket and then watch that basket.
>
> —Andrew Carnegie

Concentration in a business where a product or service has a major edge over its competitors and grows steadily is the typical backstory of most family wealth creation. Sixty-seven percent of participants in the 2019 FOX Investment Survey still own a significant stake in one or more operating businesses.[3] Not only the concentration of investment, but the concentration of time and energy, ownership, calculated risks, and equity are all components that have led a select few to the pinnacle of financial success. Ian D'Souza, Co-Founder of the NYU Stern Family Office Council and Adjunct Professor of Finance at the Leonard N. Stern School of Business, estimates that many family offices generated approximately eighty percent of their initial wealth from a control position in an operating business(es) where the founder had significant control—not a diversified portfolio, but a concentrated investment position where they have direct line of sight to cash flows.[4] When we look at the tremendous wealth of the DuPont, Mellon, Rockefeller, Phipps, Scripps, Smith, Chandler, Brown, and Bacardi families as listed in "Family Fortunes" by *Forbes* in 2004, their wealth in aggregate is impressive. However, due to several factors, including inflation, taxes, spending, generational mathematics, among others, wealth becomes splintered over generations, and as a result, family fortunes tend to erode over time. For example, the DuPonts' collective affluence was estimated at $15 billion in 2004, yet no individual member of the family qualified for *Forbes* 400 in that same year.[5] In fact, of the twenty well-recognized family fortunes, not one individual family member met the minimum to be listed on the *Forbes* 400 in 2004.

Fast-forward to 2020—if we look at the *Forbes* World's Real-time List of Billionaires, the Walton family members occupy 15 percent of the top wealthiest billionaires globally and combined have more wealth than Jeff Bezos at the number one spot. Fifty percent of the top twenty created their wealth in a technology, software, or ecommerce business. What do these data points reveal to us? Wealth is often created through a concentrated business opportunity that has a distinct strategic advantage in the marketplace and/or may be disruptive in its marketplace. Second, although the *Forbes* World's Real-time List of Billionaires provides illumination to the top wealth creators, most will find it challenging to stay at the top of the list, as only 60 percent who were listed in the top 20 remain in the top 20 a decade later.[6] The Walton family is one of a kind.

Despite the fractioning of individual wealth as it spreads down generations, the family office offers its clients the ability to pool and leverage the family's collective wealth position for greater opportunities. Being concentrated in a position may be what created the wealth, but it often is not what will sustain the wealth for generations to come. Thus, for many families, their family office becomes the mechanism to understand how to look at the risk/reward tradeoffs of different investment diversification strategies coupled with the long-term strategic goals of the family. The strategies can become very complex. Further, making the transition from one extreme (concentration in an operating business or publicly traded stock) to the other extreme (a portfolio fully diversified across asset classes and strategies) is often uncomfortable and downright difficult. It is important to understand why a diversified approach will accrue generational benefits in risk reduction over time and for the wealth creator to document his or her intended strategy and commitment to it. There will undoubtedly be moments of trepidation, hesitation, and even regret. Therefore, the family office investment executive must be prepared to handle the very strong and difficult investment-related emotions. Let's consider from the family's point-of-view what the family office must achieve from an investment perspective, and how the wealth management paradigm in the family office might measure its success.

Measuring Success

Family offices will have different mechanisms to measure their performance success. Fidelity Family Office Investment Survey found that more than a third (35 percent) of family offices measure the portfolio's success on an absolute return basis, whereas a quarter (24 percent) measure its success on a relative return basis. Fewer (less than 10 percent) utilize absolute or relative risk or annual income targets as their basis for looking at the family office's investment success.[7] Joe Reilly, Jr., consultant and advisor to family offices from Greenwich, CT, shares that the key is "apply the metrics that a family office identifies as key against their plan." He notes that investment benchmarks are important, but so are the other metrics that illuminate the true success of a family office's investment prowess. From tax efficiency and wealth transfer planning structures, to asset protection and tax mitigation, Reilly notes that investment metrics do not tell the whole story.[8] Because markets will constantly be shifting and moving, investment mandates and their metrics may likely be adjusted over time. Investment performance should, as a result, be benchmarked to a capital markets index that closely resembles the family's portfolio (although a customized index is even better); it also should be benchmarked against the achievement of the family's goals as outlined in the family review. The family review or family investment policy statement sets up the goals-based asset allocation which can then be utilized as a benchmarking tool against goal achievement.[9]

Lifestyle and Legacy

There are plenty of very in-depth, complex investment books that inform the tactical aspects of investing. For the family office focused on serving the investment and wealth management needs of the family, there are two fundamental drivers to consider in the investment approach. These are the goal(s) and motivation(s) of the family when it comes to their lifestyle needs (present) and their legacy intentions (long-term). Solving for these two functions requires the resolution of several related issues, such as taxes, inflation, investment costs, spending, risk tolerance, and return objectives. Additionally, there may be dissenting opinions from either a spouse or the next generation. See Figure 8.1 that presents the balancing act of lifestyle- and legacy investment–related goals.

FIGURE 8.1 Lifestyle Versus Legacy Investment Goals

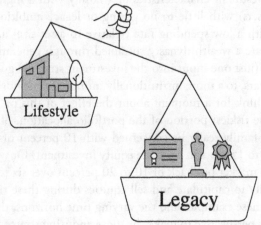

Source: © Tamarind Partners, Inc.

The graphic represents the balance that the investment approach must strike to generate adequate income under the appropriate risk tolerance and asset allocation. On the left side, lifestyle is the primary objective for the family, whereas on his right side, solving for the family's legacy is the priority.

What do we mean by lifestyle? Lifestyle represents the current availability to capital and ongoing financial needs of the individual or family client to the wealth. In Chapter 6, a broader discussion of capital sufficiency was shared about how this analysis is instrumental in the strategic planning process for a family office and can inform the strategic and tactical plan for a family. For families who require their wealth to generate a higher current income to cover lifestyle needs and existing obligations, there may be a focus or emphasis that the wealth is to be consumed and appreciated during the lifetime of the wealth holder, and less emphasis may be placed on leaving wealth to heirs, charity, or other causes.

Alternatively, the wealth holder may have created enormous wealth, yet has a modest lifestyle. These individuals may have little need or requirement for a high degree of income to fund current lifestyle needs and may have a greater ambition to focus and direct their wealth to other individuals, charities, or causes after their death. These types of individuals are often less interested or focused on spending and/or may have other sources of income from existing operating business dividends or other liquidity streams, which diminish their current lifestyle needs. Determining the family's approach to lifestyle versus legacy can be one of the most influential aspects in determining the appropriate investment strategy and will certainly influence the family's approach to developing their investment philosophy. Imagine the juxtaposed investment characteristics of a family with a high spending rate (relative to assets) with little to no gifting or legacy ambitions, versus that of a family with a low spending rate (relative to asset size) and which fully intends to create a wealth dynasty sustained through generations. The time horizon alone (just one input into the investment strategy) goes from a mortal 30 to 50 years, to a more institutionally immortal time horizon of literally 100+ years. Think for a moment about the effect of this on an investment strategy for the riskiest portion of the portfolio allocation. Should the multigenerational family really be concerned with 10 percent of their portfolio tied up for 10 to 15 years in a private equity investment? Or would or should a cyclical bear market pullback of 10 to 20 percent over six to eight months drive the family to capitulate and sell equities during these times of market stress? Given these examples and the varying time horizons, the family office can utilize this perspective to make the more enduring strategy decisions that truly reflect their goals and aspirations.

Time Horizon

> Time is really the only capital that any human being has, and the only thing he can't afford to lose.
>
> —Thomas Edison

It is stating the obvious that time is one of the most critical factors to the investment strategy for a family office. It influences the investment time horizon, how long you have to invest in order to get to a specific goal or target. On the flip side, time is like an elastic band that stretches far into the future. Just one bad investment cycle (think subprime mortgage crisis, 2007–2010) can erase what may have taken years of compounding interest to accumulate, so time can be a friend to the family office but it can also be a ferocious foe when it comes to investing. For example, when one looks at the US stock market's total returns from 1920 to 2008, we see year-to-year a wide dispersion of market ups and downs despite the average annual return yielding approximately 10 percent.[10] In the first three months of 2020, the US stock market wiped out more than three years of gains—the worst drawdown since the Great Depression—and then quickly rebounded through the following two quarters to all-time highs. The Volatility Index reached levels not seen since the pullback in 2008. Some family offices will pay a high premium to curb volatility or swings in the market, especially leptokurtosis or "fat tailed risk" that occurs when the shape of a distribution is more peaked than that of a normal or "bell curve" distribution. Through a variety of hedging strategies, and/or combinations of investment strategies, protecting and preserving the wealth amassed is often a priority for the family office.

There are three fundamental truths to investing, which are no exception to the family office. First, no matter how intelligent, trained, and experienced your investment professionals are—no one has a crystal ball to time the markets. In his book, *The Black Swan: The Impact of the Highly Improbable*, Nassim Nicholas Taleb reveals that over the past 30 years, the Standard & Poor's 500 Index (S&P) has generated a 9.5 percent per year return on average, excluding the reinvestment of dividends; yet, if you exclude the 50 worst days in that same time frame, your rate of return would nearly double to 18.2 percent. But what happens if you missed the 50 top performing days over the last 30 years? What happens to your performance is dismal, plummeting to less than 1 percent? What is remarkable is that the span of 50 days is 0.7 percent of the total days that can make the difference between double-digit returns and just about breakeven. The takeaway is that being invested over the long term will help ensure you are dollar-cost averaging, or increasing incrementally over a time period, to bring down the average cost of your position, but also safeguarding that you are invested, particularly when markets are doing well. Thus, investing with a short-term focus, or worse a day-trading mentality, is completely counterintuitive to the opportunity at hand for a family office.

The second lesson of the power of time, investing, and the family office is the obvious head start provided when the investing time horizon starts earlier. Consider the power of compounding interest, what Albert Einstein referenced as the most powerful force in the universe, and the advantage that a family can provide particularly to young beneficiaries by starting their investment futures early. If you were to invest $1,000 compounded annually at 10 percent for 10 years, utilizing a standard compounding interest calculator, the investment would yield $2,593.74, as compared to investing the same amount at 10 percent interest rate compounded daily over the same 10-year period. Contributing an additional $100 dollars a month would result in $23,421.66. The latter figure is nearly nine times greater by simply changing from annual to daily compounding and increasing monthly contributions by $100.[11] Again, it may be unrealistic to assume a 10 percent return compounded annually, not taking into account other corrosive factors such as inflation, taxes, and investment costs, among other considerations; however, there is power in being invested for the long term, which brings us to the final lesson on patient capital.

The final lesson on time is on the power of patient capital or the idea that certain assets over time will grow if the principal or the asset is left alone. A family business, trust, or operating entity built to last may be an asset considered patient capital, whereby the family may hold onto the asset even during difficult times and is willing to be patient with the asset in leaner years. Similarly, there are times when the prudent course of action is to stay invested and let the money work for you, despite swings in the market. So why does the simple principle of time provide a distinct advantage for the family office investor? They can afford to leverage time to work for them; however, there are several factors that quietly erode wealth over time, which bring a sobering reality to multigenerational wealth. Professor Ian D'Souza posits that when a family office transitions from controlling an operating business(es) to managing a diversified investment portfolio, they still maintain an illusion of a control posture despite macro and trade forces that are much more distributed. Furthermore, a family office's belief of "infinitely" long investment horizons can create an overconfidence that time will heal all investment wounds. This confuses the point that some asset classes do not have time as a critical element of the investment thesis (e.g., seed investments in start-ups where impairment is a function of the competitive dynamic rather than holding period duration).[12]

Hurdles to Growing Wealth

What are the headwinds the family office investor faces? These headwinds are no different than most ultra-affluent investors; however, they are typically in a far more complex and generationally timed fashion. Greg Curtis, author of *Creative Capital: Managing Private Wealth in a Complex World*, shares the fictitious case of $10 million left to an heiress named Edith and her improper assumption that her $10 million will compound to $2.8 billion in 50 years.[13] Edith's miscalculation in this annual compounding example is mythical. The harsh reality is that there are many forces that methodically erode wealth.

The first perpetrator is the wide dispersions of investment returns, which means that anticipating a linear, straight-line return year over year is completely unrealistic. As a result, there is a cost associated with volatility that must be accounted for. Second, the impact of inflation is a relevant variable, which is estimated to average about 4.2 percent annually.[14] As inflation increases prices around us, the purchasing power of money decreases (on a relative basis) and negatively impacts actual returns considerably. Third, taxes are a part of life, assuming you are not a tax-free pension fund or charitable endowment. As a result, the typical US investor will pay ordinary income tax on interest, dividends, and short-term capital gains and will incur capital gains tax on long-term capital gains. Curtis cites that over time, taxes may erode 2 percent per year of investment returns.[15] Fourth, just being invested can result in expenses, depending on how you are invested. From investment advisory fees, to brokerage fees, account and sales fees, exchange fees, spreads, and commissions—the multiple levels of fees that may be charged on various types of investing can further gouge into your investment return as much as 2 percent a year.[16] Lastly, spending levels (anticipated and those unanticipated) can work against total return as well. The work to simply maintain and sustain wealth over the long term is not as straightforward and simple as investing a large sum and forgetting about it for a while. Some family offices use a "scorecard approach" to model a hurdle rate of return that requires net of operating expenses, management fees, distributions to shareholders, the impact of taxes, inflation rate, and sometimes even their charitable giving. See Figure 8.2 that illuminates the types of expenses an office may incur and the type of returns needed to simply sustain their wealth over time.

Many potential approaches are available to explore asset allocation, asset location, and efficient tax-minimizing strategies; however, the purpose of this

FIGURE 8.2 Scorecard Sample

Annual Outflows	
Operating Expenses	0.5%
Management fees	0.3%
Distribution to shareholders	2.0%
Taxes	1.5%
Total Outflows:	**4.3%**
Inflation	2.0%
% needed to keep assets level	**6.3%**

Source: © 2020 M&T Bank Corporation and its Subsidiaries. All Rights Reserved.

chapter is to build a framework and understanding of the investment function in the family office. There is a massive library of exceptional investment management and asset allocation resources that delve more deeply into how and where to invest. The following section will discuss how the family office provides a different paradigm than its peer institutional cousins, the pension funds, endowments, and institutional investors.

Family Office Investing: Paradigm Shift

The family office may invest traditionally with its institutional counterparts, such as endowments or pension funds, but there are opportunities for the family and its family office that are distinct and suitable for this special type of investor. Up until 2008, many followed the endowment model, which was first utilized in Ivy League schools' endowments such as Yale, Harvard, and Princeton. Yet, after the watershed market events of 2008, many family office investors realized that they do not have to invest and operate as their larger institutional counterparts because they have different goals, objectives, incentives, and constraints.

First, a family office typically operates under the guidance of a time horizon that is longer than the traditional institutional investor's time horizon— not a function of a quarter or even an individual's lifetime, but rather multiple generations of a family. This allows family offices to have greater freedom and flexibility with asset allocation if there are not strict risk tolerance or investment constraints and/or high liquidity needs. Second, a family may have a more patient approach to investing because of their long-term approach. This means they recognize there may be volatility over the years of an assets' appreciation, but they are not looking for a short-term gain; rather, they seek growth and long-term appreciation. A study found that one of the greatest competitive advantages for the UHNW individual is their ability to gain access to exclusive investment opportunities, whereby they have the luxury of locking up capital for a longer duration of time in exchange for the higher likelihood of long-term appreciation. A survey of family offices found the respondents had an average 53 percent of their investment exposure to alternative assets such as private equity and hedge funds as well as direct investments such as real estate companies.[17] Third, risk tolerance, or the perception of various forms of risk, may vary considerably on the underlying individual investor coupled with the investment vehicle. A broader discussion of risk tolerance is to follow later in this chapter; however, the risk tolerance of an institutional investor may look very different from that of a family office. Fourth, a family office may not have to follow the strict mandates, reporting requirements, regulation compliance, and legal requirements for larger traditional investors that are required to invest in a manner that provides a certain level of diversification, hold period, income, and/or liquidity. The rigidity of these institutional models often causes unintended consequences. For example, certain institutions mandate that they cannot own non-investment grade assets in their portfolios. Therefore, these institutions are forced to sell any bond that gets downgraded to noninvestment grade without any thought or opinion to the fundamental credit orientation of the company. A family office can pursue a more flexible fixed income mandate that can take advantage of this potential (and frequent) market dislocation. Fifth, very public funds like CalPers and the Yale Endowment are subject to annual publicity and this pressure tends to pull their investment focus to the short-term. Finally, the governance requirements of reporting to a board or investment committee may not be as strict for a family office as they are for other institutional investors. Keep in mind that institutional investment mandates are often created to achieve one specified objective with a constraint to solve for the least amount of standard deviation. If we juxtapose these criteria to a family office, the family office is entrusted to invest for multiple objectives with risk metrics to include a suite of measurements far more expansive than just standard deviation, including maximum drawdown, loss probability, and up-and-down-capture ratio, among other criteria.

Institutions tend to have more concerns for tracking error and standard deviation versus some sort of market benchmark. Instead, the focus of the family office should be on the risks that most families are most concerned with, such as experiencing a permanent loss of capital or risk of a shortfall when it comes to investing for a certain period of time. In this view, families have the ability to be far more flexible with their approach and this can lead to better investment choices and outcomes. For example, a family can afford to get involved with managers earlier in their life cycle versus following on the heels of traditional institutional-type investing. There is a growing body of academic evidence that indicates that investing with early-stage managers may lead to better results. Manager criteria, such as the principals being more involved in the business at the onset and having a smaller asset base by which a portfolio manager can have greater flexibility, are key contributors to early success.

Passive Versus Active Asset Management

On the investor debate to employ actively versus passively managed portfolios, investment experts have long debated the merits of each. Based upon his extensive research into the topic, Charles Ellis, a longtime investing strategy consultant, argues that while active investing provided outsized returns in the past, a number of things have changed over time and passive investing may be the more attractive route today. Ellis argues that perhaps the most significant change agent is fee arrangements. An investor can efficiently achieve exposure to nearly any segment of the market via low-cost index and exchange traded funds. Actively managed funds, however, charge comparatively much higher fees for that same exposure. In his work, Ellis cites a study performed by Eugene Fama that revealed that after accounting for fees, 97 percent of mutual fund managers underperformed their benchmarks.[18]

Randolph Cohen, lecturer at Harvard Business School and Partner at Alignvest Investment Management, meanwhile, argues that while the passive approach may be outperforming active management generally, skilled managers who are able to differentiate themselves by focusing on specialist strategies around illiquidity, leverage, velocity, and concentration are best positioned to outperform passively managed portfolios.

A family office should consider each side of the debate in order to make an informed decision of what is the right course of action given its own unique facts and circumstances. It is important to note, however, that one is not necessarily exclusive to the other. A family's portfolio will likely include both passively and actively managed assets. As Cohen writes in an essay on the topic: "Of course, a manager who meets our high standards doesn't necessarily exist for every niche. A well-designed portfolio will employ passive strategies in markets and sectors where no stellar manager can be found. This could include both far-flung areas with few resident asset managers and highly efficient sectors of the market like US large-cap.[19]

The reality for the family office is that they do not have to play by the same rules that govern the behavior of the institutional investors, and the investment professionals leading the family office need to recognize this unique difference. They can invest in a customized, tailored approach to suit their unique needs, preferences, and styles. They write the rules.

A Practical Approach to Asset Allocation

With this understanding of the unique characteristics of the family office investor in mind, it should come as no surprise that the average portfolio is diversified with, broadly speaking, exposure to equities, fixed income instruments, alternative investments, cash products, and direct investments in business ventures.

One approach employing both an active and often passive strategy that many family offices utilize is a Barbell Approach to family office investing. In this case, the family office asset allocation has a concentration on operating entities, direct investments, or enterprises balanced by the need for more secure, liquid cash management strategies in the portfolio. Some family offices are formed as a result of successful, closely-held businesses, and the initial focus for those owners often consists of investment and ownership of a core operating business. The operating business(es) that are actively owned and managed form(s) one side of the theoretical barbell. As the operating business matures, the owners may need a portion of the profits from the operating business to redeploy into the businesses, for lifestyle expenses, or investing in new ventures. Thus, they may opt to invest the right side of the barbell in less risky, long-term, or illiquid investments, preferring to invest similarly to a treasury function.

As additional free cash flow that exceeds their liquidity needs becomes available, families may decide to expand their direct ownership platform by investing in additional operating companies. In fact, a study from Fidelity found that 98 percent of family office respondents expected to maintain or increase their exposure to investments via direct private ownership.[20] Direct investing is often seen as a more attractive route to private capital than private equity funds due to a higher degree of control and flexibility coupled with lower fees. At the same time, direct investing is quite risky; the family needs to have the ability to sustain significant losses in that segment of their portfolio. [21] Another challenge to family office investors is the "neighborhood effect"—or the behavioral finance trap of family offices trusting in their peer groups or "family office neighbors," at the exclusion of other voices, leading to "group think" and "crowdedness" risk. [22]

Despite the risks, such as the "neighborhood effect," mounting research confirms the direct investing trend associated with family offices. According to a UBS/Campden Wealth Global Family Office Survey, respondents indicated that about one-third of their portfolios consisted of direct investments with the remainder allocated to equities (32 percent), fixed income instruments (16 percent), alternative investments (12 percent), and cash products (8 percent). [23] Each family needs to take into consideration its own facts and circumstances in designing an asset allocation plan to achieve its own unique goals. This is not a one-time exercise. A family should periodically revisit its asset allocation plan to ensure it aligns with the family's needs at that time. In some cases, for example, changes are simply driven by shifting conviction for certain investment products. In other cases, these changes may be event driven. For example, there will be times where the family may decide to pivot to a more defensive position, perhaps when anticipating a market downturn. In such a circumstance, the family may decide to shift exposure from equities to cash, fixed income, and real assets.

The Investment Process in a Family Office

Each family office has its own unique approach and investment strategy; however, there are core elements to the investment process that are consistent across the family office landscape. This portion of the chapter discusses how families approach the investment process in their family office. Specifically, this section reviews the concept of an investment review; developing an investment philosophy; the role, purpose, and development of investment policy statements; and a high-level discussion of strategic and tactical asset allocation. This section concludes with insights to the manager due diligence and selection process and the ongoing maintenance and surveillance of a family office's investment strategy.

Investment Review

When it comes to prioritization of tasks in the family office, investment-focused families tend to call their attention first to the investments. Specifically, it is common for a family to have a third-party investment professional provide an audit and review of their holdings. This baseline becomes the first step of the investment review process. The investment review consists of itemizing what is owned, how assets are titled and held, and a deeper discovery process of how the family has invested historically. Are accounts primarily actively managed or passively managed, or both? Does the family have a strong bent towards a diversified style of investing or, alternatively, a higher concentration of a certain asset class, such as real estate or a family business? How have the family's investments been managed to date and who is the primary decision maker or makers? What have been the goals and objectives of the investment process and how have those goals been monitored and documented? How has the investment process been governed? Has the family outgrown its investment strategy or are they already on the right investment course? How has the family monitored performance? Which key investment metrics mean the most to the family? How does the family interpret risk/ reward trade-offs and what is their risk tolerance level? Does the family perceive they are taking too much, too little, or just the right amount of risk as it relates to their goals, objectives, and time horizon? How much is the investment approach driven by mitigating taxes? How tax efficient is the investment strategy? How sensitive are the owners to paying taxes? How does the investment strategy connect to the current state of the owners' estate plans? These are all critical questions that a family office should be prepared to answer during the investment review process. These are just some of the types of questions to be answered in the upfront investment review process. The answers to these questions will undoubtedly inform the next step, the development of the family office's investment philosophy.

Investment Governance

Investment governance takes many forms within a family office, and largely depends on the overarching investment philosophy or the guiding values, principles, and beliefs that inform and drive the investment decision-making process. Establishing an investment philosophy that clearly articulates the values associated with an individual's or family's wealth provides overarching guidance to both the strategic and tactical asset allocation. The investment philosophy is not static, but rather reflects ongoing changes that impact the family owners and their investments.

In addition to the evolving investment philosophy, a family's investment philosophy may also provide guidance and wisdom from wealth creators to the intent, purpose, and how the wealth is to be stewarded. These stories and values impart influence to how wealth should be viewed by recipients, as well as impact how it should be invested. Some families may have a strong spiritual or faith-based relationship to their wealth that may also be reflected in their investment philosophy. Items covered in the previous sections are also part of developing the investment philosophy; for example, patient capital, lifestyle versus legacy, and the family's ability to customize and function in a unique manner when it comes to investing are all important guideposts for their investment philosophy. There is no right or wrong investment philosophy; rather, think of it as a spectrum to customize to the belief system around investing of the family. Once the overarching investment philosophy has been identified, devising investment objectives is an important step in formalizing the investment approach.

Families address investment governance and its related issues in many ways from a founder or first-generation approach to a more institutional model. It is not about the model per se, as no one model is strictly preferable to another as all family circumstances are different. Rather, investment governance practices evolve, and new governance models should be considered as family circumstances change. Successful family investment governance has as much, if not more, to do with successful implementation as it does with the choice of the model.[24]

See Figure 8.3 that outlines some ways families approach investment governance and the pros and cons of each model.

Developing an investment philosophy can be quite challenging for a family especially with little or no interest or experience in investing. This is particularly true in the second and succeeding generations where the patriarch or matriarch's investment views prevailed. "A clearly articulated investment philosophy is fundamental to a cohesive family office investment program. Many families miss this first step and move right into implementing an investment strategy.[25] Starting the conversation among family members is often difficult. So, keeping it simple is often the best course of action. A family's exploration of its investment philosophy usually involves:

1. Reviewing the overall family mission, vision, and values statements
2. Defining the purpose of the investment assets
3. Defining the amount of the family's investable assets
4. Determining how long the investments are to last
5. Discussing likely additions or withdrawals
6. Discussing income and liquidity requirements
7. Discussing investment beliefs
8. Defining what risk means
9. Identifying ways that the assets can be managed
10. Discussing preferences for control over investment decisions

FIGURE 8.3 Family Investment Governance Models[26]

MODEL	CHARACTERISTICS	STRENGTHS	WEAKNESSES
Patriarch/Matriarch (G1—First Generation)	G1 has investment decision authority. May work with a close team of key advisers.	High locus of control; streamlined decision making.	Key person risk: Void of authority if death, disability, or lack of interest. Idiosyncratic investments. Limited investment perspective.
Family Leader/Branch (G2—Second Generation and beyond)	Investment decisions guided by individual or family branch with investment interest, knowledge, and/or experience.	Investment decisions led by experienced family. Represents all branches. Focused and efficient decision making.	Responsibility for global financial well-being of family. Continued decision-making authority by individual or group may cause resentment. Communication/Privacy/Disclosure issues.
Ownership/Beneficial Interest (G2—Second Generation and beyond)	Separated approach; Each family member/family branch makes own decisions for assets—either outright or in trust.	Direct input on preferences and needs. Focused on the individual and privacy.	Limits efficiency and economies of scale in investing. Complicates investments through pooled entities and trusts. Investment skill and experience among family members varies.
Generational Investment Committee (G2—Second Generation and beyond)	Family Investment Committee with branch and generational representation. Consultation with outside investment advisors on a nondiscretionary basis.	Closer connection with family wealth. Platform for educating the younger generations. Different perspectives and ideas.	Decision making can be slow. Administrative support is needed to co-ordinate and execute decisions. Family tensions may be brought into the IC and reduce efficiency. Privacy/Disclosure issues.
Trustee Model (G2-3+ — Second/Third Generation and beyond)	Non-family trustees participate on investment committee or with a corporate co-trustee.	Impartial input from trusted advisors/fiduciaries. Focused on investment decisions and confidentiality.	Outside leadership means family may lose their voice on many decisions. Family needs to be comfortable with outsiders making decisions.
"Institutional" Approach (G2-3+ —Second/Third Generation and beyond)	Delegated investment authority to the family office investment team or investment consultant. Investment Committee chaired by an outside professional. Family branch represent with outsiders on the Investment Committee.	Unbiased, impartial, and focused on the family investment program. Responsibility clearly defined. Maintains confidentiality.	Collective family interests supersede individual family households; family input may be diminished. Family comfortable delegating investment authority. Less communication.

Source: Kathryn M. McCarthy

The family's investment philosophy informs the investment objectives and investment policy discussed in the next sections.

Investment Objectives

Investment objectives are the functional goals established by the family for their wealth. These investment objectives provide the guidance of how the wealth is to be invested and to achieve specific goals. Investment goals may range from targeted, such as leaving a certain amount to beneficiaries or charities, to strategic, such as growth of assets for future generations, preserving capital, or income generation. The investment objectives, like the investment philosophy, are typically included in an investment policy statement. Further, investment objectives for family portfolios may range from conservative with a focus on wealth preservation to aggressive and growth-oriented with aspirations for the next generation in mind. The objectives tend to shift as the family office matures. Respondents to a recent survey revealed an inherent bias toward conservatism for families in their third or greater generation who indicated wealth preservation as their top priority (60%) followed by wealth accumulation (36%). Conversely, families in their first or second generation reported that they put less emphasis on wealth preservation (41%) than wealth accumulation (49%).[27] Secondary goals may be to minimize expenses, achieve estate planning efficiency, engage with high-quality advisors, increase transparency into the investment due diligence process, enhance family decision making, and/or target social impact with the family's investments. Holding conversations with owners to understand investment objectives and preferences will enable the family office advisor to construct an investment approach that is aligned with the clients' values, goals, and risk tolerance. Once there is a clear understanding of the investment objectives and their associated time horizons, the family office is ready to compile their investment policy statement.

The Investment Policy Statement

The investment policy statement (IPS) is a quasi-legal document that varies in length and provides the guidance and goals for the way the wealth is to be invested.

An investment policy statement usually articulates the overarching guidelines for the family's investment as opposed to an investment mandate for a specific account. The IPS includes a description of the investment asset allocation, risk parameters, comparable benchmarks, and requirements in terms of liquidity, investment preferences or constraints, as well as the time horizon.

Jean Brunel, a leading investment, and wealth advisor and managing principal of Brunel Associates, likens the construction of an investment process to that of a pilot devising his or her flight plan. Brunel writes,

> The flight plan tells him or her where they are going, how they are going to get there, and what will be the intermediate targets along the way. Similarly, investors need a plan that sets out what they are seeking to achieve, how they are planning to achieve their goals, and what intermediate targets may be needed. The latter is particularly important. It reflects the contraction that seems inherent in the very long-term nature of the wealth management process when dealing with multiple generations, on the one hand and, on the other hand, the need to review investment performance at considerably more frequent intervals. Consider the risks: Simply focusing on long-term goals can lull investors into a sense of security, or incite selected managers to see open-ended long-term mandates, with little or no short-term accountability. However, the alternative is too sharp a focus on short-term performance, which can play directly to the psychology tendencies of individuals to be momentum players.[28]

There are several benefits to implementing an investment policy statement as part of one's investment process. First, it can establish clear expectations and articulate what the goals, objectives, and guidelines are for how a pool of wealth is to be invested. Kathryn M. McCarthy shares that "the investment policy statement is the cornerstone of family investment governance. I am seeing more family offices with a robust IPS."[29] According to Campden Wealth's Global Family Office Report (2019), investment guidelines (a definition for strategic asset allocation across the investment universe) are the most prevalent governance structure that the family office has in place (74 percent of respondents).[30]

Second, it provides guidance to the family office investment professionals that can be the basis for ongoing discussions as the needs and preferences of the client changes. Third, it often provides further insight to the investment guidance for the wealth than what may or may not be articulated in the IPS itself. Fourth, it helps to document decision-making points along the investment management timeline. Over time, the goals and objectives for the family may change and likely so will the global financial markets evolve. The investment policy statement is not a fixed document; rather, it will evolve over time. Figure 8.4 provides a framework for an investment policy statement. There are four essential components of an investment policy statement including its (1) Scope and Purpose, (2) Governance, (3) Investment, Return, and Risk Objectives, and (4) Risk Management.[31]

FIGURE 8.4 Investment Policy Statement Framework

1. **Scope and Purpose**
   - Establish context by identifying the source of the wealth.
   - Define the investor (an individual, family branch, trust, or other entity) and identify the assets to be invested.
   - Define the roles and responsibilities of the key participants including the investment committee.
   - Identify an organizational structure for investing, e.g., investment advisor with or without discretionary authority.
   - Set forth a standard of care for advisors.
2. **Governance**
   - Specify who is responsible for determining investment policy, executing, and monitoring the results.
   - Describe the process for reviewing and updating the IPS.
   - Describe the responsibility and process for engaging and discharging advisors.
   - Assign responsibility for determining the asset allocation including defining the criteria for the development of the investment assumptions.
   - Assign responsibility for risk management, monitoring, and reporting.
3. **Investment, Return, and Risk Objectives**
   - Describe the overall investment objective.
   - Identify asset classes and performance objectives for each.
   - Define distribution/and spending policies.
   - Establish a policy portfolio as a basis for performance and risk assessment.
   - Define the risk tolerance of the investor.
   - Describe constraints (time horizon, liquidity, tax considerations, use of leverage, currency).
   - Describe other constraints (ethical considerations, proxy voting policy, securities lending).
4. **Risk Management**
   - Establish performance measurement and reporting accountabilities.
   - Specify appropriate metrics for risk measurement and evaluation.
   - Define the process for rebalancing portfolios to target allocations.

Like a family office's charter or constitution, the investment policy statement should be routinely reviewed and integrated into the ongoing investment discussions and decision-making process. A written acknowledgement signed by the responsible parties formalizes its status as a key family governance document. By capturing the goals, objectives, assumptions, and investment process, the investment policy statement becomes the written artifact between investor and advisor that is a dynamic tool to help capture the family office's investment road map. It is also important to note that in some multigenerational families, there may be more than one global family investment policy statement. Different generations, differing risk tolerances, multiple entities like family foundations, and diverse goals and investment objectives require more specific policy and guidelines.

Investment Committee

Many family offices govern their investment process with an investment committee. For some, this body comprises family and non-family members, while others prefer to assemble a team of outside investment professionals. The investment committee typically reports to a board of directors for the family office. Its role is to advise on the investment approach, the asset allocation, to oversee and/or provide oversight to the leadership and investment advisory of the single-family office. The investment committee may also function as a sounding board and idea generator of new ideas and challenge the assumptions help by the leadership within the family office. The investment committee may be an important validator and/or provide recommendations and corrective actions should the investment process go astray. Not all families have an investment committee; some prefer a less structured approach to garnering feedback from family owners and/or outside wealth management professionals. However, increasingly, there appears to be a greater adoption of a governing body of advisors to the investment process to aid in risk management, as well as to provide outside points of view to the family's investment mandate.

According to the 2018 FOX Global Investment Survey, the use of an investment committee led to higher returns and satisfaction. Three of four family office survey participants (77 percent) use an investment committee, with nearly all (96 percent) comprised of at least one family member, and 77 percent having at least one external advisor. Those offices that utilize an investment committee achieved significantly higher 2017 portfolio returns than those without (15.8 percent versus 11.3 percent) and were more likely to be "very satisfied" with their 2017 investment performance. Two-thirds (65 percent) of the surveyed family offices that use an investment committee reported that they were "very" satisfied with 2017 investment performance versus only 36 percent of offices without an investment committee citing the same level of satisfaction."[32]

A best practice is to have a job description and criteria outlining what experience, knowledge, certifications, or advanced degrees make an individual qualified to be on the committee. Further, the committee must operate with a clear understanding of the appropriate amount of discretion for their advisor (whatever has been agreed to particularly in outsourced CIO arrangements). Finally, the investment committee must act responsively to allow for the strategy and execution to be able to take advantage of the short-term opportunities or dislocations that may arise.

Why Would a Family Establish an Investment Committee (IC)?

There are many reasons why families establish investment committees. The primary reason is to improve and professionalize the oversight of the family's investment program. Many times, the IC steps into the shoes of the founder or senior generation. Other times it is considered a forum to involve family members and educate them about their investments. Overall, the investment committee is held responsible for the investment function of the family office.

How Does a Family Establish an Investment Committee?

The directive usually comes from the family office board since most invest-ment committees report to it. In some complicated, multi-trust situations, the directive may come from the trustees. A search begins through informal net-working or by employing a search firm. In formal searches, a position descrip-tion is developed by the family office and the board conducts the search. "Many families develop their investment committees starting with one or two people and enhance committee membership as needed. I sit on several family investment committees and the optimum number is three outside profession-als plus several family members," says Kathryn McCarthy.[33] The professional skills needed for a well-functioning investment committee vary family-by-family depending on how the assets are invested and whether there is an inter-nal CIO and/or an investment team. Generally, IC members are qualified, experienced investment professionals, but not necessarily experts in one area. The theory is that experts can be hired as needed. Members should be com-mitted to the family and the investment process. In addition, there needs to be a strong chair to set the agenda and often manage family expectations.

Critical to the functioning of the IC is the development of the invest-ment committee charter. It defines the scope and authority of the members. In addition, the IC charter formalizes meeting schedules, term limits, and committee composition and addresses conflicts of interest. Figure 8.5 pro-vides a sample investment committee charter.

How Does an Investment Committee Usually Operate?

Investment committees generally meet three or four times a year. Meetings can last for anywhere between three to four hours or to a full day. The first

FIGURE 8.5   Sample Investment Committee Charter[34]

PURPOSE:

This Investment Committee ("Committee") is established to advise and provide oversight of the investment management processes and to direct and oversee its investment program(s) in compliance with objectives as set out in the Investment Policy Statement.

The role of the committee will include:

- Reviewing investment policies and guidelines;
- Ensuring compliance with the Investment Policy Statement;
- Monitoring the management of the investment program to ensure a healthy investment process complying with investment policies and guidelines;
- Developing new investment ideas and strategies and identifying and recommending appropriate asset managers to implement those strategies.

SCOPE OF AUTHORITY:

It is expressly understood that the ultimate authority of the Investment Committee is advisory in nature. The Executive Committee of the Family Office Board has sole authority for making final decisions.

COMPOSITION:

The Committee will consist of not less than four members and no more than six members. At least three members of the Committee will be experienced investment professionals. The Committee will elect its Chairman. The initial term for external members will be one-year renewable for two additional three-year terms. Terms can be extended as needed.

MEETINGS:

The Committee shall meet either by phone or in person four times per year, with additional meetings by phone or videoconference as may be necessary and appropriate to fulfill the responsibilities described below. At least one of the four meetings must be held in person. The Committee Chair will call for the meeting. Minutes will be taken at each meeting and circulated to the IC.

KEY DUTIES AND RESPONSIBILITIES:

To fulfill its purposes, the Committee shall undertake the following:

1. Review and recommend for approval investment philosophy and objectives, policies and procedures, long-term asset allocation targets and ranges.
2. Provide insight on investment strategies and identify and recommend investment managers as needed.
3. Ensure that investment policies and procedures incorporate appropriate risk management benchmarks to track market, liquidity, and other investment risks.
4. Review and approve performance evaluation methodology, including benchmarks, and evaluate investment performance of the portfolio and asset managers at least annually.
5. Review and recommend the valuation policies and the fair values used for monitoring the pricing of investments at least annually.
6. Report to the Family Office Board quarterly and other family enterprise boards on request.
7. Review the IPS considering performance and market conditions at least annually.

(Continued)

8. Review and recommend new investments and exits from existing investments as appropriate, and in line with authority limits.

9. Review the overall budget for the investment function and the fee structure of major service providers and asset managers at least annually.

10. Review the Investment Committee Charter and recommend changes if needed at least annually.

11. Review internal staffing and other investment related needs of the family office.

12. Meet with prospective and existing investment/asset managers and other service providers from time to time

13. Track variances from the approved asset allocation and review management recommendations for any changes in the long-term asset allocation.

CONFLICTS OF INTEREST:

Committee Members should disclose all potential conflicts of interest as soon as they become known and are expected to recuse themselves from any final decisions where they have a conflict of interest or potential personal gain.

COMPENSATION:

Each non-family committee member will receive an annual retainer.

ADDITIONAL ACTIVITIES:

The Committee shall perform any other activity that is consistent with this Charter as considered appropriate.

meeting of each year is usually longer as it covers more discussion on the previous year's performance and the coming year's investment strategy. How time is spent is of great importance to the effectiveness of the investment committee. Also, the role of the IC Chair is critical to the success of the committee. The most effective IC Chair sets out a clear agenda for each meeting, ensures materials have been sent out in advance, and encourages input and discussion from the committee members.

While meeting agendas will vary based on markets and particular circumstances, most meetings will cover these topics as the standard part of the agenda:

1. Investment performance assessment and performance attribution.

2. Macroeconomic assessment and related tactical asset allocation moves.

3. Monitoring compliance with the investment policy statement, especially focusing on risk level, liquidity, asset allocation, currency exposure, and manager sizing and concentration.

4. Assessing the internal investment team and/or external investment advisor's processes (e.g., risk management, manager due diligence, tactical moves).

5. Other topics considered by the investment committee on a less frequent basis include:

- Revisiting the family's goals and objectives and alignment with the investment portfolio processes (e.g., incorporating social impact and responsible investing).
- Reviewing individual asset classes and strategies.
- Assessing internal and external investment advisory/OCIO resources.
- Reviewing investment committee membership, tenure, roles, and meeting process.
- Reviewing investment reporting and communication.
- Assessing the family risk tolerance.[35]

Strategic and Tactical Asset Allocation, Manager Selection, and Investment Monitoring

With goals-based planning in mind, coupled with how the family has crafted its investment policy(s), how then does one derive an asset allocation strategy designed to produce the maximum level of return for any given level of risk tolerance? The strategic asset allocation process refers to the overall macro approach to designing and constructing the family's asset allocation. What are the primary considerations when deriving the strategic asset allocation? Most family offices focus on liquidity, diversification, and risk management considerations in relation to the goals and objectives established by the client to drive the appropriate allocation. These considerations are further informed by the client's risk tolerance, which is often assessed by one's reaction to the worst drawdown scenarios. How would you feel if you lost 10 percent, 20 percent or more than 30 percent of your wealth in a market cycle? This is just one gauge of assessing an individual's risk tolerance, and full analytics and questionnaires are available. Another component to strategic asset allocation is to make sure the portfolio is both balanced and efficient. Oftentimes, family offices utilize capital market assumptions for asset-class returns (on a forward-looking basis), which can materially inform the right strategic asset allocation mix for the client. As mentioned earlier, not all families must fit the model of institutional-type investors, yet they need to create assumptions and an understanding of why they invest the way that they do.

Tactical asset allocation refers to what occurs on a day-to-day basis with investment management and oversight. Another way to conceptualize the tactical asset allocation is to look at it as the incorporation of how the family's views of the current market environment influence how the family makes tactical asset allocation decisions to overweight their strategic targets to equities, or perhaps underweight their neutral target to high-yield bonds. Tactical asset allocation moves are typically described as being 6 to 18 months in duration and are meant to take advantage of an opportunity or mitigate an identified risk seen in the capital markets. What are the tactical steps that support your strategic asset allocation? What sources of information do you utilize, survey, and scan to assess and determine opportunities and to validate asset selections? Why is the tactical underlying process as critical as the overall strategic process? The tactical approach to asset allocation must reflect and mirror the intended goals of the strategic allocation process. It requires rigorous fact-checking and constant monitoring to ascertain the timing to make tactical steps to buy or sell securities, and/or to utilize other instruments such as debt, direct investing, and/or hedge funds.

Manager selection and surveillance is another primary function of the family office.[36] This is the process by which family offices conduct research, front office and back office due diligence, and to understand how managers establish their niche specialty or specific market strategy. Each family office may conduct their research in-house and/or may outsource components of the process. Some family offices develop a niche expertise in one area or type of investing, for example, real estate development, high tech, or biomedical. Other family offices may have a core area of expertise stemming from how the wealth was created in a certain line of business, such as manufacturing. It is critical to understand the quantitative aspects and the qualitative components of each manager, such as his or her investment philosophy, the quality of his or her risk controls and back office operations, and—most importantly—the character of his or her key decision makers. There are a number of ingredients to becoming a successful investment manager, including the manager demonstrating a consistency to their investment approach over numerous market cycles, demonstrating a strategy that over time has provided above-market returns (alpha) and strong back office and front office compliance with all governing agencies. These are the hallmarks of elite managers.

Once the strategic and tactical allocation is in place and the sourcing of investment managers is completed, the ongoing oversight, risk management, and evaluation of the investment process in the family office are critical to the end result. Specifically, the oversight, risk management, and evaluation are continual processes that occur on an ongoing basis for both the managers and the markets. Identifying qualified investment professionals to build, cultivate, and develop the strategic, tactical, and investment due diligence and then to monitor the investments are vital aspects to the risk management of the family office. As discussed in Chapter 9 on talent management, the expense to hire this type of talent can come with a fairly high price tag and more family offices are looking to multi-family offices and other providers to solve for the investment oversight. The following section provides a broader discussion of the role chief investment officer.

CIO Function: In-House Versus Outsourced

The Chief Investment Officer (CIO) role leads the investment function in the family office, taking direction from the key family leader(s), the Chief Executive Officer (CEO), investment committee and/or a board of directors. Depending on the investment governance, sometimes the CIO directs investment decisions and reports back to the family or board; in most cases the CIO makes recommendations to family leadership or a board, who then advises and provides the final say to the investment allocation. Because the CIO's primary responsibility is to maintain and grow the existing wealth, most CIOs operate within guidelines and parameters of how the family prefers to invest, assumptions related to risk, what asset classes to invest, and a clear understanding of lifestyle, liquidity, and tax constraints. Because the family is in the business of staying rich versus getting rich, the CIO is typically operating under guidance that is oriented toward wealth preservation rather than aggressive growth. No family wants to put at significant risk the wealth that may have taken one or possibly several generations of financial investment or business success to acquire in the first place.

The CIO has five distinct functions. The first function is assessing the underlying assets (i.e., operating businesses, limited partnerships, concentrated stock positions, etc.) and how to invest, considering their tax, legal, risk management, and liquidity constraints/requirements. The CIO also translates and deciphers the families' investment objective and philosophy into a disciplined and results-oriented investment strategy. The CIO must interpret and understand the wealth objectives of the family, often influenced by the first-generation wealth-holder, where the wealth may be consolidated. Yet, the family ownership group becomes more complex over generations, and the CIO must discern subfamily investment goals involving multiple beneficiaries, various time horizons, and different expectations for the wealth.

The second function of the CIO is to act as the majordomo for the family office's investments. A majordomo is defined as "a head steward of a large household (as a palace) or a person who speaks, makes arrangements, or takes charge for another; broadly: the person who runs an enterprise." This individual advises at both the strategic and tactical levels. As the majordomo, they are empowered to act on the family's behalf when it comes to investing with the close oversight and involvement of the family. The CIO thinks about the strategic decisions for the investment allocation both short and long term and the potential investment risks associated with various strategies. Many families in the second and third generations see a proliferation of illiquid assets in their portfolio, such as real estate, direct investments, private equity, and/ or business ownership. With a wide array of investments, the CIO must have expertise and knowledge over a variety of asset classes and types.

The third function of the CIO is as the overseer, organizer, and implementer of the investment process. The CIO builds the investment process for the family office investments to also mitigate decision risk. They help articulate the governance process, which is fundamental for its risk controls. They lead the process to identify, select, diversify, and monitor the money managers. Increasingly, family offices utilize outsourced consulting firms that specialize in alternative and other illiquid investments, which can maximize returns for a subset of the family's portfolio. By creating the financial strategy for the family office, the CIO directs the investment policy statement creation, outlines the investment constraints and parameters, and establishes the comparative investment benchmarks. The CIO works in conjunction with the investment committee as well as with the investment research professionals and consultants who conduct the back and front office due diligence on underlying investments. The CIO's success is in large part a function of the effectiveness of the family office investment process, the communication and governance systems, and the underlying investment talent in-house and/or outsourced.

The fourth function of the CIO is to liaise between the investment world and the family. The CIO has the pulse on the markets and is connected to leading money managers that are mandated by the family. Not all family offices expect the CIO to make direct investments in specific equities, for example. Rather, they may be working with several underlying money managers who are experts in a specific investment strategy such as long–short, growth, emerging markets, and subordinated debt, among other sub-strategies. The CIO provides recommendations to tailor and fit the portfolio construction based on the current market environment. Thus, the asset allocation may be conceived by the CIO with inputs on the current market environment or the capital market assumptions. Typically, the family leadership, family board, and/or investment committee will support or challenge these recommendations.

Finally, the CIO has the responsibility of mitigating investment risks for the family office. The risk management function is a critical aspect of their role. In addition, the CIO makes sure the family has a well-diversified investment portfolio of reputable money managers who have proven track records, a lens towards risk mitigation, and integrity in their process. The CIO's approach to the investment process will typically scrutinize, question, and constantly test all assumptions and inputs of the asset allocation model, the portfolio construction, as well as at the manager selection level. The CIO asks investment managers who their clearing firm is, who their legal and accounting counsels are, and who their prime broker is in cases of alternative investment managers. Establishing investment risk metrics and analytics that are monitored routinely will help to surface risks in advance of a major catastrophe. Not all family offices are building a family office structure with in-house investment capabilities, and instead are opting to outsource the chief investment officer function.

As an alternative to building out the investment function in-house, families are increasingly opting for the cost benefit of outsourcing all or a portion of their investment management function. Where attracting and retaining top investment talent is at a premium, one North American family office shared, "It is challenging to attract top talent to our small coastal community. In turn, we outsource a lot. We have a money manager, a relationship manager, and a traditional broker/dealer. We own a variety of stocks, international and municipal debt, and we have invested in a fund. It's all the things that I don't have the expertise to invest in or time to manage. We've been very pleased with the results."[37] See Figure 8.6 from Campden UBS Global Family Office Study that outlines the most frequently investment related activities that are outsourced services.[38]

FIGURE 8.6 Inhouse Versus Outsourced Investment Related Family Office Services

Investment related activities	In-house	Outsourced	Both	% In-house if "Both"
Asset allocation	73%	11%	17%	57%
Risk management	64%	12%	24%	50%
Manager selection/oversight	66%	11%	23%	58%
Private banking	25%	63%	13%	50%
Traditional investment	55%	20%	25%	52%
Alternative investment	58%	14%	28%	52%
Real estate	58%	20%	22%	56%
Investment banking functions (deal sourcing, due diligence, capital structuring, exits)	39%	20%	41%	46%
Financial accounting/reporting	64%	13%	23%	67%
Global custody and integrated investment reporting	24%	52%	24%	59%
FX management	48%	45%	7.1%	45%
Philanthropy	65%	15%	20%	49%

Note: Figures may not total 100% due to rounfing

Source: UBS and Campden Wealth, The Global Family Office Report 2019, © 2019 Campden Wealth Limited, p. 66.

Robert Casey, Editor-in-Chief for the UHNW Institute and long-time family wealth industry observer, notes that outsourced CIOs as a group provide four distinct types of services, though clients do not necessarily use them all. First, they operate as investment consultants, providing high-level advice on investment policy, asset allocation, portfolio construction, and performance analysis. Second, they may function as investment planners, managing liquidity and cash flow needs, doing tax overlay management, and integrating investment strategies with financial planning goals. Third, they often serve as managers of managers, providing manager research, selection, and evaluation. Fourth, they may provide asset management services, often for alternative investment classes and/or pooled investment vehicles. Tom Livergood, Founder and CEO of The Family Wealth Alliance, has shared that the outsourced or external CIO model is a "Scalable Pillar" of family office operations. Tom shares that the first issue is a function of talent. "There remains a gap in top-tier talent at the senior CIO level in the family office space. This talent has migrated to larger firms with more sophisticated investment resources and more elaborate compensation packages. As a result, smaller family offices may retain an outsourced CIO for less than what they could build it in house."[39] The second driver is the cost to scale justification. To truly warrant building a fully integrated investment platform in a family office, most families need at least $1 billion. With the fractionalization of wealth over generations, the erosion of family principal due to inflation, taxes, and the increasing cost of living, more and more family offices are entertaining and assessing when and if they may outsource this key function of the family office. Yet, a primary driver for the growth of the outsourced CIO model is the expense difference in particular for smaller single-family office clients.

What are the asset-based fees for an outsourced CIO? Because multiple providers may consider themselves able to render this service, there are differences between pure investment firms and multi-family offices functioning as an external CIO. For example, rendering the outsourced CIO function becomes less expensive the more assets that are under advisement. An external CIO study found that outsourced CIOs charged on average 73 basis points (bps), or 0.73 percent on assets under management, as compared to a multi-family office who charges on average 85 basis points (bps) for $10 million or less invested. The fee structures decline at various breakpoints, dropping to 53 bps for investment firms and 72 bps for multi-family offices for $10 to $20 million of assets under management. For family offices with larger pools of wealth, the fee structures further declines, dropping to 41 bps for investment firms and 44 bps for multi-family offices for $50 to $100 million of assets under management.[40] With assets in excess of $100 million, most outsourced CIOs are willing to negotiate the fee even further.

Although it has grown more mainstream, there are still several family offices not interested in the outsourced CIO model. These types of single-family offices tend to have a well-established investment process and dedicated investment team of professionals. Family office owners who prefer to be more engaged and directly involved with the oversight, manager selection, and/or investment process may prefer to have these investment professionals dedicated to them in-house. Finally, the family offices who have the scale are not as concerned regarding sustainability of the family office operations compared to those fully integrated single-family offices with under a $100 million who may have more challenges transitioning multiple generations of family owners and maintaining their service offering so it is competitive to outside firms. The outsourced CIO model is not right for all families; however, it is a trend in the investment family office landscape.

Conclusion and Final Thoughts

The family office investment process is complex and unique in every family office circumstance; however, there are certain keys to its success. The first one is to identify goals and determine if they are needs or wants. The second element is to understand the levels of risk, complexity, and pervasive headwinds (taxes, inflation, generational mathematics, etc.) that need to be factored into the approach. The third key is to determine if the investment function is the primary driver of the family office, and thus the capabilities must be built in-house, or if the investment function is solved with an outsourced CIO model. This chapter has provided insights to how the family office may have a unique investment paradigm and does not have to operate by the same rules as its institutional cousins. Further, it provides a perspective on the patient capital opportunity that having a longer time horizon and significantly more capital can provide for a family office. Finally, this chapter outlines the investment function of the family office, including determining investment goals, the role of the investment policy statement, investment governance, the application of goals-based planning, and the strategic and tactical allocation process. There is no one right answer to the family office investment question, but rather a range of opportunities so families may customize their investment platform to their strategic goals and long-term aspirations. Thank you to Kathryn McCarthy, Ian D'Souza, Kevin Morrissey, Michael F. Black, and Bob Casey for their insights shared in this chapter.

Notes

1. This chapter focuses on the unique aspects of the investment process as it relates to the family office; however, it does not provide specific or comprehensive advice or counsel to the fundamental basics of investing, asset allocation, manager selection, back/front office due diligence, asset location, or tax sensitive investment strategies.
2. From an interview with James E. Hughes, 2012.
3. Family Office Exchange, "2019 FOX Investment Survey," Chicago, Illinois, 2019. https://www.familyoffice.com.
4. Correspondence with Ian D'Souza Adjunct Professor of Finance at the Leonard N. Stern School of Business, April 2020.
5. Peter Newcomb, "Family Fortunes," *Forbes* (October 11, 2004).
6. *Forbes* World's Real-Time List of Billionaires as of April 4, 2020 https://www.forbes.com/real-time-billionaires/#5d24ae6c3d78
7. Michael F. Black and Matt DaCosta, How Family Offices are Balancing Increased Cost and Complexity, pg. 1, Fidelity, 2019.
8. Interview with Joe Reilly, consultant and advisor to family offices from Greenwich, CT, April 2020.
9. Lisa Niemeier, family office consultant and former founder of graymatter Strategies, LLC personal correspondence with Kirby Rosplock, 2019.
10. Roger G. Ibbotson and Rex A. Sinquefield, "Stocks, Bonds, and Inflation: Year-by-Year Historic Returns (1926–1974)," *Journal of Business* (January 1976); Ibbotson® SBBI ® 2011 Classic Yearbook: Market Results for Stocks, Bonds, Bills, and Inflation 1926–2010, Morningstar.
11. To examine various compounding interest scenarios, visit www.thecalculator site.com.
12. Correspondence with Ian D'Souza Adjunct Professor of Finance at the Leonard N. Stern School of Business April 2020.
13. Greg Curtis, *Creative Capital: Managing Private Wealth in a Complex World* (Lincoln, NE: iUniverse, 2012), 60.
14. Ibid., 61.
15. Ibid., 62.
16. Ibid., 62.
17. Wendy Spires, Family Office Focus: Efficiency in Accounting and Investment Analysis, pg 5. Family Wealth Report, London UK, 2019.
18. Tom McCullough and Keith Whitaker, *Wealth of Wisdom: The Top 50 Questions Wealthy Families Must Ask* (West Sussex, UK: John Wiley & Sons, 2019), 129.
19. Ibid., 139.
20. Michael F. Black and Matt DaCosta, How Family Offices are Balancing Increased Cost and Complexity, pg. 1, Fidelity, 2019.

21. Kirby Rosplock, *The Complete Direct Investing Handbook: A Guide for Family Offices, Qualified Purchasers, and Accredited Investors* (Hoboken, NJ: John Wiley & Sons, 2017), 122–124.

22. Correspondence with Ian D'Souza Adjunct Professor of Finance at the Leonard N. Stern School of Business April 2020.

23. Campden Research, The Global Family Office Report, pg. 17, Campden Wealth Limited, London UK, 2019.

24. Correspondence with Kathryn M. McCarthy April 2020.

25. Correspondence with Kathryn M. McCarthy, April 2020.

26. Figure was adapted from various sources including Cambridge Associates on Family Governance: Best Practices, memo dated October 13, 2009, and the Family Decision-Making Report produced by Campden Wealth and Morgan Stanley Private Wealth Management, 2016.

27. Michael F. Black and Matt DaCosta, How Family Offices Are Balancing Increased Cost and Complexity, pg. 7, Fidelity, 2019.

28. Jean Brunel, *Integrated Wealth Management: The New Direction for Portfolio Managers,* 2nd ed. (London: Euromoney Books, 2006), 220.

29. Correspondence with Kathryn McCarthy, April 2020.

30. Campden Research, The Global Family Office Report, pg. 72, Campden Wealth Limited, London UK, 2019.

31. The IPS framework is based off the CFA Institute's 2010 publication "Elements of an Investment Policy Statement for Individual Investors" and its approach to IPS construction.

32. 2018 FOX Global investment survey, the use of an Investment Committee Lead to Higher Returns and Satisfaction.

33. Correspondence with Kathryn McCarthy, April 2020.

34. Sample Investment Committee Agenda provided as a template from Kathryn McCarthy, April 2020.

35. Sample agenda for an Investment Committee adapted from the Investment Committee Best Practices, Stan Miranda and Brendan Corcoran, Partners Capital, Second Quarter, 2017.

36. Managers are defined as outside, third-party investment managers hired to implement an investment strategy on behalf of the family.

37. Campden Research, The Global Family Office Report, pg. 64, Campden Wealth Limited, London UK, 2019.

38. Campden Research, The Global Family Office Report, pg. 66, Campden Wealth Limited, London UK, 2019.

39. Personal Correspondence with Tom Livergood, CEO, The Family Wealth Alliance.

40. Ibid., pg. 13.

CHAPTER 9

Family Office Operations and Information Technology

John Rosplock
COO and CFO, Tamarind Partners, Inc.

Robert Kaufold
President and Chief Risk Officer, Cauldera LLC

Operations and information technology are vital components of modern family offices. This chapter reveals insights into operational and technological advancements in the family office realm as they relate to privacy, security, document sharing, back office operations, reporting, and technology. With insights from leading information technology, security, operations, and risk experts, this chapter frames a logic and approach to the due diligence, technology selection, building, and maintaining of a smart family office infrastructure based on the goals and aspirations of the family members it ultimately serves. The chapter concludes with an assessment of operational requirements for the twenty-first-century family office to help them evaluate the level of complexity to help guide family office infrastructure needs.

Family Needs Drive Family Office Systems

The needs of the family should come first as it relates to designing the family office operations and information technology infrastructure. When families guide their family office or external advisors to their goals, an operational infrastructure that provides the best information flow can be designed. This enables the family office to guard against risks to the family's human, intellectual, and financial capital, and enables the family to make thoughtful and timely decisions. Most readers agree with these statements; however, the truth is that many family offices were formed to complete specific tasks related to investments, business, legal, or estate structure needs (i.e., addressing accounting needs, providing bill payment services, tax preparation, or investment management). Form often follows function, which then drives the organizational chart of the family office.

The family office infrastructure and operational needs are typically an afterthought to accomplish and/or accommodate the task(s) at hand. However, what is needed is to create a flexible infrastructure that helps achieve those family objectives in the near-term with the long-term in mind.

This is no easy or inexpensive task. In 2019, the Campden UBS Family Office Report surmised that family offices spend approximately 41 basis points in three operational areas: general advisory, professional services, and administrative activities.[1] These costs include both insourced and outsourced providers and make up about 62 percent of the total costs of the family office. Given the expense, families constantly debate the value of administrative services and seek efficiencies that lead to reduced costs. For many, technology is the answer. However, solely focusing on mitigating operational and administrative costs may inhibit the family office function and providing the core services and information to the family that it needs. Rhona Vogel, CEO and Founder of Vogel Consulting in Milwaukee, an independent, multi-family office firm, shared that "operations, reporting, and planning are at the heart of most family offices—they just don't want to admit it."[2] Other topics, such as investment management, manager due diligence, asset allocation, and wealth transfer planning, will receive a lot more interest at conferences; yet, Vogel observes that most family offices spend most of their time overseeing accounts, managing data feeds, performing accounting oversight, and illustrating account information in a way that is user friendly and instructional to the family. Therefore, it is imperative that a family invest and maintain an operational infrastructure sufficient to handle the transactional volume and data analysis needed to manage family assets, archive family history, and make timely and informed decisions that enhance the human, spiritual, and intellectual assets of the family.

This chapter explains why an efficient, resilient, and adaptive operating and administrative system is crucial to the long-term success of the family it serves. The chapter demonstrates how it can be achieved, especially for families that have engaged in the visioning exercise in Chapter 3. That information is a critical starting point for any family office when considering their operational infrastructure.

Family Office Operations

The life cycle of a family office increasingly becomes more complex overtime; balancing infrastructure, processes, and leadership needs, and family office operation considerations is the challenge. As the complexity increases, the infrastructure and processes must be evaluated and improved upon.

The technology available is continuously being improved, therefore the family office must spend time and resources to keep legacy systems up to date and evaluate newer technology that meets the needs of the family office. To follow are the critical family office operations and functions.

Accounting

As complexity grows, the accounting requirements increase. A key factor in understanding the accounting software is identifying the type of family office model for which the solution is solving. A focus of accounting software is investment accounting. This software automatically pulls data from feeds which create general journal entries into the ledger. Alternatively, accounting software that manages the operations, trusts, and complex partnerships is ideal for families with a focus on operating companies or illiquid assets.

Reporting

In general, there are three categories of reports:

1. *Tax and compliance:* These reports are mandatory to complete but, in many cases, do not provide much value to the strategic planning processes of a family. These reports are typically provided to tax, legal, and accounting advisors on a quarterly basis to ensure compliance. These reports also alert the family to the potential impact that contemplated changes in regulation could have on the family's financial assets.

Examples include:
- Tax returns and related tax return supporting schedules
- Individual partnership accounting statements
- Private foundation supporting schedules to monitor compliance with 5 percent distribution rules
- Political contribution monitoring and reporting

Other than the family and the family office, readers of these reports will include tax advisors, legal advisors, and government and regulatory agencies, as appropriate.

2. *Wealth management planning:* The family should always know where their assets are located (i.e., which bank or custodian), who has the ability to execute transactions on the family's behalf, and who has the ability to speak to advisors on behalf of the family. Operationally speaking, these financial and investment professionals are focused on reviewing transaction activity and show how assets have changed between periods. Various financial and investment reports are prepared at least quarterly but may be prepared more frequently depending on the level of activity and/or the nature of the investment.

   Examples include:
   - Budget versus actual expense analyses
   - Detailed balance sheets by asset geographic location
   - Detailed transaction information summarized by vendor
   - Detailed transaction information by specific investment
   - Annual review of authorized signatories at all financial institutions

   These reports are most important to the family, but also have importance to the trustees and beneficiaries of specific trusts who have fiduciary responsibility for assets in those structures.

3. *Strategic planning and analysis:* These reports aid the strategic planning, showing how assets have performed over periods of time and giving insights into long-range strategy. These reports are often very compelling for the family to benchmark long-term goals and objectives.

   Examples include:
   - Multiple year budget projections, consolidated, by business and respective family
   - Investment review of previous 10-, 5-, 3-, and 1-year periods and projections for future periods, as deemed reasonable
   - Investment expense review, by advisor compared to performance
   - Trust valuation projections for 20, 30, and 50 years
   - Trust and estate projections for each generation
   - Tax expense strategies and projections

Often these reports are very important to the family and family office, but they also hold key information for trustees and beneficiaries as well as investment, legal, and tax advisors.

The next section explores in greater detail three specific operational functions including: financial reporting, data management, and decision archiving.

Financial Reporting

All bank statements, custodian statements, and credit card statements are available for download into most software packages. This has greatly shortened the time it takes to code and enter accounting transactions. Time is taken upfront to develop financial templates used to receive the data from different sources, which are then summarized and coded based on general ledger codes within the applicable accounting system.

But the key to financial reporting is understanding the audience, including members' level of knowledge within a specific area and, most importantly, the format in which they are best able to digest the information presented. Although focusing specifically on family members, there are other groups to consider. These include, but are not limited to:

- *Trustees:* Most families have multiple trusts that have been set up over time. Families have entrusted a trustee to administer the parameters of the trust and be responsible to its beneficiaries. The trustee has a fiduciary responsibility to the beneficiaries of the trust they oversee and therefore should be receiving financial, tax, and investment reports as they pertain to trust assets on a regular basis.
- *Beneficiaries:* The information provided to beneficiaries will vary, depending upon the reporting parameters established in the trust agreement as to when the beneficiary is eligible to receive information regarding the trust. For the purpose of this section, assuming that a beneficiary has been properly trained and prepared to receive trust information, he or she should expect to receive similar information as the trustee with one addition. The family office would be expected to provide expense information to the beneficiaries so that they can analyze their personal spending so as to be able to give the trustee information needed for the calculation of distributions.
- *Investment advisors:* The investment approach for the family office is discussed in greater detail in Chapter 8. For this section, the key information for investment advisors focuses on cash. The family office should provide regular cash projections to the investment advisor to ensure that the family has appropriate liquidity to meet its needs. This information is critical

to the investment advisor, so he or she can plan appropriately and execute transactions in an orderly manner to better preserve the value of the portfolio and avoid selling assets at inappropriate times.

- *Tax advisors:* It is critical that family offices accumulate tax-related information throughout the year and communicate that data to their tax advisors on a timely basis, especially in a complex system. As tax rules continue to evolve, keeping the tax advisor up to speed with the business and investment activities of the family throughout the year can save families a significant amount of capital. Interacting with the tax advisor throughout the year will save time, and therefore expense, during the tax preparation process when the tax advisor's time is at a premium.

- *Legal and insurance advisors:* Families continuously change and, as such, so do the risks to the family. The family office will typically keep in touch with these advisors annually, updating them on changes to the family, new projects, significant purchases, or business ventures so the advisor can build support that best protects the human, intellectual, and financial property of the family.

- *Government and regulatory entities:* Throughout the year, there are many different tax and regulatory filings that need to occur on a timely basis. The family office ensures that the information is collected and reported on a timely basis in the manner prescribed by the specific agency.

Technology is paramount to financial accounting and reporting. It should be noted that there are numerous systems that can be tailored to meet the needs of families. However, before the search for that system starts, it is critical for families to understand the inputs into that system and the desired outputs. These systems are generally expensive (not to mention time consuming) to set up and to maintain, but in the right environment they can yield an immense amount of efficiency. When it comes to data integrity, the old mantra holds true: garbage in equals garbage out. Investing in a sophisticated accounting system will make the family office infrastructure more complex. Therefore, the purpose of that system should be well understood before any system is evaluated.

Data and Decision Archiving

Families of wealth have data management needs that are greater than just reporting on investments and bill pay. Families today also want a repository that can be accessed remotely to manage their personal assets and personal information. Solutions can range from simple cloud-based software like Dropbox to fully customizable software designed specifically to meet the needs of each family member.

The family office has the responsibility of storing the finished product that includes summaries of meetings held, decisions made, and the factors surrounding those decisions. This information should be stored in one place, easily accessed by the family when needed from any location. It is this history that multigenerational families will come to rely upon to make clear decisions as they continue their journey.

Let's consider additional functions of the complex family office both individually and their technology opportunities.

1. The family office actively manages its own assets with possible support from an independent investment advisor. Creating the baseline for broader family wealth management is imperative. In this case, however, since the family is responsible for managing the assets, a technology platform is required to monitor activity and to provide information for the family to make decisions. It is also needed to ensure that important information is received and processed on a timely basis, possibly daily.

   A perfect example is a private equity investment capital call notice. To ensure that the notice is processed in a timely manner, the appropriate family office representative must receive the notice, accumulate cash from the investors in the specific investment, and then forward the cash to the investment entity.

   This may not be as easy as it sounds, as in many cases, the family will set up separate partnership structures to invest in a single private equity investment. In this situation, the family office coordinates with all the members to inform them of their pro-rata share of the capital call and accumulate the funds before forwarding onto the investment company.

   Having a system that allows the family office to quickly understand the investors of a particular investment, the process for them to forward the needed cash, and the timing of the capital call are critical to meet the deadlines imposed by the investment company. It is additionally important to make sure that each investor maintains appropriate liquidity to cover the capital call when it is received.

2. Reviewing trust and estate structures to understand if the system in place supports the family's goal of asset preservation. Due to tax, legal, and regulatory changes, frequently reviewing changes that may impact the family's reporting, archiving, and data management is pivotal.

Efficient family offices may produce two reports on an annual basis. The first is a flow chart that illustrates how family funds flow from the wealth creator to the youngest generation, for example. It shows where estate taxes will be paid and, most importantly for the family, where the financial assets end up after all the planning is executed. This is a very useful tool to remind the family the result of their estate planning.

The second report is a projection. Using a flow-of-funds flowchart, the family office can produce an analysis that shows how the investment strategy will affect the assets over time. This is a very useful tool to look at annually as new information, such as actual spending, will directly impact the portfolio growth projections. This is a helpful report for the senior generations when planning for future distributions to the youngest generations, so they can understand the financial assets that could ultimately be available to those beneficiaries.

These reports take time to produce initially but become valuable annual markers for family discussions surrounding their trust and estate strategies.

3. Managing co-investment structures and strategies. Industrial families such as the Rockefellers and the Phipps saw value in combining assets within the family to make investments. This collaboration allowed the families to make larger direct investments but also spread the financial risk across multiple pools of resources. It also allows for smaller investment pools to participate in investments that they would not necessarily be permitted.

However, this creates technological complexity because all that is combined must be allocated, either for specific financial reporting or for tax reporting. The Phipps family started Bessemer Trust to handle this work (amongst other things). The family may not need to establish as sophisticated an infrastructure but may require a smaller scale system and software to gather the data and complete proper allocations of income, expense, and investment value.

Family Office Management

Global management of the family office and the family is a newer area of technology available. Most of the solutions have been created by a family office or a service provider to provide functionality unique to the needs of a family of wealth and family offices. These solutions focus on managing the lives of the family members, provide access to the family members for decisions through a cloud-based portal or dashboard, and provide a tool to provide seamless communication between the family, family office, and key service providers.

Security

Family offices and families have varying policies and protocols when it comes to security and risk management. Security and risk management has grown exponentially in the digital age, becoming an area of focus especially true for families opting for a virtual family office approach. When speaking to families and key employees most say they have security systems, and everything is fine. The next question is do you have a security plan and manual in place? Almost everyone indicates that they do not know, or they do not need one. Security for a family office is not just protecting the family office data behind firewalls anymore. Security also includes policies and technology to monitor employee behavior, family privacy, and personal security. Solutions are good only if they are used; therefore, policies, protocols, training, and monitoring must occur. Annual audits and risk reviews of the technology and monitoring threats ensure that updates are implemented routinely. Larger family offices may consider hiring an outsourced security officer.

Solutions available to families and family offices to protect against threats are:

- Identity theft and financial fraud monitoring
- Laptop, tablet, and mobile protection
- Password monitors and protection
- Encrypted email and text
- Cyber event monitoring and protection
- Network monitoring, firewalls, and protection
- Social media monitoring

Other Technology

There are several other solutions a family office may want to evaluate including the following list:

- VoIP versus legacy phone systems
- Website hosting versus outsourcing
- Email archiving
- Online scheduling
- Web conferencing
- Payroll administration

- Employee benefits, HR, and insurance
- Concierge and travel
- eSignature
- Project management
- Internal communication solutions

Assessing Operational Complexity

Now that the family office operational functions and technology segments have been discussed, what do you need for family office operations to be successful? First, examining the complexity of a family and their family office is a pertinent exercise. Chapter 6 provides insights to gathering key ownership documentation as well as insights about the family with respect to its human capital, financial capital, legal, enterprise and estate planning, and risk management information. Once complexity is mapped and understood, it is necessary to examine the accumulation of data that supports an efficient and meaningful reporting process and successful operations and promotes collaborative, helpful feedback loops for the family, its family office, and the advisors along the way. How information is organized, coded, and stored in a repository or document storage platform by the family office and made available to all family members, regardless of their location, is imperative to assess.

Complexity is not correlated to the amount of financial wealth. In truth, the size of the financial wealth simply creates the opportunity for complexity. It is up to the family to determine how complex they want their infrastructure to be. Complexity is not an evil to the family office. It was created with good intentions, such as asset preservation, transfers between generations, estate tax mitigation, or protection of family privacy. Its purpose simply needs to be understood so that the operational system built by the family office can provide the compliance, strategic support, and information needed to manage the infrastructure. It is important to begin to understand how complex the family may be. The family office complexity assessment is in Appendix A.

This assessment only begins to lay out the complexity of the family and the needs of the family. It is a tool for the family to begin a discussion of what information needs to be managed and to identify potential weaknesses where expert advisers may help build the family office infrastructure.

This exercise may also reveal that the family office infrastructure needs on the surface seem complex but may not be so. For example, the family may have many investment positions in different asset classes. However, they may have given total investment discretion to an outsourced CIO. In this case, despite the number of investment positions, the system to support the investment function is less complex, as the family needs only to monitor and maintain due diligence on the outsourced CIO, instead of each individual position. However, they are not completely out of the forest, because if each of those investment positions produced tax return documents (i.e., 1099s or K-1s), then complexity reenters the equation. Sometimes, the assessment can provide the ability to understand different approaches to organize the infrastructure needs. For example, if a central repository may be desired, due to the need to confidentially share documents, then exploring systems that have that as a capability to decrease the number of documents being emailed, scanned, or shared may help to decrease complexity.

With the information from the family office complexity assessment, one can begin to understand the operational functions needed to respond to the given level of complexity. Provide a score of 1 for simple, score of 2 for complicated, and score of 3 for complex to each question. If the question is not applicable, score it with a 0. Add up the scores by each section to determine where the family lands within the complexity graph. Use your responses from the complexity assessment to determine which quadrant the family office fits. See Figure 9.1 for the Complexity Graph.

FIGURE 9.1 Complexity Graph

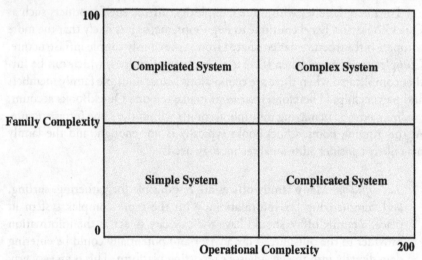

Source: © Tamarind Partners, Inc.

Simple to Complex Systems

In a *simple system* consider an off-the-shelf product, such as QuickBooks, combined with Excel for ad-hoc type reporting, which may be the best option. This approach takes care of the general accounting, bill pay, and family balance sheet construction. It also provides the transaction level detail needed by the tax accountant. It is also going to inform whomever you hire, as most every bookkeeper, accountant, and bill payer has experience with these universal accounting applications.

Off-the-shelf technology, combined with the asset reporting available from the family's private bank or custodian may be sufficient to meet the financial asset, liquidity, and expense reporting needs of the family. Yet, some families may determine that they have specific requirements or needs and prefer to build a more customized system. Customized accounting systems will be discussed a bit more within the more complicated case that follows.

Increased complexity leads to the need for more *complicated systems*. In this case, a family being served may be growing and contemplating work for the second or third generations. External inputs from banks, custodians, or other outside advisors start to creep over fifteen inputs and reporting frequency moves closer to monthly. There are many (but not an overwhelming number of) transactions processed monthly. In this case, a small family office staff supported by outsource providers would be put in place.

For many families with more complexity, off-the-shelf products such as QuickBooks and Excel continue to reign supreme, as it is likely that the more complex infrastructure has emanated from a previously simple infrastructure. Complexity increases when there is an increase of entities, which can be further complicated when there are transactions across multiple family members and partnerships. Therefore, instead of managing one QuickBooks account, you may now be managing multiple accounts within the same infrastructure. At this tipping point, QuickBooks typically is not enough, and the family may likely consider additional technology needs.

1. *Tax software:* Many family offices are responsible for gathering, sorting, and summarizing tax information. With the more complex system in place, a family office should have the capacity to act as the information provider to the outsourced tax advisor and potentially could be entering data directly into the tax advisor's reporting platform. This is an easy way to save the family office some expense, as it typically replaces the work of an associate at the tax firm with internal staff. It also allows the family office to learn more about the tax process so to be better able to provide strategic tax advice during the year.

2. *Investment tracking software:* Depending on the level of involvement, the volume of data, and the frequency of reporting needs, the family may consider investing in tracking software to monitor investment activity, track private equity commitments, as well as the ability to model cash flows for specific investments or asset classes. The absolute key to this decision has to do with the format, quality, and timing of the information that is received from each investment manager and the ease (or complexity) of uploading that information into the software package. Families should seek professional advice here, especially in the more complex infrastructure system, to ensure that software purchased produces the desired results. There are plenty of examples of wasted time and money implementing a system that simply did not produce the anticipated results or the required information.

It is important to note in this instance that costs to update and maintain the software could be significant. And the cost to transition data between systems, if a family were to change their mind, could also be considerable. In short, tread carefully and make sure that you have a firm understanding as to the purpose of the reports, the information desired, and the ongoing support needed to maintain the systems in place.

Some family offices decide to outsource one or more complicated technologies as an alternative option to managing in-house. Many families may not want to manage the reporting infrastructure needed to manage the family's assets. More importantly, families may not know exactly how to build the broader family office technology infrastructure or to hire the people to complete the work. Many multi-family offices provide this core service to families. In this case, the family decides that it does not want to build, maintain, and manage a technology infrastructure or a full-time staff. What is given up in personalized service is rewarded with cost efficiencies while maintaining high-level reporting. For families, this is a very important decision where the right relationship is seen as beneficial to the family as well as the multi-family office. It is important to note that a family's responsibility for oversight and input do not diminish when outsourcing reporting, accounting, bill pay, or other technology solutions. In fact, third-party oversight may be more intense! However, for families transitioning from a simple system to a more complicated system, an outsourced relationship such as multi-family office may be a viable and efficient option to consider.

The *complex system* is one where the family being served has grown to where three generations of the family are utilizing the services of the family office. Trusts that had been previously established begin to make distributions to beneficiaries. External inputs from banks, custodians, or other outside advisors start to creep over 25, reporting frequency moves to monthly with some risk reporting (such as liquidity or information on concentrated asset positions) available daily and real-time. There are a sizeable number of transactions processed daily. Automation, workflows, reporting aggregation and consolidation, analytics, and partnership accounting are required, and even if only one of the items needs customization, the system may migrate from simple to complex.

For a *complex system* to work, a family office must put in place responsible, trusted individuals to act as the data gatherers, interpreters, protectors, thinking partners, aggregators, organizers, and governors to implement and support the technology infrastructure of the family office. Chapter 10 discusses human resourcing, recruiting, and talent management in more depth.

Complex System Technology

There are two focal areas to develop within the *complex system* of a family office. The first is the reporting process that gathers, summarizes, reports, and ultimately archives information for the family. The second is the feedback loop between all parties involved, which are critical to the long-term success of the family. Start by looking at the construction of a reporting process shown in Figure 9.2.

Data accumulation is the start of any reporting process. Start with internal data accumulation by gathering the formation and governance documents of the family. To start to digest the information of a *complex system*, read the documents that govern these entities (such as partnership agreements, trusts, and related tax returns) to understand the activities, ownership, withdrawal rights, and reporting requirements of each instrument. Why are these documents so critical to the family office operations? Typically, within trust documents or operating agreements are corporate and/or familial governance obligations and the rules that provide direction and guidance that help form the family office's operations, reporting, and information management. These legal agreements often have embedded within them the governing principles that the family office needs to operate within.

Once the documents are read and understood, the family office maintains operational compliance with these documents and ensures that tasks required by these established structures are completed in a timely manner. A schedule is maintained to ensure that all documents are reviewed periodically by the family to ensure that the provisions included in these documents are still relevant to the family's activities. Some families continue to coordinate and organize

FIGURE 9.2 Reporting Flowchart

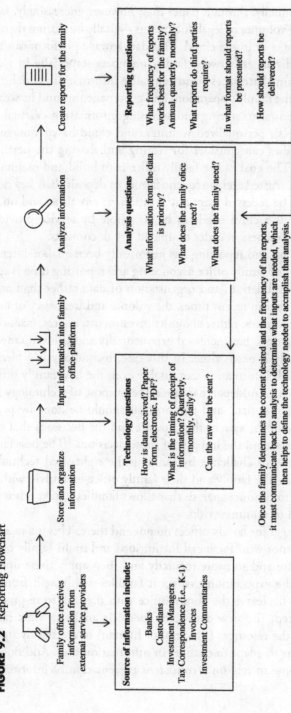

Source of information include:
- Banks
- Custodians
- Investment Managers
- Tax Correspondence (i.e., K-1)
- Invoices
- Investment Commentaries

Family office receives information from external service providers

Store and organize information

Input information into family office platform

Analyze information

Create reports for the family

Technology questions

How is data received? Paper form, electronic, PDF?

What is the timing of receipt of information? Quarterly, monthly, daily?

Can the raw data be sent?

Analysis questions

What information from the data is priority?

What does the family need?

What does the family need?

Reporting questions

What frequency of reports works best for the family? Annual, quarterly, monthly?

What reports do third parties require?

In what format should reports be presented?

How should reports be delivered?

Once the family determines the content desired and the frequency of the reports, it must communicate back to analysis to determine what inputs are needed, which then helps to define the technology needed to accomplish that analysis.

Source: © Tamarind Partners, Inc.

245

these documents manually, through paper files; however, increasingly, families are managing the volumes of legal documents digitally by storing them on virtual private networks or in the cloud. This data storage platform can help families bridge the distances between family members (especially in global families), provide immediate access, and centralize information, which then streamlines some of the family's operations and governance around its wealth.

Technology is central to storing and accessing information. Virtual Private Networks (VPNs), personalized websites, and cloud-based storage are all options that families can consider for storing and sharing the pertinent family information. The goal of the family office is to build and maintain a private, confidential, trusted archive for the family to deposit their key documents that then can be accessed from any location, at any time, and on any device. The document archive needs to be accessible by service providers, select employees, and owners in order to upload key documents.

Data accumulation and reporting has historically been a labor-intensive process. In fact, most of family office accounting and reporting time is spent in accumulation, consolidation, and organization of data rather than actual analysis. Add to this that in recent times, the volume and frequency of information that a family receives, either about its investments, estates, taxes or its human resources practices, has increased exponentially and is instantaneous. However, proper analysis needs time. In this case, technology is a blessing and a curse. Too much information can disable even the best family offices. Joe Lonsdale, Founder of Addepar, has noted the purpose of technology is to gather, sort, and organize data, and that analysis should be done by people who have knowledge of the system they operate and the decisions that need to be made, and understand the impacts of those decisions.[3] The best family offices strive to meet this challenge by building the right-sized technology platform that provides the family and their family office executives with the information needed to conduct analysis that allows families to take advantage of opportunities and to minimize risks.

The data challenges for family offices do not end there. This is a race that the family office cannot win. Financial institutions and multi-family offices update their hardware and software regularly and then apply these updates to all clients, with the expectation that most families will benefit from the improved metrics. This leaves the family office with the task to re-program their systems to accept the new data feeds for their analysis. Most family offices do not have the resources (financial or human) to constantly update their internal systems to adapt to changes in information flow. Additionally, families typically come to rely on a consistent presentation of information.

Therefore, the family office must first interpret changes to the information flow and then integrate them into the reporting process for the family to ensure that key information is presented in a consistent and applicable format.

In order for any systems to be successful over the long term, good feedback loops need to be in place to ensure that information flows freely among the appropriate parties and that changes to the systems, which are inevitable, can be integrated without significant disruption. A communication process to link the family office formally to the family and outside vendors, advisors, and consultants is a critical component of a robust system. (See Figure 9.3 Family Office Feedback Loop.)

FIGURE 9.3 Family Office Feedback Loop

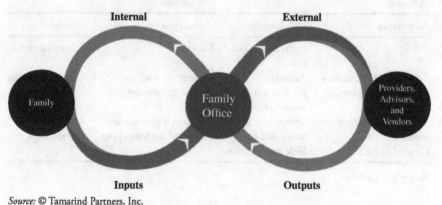

Source: © Tamarind Partners, Inc.

Operations Lens to Insourcing Versus Outsourcing

When a family office decides to utilize information technology, the family first needs to determine who is responsible for completing the technology tasks with respect to the family office. The family has the choice to build the system with inhouse staff within the framework of a family office or to outsource the operating functions.

In most cases, family offices may utilize a mix of internal staff and outsourced support for family office operations. Apart from the largest family offices, internal staff members tend to be generalists, professionals that have a strong working knowledge of finance, accounting, personal services, and philanthropy that can respond to multiple requests from the family. In these cases, internal staff is supplemented by external specialists that provide specific knowledge and expertise as needed. Examples of external experts are tax professionals, investment advisors, insurance providers, and human resource specialists. These external service providers supplement the knowledge of the internal staff while being managed by the internal staff. Their work is impermanent, usually focused on specific tasks or needed insights, and once the knowledge is integrated, the service is no longer necessary. Although impermanent, an external service provider may be engaged for many years, especially in the fields of tax and investment. There are some advantages and disadvantages of insourcing versus outsourcing family office operations and technology. Table 9.1 outlines the advantages and disadvantages.

TABLE 9.1   Insourcing Versus Outsourcing the Family Office Operations

In-house		Outsourced	
Advantages	Disadvantages	Advantages	Disadvantages
Privacy	Human resource cost	Cost	Privacy concerns
Personalized attention— single point of contact	Turnover Having enough redundancy	Continuity with high-quality technology	Canned reporting
Ad-hoc, strategic reports available	Technology maintenance and costs	Potential higher quality personnel for lower price	Multiple client relationships
Control of data	Risk management		

Source: Rob Kaufold

The management of family office staff and external professionals is constant to ensure that value is being received for the price paid for the technology. An external outsource provider example is a technology or systems consultant. This situation would arise if the family decided to implement or improve a technology infrastructure to add services and capabilities to the family, manage, and report on family activities, and maintain the family archives. The review and recommendation of an appropriate system may be outside of the expected scope of an internal staff and therefore would be worthwhile to hire external experts to assess complexity and recommend and install a technology system. This work is ongoing and ever changing; often external consultants train the internal staff to use the system and eventually exit the family office when the technology project is complete. Other examples include completing periodic appraisal evaluations of the family's illiquid assets or assisting with the sale of a family business or significant asset. In all cases, there is a specific expertise needed to execute this technology function that is frequently outside of the regular operational responsibilities of the family office.

Technology Considerations: Buy or Build

Once the family office determines what technology it is trying to solve and who performs the work, the family office needs to scope requirements. Based on the current technological state of the family and the family businesses, it will want to map the preferred infrastructure future state with the new technology. Next, the decision must be made whether to modify the current technology, move forward with new technology, use a combination of old and new technology, or build a custom solution. Most families that have an operating company are already using technology and some may decide to use the same technology for the family office. However, the technology needs to be kept separate between the family office and the family businesses. Deciding who the decision-makers are during the process is important and a family office should not go down a path where users of the technology are excluded from the decision process. Unfortunately, it is common for large organizations to have senior staff make all the decisions without the input and/or participation of the end users or administrators. Another observation is that families who have grown their operating businesses tend to not update their technology to the current versions and/or have technology that has never completely being utilized.

Before a family office can begin to evaluate technology, the family office needs to create a baseline of the current technology being used by the family office and the family businesses. The information gathered is very useful in measuring the improvement of the new system, but the evaluation will also bring to light inefficiencies. The current technology might not be fully utilized or set up correctly, the current database could be set up incorrectly or the data corrupted, and the business processes might not be followed or are non-existent. Sometimes fixing the issues discovered during the baseline process will address the needs of the family office without having to evaluate new technology.

An example is a family who has acquired illiquid assets (real estate, bank, trust company, etc.) over a number of years and, when the overall complexity of the illiquid assets were small, the family did not need to utilize all the features in the technology solution. The family then grew to over 30 companies, and decided to separate the family business from the family and create a family office. The family began the process of looking for technology for the family office that would support the needs of the family, but the family never looked at the current technology as an option since the way the technology was implemented it did not meet the needs of the family. However, after looking at new technology, the family realized that the current technology they had actually performed most of the requirements they needed but was never updated as the family businesses grew, and the family employees were never fully trained on how to use all of the features. In this example, the family needed a document management system and reporting consolidation with analytics. The system could perform these tasks, but the family instead purchased other software to handle these tasks. Hiring a consultant who is an expert with the technology or communicating with the technology provider on a yearly basis is a recommended approach to being aware of new features and updates to any technology.

Family offices that decide to build their own solution can design a system that does exactly what they want but at a high cost, added risk, and timing issues. Most of the technology designed specifically for the family office was created by a family office who then decided to license the technology to other family offices with similar requirements and needs. Understand, if you work with a third-party vendor to build your customized system, it is important to check the contract to understand if they have rights to co-own the new advancements or system that is created. There are cases where vendors will turn around and commercialize the concept spearheaded and paid for by a family office, and then make it proprietary to sell commercially.

New Technology Due Diligence and Onboarding

Understanding the different technologies on the market today is a daunting task for any family office. External resources are best used to help the discovery process by shortening the time to understand the functionality of the technology and can help to reduce the overall cost of the project.

Technology solutions come in two forms which a family must decide between: an all-in-one solution or an à la carte systems design.

À la carte systems allow the family to pick and choose different technology for each requirement, which allows the family to only pick the functionality needed reducing the overall cost. It allows the family to choose a technology that is a leader in the functionality. À la carte systems overall tend to be at an overall lower cost. However, à la carte systems create more risk, require a clear understanding of how the data will flow between the systems, and potentially take longer to onboard.

All-in-one systems will perform collectively all the tasks required and have core functionality that is done above the industry average. Because the system is designed to tackle all aspects, it often does not do anyone of them outstandingly. All-in-one systems tend to allow for third-party applications that can be purchased as an add-on to provide additional functionality. The large systems Salesforce and Microsoft Dynamics each have an application marketplace to purchase add-ons as an example.

Evaluation of Technology

The evaluation process utilized by Tamarind Partners starts with understanding the impetus for the creation of the technology, the system, and underlying software. Answering questions such as: Who created the software? Tamarind breaks this down into three category types: family office, institution, or retail. Technology designed by a family office tends to better serve the needs of a family. Institution designed technology usually is intended for large family offices or corporations and does not tend to cater to the unique needs of the family office. The pricing model, which is discussed later, also tends to be rigid and does not favor the family office and smaller businesses. Retail has one purpose which is to sell mainly off-the-shelf technology and services, such as QuickBooks, which tend to provide less customization. However, retail systems may have third-party add-on applications that ultimately may allow for unique system designs that meet family's needs. Pricing tends to be rigid but is clearly defined upfront.

Pricing models must be clearly understood for each technology. The pricing model falls into four types:

1. *User-based:* Most family office–designed systems tend to price based on the number of users (or seats) who will need access to the system. Each technology provider may have a different definition of a user. Therefore, have each provider clearly define what a "user" is because it can significantly impact the cost. Be aware that most user-based models require a minimum number of users. Some providers offer a tiered pricing structure for users who only view and pull reports versus executing administrative tasks.
2. *Annual license:* Most institutional and retail systems are based on an annual license. A tiered fee structure, usually based on complexity, will determine the overall cost.
3. *AUM-based:* Some institutions base pricing on the amount of liquid and illiquid assets managed by the system. Financial systems commonly use this pricing model.

4. *Purchase:* Very few technology systems still use the purchase-pricing model (one-time purchase). Some systems do, but be careful because these systems tend to charge an annual "maintenance fee" along with additional fees for support.

Other pricing considerations include onboarding and hidden costs. Some all-in-one systems can cost more than two times the annual licensing fee. Hidden costs include customer support services, hosting services, maintenance, upgrades, data services, and the number of data feeds coming into and out of the system.

Besides understanding the pricing model, other important questions to be answered when evaluating technology are:

Business Demographic Questions

- Who owns the technology? How is the business capitalized? For family office–designed technology, understanding who owns what can prevent headaches down the road. For example, a software company created a family office technology platform and then decided to commercialize it. Yet, after being on the market for less than five years, the technology platform was pulled by the original family office from the market as they decided they did not need to commercialize it. The family office had partnered with a private equity company, who made the decision to close the business as the return did not meet expectations.
- Is the business profitable? Is there any debt?
- What is the current number of clients? How is a "client" defined? How many clients are family offices, multi-family offices, and RIAs?
- What is a typical client? Who is the technology designed for?
- How many clients are added annually, typically? How many clients are lost and why?
- What improvements and updates are being implemented and how often are they released? Has the provider sent a development roadmap of updates.
- What is not included in the price? Are there any add-ons available?
- Who owns the data? Can data be used by the provider for any purpose (e.g., provider software analytics, marketing, etc.)?
- Have there been any key personnel turnover?
- How many employees do you have? How many employees work in sales, development, tech services, and support? Where is support services located?
- Who are your major competitors?

- What are your core competencies? What is the software trying to solve? What are the weaknesses of the software?
- What three good and bad things would a client say about you?

Onboarding Questions

- How long is the process?
- What support is provided?
- Are there any added costs?
- Is the software built on another platform (Salesforce, Microsoft, etc.)?
- Ideally, how many people are needed to operate the software?
- Is there a minimum term for a contract?
- What is the process to terminate the contract?

Asking the right questions about the actual technology is very important. Make sure to ask for samples of reports, screenshots, demos, and any other material that may be of help. Depending on the type of family office structure, make sure to ask direct questions regarding each of the following pertinent sections and items. See Appendix B for the Family Office Technology segments.

The process of installing the technology tends to follow the basic steps of a project plan. The software provider should lead the onboarding process, but make sure the technology administrator of the family office is involved with all steps. Utilizing a third-party vendor for onboarding is another alternative. Typically, the onboarding process will take a minimum of six weeks and for more complex systems up to eighteen months to be completely onboarded. Sometimes the process may take longer if there is a high degree of customization or interruptions during the onboarding process.

Onboarding Steps

1. Contracting and service level agreements are negotiated and executed
2. Scope the project
3. Define the current state of the family office and technology
4. Determine the data feeds to be connected to the new system and where the feeds originate
5. Define the legacy data that will need to be imported
6. Configure the system
7. Beta test the system while running the legacy systems in parallel
8. Review and edit the reports

9. Document the operational procedures and create a user manual
10. Train and educate the users of the system

Keys to Success

There are many critical issues, whether operational or technological, that can prevent a solution being successfully implemented. It can only take one oversight or error to undermine the technology solution. One of the most important success factors is the complete buy-in by the family, family leadership, and executives implementing the system. By including the users of the technology early in the vetting, selection, and onboarding process, their knowledge of the day-to-day operations can inform the technology transfer. Taking the necessary time to evaluate the technology and not make a judgment based on one demo, phone call, or presentation is a best practice.

For example, when a family office was evaluating a technology solution and the provider focused on only one aspect of the platform, the family owners were turned off and discounted the software. The provider did not understand the audience of the demo and focused on the data and technical items. The family decided that the solution would not work and refused to entertain another demo from that provider even though the solution was an excellent fit.

Another best practice is determining early who the family office champion is in the sourcing and vetting process. By providing this person actionable authority, not just responsibility, to implement the solution is critical. Making the project a priority and communication of milestones, tasks, and the timeline will prevent the project from stalling, which could delay the launch.

An important key to success is making sure that the technology in a family office is implemented properly with its users fully trained. Taking shortcuts and deciding to add functionality later never works as planned and ultimately costs more in the end. Being transparent with the onboarding team will prevent issues that will slow down the process. Finally, a best practice for ongoing maintenance of technology and systems is to develop an annual technology assessment. To follow are critical operations and technology questions to consider ongoing:

- Is technology supporting or detracting from the family office management?
- What are the current family office technology trends and where are they headed?
- What are the greatest security risks and concerns when it comes to operational oversight and management of the family office?
- What are the key issues when it comes to document management, storage, and distribution for the family?

- What separates the exceptional family office operations from the average? What are the best family offices doing more, better, and differently when it comes to their operations and IT?
- What protocols and procedures or best practices are other family offices doing?
- What is the total cost of ownership and the return on investment of technology?
- How much is the family office willing to spend (both in time and money) on the family's technology platform? How much is the family willing to commit to maintain that system for the long term?

Conclusion and Final Thoughts

This chapter provides context that can help frame operational infrastructure to promote the well-being of the family, support their journey, and give the insight needed to ask the right questions when it comes to creating the most efficient and effective family office system. Several concepts have been introduced that inform the operational and technological solutions for a family and their family office. Evolving a simple fact pattern of a family office to the most complex fact pattern, infrastructure needs will vary depending on the level of known versus anticipated complexity. The primary goal of all systems is to keep the infrastructure as simple as possible without sacrificing control or transparency, while mitigating potential operational conflicts and/or complexities in the future.

Again, infrastructure is driven by complexity, and complexity is a considerable driver in the cost to operate the family office. Families need to understand their own family complexity and information needs before investing in sophisticated systems; otherwise, unnecessary expenses will be incurred. Families must also acknowledge their technological capacity and tailor systems to support the ideal way that a family processes information. The industry-recognized "best system" may not be appropriate to facilitate family conversations, learning, or decision-making. Technology enhances the work of the family office and provides greater levels of control, security, and insight for the family. Given these realities, families must assess their capacity to build and maintain a system. This gets back to a previous point. The constant state of change in technology may be a prohibitive hurdle for all but the most complex families. As such, multi-family office options for some or all of the family office functions may prove more valuable for the less-complex structures. Any infrastructure created will have to adapt eventually to the changing needs of the family, to environmental changes, and to technical advancements that will introduce complexity to even the simplest of systems.

Instead of perfection, the family office's infrastructure and underlying systems should strive to be resilient to best protect the family interests, adapt to its evolving needs, and promote its growth. A family with an efficient, resilient family office infrastructure, and a solid technology plan is a powerful force that sets the groundwork for multigenerational success.

Notes

1. Campden UBS Global Family Office Report, 2019.
2. Correspondence with Rhona Vogel, Founder and CEO of Vogel Consulting, April 2020.
3. From personal correspondence with Joe Lonsdale, Cofounder and Executive Chairman, Addepar, Inc., 2012.

CHAPTER 10

Family Office Talent, Compensation, and Recruitment

Kirby Rosplock, PhD

This chapter focuses on the talent and staff of the family office, and also discusses compensation, recruitment, and human resource management (HR) to align the business strategy and objectives of the family office with HR practices. This means aligning the vision, mission, goals of the family members served, the services offered, and the business operations with the HR strategy. Doing this effectively requires a proactive, hands-on approach to staffing, developing, incenting, rewarding, and retaining your staff. Typically, responsibility for these tasks falls on the family office leadership, versus a human resources manager, which might be found in larger corporations.

Talent management, recruiting, and retention, which are critical for short- and long-term family office establishment, continuity, and performance, have been under-discussed topics in the family office realm. This chapter offers insights on how talent in this evolving market is increasingly valued. In fact, a recent family office study noted increasing compensation for all family office roles.[1] The Morgan Stanley and Botoff Consulting report found that 87 percent of the family offices review and adjust staff compensation annually. Nearly 40 percent of family offices reported salary increases between 4 percent and 10 percent or more, outpacing the national average of 3 percent, with 55 percent of the largest offices (those with $1B+ AUM) granting salary increases greater than 4 percent.[2]

This chapter provides a glimpse into talent management best practices within the family office. Profiling the typical family office professionals and what makes them first class, this chapter also explores key issues related to compensation and identifying, retaining, and incenting personnel. It provides an HR discussion on the keys to employee retention and satisfaction and the importance of performance management. Finally, it shares considerations regarding family and non-family executives at the helm of a family office.

Introduction

Staffing a family office is challenging, as those individuals with experience with more than one family office are limited. Although the precise number of family offices is not known, there are at least 5,000 in the US alone, and Ernst & Young estimates the global population of family offices to be at least 10,000.[3] These numbers would double if you include embedded family offices (those housed within operating companies). Thus, the actual number of professionals who have worked in a family office setting is small relative to those in the wealth, banking, and investment industries.

The professionals who ascend to a leadership rank in the family office are well-seasoned, expert advisors, or consiglieres, in whom families have supreme trust and confidence to manage their complex financial lives. These prized professionals do not typically follow a linear career path; rather, they develop a certain expertise in investments, tax, legal, estate planning, financial planning, accounting, or wealth transfer planning.

Serving the ultra-affluent family in a family office has both opportunities and challenges and is certainly not a predictable work experience. Family office professionals, at their core, often have a service orientation. One family office executive shared, "I know I am a pleaser. I derive great satisfaction from making this right for my family. It is the ultimate mark of success." This desire to serve families is their top priority, and often has prompted them to opt out of commission-based or sales positions in larger financial institutions that traditionally afford higher bonus structures, perks, or incentives.

Most family offices are small with 10 to 15 employees or less, so family office talent also tends to enjoy working in smaller teams. However, family office talent that gravitates to the larger MFOs may also be connected with a financial or banking institution. Those MFO firms with more than $15 billion assets under management (AUM) employ hundreds of professionals; for example, BMO Family Office employs approximately 100+ staff, PNC

Hawthorn Family Wealth employs approximately 200+ professionals, and JTC Private Office has more than 700+ employees, according to their websites. Medium-size MFOs with $5 billion to $15 billion AUM may have far fewer employed, in the neighborhood of 50+ employees. The smaller, boutique MFOs generally employ fewer than 25 employees and typically have less than $1 to $2 billion AUM. MFOs vary considerably in size, depending on their number of clients, assets under management, and whether they utilize a product-driven or an integrated-advice model. Although the MFOs are more visible to the lay consumer due to their marketing and public relations efforts, Robert Casey reports that less than 8 percent of family offices are MFOs.[4] Despite the percentage of multi-family offices being less than 10 percent of the overall family office population, due to the larger institutional multi-family offices, more family office employees have had experiences inside of a multi-family office than a single-family office. Because the formerly closed-door environment of a family office kept its presence under the radar for most investment professionals, the added public awareness from the growth of the sector has resulted in increased interest in the multi-family office field. During interviews with family office recruiters and search firms for this edition of the book, it was revealed that increasing numbers of families have been searching for dedicated, family office professionals who will act as agents, advocates, and even intermediaries for the family. If the scale of the family office does not justify having dedicated individuals in niche specialties, certain business operations (e.g., tax, legal, or compliance) may also be outsourced.

Family Office Staffing

Staffing is moderated by how the family builds and sustains its wealth. Tamarind Partners characterizes two primary archetypes: enterprising families, that grow wealth through operating companies, and investing families, that grow wealth by investing in private and public markets. Once this is determined, the basic family office structure is selected, ranging from a virtual office, where the technical functions of the family office are outsourced; an embedded office (for operating-type families), where resources for carrying out the family office functions are shared with the operating company; or a fully built-out office, where dedicated staff carry out the range family office functions. The chosen structure influences subsequent decisions regarding staffing and the organization chart. (See Figure 10.1.)

FIGURE 10.1   Family Office Orientation

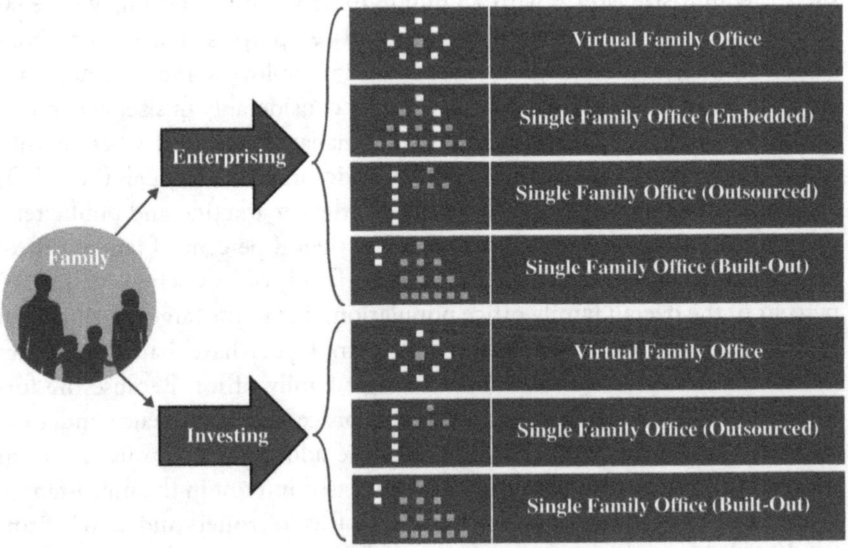

Source: © Tamarind Partners, Inc.

For this reason, the saying goes that if you have seen one family office organizational chart, you have seen one family office organizational chart. No two family offices are structured and staffed in precisely the same way, leading to unique organizational charts from one office to another. What might be key staff in one family office setting may be considered non-essential to another. Smaller family offices may opt for a virtual structure and just one to three personnel such as a bookkeeper, president, and administrator. Many larger, multifaceted families prefer or demand more complex structure tailored to their particular wealth management planning, business, and family goals. For example, if the family administers a number of trusts and partnerships that require significant fiduciary and trust administration, the family office may include more wealth advisory professionals, such as an estate planning attorney, tax accountant, or risk management advisor. An investing-type family may focus its recruiting efforts on attracting family office professionals with investment experience and credentials such as Chartered Financial Analyst (CFA®) or Certified Financial Planner™ (CFP®). Figure 10.2 presents one example of how a medium to large Family Office may set up its organization.

FIGURE 10.2 Sample Single-Family Office Organizational Chart

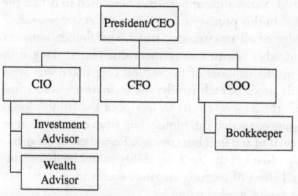

Source: © Tamarind Partners, Inc.

Single-Family Office Organizational Chart

Although there are many possible variations of a family office's organization chart, it is helpful to consider the family office roles that may appear in the various family office organizational structures.

President/CEO

The president or chief executive officer (CEO) is the primary steward of the family's assets and reports to the board of directors, often consisting of family owner shareholders, investment professionals, and/or non-family wealth experts. The president's key responsibilities are to orchestrate the varied family office activities in service of the family's mission and vision. To do so, short-term goals and efficiencies must be achieved while keeping a long-range view of the family, its wealth, and multigenerational goals and objectives. The president is the family's primary representative, providing continuity and stability for the family and holding the family office accountable. Achieving such continuity requires the president to be a versatile change agent, helping the family and family office navigate the inevitable family transitions and consequent human resource management shifts that occur over time, so the family office evolves with the family. For example, the president must anticipate needed technology, human resources, or other changes that allow the office to grow and add new structures to the system without disrupting processes already in place.

To do this, the leadership typically engages in all aspects of the family office and successfully inspires, leads, and oversees the family office employees in their respective tasks. Various metaphors have been used to depict the kind of individual needed in this primary role, such as the *expert generalist*,[5] who has broad knowledge of all investments, trusts, and foundations, tax and estate planning, and other wealth management disciplines, along with in-depth specialization in one or more of the vertical core functional areas depending on the specific needs of each family; the *quarterback,* who coordinates and optimizes all the players' efforts in service of the family's long-term objectives; or the *grasshopper* that can nimbly hop from one situation to another, contributing direction and insight as needed. Regardless of the metaphor used, the leadership often has the uncanny ability to troubleshoot situations, link the cause and effect of seeming disparate events to one another, and rapidly marshal and deploy needed resources.

Accordingly, the CEO needs to be highly experienced, with ample general management, business management, and people management experience—and the good judgment that comes with such experience.[6] Lisa Ryan, executive recruiter and human resource consultant to family offices, offered the guideline that qualified candidates for the CEO position in a family office with at least $250 million in assets should have between 10 and 15 years of experience. Offices with upwards of $500 million in assets should seek candidates with at least 15 years of experience. These recommendations align with recent survey findings from Botoff Consulting and FORGE, which highlighted that 41 percent of non-family CEOs and 65 percent of family member CEOs had more than 10 years tenure in their roles.[7]

Particular knowledge, skills, and abilities needed in these professions include knowledge of the disciplines of wealth management, tax, financial management and reporting, investments, foundations and philanthropy, trust and estate planning, and risk management as well as awareness of how these disciplines interact; knowledge and competencies related to family dynamics, such as the ability to facilitate critical family discussions, engage multiple family members and generations, and educate and motivate the younger generation; and strong leadership, communication, and execution skills.

The qualifications needed in the CEO of one office will vary from office to office based on culture, style, offering, and type of office. For example, some offices will need a CEO with deep financial, accounting, or legal background, with less emphasis on specific business segment or sector. Family offices created by individuals with finance backgrounds frequently opt for CFO-type CEOs with strong competencies in cash flow, business management, and accounting, personal accounting, partnership, and LLP interests as well as estate planning.[8] Furthermore, the right CEO for a family office that runs multiple operating businesses likely would not be the right CEO for a family office that invests primarily in public markets.[9] This emphasizes the importance of tailored recruiting practices for key roles in the family office—particularly given the challenges of determining how much experience and what qualifications the executive for any particular office needs. While the ideal CEO candidate has had multiple experiences, their career path can vary. While some start as a tax CPA, others start as attorneys or other wealth management staff, then broadening their knowledge by working in progressive leadership capacities. A helpful rule of thumb is that as the size of a family's asset base grows over time, so do the number of entities and typically the size of the family tree. To handle this high level of complexity, strong judgment and experience are necessary qualities in the family office chief executive.

Chief Investment Officer

Another senior position in a family office is the chief investment officer (CIO). The CIO plays a critical role in establishing the investment process, philosophy, standards, goals, and objectives for the family office. Although some family offices adopt an aggressive investment mandate, most CIOs focus on wealth preservation through modest but respectable annual investment performance that yields sufficient returns to family investors after taxes, depreciation, and amortization of the assets.

Given this chief mandate, the CIO is responsible for designing and executing an investment plan guided by the family's investment policy statement. As part of this, the CIO monitors known, family-accepted concentrations in entity ownership, industry sectors, and/or geographic regions; oversees governance process regarding which investments fit into the overall family office investment strategy; and challenges the family to evaluate other options and directions when warranted.

The CIO also is a central figure in sourcing and vetting quality deals and investment opportunities, harvested from relationships of trust.[10] The CIO often calculates wealth projections based on the assets under management to help the family assess its liquidity needs, manage its trust and estate plan, and prepare for tax payments. The CIO must understand, evaluate, and interpret the short-term volatility and global market conditions with a long-term investment horizon and provide investment performance data to the family. They also coordinate investment performance accountability by wealth managers within and outside the family.

CIOs may also provide proactive risk management, including identifying and mitigating investment risks as well as communicating them regularly to family and weighing in heavily on the asset allocation strategy as a function of the risk/return profile for the portfolio. During this work, they interface and communicate with multiple generations of family members, family office staff, and outside advisors.

This broad range of responsibilities requires them to be capable and competent in a variety of investment functions. As a foundation, they must possess generalist finance skills and understand the broader macroeconomics of the marketplace along with microeconomics of specific investments, such as commodities or futures. Accordingly, the CIO typically has a keen strategic and tactical understanding of investment diversification, asset allocation, and portfolio management and an insatiable appetite for investment due diligence. CIOs typically have 20 or more years of progressive experience in the investment industry, and most have either advanced degrees or professional certifications. Survey findings from Botoff Consulting and FORGE reported that 81 percent of CIOs have an MBA and 42 percent have CFA® designations.[11] Specialized knowledge in the family's most relevant investment areas (e.g., impact investing, specific industry, or stage-based direct investing) may not be required, but it is often a key leverage point for this role.[12]

Additional specific qualifications and responsibilities for CIOs vary based on whether the SFO predominantly allocates to managers or engages in direct investing itself. In allocator-type family offices, the CIO needs to be, first and foremost, excellent at planning, organizing, sourcing, due diligence, monitoring, and validating and reporting on all investment activities. The CIO needs to source best-in-class money managers who execute the actual investing of a particular allocation, such as cash management, bonds, equities, real estate, and commodities. In addition to (or instead of) traditional long-only managers, alternative investment managers may be selected for a given allocation to add shorting, leverage, and derivative strategies. Meanwhile, CIOs of direct investing-type family offices need significant direct investment expertise and an extensive network for sourcing unique deals.[13]

Chief Financial Officer

The chief financial officer (CFO) is responsible for establishing and overseeing systems, processes, and procedures to ensure the effective and efficient operation of the family office financial functions. Domains of responsibility include income tax strategy, planning, and compliance; investment analysis, tracking, and performance reporting; estate planning and legal services; cash management, forecasting, budgeting, and financial reporting; foundation administration; trust and estate administration; and insurance and risk management.

In addition to managing the tax-related concerns of the family office, the CFO is also responsible for the family members' personal tax issues and returns (including family trusts and partnerships). This often includes coordination with the family's in-house or external legal counsel and with the CIO to understand and link the investment strategy to tax planning. In certain nuanced tax planning circumstances, the CFO will outsource to and coordinate with appropriate tax and accounting advice.

The CFO also is responsible for establishing a robust reporting system that provides ongoing oversight and control of capital and then communicating vital financial information (e.g., financial statements, net worth analyses, cap tables) to family members and other key stakeholders who may not have a finance background. The CFO also may provide financial education to next-generation family members as well as manage liquidity of various entities, such as bill paying for the family office and the family, managing lines of credit, issuing business and family loans, and making cash distributions to family members also fall within the CFO's responsibilities.[14]

Other special roles carried out by the CFO include developing and tracking Key Performance Indicators, monitoring financial accountability, acting as the family's primary risk officer, and assisting in evaluating business and real estate opportunities for the family.[15] One CFO of a family office shared, "Our role as CFO provides the coordination and planning of the financial planning for the macro lens. We can drill down and advise on a project, investment, or trust perspective, but can help a family understand where they are relative to where they are trying to get to go."

To successfully carry out these roles, the CFO should possess generalist knowledge in multiple relevant areas, such as investments and legal (not under the primary purview of this role), in addition to specialized knowledge in accounting areas, such as transactional accounting, budgeting/forecasting, complex multigenerational estate planning and financial planning, taxation, and financial reporting. Traditionally, CFO candidates have a strong combination of business and personal accounting background, as well as CFO experience in a successful private company.[16] As with family office CEOs and CIOs, research shows that CFOs also have strong educational and professional backgrounds, as 81 percent reported having an MBA and 86 percent with a CPA.[17]

A CFO is essential for families with substantial business interests and/or significant personal, trust, and partnership accounting requirements. The CFO reports directly to the president; however, if there is no CFO, the CEO may carry out the responsibilities described in this section, possibly with the assistance of data from internal staff (e.g., CIO, bookkeeper, accountant) and external providers.

Chief Operations Officer

The chief operations officer (COO) is responsible for all the operational oversight of the family office. This individual keeps vigilant oversight of the infrastructure, systems, and operational processes. From accounting oversight to compliance and regulatory concerns, depending on the scale and complexity of the family office operations, the COO may wear several different hats. These include head of IT, security, front- and back-office operations, and senior counsel in charge of reviewing contracts, agreements, and partnership documents in addition to overseeing risk management protocols. The COO oversees reporting and reconciliations and often may oversee aspects of compliance and regulatory issues. COOs must be hands-on and integrally involved in the management of the inner workings of the family office. The COO is focused on data management—from how it is accessed and by whom to how it is gathered, stored securely, and managed over the long term. COOs are students of operational risks and often work integrally with compliance and/or risk advisors.

Investment Advisor

The investment advisor is both a technician and a relationship manager with hands-on advisement to the family. This individual often has one or more designations such as Chartered Financial Analyst (CFA®), Certified Investment Management Analyst (CIMA), or Chartered Investment Counselor (CIC). The investment advisor works closely with the CIO on the investment approach of the family office and then translates it into the specific needs and allocations for each underlying family. Investment advisors provide investment advice, management, and oversight to all the investment aspects of each family client. They are concerned with the risk profile of their client, tailoring the investment policy statements and understanding liquidity needs and tax implications. They are also focused on understanding liquidity and cash flow needs and the timing of those cash outlays.

Tax Accountant and Bookkeeper

The tax accountant will organize and maintain oversight of the tax documentation (K-1s) required for preparation in filing annual tax returns. The bookkeeper will maintain daily general ledgers to make sure that all the accounts balance and are reconciled daily. Bookkeepers also monitor capital inflows and outflows to make sure accounts balance. Both roles are critical to the high functioning family office. Some family offices may outsource one or both functions, although it is not uncommon to see both roles managed internally in a larger, more complex family office.

Wealth Advisor

The wealth advisor is an expert in tax, estate planning, and accounting. Wealth advisors may have designations such as Certified Financial Planner (CFP®) or Chartered Financial Consultant (ChFC). Wealth advisors will inform the family on matters of wealth transfer, estate planning, fiduciary concerns, taxes, and multigenerational wealth management planning. They work closely with the investment advisor to execute strategic planning that is complementary to the investment and portfolio management. They often are the liaison to work with risk management specialists and insurance advisors for matters such as life insurance, asset protection, loss mitigation, property and casualty insurance, among other insurance products and strategies.

Gender and Family Office Executives

Although women comprise 44.7 percent of the employee population in S&P 500 companies and receive more college and advanced degrees in developed countries than men, significant gender disparities remain with regard to pay and advancement, particularly in senior leadership roles.[18] Women held less than a quarter (24 percent) of senior roles across the world in 2018, a decrease from 25 percent in 2017.

Similarly, although one-third of reported family office executives are female, fewer women occupy CEO and CIO roles—26 percent and 18 percent, respectively. The mix of male/female executives is closely balanced in the CFO and COO roles. In all roles except COO, the percentage of females in executive roles decreases significantly if they are family members. For example, a recent study noted that only 6 percent of CIOs and 17 percent of CEOs are female family members.[19] Closing the leadership gender gap is hopefully an area due for course correction in the coming decades for the family office as more women are given the nod to step up.

I have personally had an opportunity to work with several rising generation women family office owners and operators stepping into their power in a leadership capacity. One of the greatest challenges these women face is common for any career executive woman—balancing the desire to start a family, perhaps get an advanced degree, hone their professional skills, and staying loyal to the needs of their family. The family office domain, on one hand, may provide more flexibility, virtual opportunities, autonomy, and advancement opportunities for women now and in the future. It also has historically been more dominated by men, and less welcoming to new entrants. The opportunity for gender to refresh and reinvent leadership norms in the family office is today's reality. A recent conversation with a family patriarch reinforced this shift. He shared that his family unanimously agreed that seeking a credentialed, seasoned, and experienced woman CEO for the family office was a priority to them. More and more, women are being invited to the family office boardroom or to the C-suite.

Recruiting Family Office Talent

The success of a family office ultimately hinges upon the expert professionals who serve the family. However, recruiting this talent is challenging, as there is no formal training ground for family office professionals and the needs vary so greatly from one family office to another.

While some families may initially try to find the talent on their own or grow their own talent, Linda Mack, founder of the executive search firm Mack International, warns that this can be a costly gamble, as principals often struggle to find or fail to uncover the best candidates for their situation. Therefore, many other families retain specialized recruiters who focus on placing top-tier, senior-level professionals, especially for the key roles of CEO, CIO, CFO, and COO.

One seasoned executive recruiter shared that it can be quite difficult to assess whether executive candidates have the judgment required to handle the unknown and unexpected issues that regularly surface in family offices. Experience in years is an inadequate metric. Instead, a deep understanding of the nuances of each candidate's background and experience must be developed. The executive recruiter admitted, "I have erred in thinking that an individual did not have enough experience for a role, and I have erred in thinking someone was 'too seasoned' for a role. Once, I was concerned about placing an individual with 17 years of experience as the CEO of a multi-billion, multigenerational family office. He had started his career in tax accounting and had then run the family office operations for a multigenerational, business-owning family. Although he was young, he was an old soul due to his personal background, and he was mature beyond his years." This individual ultimately was hired for the CEO role and reportedly has been extremely successful.[20]

Tamarind Partners advises that successfully attracting and later retaining family office talent begins with robust human resource management practices, including the development of appropriate job descriptions; management, compensation, and reporting structures; performance management systems; and onboarding, development, and advancement opportunities.[21] Before one even gets to the point of recruiting, a family has to understand and define roles, shaping how the associated functions and outcomes will help the office do more, better, or differently. Is it a new hire for a new role? An expanded hire of a prior role? Or is it a role that combines multiple roles?

Linda Mack shared that she utilizes a 360-degree approach to create family office staff roles and job descriptions. Not only does she solicit the input of the internal and external family and non-family stakeholders with whom the candidate would interact, but she also conducts an in-depth study of a family's needs, objectives, values, and culture. These data points are used to compose the position and ideal candidate profile. Mack looks to determine if there is clarity, consensus, and alignment regarding the position and ideal candidate profile.[22]

Management, compensation, and reporting structures should reflect open door policies; defined operating norms; reporting hierarchies and career tracks; and strong alignment between roles, responsibilities, and compensation. Creative compensation options rather than simply more money also should be considered.

New hires should be educated and onboarded to the unique culture of the family and the family office. An employee handbook should be created and regularly updated to reflect the needs and norms of the SFO. Performance management systems should be used to track and reward staff performance. Moreover, family office staff—particularly entry- and mid-level staff—need to have opportunities for professional development, cross training, and advancement.

Finding a Good Chemistry and Culture Fit

Once a short list of qualified candidates is created through initial screening for background and competencies, the interview and vetting portion of the process begins. It is critical for family office candidates—particularly those in leadership roles and advisory capacities—to interview with the key executives and family members as well as by the outside providers, service teams, and/or institutions that they will interface. Remember—even if the individual has all the talent, experience, and acumen in the world, no amount of training or coaching can compensate for the relational aspect. Cautionary tales abound regarding how highly qualified family office executives' effectiveness is thwarted in the absence of strong connection and rapport with the individual family members.

Family office executive search professionals, like M. J. Rankin and others, emphasize that chemistry fit with the family is pivotal to the family office professional's success, as their technical and industry qualifications are givens at this level.

The following story illustrates how chemistry fit and culture were important factors when being considered for a family office leadership role.

Anne Etheridge had experience in fundraising and philanthropy and dreamed of the chance of working for a family office with a family foundation with similar values to her own. One day in 1990, an anonymous advertisement in the *Los Angeles Times* caught her eye:

> Seeking manager, family office, philanthropy. Send resume to S. Lee, P.O.
> Box 423, Los Angeles, CA

Skeptical but intrigued, Etheridge applied. She soon received a boilerplate response with a lengthy questionnaire, which she also completed hesitantly. A few weeks later, she was summoned to a meeting to her pleasant surprise with a Mr. Peter Norton, who told Etheridge he was selling his technology firm and needed to establish a family office to manage his newly established wealth. He and his wife also had a nascent family foundation.

The interview proceeded with a collection of seemingly odd questions, such as "Do you have a dog, and would you bring the dog to the office?" "Can you drive a manual (stick shift) car?" "Did you grow up on a farm?" The wisdom of these questions became evident to her only later: Bringing her dog to work suggested she could be available for long hours, as needed. Mr. Norton theorized that people who learned to drive the more difficult manual (versus automatic) transmissions were enterprising and open to learning. (Practically speaking, they also would be able to drive Mr. Norton's Ferrari to the auto shop when needed.) Mr. Norton further speculated that individuals who were raised on a farm possessed self-confidence and self-reliance. A subsequent conversation with Mr. Norton's wife similarly focused on her character, interests, passions, how she spent her free time, and what mattered most to her. Yet at no time did they discuss her technical or managerial qualifications! Upon conclusion of these discussions, Mr. Norton told Etheridge he would let her know in the coming days with a response. Three hours later, Etheridge was hired. Before agreeing to the role, she returned to craft the specific terms and responsibilities of the role and her compensation.

Perhaps Etheridge's story is one of a kind, but I suspect not. Many wealth creators are highly private and want to interview numerous candidates to find the right one. What gave Etheridge a leg up over the 250 other applicants for the job? She possessed traits and attitudes the Nortons valued, including being a self-starter, practical, experienced, philanthropic, authentic, direct, mission driven, and interpersonally adept. Yet it required in-depth conversations for all parties to gauge fit. Etheridge has since retired from being director of the Norton family office, but her unique hiring is telling of how nuanced family office recruiting and onboarding into a family office may be.

Although many family offices seek to gauge chemistry and culture fit using handwriting analysis or psychological testing such as Keirsey Bates or Myers Briggs Type Indicator, it is important to be aware that such assessments may lead to a damaging or misleading label that overshadows the individual's true fit in the organization. Psychological profiling assessments, albeit useful, are best employed in the later stages of the search and to affirm aspects of the individual's style and personality. Finally, although good fit is critical to staff effectiveness, it also can help family offices avoid costly turnover. Low turnover means employees tend to develop deep experience, loyalty, and strong working relationships with one- or two-family offices, although it can come at the cost of broader industry-wide experience. Family office compensation research reflects this stability, as a study found that turnover in senior family office roles appears to be relatively low, with 41 percent of family offices reporting CEO tenure of more than 10 years.[23]

Background Checks

The final critical ingredient to any recruiting process is candidate background checking. Risk management and safekeeping the family's assets, records, reputation, and well-being are key responsibilities of the family office. Because employees will have access to potentially very private and confidential information, the importance of conducting thorough background checks on your employees cannot be overstated. In addition to criminal background checks, financial screening and/or credit checks are often common. A family office may ask a candidate to openly and voluntarily agree to a pre-hire drug testing, too. Pre-screening by the family office's legal representatives, trustees, or fiduciaries is quite common, so do not take it as an insult if you are asked. Executive recruiters rarely are part of the background checks, as typically more advanced screening is requested as a candidate is in the final consideration phase.

Compensation

Family office talent comes at a cost because these are prized individuals regardless if they are C-suite or at an analyst level. There is a myriad of risks associated with hiring an individual who is underqualified with the hope he or she may grow into the position. Appropriate compensation is a critical, strategic tool that families employ to enhance family office operational and performance alignment.

Family office compensation for CEOs and CIOs in the family office varies based on the nature, size, and scope of the family office as well as how the family envisions working with a family office professional. For example, based on limited market data from published compensation research, CEOs of small family offices command $300,000–$600,000, while CEOs of larger family offices (or of small-family offices with a more complex fact pattern) earn $500,000–$3,000,000, inclusive of base salary, short- and long-term incentive bonuses, deferred compensation, and, possibly, co-investing opportunities. Because family offices are competing for top talent with global institutions, they must have compensation plans capable of attracting, retaining, and motivating these individuals, indicating that compensation should receive ongoing attention.[24] Accordingly, almost all family offices awarded base salary increases for 2019, with nearly 40 percent of family offices reporting increases that outpaced the national average.[25]

In general, executive compensation packages are determined by their position (i.e., strategic versus operational) and the defined role's focus (i.e., investment, operations, acquisitions, administration). Perhaps most importantly, compensation is guided and influenced by the family's principles and values, and by each family office's goals (i.e., to maximize investments, acquisitions, or private equity). Thus, CEO compensation can vary widely from office to office, and this is reflected in some of the variances in compensation reported by research organizations:

- *CEOs:* A limited-scope, global research study indicated that average CEO base salary worldwide was $335,000, a 3.7 percent increase from 2018. Average bonus is 48 percent, yielding a total compensation of $496,000.[26] A similar industry study reports compensation figures based on 491 executives of 323 US family office firms they surveyed. In the 2019 Botoff Consulting and FORGE survey, average base salary for CEOs was $442,943, although compensation for executives increases as AUM increases, especially from a total direct compensation perspective. This study reported base salaries averaging $1.26 million (in the ninetieth percentile) for CEOs of firms with at least $1 billion AUM, compared to $440,000 for CEOs of firms with less than $100 million AUM. [27]

- *CIOs:* A global research report indicates that average CIO base salary is $266,000 ($399,000 including bonuses).[28] Similarly, another study reported a CIO salary range of $250,000–500,000, while another industry report indicated an average base CIO salary of $420,415. Due to the nature of the underlying assets managed by CIOs, the bonus structures for CIOs vary greatly. While allocator CIO bonuses average $200,000–600,000, direct investor CIO bonuses and deferred compensation from incentive allocations in deals they source can yield total compensation upwards of several million dollars. Both CIO types may have co-investing opportunities with the family.[29] Furthermore, it should be noted that most family offices hiring in-house CIOs are typically building an investment platform for assets in excess of a billion dollars. The price tag to hire this elite talent is not for the faint of heart. These seasoned professionals can command a base salary starting typically at $500,000 and go far north of a few million in certain cases. This cost often can seem nominal to families investing a billion dollars, as it comes with the leadership of an investment sage in a league of his or her own.
- *COOs:* A global research report indicates that the average CFO base salaries are $213,000, and $277,000 including bonuses;[30] whereas, another published compensation report indicated a higher COO average salary of $379,369. [31]
- *CFOs:* A global research report indicates that the average CFO base salaries are $208,000 ($275,000 including bonuses).[32] Other reports indicate a similar base salary range of $175,000 to $250,000, with total compensation (i.e., base plus short- and long-term bonuses, deferred compensation, and possibly co-investing opportunities) ranging from $300,000 to $550,000.[33] Another industry report found higher base salaries in their research, reporting an average salary of $277,953 for CFOs.

While this section cites total compensation with bonuses based on role associated with their function, it is important to note that bonuses in family offices often are discretionary. Over half of global respondents characterized their team members' bonuses as discretionary, compared to just 9.0%–15% describing them as formulaic. Nevertheless, family offices appear to be increasingly using discretionary bonuses. In UBS/Campden research, 44 percent of surveyed CEOs and 35 percent of CIOs received a discretionary bonus this year, compared to only 32 percent and 20 percent, respectively, of those surveyed last year. Other tactics include a mixed approach, whereby the bonus is an amalgamation of both discretion and formulaic targets or proportional profit sharing.[34]

A final takeaway is that whatever the compensation structure, it must align with the role, function, and scope of responsibilities for the professional. One example of this phenomenon occurred when a family office failed to align compensation of an executive as its family office mandate shifted. The principal had built the wealth through direct investing with the aid of a gregarious executive team. He decides to move from an active, direct investing strategy and fully built-out structure to a more passive preservation strategy and managed account strategy with outside providers. Over time, the founder desired to work out many of his private equity positions by redeploying that capital into more conservative investment strategies that did not require such active management. This dramatic shift meant that the focus, nature, and scope of executives' roles, particularly for his CIO, were changing dramatically—namely, the family no longer needed strong subject matter expertise on investment banking, deal sourcing, vetting, structuring, monitoring, and execution of direct deals. Instead, it needed an expert generalist who could wear several hats, who could identify and select investment managers, consider the investment strategy, diversification, and portfolio allocation, and sit on the investment committee, and whose compensation package was based less on incentive with co-investment opportunities and more on salary. Tamarind Partners supported the client as they retooled their office and their service offering, and also offboarded their long-time executive in a respectful manner. Reworking the job description, and right-sizing the compensation package, Tamarind Partners then directed the client to several recruiters to interview and ultimately select to conduct a search for their next family office leader. Fast-forward: The founder was able to make a major transition from operator, board participant, wealth creator, and manager to focusing his time on his family, philanthropy, his civic duties, and personal hobbies. An expert generalist-type leader was eventually identified to help the family office transition, meaning many of his direct investments were divested. Now the family office is more focused to serve both first and second generations of the family and their growing philanthropic and foundation endeavors.

Methods for Determining Annual Incentives

Most family offices awarded discretionary bonuses to their employees for 2018, although a growing shift to formalized annual incentive plans is evident. Half of family offices reported the use of long-term incentives for their executives, with a majority of those using either one or two types of long-term incentive (LTI) plans. Although some experts warn that incentivizing professionals in a variable manner can lead to excessive risk-taking with investment portfolios, other families contend that investment performance is one of the few ways for investment professionals to really demonstrate their value. Overall, family offices have reported that co-investment opportunity and deferred bonus/incentive compensation are the most prominent vehicles used for long-term incentive plans.[35] LTI plans are growing in popularity and are used for a variety of reasons, such as attracting top candidates and building engagement and retention among existing staff. LTIs include phantom equity, supplemental deferred compensation (for CEOs and CFOs), co-investing opportunities (for CEOs, CIOs, and COOs), carried interest (for CIOs), and transaction bonuses (for CEOs, CFOs, and COOs).

Roughly 80 percent of family offices provide annual bonuses, and 42 percent pay annual incentives.[36] These incentive strategies tend to be most popular in offices with AUM of $1 billion or more. In other words, the more AUM, the more employees, and the more likelihood of a structured compensation process with less variability in timing and awarding of incentives. Furthermore, nearly 30 percent of all family offices reported they paid higher incentive amounts than the previous year, indicating either that family office staff are meeting or exceeding annual goals or that family offices are increasing the competitiveness of their compensation—or both.

It is important to note, however, that the wide use of discretionary bonuses suggests that less than half the family offices surveyed align their incentive programs with best practices regarding use of a formalized plan or a mix of discretionary decision-making and a formalized plan. Botoff Consulting founder Trish Botoff noted, "As the industry matures, we have seen executive compensation practices become more sophisticated, with greater SFO adoption of structured incentive plans that can enable family offices to better drive performance and enhance the vital alignment between the family and family office's strategy."[37]

Botoff offers the following guidelines for creating structured incentive plans:

- Select the roles that will participate in an incentive plan.
- Define the incentive opportunity (usually as a percentage of base salary).
- Identify the performance categories that will be evaluated for incentive determination.
- Create the performance targets and expectations for threshold, target, and maximum payout levels. Care should be taken to align these metrics with the family's strategic direction.
- Determine the performance period that will be assessed and the payout timing.

Managing Family Office Talent

After the perfect candidates are hired, and are on your payroll, how do you ensure they are successful? Let us imagine that your new employees are settling in nicely and appear to be working well with their peers and the family. Now, fast-forward six months into the future and some hiccup arises. You look back and realize that you really had not established clear reporting hierarchy expectations, had no onboarding plan, and had not outlined the role or set performance metrics or performance goals. To follow are four human resource management areas that may help a family office avoid such pitfalls.

Role Clarity and Job Description

Providing family office personnel with a clear understanding of their roles and functions is a necessity. Creating a document that outlines the scope of the role, its function, and a general description of the tasks associated with the position will provide necessary boundaries for the position. It can assist in clarifying what the role responsibilities and performance objectives are. It identifies the areas where the individual has control and authority and may also identify what areas the individual is in a supporting, collaborative role and is a resource to others. It may also identify what percentage of time should be allocated to different functions. Revisiting the job description annually should be a part of the performance management discussion as the job description can also help identify how and if the role is evolving and changing. Further, this review can identify development areas for further education, training, or skill-base building. Having role clarity and an established job description can be an instrumental material in the ongoing performance management of family office employees.

Reporting Hierarchy and Authority

Employees who have a clear understanding of the chain of command and respect the hierarchy are going to be more successful. As most family offices have smaller organizational charts, new employees, especially those who are higher in status, need to know who reports to them and who they report to. Often the family client may be who they serve, but a functional manager is who determines the employee's performance and evaluates their growth, development, and success. When family is wearing multiple hats as owner, client, and manager, the clarification around hierarchy, authority, and the reporting structure is even more imperative. Further, employees need to be provided with their boundaries: Some will have a wide latitude and access to client information, while others may only have access to specific records, reports, or documents. Understanding the permissions, access, and structure is incredibly important from both a human resource perspective but also a risk management perspective.

Performance Management

It is never too late to establish a performance management program for your family office. It is a myth that a family office can be too small to warrant one. In fact, performance management is paramount in establishing alignment between family office leadership and family office professionals to make sure that their individual mandates, roles, and responsibilities contribute to the family office's overall strategic plan. Whereas an individual's performance goals may be open, such as to "meet or exceed my client's expectations" or to "conduct quarterly calls and meetings with all my families," performance metrics are tangible and measurable. For example, if your goal is to have high client satisfaction, then your performance metric might be to achieve a 90 percent or greater client satisfaction rating from a random subset of family clients. Thus, management would need to engage a random subset of clients in a short interview or survey to garner their feedback on their client experience. For larger MFOs, engaging a third party to anonymously sample your clients can be incredibly valuable periodically.

The power of performance metrics is threefold. First, performance metrics keep both family office professionals and managers on the same page when it comes to individual goals and measurable actions to demonstrate the achievement of those goals. Second, it helps inspire and enhance the job performance of family office professionals because they are clear on what they need to do in order to succeed and how they will be rewarded for their accomplishments. Third, it reduces stress. When professionals are unclear of how they will be compensated or evaluated, it can take a toll on the culture and morale of the family office. This lack of clarity and uncertainty can breed distrust and anxiety. In worst-case scenarios, family office professionals will leave in search of employers who provide greater security and clarity in terms of goals and metrics that are achievable and realistic. The case study is of a fictionalized family office that emphasizes the importance of strong talent management practices.

Communication and Trust

Another critical area for family office employees is to be empathetic and patient and demonstrate strong communication. Many family office executives interviewed could not emphasize enough how building the skills in the family office to have healthy, open communication among employees and family members, both informally and formally, is critical for them to resolve challenging situations when they arise. The family office executive can effectively model that behavior and provide guidance and encouragement to engage the family in a safe, open forum. If family office executives are not empathetic, open, and attentive, family can perceive they are not truly open to the family's interests and may assume the family office executive is actually operating in his or her own best interests or following the path of least resistance. Moreover, it is important to remain objective and to pursue a course for the family that is in the best interest of the overall family and not just for one or two branches or generations of the family. This requires the executive to strike a delicate balance because the financial controlling interest may reside within a few family members or among the members of one generation. Thus, the family office executive must balance serving the board and family stakeholders, even when advising and making recommendations that may not always be popular to powerful contingents in the family. Straining the trust between the family executive and the family can be the straw that breaks the camel's back. The family office executives who can moderate, model diplomacy, and manage friction when it arises, mitigating conflict before it erupts, are most likely to succeed. Perhaps the greatest skill of a successful family office employee is not technical at all; it is mastering effective communication and building enduring trust with the family.

Recruiting Internationally

While the specific issues may vary across world regions, disruption and uncertainty are rampant in every market. Whether the Brexit and shifting tax regulations in the UK, or political risks and other strains in the Middle East, or ever-evolving US trade policies, or health crises such as a pandemic, wealthy families around the globe are seeking assistance for the increasingly complex forces and regulations affecting their growth and preservation of wealth. Family offices are responding by becoming more agile and attuned to the concerns of their particular region. Moreover, although talented professionals are increasingly flocking to family offices as a viable career, recruiting, compensating, and retaining the best professionals remain as the primary issues for family offices around the globe. Compensation is a particularly challenging issue because of the lack of publicly available, credible data, and the idiosyncratic nature of family offices. Thus, variation across regions in expected. Research indicates that CEOs in North America receive the highest base salaries ($408,000), followed by those in Europe ($323,000), emerging markets ($314,000), and Asia-Pacific ($225,000). CEOs in North America also received one of the highest bonuses as a proportion of their base salaries (52 percent).[38]

The Global Family Office Compensation survey found that CEOs are paid the highest in the Middle East, followed by United States, United Kingdom, and Asia Pacific. The survey also reveals that discretionary bonuses are the most common means to reward staff; most global family offices surveyed pay their staff a discretionary bonus between 21 and 30 percent of the base salary. In Asia Pacific, the family office pays the highest discretionary bonuses—31 to 50 percent of base salary.[39]

Case Study: Setting Up the Office

Richard was a banker for a wealthy family for many years. The family patriarch (James) had developed a close relationship with him and one day invited him to head up his family office. When James asked Richard to lead their family office, he felt very confident and qualified for the position, considering his in-depth knowledge of the family and their complex banking history. Once he had assumed the role, however, he discovered that he only knew a fraction of the family's entire story. In particular, he experienced significant disorientation given the family's offshore holdings and entities globally. Unaware when he agreed to the role, he soon discovered that James did not actually have a family office structure.

Richard called Tamarind Partners for advice on his role and the fact that the office was essentially a blank canvas. In contrast, within his banking role, he had extensive resources, tools, risk controls, and guides. Now in this role, he did not even have a job description or clear understanding of the scope of the family office domain or his executive authority. Working with Tamarind Partners, he learned it was critical to first create a 90-day plan to establish his action items with the principals and how he was assessing the critical business, financial, investment, tax, legal, accounting, resourcing, estate planning, and family service needs. Prioritizing those issues and providing education and information on best practices for the principal of other comparable family offices similar to theirs were also included. Tamarind Partners worked with Richard on the position requirements so he could provide the patriarch with a draft job description, which clarified his role, oversight, and management responsibilities, expectations, goals, metrics for being evaluated, and milestones (near-term and long-term). Knowing that he was building out the family office, he worked with Tamarind Partners to develop a roadmap of his scope of work and approach. Richard then provided James with a framework, roadmap, and focus on the early setup needs of the family office.

The family office continually evolves and, as a result, job descriptions, goals and objectives, metrics, and other features of the office need to evolve with it. A final consideration is establishing feedback loops for the executives so that they have a pathway for expressing issues and needs. This is particularly important because most of the individuals coming into this role have service backgrounds and are conditioned to say yes to the family, even when they should say no. Therefore, structures need to be in place that promote honest feedback, dialogue, and reasonable expectations.

Family or Non-Family at the Helm

With recent compensation research reporting that 40 percent of family offices are led by a family member,[40] there are varying schools of thought about who should hold this critical post. Some individuals interviewed believe a family member needs to lead the office, whereas others preferred having a non-family member expert lead. The latter was the case in families where deep expertise in wealth management within the family's talent pool was lacking; another study found that only about one-third of CIO roles are held by a family member. All other roles can be staffed as the family wishes, either by family members or non-family members; but more often, non-family members comprise the advisory roles in most family offices.

With a significant number of family members occupying the corner suite, the family office president is often a wealth creator or second-generation owner with enough personal wealth to justify a family office. These individuals are charismatic family leaders with the influence and relationships to engage a broader family group and to lead and direct co-investment through a family office structure. The larger the office is in terms of assets under management, the more likely that C-suite roles are non-family professional managers. In contrast, for small family offices (those reporting less than $100 million in AUM), half of CEOs and 40 percent of CIOs identified as a family member.[41] In these cases, the family engagement may often be higher because a family member is directly leading and involved in the day-to-day management and decision making for the family's wealth.

When the president is not a family member, they may have worked with the family for some years in the family business or as a wealth advisor, estate planner, or an investment consultant. They have often been recruited and hired into the family office as a trusted advisor and counselor to the family.

Hiring a non-family office executive may be more of a process than grooming and recruiting within the family for family office leadership. In fact, family members are playing an increasingly critical role in the talent management of a family office, and several family offices interviewed for this book were led by one or more family members. Some assumed the role of CEO, president, or chairman, whereas others were the CIO or family liaison, coordinator, family council chair, or advisor. In certain families, a natural leader emerges with the technical skills, experience, and ambition to fill a role in the family office. In other families, the family appoints or elects a family member to come into an executive role. In any case, the circumstances leading to the involvement, management, and leadership of a family member in their family office always has a unique backstory.

Family Member Compensation

In addition to role clarity, family leaders in the family office appear to have differing opinions on compensation for family member executives in the family office. Many research studies as well as my own interviews with family office leaders indicate that family member compensation varies considerably based on age, experience, technical expertise, and role within the family office or family business. Moreover, family member compensation often is lower than non-family member compensation, and some family members actually prefer *not* to take a salary—particularly those senior family members who are not interested in having any more taxable income added to their estate. Instead, they feel a duty and responsibility to oversee, preserve, and steward the wealth for future generations.

In the case of smaller family offices, those under $100 million, more often than not the family member executive is compensated at competitive rates or slightly less. Sometimes, this is because family member clients discount the value their family member executive contributes, particularly those who step into the role with less wealth advisory experience and those who are transitioning from a business background and have no direct family office experience. This discrepancy in pay may create friction and eventually lead to resentment if the family is not able to have an open and honest dialogue on the value and appropriate compensation of a family member in a family office role.

It is evident that working in a family office when you are both a family member and client is not an easy task; however, it can be a very rewarding and enriching experience. A number of interviewees described the fulfillment and joy of seeing their family prosper knowing the success of the family office had a major input into their day-to-day lives. In many regards, the family office is the one constant for families whose complex lives continue to evolve. Being employed as a family member in the family office, similar to a family member involved in a family business, can allow family members to imbibe the values, ethics, and beliefs of the family into the operations of the family office.

Conclusion and Final Thoughts

Some of the most invaluable assets in a family office are the professionals who work for the family. The need for skilled, experienced professionals whom the family can trust and who serve their best interests is in high demand. These individuals are proactive, anticipating the ever-changing realities of family wealth; key executives in the family office need to be cultivated and developed as the family evolves and grows in order to have a great enough pool of talent for family offices to draw. Identifying best-in-breed talent involves a focus not just on the right skill set, but also on the chemistry fit, experience, and compensation to reward and retain. A family office executive ideally becomes a trusted advisor, mentor, gatekeeper, protector, and leader and also a long-term, committed employee of the family. Offering an appealing compensation package will attract talented individuals; however, a family must be careful to compensate and incent individuals not only by their roles but also in a way that is in line with the family's values and goals. It must create a structure that allows employees to thrive and succeed with guidance, expectations, and clear measurements for their role. This involves defining individuals' job descriptions, providing performance indicators for their roles, and compensating accordingly. Creating opportunities for personal and professional growth can enhance how they serve in the family office. These are the keys to successful talent management in the family office.

Notes

1. Botoff Consulting, LLC, Aligning Compensation and Family Office Goals, September 29, 2015; UBS/Campden Research, The Global Family Office Report, 2019; Agreus, USA Family Office Compensation Benchmark Report, 2018.

2. Botoff Consulting, Morgan Stanley Family Office Compensation, 2019. Available at https://www.morganstanley.com/cs/pdf/9528132-FOR-Compensation-Report-Broch.pdf.
3. EY Family Office Guide, 2017.
4. Robert Casey, State of the industry report—single family offices take their turn on center stage, December 2018, www.globelawandbusiness.com.
5. Correspondence with Linda Mack, Founder, Mack International, April 2020.
6. Correspondence with Lisa Ryan, Principal of Lisa D. Ryan, LLC, January 2020.
7. Botoff Consulting and FORGE community. 2019 Single Family Office (SFO) Executive Compensation Survey, December 2019, p. 13.
8. Texas Family Office Association, LLC (TFOA), Creating a Single Family Office to Manage Your Family's Interests, 2019, p. 20.
9. Ibid, 18–19.
10. Tamarind Partners, March 27–29, 2019, Family Office Staffing: Organizational Charts, Roles & Responsibilities Presentation.
11. Ibid.
12. Botoff Consulting and FORGE community, 2019 Single Family Office (SFO) Executive Compensation Survey, December 2019.
13. Texas Family Office Association, LLC (TFOA), Creating a Single Family Office to Manage Your Family's Interests, 2019, p. 20.
14. Creating a Single Family Office to Manage Your Family's Interests, 2019, p. 20; Tamarind Partners, Family Office Staffing: Organizational Charts, Roles & Responsibilities Presentation, March 27–29, 2019.
15. Texas Family Office Association, LLC (TFOA), Creating a Single Family Office to Manage Your Family's Interests, 2019, p. 20.
16. Ibid., 19.
17. Botoff Consulting and FORGE community, 2019 Single Family Office (SFO) Executive Compensation Survey, December 2019, p. 14.
18. Blumenstein & Bennett, 2018; Catalyst, 2018; National Center for Education Statistics, 2015; U.S. Census Bureau, 2015.
19. Botoff Consulting and FORGE community, 2019 Single Family Office (SFO) Executive Compensation Survey, December 2019.
20. Correspondence with Lisa Ryan, January 20, 2020.
21. Tamarind Partners, March 27–29, 2019, Family Office Staffing: Organizational Charts, Roles & Responsibilities Presentation.
22. Correspondence with Linda Mack, 2020.
23. Botoff Consulting and FORGE community, 2019 Single Family Office (SFO) Executive Compensation Survey, December 2019, p. 13.
24. Texas Family Office Association, LLC (TFOA) Creating a Single Family Office to Manage Your Family's Interests, 2019, p. 18–19.
25. Ibid., 20.
26. UBS/Campden, 2019, The Global Family Office Report, 2019.

27. Botoff Consulting and FORGE community, 2019 Single Family Office (SFO) Executive Compensation Survey, December 2019.

28. UBS/Campden, 2019, The Global Family Office Report, 2019.

29. Texas Family Office Association, LLC (TFOA), Creating a Single Family Office to Manage Your Family's Interests, 2019, p. 19.

30. UBS/Campden, 2019, The Global Family Office Report, 2019.

31. Botoff Consulting and FORGE community, 2019 Single Family Office (SFO) Executive Compensation Survey, December 2019.

32. UBS/Campden, 2019, The Global Family Office Report, 2019.

33. Texas Family Office Association, LLC (TFOA), Creating a Single Family Office to Manage Your Family's Interests, 2019, p. 20.

34. UBS/Campden, 2019, The Global Family Office Report, 2019.

35. Botoff Consulting and FORGE community, 2019 Single Family Office (SFO) Executive Compensation Survey, December 2019, p. 3

36. Ibid., 17.

37. Correspondence with Patricia Botoff, Botoff Consulting, April 2020.

38. UBS/Campden, 2019, The Global Family Office Report, 2019.

39. Correspondence with Paul Westall and Tayyab Mohamed, Agreus Group, April 2020.

40. Botoff Consulting and FORGE community, 2019 Single Family Office (SFO) Executive Compensation Survey, December 2019.

41. Botoff Consulting and FORGE community, 2019 Single Family Office (SFO) Executive Compensation Survey, December 2019, p. 11.

CHAPTER 11

Governance Issues for the Family Office

Barbara Hauser, JD

Independent Family Advisor

Kirby Rosplock, PhD

In this chapter we address the importance of "governance" in two contexts. First, we examine the importance of governance in the family office itself, an often-neglected topic. Second, we describe the features of good governance for the family.

Why is governance so important? By having a good awareness of the benefits of good governance, the family office can play a very important role in keeping the family cohesive, which is certainly a great goal for the long-term continuation of the family (and also for the family office). This cohesiveness emerges from carefully designing the decision-making procedures that will be followed by the family and by the family office. Today these topics fall into the category of family governance, which is explored in more detail in this chapter.

In the same way that countries have their own systems of governance, so do families. Some are more successful than others (e.g., dictators risk being overturned, whereas elections and constitutions typically are respected by those who created them). The best family offices are proactive and have good governance procedures and decision-making processes that help the family function well. During an interview for this book on the role of governance and the family office, Jay Hughes shared, "The great political philosophers understood that politics is only about joint decision-making. That's all it is.

That's why Aristotle said the foundation of any government is the family bricks in the bottom of that foundation. Are they functioning? Are they making joint decisions together?"

This chapter covers those governance procedures applied to the family office, and to the family itself.

Governance Issues for the Family Office Itself

Most traditional family offices focus much more on how they oversee financial investments than they do on running the office as a business that follows best practices in corporate governance. This would include the hallmarks of good corporate governance: transparency and accountability. (See the model OECD corporate governance principles.[1])

A lot depends on the stage of the family office and of the family. The governance issues for a new office with a relatively small family in its first generation of wealth management are not as complex as for an established office that serves multiple generations of the family. For example, key wealth decision makers in a first-generation family are typically the matriarch and/or patriarch. When families with multigenerational wealth evolve to the second generation of decision makers, the family tree may have expanded to a group of siblings.

As the family office becomes accountable to a larger group who may not have the same interests, the complexities of giving voice and having decision-making authority increase. This highlights the need to have good policies in place—to avoid ad hoc decisions or preferences that can create tension, resentment, and animosity among family members.

Benefits of a Good Board

The standard mark of good governance in any business is the quality and involvement of its board. A study found that fewer than half of families with a family office have advisory boards or boards of directors in the family office (48 percent).[2] And even fewer family offices have an effective (or independent) board that has regular meetings.

At the outset, the family should spend time to clarify their goals and expectations for the family office. The family should be able to explain their priorities to the family office. This will help the family office to carry out the goals of the family.

A study by the Family Office Exchange concluded that not only are good boards for family offices important, they are indispensable:

> Serving as an accountability checkpoint, boards can assure that structures are established to help uncover risks and, once detected, have policies that help to mitigate exposure. Consequently, the board in its governing capacity plays a significant role in preserving family wealth and sustainability.[3]

The board is also critical in legal terms. The board is responsible for the overall management and direction of any company. Some say the global financial crisis that began in 2008 was due to lack of attention and oversight by the boards of financial institutions.

In the family office, the board can be helpful in areas that are like those in other businesses. We can learn from the extensive work that has been done on a global level and apply them to the family office.

For example, in the Organization of Economic Co-operation and Development (OECD) model principles of corporate governance, the board should be responsible for eight key functions:

1. Reviewing and guiding corporate strategy, major plans of action, risk policy, annual budgets and business plans; setting performance objectives; monitoring implementation and corporate performance; and overseeing major capital expenditures, acquisitions, and divestitures
2. Monitoring the effectiveness of the company's governance practices and making changes as needed
3. Selecting, compensating, monitoring, and, when necessary, replacing key executives and overseeing succession planning
4. Aligning key executive and board remuneration with the long-term interests of the company and its shareholders
5. Ensuring a formal and transparent board nomination and election process
6. Monitoring and managing potential conflicts of interest of management, board members, and shareholders, including misuse of corporate assets and abuse in related party transactions
7. Ensuring the integrity of the corporation's accounting and financial reporting systems, including the independent audit, and that appropriate systems of control are in place—in particular, systems for risk management, financial, and operational control, and compliance with the law and relevant standards
8. Overseeing the process of disclosure and communications

Although it is unlikely that family offices are this structured, the OECD principles can serve as an aspirational goal to be a well-run office. We have seen an immediate improvement in the professionalization of a family office when there is a board to whom the management reports on a regular basis.

As mentioned above, one critical function of the board is to hire and fire the CEO. In many traditional family offices, however, the CEO role has quietly evolved from a professional advisor relationship with the senior members of the family, rather than from any oversight and election by a board. It becomes quite difficult to confront the CEO and suggest changes much less to ask the CEO to leave.

A proper board (to use the British adjective) is elected by the owners of the family office (see Chapter 5 on the various legal structures of a family office). Their terms and duties are spelled out in the relevant corporate documents (such as in the by-laws). Many families prefer to have an odd number of board members to prevent stalemates during voting. For a single-family office (SFO), the right number in our experience seems to be between five and seven board members. The board should meet at least quarterly, with written agendas and written minutes. When the family office is fairly new, and the family consists of first generation, the board function can be simplified, but we recommend following the model of quarterly board meetings to instill a regularity, which can become more complex as the family becomes more complex.

Importance of Independent Directors

Again, looking at public (listed) companies for guidance, it is clearly a best practice in corporate governance to have independent directors. Professor John Ward, a leading family business researcher, author, consultant, and educator, recommends a minimum of three independent directors for family businesses. However, in our experience few family offices are ready to include so many outsiders in their private financial business.

Research shows that most family office boards are composed of family members (on average, four) with only one outside non-family board member.[4] It should be a goal to add non-family board members over time. In choosing an independent director, the office and family should look for someone who is familiar with the family office world.

The family office is a unique environment, and a candidate for a director might not appreciate that factor. For example, one family added a seasoned independent director who immediately focused on loss assets, such as the yacht. He thought it would be an obvious decision to get rid of it, not appreciating the meaning it had to various family members.

Interim Stage of Advisory Board

For those family offices that hesitate to share family financial information with outsiders, an interim step can be to create an advisory board for the family office. Candidates are likely to be pleased and flattered to join as advisory board members. If chosen well, their advice and oversight could add a very positive and professional level of management for the family office. An advisory board can prepare the family to establish a proper board in the future. They can use the advisory board as a first step to having an active board and see how comfortable they are (or are not) in sharing certain information and in receiving helpful input by the board.

Accountability to the Family

Often the family office management grows into its position in a gradual way, beginning as professional advisors to the senior family members. It is common for those senior family members to prefer not to share much financial information with younger family members. Their long-term advisors generally follow those preferences. Over time, though, this is not a successful governance practice. The crucial hallmark of transparency needs to be honored. Good governance includes much more financial accountability to all of the family members. Sheltering family members from the responsibilities of wealth ownership disempowers them to be engaged and accountable for their actions. In order for families to be successful with building strong stewards of the wealth, creating an expectation, a process, and opportunities for family members to grow into their responsibilities is a function of prudent family governance.

Participation in Long-Term Strategy

As mentioned previously, a primary responsibility of a good board is to set the long-term strategy of the office. The board can only try to do this if the family has shared their vision and mission.

Engaging in the strategic planning process is a multipronged approach. It requires a clear understanding of the current state of the family, which is discussed in Chapter 6. Further, it requires an understanding of where the family desires to be not just one year or five years in the future, but in two or three generations. Conducting a visioning exercise as described in Chapter 4 may be a helpful exercise to inform the board about the long-term strategy of the family office. By understanding where the family desires to be two or three generations out, the family office can begin to develop a long-range strategic plan that provides a general roadmap to get there.

Next Generation Issues to Address

The next generation in wealthy families is a category that receives a lot of current attention. A family office study finds that a third (36 percent) have management roles within the family or sit on the board (25 percent).[5] Timing wise, 28 percent of next-generation family members are involved and taking over control of their family's wealth with North America and Europe ahead of emerging markets and Asia-Pacific.[6] For the senior generation, the concerns are generally whether or not the next generation is well equipped to control and take responsibility for the wealth. All wealthy families are concerned about falling prey to the global proverb of "shirtsleeves to shirtsleeves in three generations."

The board could examine the alternatives for strengthening and supporting the next generation. There are many outside educational programs, including those offered by financial institutions. See Chapter 12 for a broader discussion of developing the next generation of wealth stewards. The board may also support the concept of having the office create a tailored educational series for the next generation. For example, one family has been training the next generation to become trustees in the future. In the process, they are learning more about how trusts work and the different roles of the trustees and the beneficiaries. Families have a complex challenge to prepare and empower, yet also provide opportunities for future family members to find their own way. They need to be informed, but also independent of the prior generation.

Another great learning opportunity for the next generation is to become involved in the family's charitable activities. Often there is a charitable foundation created by the family and administered by the family office. One family hired a consultant to develop a plan for gradual involvement by the next generation based on their talents, interests, and available time. Philanthropy and involvement with shared family giving is an important opportunity for family members to engage in decision-making for the family. Chapter 14 provides a broader discussion of the power of philanthropy, legacy, and impact investing.

Succession Planning for the Family Office and Its Executives

Another governance issue is to be sure that there is a succession plan for the executives in the family office as well as a succession plan for the family office. These are topics that are often not addressed by the family office, in part due to how the current management evolved into their positions and/or how family owners are engaged and involved with the business management of the family office. Again, the board may bring up this topic and oversee the planning.

Succession planning is one of the most challenging transitions in a family office and may be why only about half (54 percent) have a written succession plan for their family office according to a Campden UBS family office research study.[7] Succession planning in the family office is challenging for several reasons. First, it requires one generation of leaders to recognize their own mortality. For many first-generation wealth creators, the owning and operating of their family office is closely knitted to their personal identity and to the pride of what they have created for themselves and their offspring. The reality of stepping away from what they have worked so hard to create and relinquishing control, authority, and oversight for the family wealth and the office can deal a significant blow to their perceived stature and role in the family.

Second, family owners and leaders may be challenged by envisioning and/or identifying who will assume that role and how/if this new generation of leaders will make decisions. Will or have they learned from their predecessor and will they carry on the mantle of the prior leadership, or will they embark on a new pathway to govern the family office?

Third, transitions are not simply a one-time event. Rather, there is typically a series of transition steps in preparing and grooming a leader to come into a role and an incumbent to wind down and transition responsibilities, so that the governance structure shifts and adjusts for the new circumstances. Transitions may take several years for family offices that engage in the planning process in advance of the actual succession. In many family offices, there may be an overlap of leadership between the retiring executive and the incoming family office executive, which can create an entirely new dynamic as the baton is passed. Yet in far too many cases, families have been forced to deal with the challenging, stressful, and daunting task of on-the-fly transitions. These transitions are sudden, and families typically are surprised by and unprepared for them.

One study suggests that the majority of family offices (7 out of 10) are led by a family member.[8] Why do so many family members end up as the CEO or president of their family office? For the first-generation wealth creators, the family office typically becomes the new family enterprise for them to chair and lead. The assets they have generated through the sale of a business, an executive retirement package, or other windfall often consumes their energy to manage and oversee. For subsequent generations who are inheritors or beneficiaries of wealth, a deep sense of responsibility and stewardship often influences their career path to assume a leadership position. Yet not all families have a family leader who is equipped and ready to assume the leadership mantle. Further, some families determine that an outside family office executive is preferred as they are independent of the family and may provide an objective perspective for the family. In either of these scenarios, there is not one way that is better or worse, rather just different.

After interviewing several family office executives, mostly family and certainly a number of non-family leaders, some themes around succession in the family office executive began to emerge.

First, family offices that appear to weather the succession the best are those, not surprisingly, who accept and anticipate leadership change as a normal course of business. In other words, they have built into the strategic planning process the expectation that all individuals in a leadership capacity (President/CEO, board, family council, etc.) must engage in planning how they will prepare the family office when their tenure comes to a close. This mindset naturally informs the overall strategic plan and the family ethos as a whole. Thus, the family creates an expectation that the wisdom, experience, and values of the leadership directly inform those of the incoming successor. Like weaving a tightly knotted carpet, there is no break or interruption to the family office operations as one leader segues into the role and the other transitions out.

Second, interviews reveal that many family offices transition the president/CEO to a chairman of the board role in order to retain their counsel, wisdom, and advice in the coming year or so. Depending on the age, experience, and abilities of the incoming leader, the predecessor may also mentor and/or advise their successor. Although there is a clear transition, these successful mentors do not lead for the successor; rather, they become a sounding board and provide advice and wisdom to help inform the decisions made by the successor. Allowing the new leadership to grow into and build confidence in the role is critical to their long-term success. Further, it helps establish them as the new visible leader to the family and other family office executives.

Third, family offices should always have a contingency leadership plan. The Coronavirus Pandemic of 2020 only heightened families' awareness for how unpredictable and rapid change may take place. A contingency plan outlines what steps to follow in the rare circumstance where a family office executive becomes incapacitated. The plan is typically developed in conjunction with key family owners and senior family office executives and is shared with family stakeholders. An interesting phenomenon was observed with a private group of family office executives in the Midwest. For sudden, unexpected situations where a family office leader was incapacitated and/or passed away, the other family office executives would step in and assist the individual family office in leadership transition. They might assist with the day-to-day operations during this interim, as well as help the family with the executive search process to replace and/or aid in the grooming and mentoring of the incoming family office executive to assume this role. Family offices coming to the aid of other family offices during a difficult time was a rewarding discovery and illustrates how family offices can work collaboratively and collegially.

Although there are stories of senior family office leaders who are hesitant to give up their post for fear that their offspring are not capable to lead the family office, not adequately groomed, or worse yet, not competent to lead, other families immediately recognize that the succeeding generation has not demonstrated a genuine interest or ability or reached an age and/or skill set to be tracked for a leadership role in the family office.

For these families, identifying a bridging non-family office executive increasingly becomes the preferred path. After several interviews with non-family executives, one clear and distinct observation is the level of objective professionalism and profound wisdom that a well-seasoned, non-family member executive can bring to a family's family office. Bringing their experience and wisdom from the best practices of other family offices, these individuals can elevate the sophistication with which the family office is managed and operated. This is not to say that a family member may not bring these same qualities, but the non-family office professionals who have dedicated themselves to a family office track often demonstrate a keen awareness, sensitivity, and pragmatism to the stewardship of the family's wealth.

Governance for the Family Itself

Although governance is often associated with corporate structures and management, there is also the governance that exists unique to each family. This section discusses the nature of a family's decision-making process, what the hallmarks of a strong governance process are, what the benefits of good governance are, and how to develop your family's governance system. The latter portion of this section identifies important constructs, such as the role of a family council and a family constitution, as tools to foster and promote positive family decision-making.

Dennis Jaffe, in his book, *Borrowed from Your Grandchildren: The Evolution of 100-Year Family Enterprises*, finds that participatory governance is key to keeping the family together:

> [B]y the second or third generation, the culture shifts to become more transparent, open and collaborative. This entails having clear policies, practices and organization to set goals, define leadership, make decisions and hold people accountable. The family culture shifts from family to business first, a more professional orientation to business and investment, and also toward transparency and collaboration.[9]

Jaffe's research on the role of governance practices in intergenerational success revealed that governance systems and other best practices were increasingly adopted and vital with each succeeding generation. For example, whereas only 13 percent of second-generation families engaged in next-generation education, 71 percent of the third-generation and all five-generation plus families did so. (See Table 11.1 and Figure 11.1.)

TABLE 11.1   Family Practices by Generation

Practice Generation	G2	G3	G3-4	G4	G5+
Family Governance					
Family Council	63%	71%	100%	85%	100%
Family Constitution	25	43	71	96	100
Next Generation Education	13	43	71	75	100
Exit Policy	0	43	43	85	100
Enterprise Practices					
Independent Board	25	71	85	96	100
Nonfamily CEO	25	28	43	25	100

Source: Dennis T. Jaffe, *Borrowed From Your Grandchildren: The Evolution of 100-Year Family Enterprises.* Copyright © 2020 John Wiley & Sons, Inc. Reprinted with permission of John Wiley & Sons, Inc.

FIGURE 11.1   Evolving Family Governance Practices Over Generations

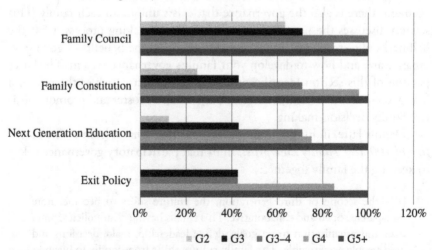

Source: Dennis T. Jaffe, *Borrowed From Your Grandchildren: The Evolution of 100-Year Family Enterprises.* Copyright © 2020 John Wiley & Sons, Inc. Reprinted with permission of John Wiley & Sons, Inc.

Analysis of Existing Decision-Making Process

Every family has developed a way it makes decisions. Some families prefer a more informal, casual style of decision-making, while other families prefer to articulate, document, and follow a stricter process for making decisions. Neither way is better or worse; rather, different styles may be better for different families. With that said, as families become larger and more complex with additional family members, it can be helpful to formalize information sharing and the process for decision-making purely from an administrative perspective.

A recent Campden UBS research study found that almost half (47 percent) of family respondents said the next generation was currently either somewhat (29 percent) or very (18 percent) unprepared for future succession, suggesting that additional education and onboarding was needed.[10] However, the study also reflected that many were in the midst of a generational transition, as 28 percent of respondents of the Next Generation took control of the family wealth within the last 10 years, and 37 percent are expected to take control within the next 10 years. The study also found that 36 percent are already in executive or management positions within the family office and 25 percent sit on boards.[11] Because of the uncertainty for the next generation to take the reins for the wealth, decision-making more often resides with the more senior generation. Unsure if adult children are truly prepared, grantors may hold off passing along wealth until children are well on into their adult life.

In first-generation families, parents typically are the primary decision makers; however, in the second generations and beyond, the leadership within the family may vary considerably. In some families, the oldest son is given the right and the resources to lead the sibling group, a system commonly known as primogeniture.

However, research indicates this practice may be antiquated, as most parents (mothers, 95 percent, and fathers, 97 percent) prefer to distribute wealth to their children equally.[12] With this in mind, sibling inheritors will have to develop an understanding and process for involvement, with information sharing as well as decision-making with the other siblings. Ivan Lansberg, a family business expert, refers to the second generation of leadership as a *sibling partnership*, as the sibling group typically must work closely together to make decisions as a unit.[13]

From the second to third generation of wealth ownership, the governance in the family grows in complexity, moving into what Lansberg refers to as a *cousin consortium*. The decision-making may now be spread across a series of cousins from various branches of a family. Communication, information exchange, and a clearly articulated process of governance become key elements. Informal decision-making at the first-generation wealth/business owner phase is commonplace; however, it does not typically work as well in second and later generation families. Instead, a formal process from the leadership in the family is critical to engage, involve, and create a sense of belonging among family members.

Edouard Thijssen, a third-generation member of a Belgian business-owning family, identifies firsthand with these issues. In Thijssen's family, ownership had been divided and transferred across numerous cousins representing different amounts of ownership in the portfolio of companies owned by the family. Seeing the challenges of managing all these complex relationships in his own family, Thijssen conceived of and built a virtual information hub for sharing information online among his family members. This platform helped his family to bridge the distances between family members and to access and centralize information that helped to streamline some of the family's operations and governance around its wealth. His company, TrustedFamily, provides a secure online portal for families in business and their family offices. Thijssen offered the following:

When family is spread out all over the world in different countries and cities, it is difficult to always meet in-person. His virtual platform allows families to connect around the issues they share as a family and selectively dialogue on specific agenda items. For example, the family council, family board, the family foundation, or the family assembly are able to share information to its select members.

Here, the family office and family share a common mission to gather, store, and make available key information for all family members so that key strategic and administrative discussions can be had at any time, from any location.[14]

Since the pandemic of 2020, virtual infrastructure to support governance is key and having access information and storing it in a digital vault or cloud-based site is paramount. The section that follows expands further on transparency, accountability, and family member participation as hallmarks of good governance.

Hallmarks of Good Governance: Transparency, Accountability, and Participation

At the public company level, the two key hallmarks of good governance are transparency and accountability. In a family setting, however, it seems crucial to add a third: participation. In order to keep the family together for a long time in the future, it is really important to always involve at least two generations in creating their governance system.

As in most fields, it has been an often-painful lesson that top-down planning does not produce lasting effects. Many families have constitutions or other series of rules (e.g., protocols, charters, mission statements, value statements, etc.); however, when the younger family members do not participate in their creation, they have no strong loyalty to adopt them.

Benefits of the Family Creating Its Own Governance Process and Structure

Just as participation by younger family members is critically important, so is the overall process of having the family create its own governance structure. When the governance (e.g., any decision-making process) is imposed by a patriarch, it is not likely to last after the patriarch is gone. The next generation did not participate in creating it, so they have no automatic loyalty to the system. In fact, if they have resented the way in which they have been consistently excluded from many decisions in the family, they may actively resent the system.

Just as top-down systems do not last well, so also do outside systems not last. This refers to a governance system that someone outside of the family writes for the family. Unfortunately, many families have hired outside advisors to create a governance system for them. (After we speak about family constitutions, for example, it is common that someone will ask if a consultant can write one for them. The answer is yes, they can write them; but it will not provide the same experience or the same output as engaging the family in this process would. Thus, it is recommended that the content is best to come from family while utilizing an outsource facilitator or consultant to guide the process.)

The fatal flaw in a constitution written by an outside advisor is that the provisions are not connected to the family, so it has no real meaning to the family. The constitution is put in a drawer and the family continues as before. (One of our most valued feedback comments was from a family member who said, "When I read our new constitution, it sounds so familiar . . . it really is ours.")

The reason that good family governance is so important is that it can provide the cohesiveness needed if the family is to continue together for several generations. (If the family has no real interest in staying together, there is no need for a good governance system or for a family office.) Interestingly, by going through the process of creating a family constitution, the family is learning in a hands-on way how to work together and to make decisions together.

How to Create the Family Governance

How a family creates its own governance system is by following a process that has worked for many families and in many countries. Many families agree that they do need an outside advisor to guide and facilitate the process.

If a family member tries to play that role, the group dynamics are likely to interfere. For example, if the patriarch is the process leader, the family members likely have learned a behavior of not questioning his authority—with the result being that the rest of the family will not feel any particular loyalty to the decisions.

If any other family leader plays that role, the siblings are quite likely to resent him or her. Finally, the goal is for each family member to participate, and it is nearly impossible to lead a meeting or discussion and also participate in it. The roles are too different.

When looking for an outside advisor, an important factor is their experience with other wealthy multigenerational families. (Families have received proposals from large global corporate consulting firms whose core skill is corporate strategic planning with listed companies, but who say yes of course they could include family governance.)

The outside advisor will be able to present back to the family the objective description of how they are doing as a family in their current decision-making process. The experience with other families will be a great additional resource for the family. In some cases, the non-family family office executive or the family's estate planning attorney may be able to facilitate the family meeting. The preferences vary depending on the nature of the family and their most trusted advisors.

In the event of an outside consultant, the first step is for the outside advisor to have private interview sessions with each family member. This is to get a sense of the various issues that are circulating within the family, many of which are just not shared with other family members for a variety of reasons. Often the family member has had no one to talk with who has a background of understanding many similar families.

Those issues that seem to be more about very personal issues are set aside (in a similar way that the United States has a Bill of Rights, protecting personal areas that the state should respect and/or leave alone). The issues that involve the larger family are the important ones to evaluate.

Next, the outside advisor makes a written report of the issues that could be addressed. This is usually done without mentioning any names or criticisms, but which includes enough information to describe those issues. The family reviews the report and decides with the outside advisor which of the issues to place on an agenda for a formal family meeting.

Family meetings are a critical component of the governance of a family. Some families attempt to pull together a family meeting during a vacation or a family gathering, such as a wedding or anniversary. However, most families interviewed with a long success track of family meetings identified that dedicating the time just for the family meeting was important. In a family office study most families host regular family meetings (84 percent).[15] Formal family meetings provide a forum for family members to discuss the business issues of the wealth in a structured and professional manner. Although most families had their very first family meeting around a kitchen table, as families evolve and more family members are added generation over generation, formalizing the family meeting can make the discussions more efficient, effective, and streamlined.

Family Councils

One of the first topics to be addressed at the formal family meetings is whether or not they want to create a family council. This depends in part on the number of family members and the number of branches in the family. At one extreme, a family with 400 living members in the Gulf region formed a family council of 12 representative members. Another family with five involved family members decided that they should all be on the family council, and it would be structured for the next generation when branch representation would begin.

Approximately half of family offices (44 percent) have a family council that meets about four times on average a year composed of six members.[16] The family council acts in a way that could be compared in countries to the role of Parliament, the Diet, Congress, and so on. On another level, it could be compared to the role that a board plays in a business. One word of advice when it comes to family council success is that the council has a clear role in the family decision-making process and an action associated with its presence. First, a family council has to be supported by the family when it comes to participation and membership. Setting up a governing body such as a family council just for the sake of having representation will not lead to a productive end.

A family council is most successful if there is a clear understanding by the family, board, and family office executives of its role, its authority, who it represents, and how it is to work with the other governing and leadership bodies. Further, we have heard families discussing all too frequently how they had a family council that lost its steam.

Family councils that are working towards a project goal, for example, tend to build greater energy and buy in than councils that are not in any state of action. For example, one family had its family council create a survey to gather feedback from family members regarding the direction, leadership, and strategic planning for their family enterprise. The survey feedback surfaced important concerns with the leadership and the direction of how the family enterprise was being managed. As a result, the lack of confidence represented through the council's survey of the combined minority interests triggered certain leadership and board members to step down.

Although some councils play a more pronounced role in the governance of the family enterprise, other councils may have a focus to build cohesion, harmony, and connections across family branches. Another family council was asked to plan how to keep the family knitted across various geographies, time zones, and age groups. They inspired a family to involve the younger generations via a family blog that engaged younger family members to share more with the broader family. They also hosted an annual family retreat, which brought family members together to celebrate their heritage, and also to embrace their future as a family unit. From activities to build trust, such as ropes courses and obstacle courses, to educational forums to bolster financial skills, entrepreneurship skills, or communication skills, the family council was tasked with creating an experience that kept family members coming back for more.

Family Constitutions

Once the family meets, an important topic is whether or not they want to create their rule-making structure. On a country level, this structure would be called a constitution. The purpose of a constitution is to determine which decision-making bodies should exist along with what decisions they would be authorized to make on their own and which they would need member approval for. A good outside advisor would encourage them to write their own preamble about why they are creating the constitution. The subjects dealt with in the constitution can be as individual as each family is unique. The length can vary from 3 pages to as many as 55.

There are three important characteristics of a strong, robust family constitution.

1. Families who engage family members for the input and creation of the constitution tend to have greater buy-in by the family. In other words, where there is low or no involvement of family members in the drafting of the document, there is low or no commitment to the principles outlined in the constitution.
2. The family constitution is a living document. Families who periodically evaluate the charter and review the terms as it applies to the family today tend to abide by their family's constitutions. Some families will amend their constitution as changes or events occur in the family. It is important to make this a dynamic governance document that evolves as the family also evolves. One family we know reads their family mission, which is at the front of their family constitution, at the beginning of every family meeting.
3. Family constitutions do not have to be overly complicated and dense. Some families prefer to sketch out their purpose or preamble to start and identify over time the additional areas where they want to provide more definition. One family office shared its experience of how they created the constitution slowly over time and then, as life events occurred, such as the marriage of a daughter and birth of a grandson, they expanded on the norms and expectations of family members around different subjects.

There is no time frame for creating a constitution. It is helpful to have a committee or an advisory group or even the family council tasked with moving along the process of creation. Without owners of the constitution project, families may lose momentum and the drive to get it to a more formalized state.

Family constitutions may encompass a wide array of provisions and topics depending on the family. Following is a compilation of areas that may be included in a family's constitution.

Sample of Family Constitution Contents[17]

- Preamble or Statement of Purpose
- Family Membership and Responsibilities of Members
- Family Vision or Mission
- Family Values, Beliefs, or Principles

- Family Entities, Structures, and Processes
- Family Governance Protocols
- Family Meetings
- Family Office Board
- Family Council
- Family Business Board
- Investment Advisory
- Asset Management Board
- Risk Management or Asset Protection
- Family Philanthropy and/or Foundation Board
- Family Office Governance
- Family Bank and/or Family Co-Invested Funds
- Family Business Ownership
- Guidelines for Ownership, Inheritance, Succession
- Family Education Oversight
- Stock Agreements such as Buy/Sell Agreements
- Family Employment and Compensation Policies
- Family Gatherings
- Memorialization of Family History
- Conflicts of Interest

The following case study shares family governance insights from two members of the family who represent the fourth and fifth generations of an enterprising and philanthropic family.

Kettering Family Governance Case Study

The following case study shares insights from Charles F. Kettering, III ("Charlie") and his son, Grant Kettering, members of the Kettering family's fourth and fifth generations. Here is the family's story and insights into a modern family office and its governance practices.

History of DELCO

Charles F. Kettering was born in 1876 into a prosperous but humble farming family that had immigrated from Germany to Ohio in 1837. He grew up as a farm boy and worked various jobs, including installing telephone lines, to finance his own education. After several fits and starts due to persistent poor eyesight, he eventually received a degree in engineering from Ohio State University in 1904 and took a job at National Cash Register (NCR) in

Dayton, Ohio. At NCR, among other work, he invented a simplified credit approval system and electrified the cash register.[18] Prior to that, cash registers required a hand crank to open the cash drawer.

Inspired by these early achievements, Kettering and several associates decided to try to address a similar problem for the automobile, which at that time also needed a hand crank to be started. Working out of a barn, they spent nights and their free time beginning to develop what was to become the battery ignition system and self-starter for the automobile. When their first commercial order for 5,000 ignition systems came from Cadillac in 1909, Kettering, along with Edward A. Deeds, formed the Dayton Engineering Laboratories Company (DELCO). The self-starter was finalized in 1911 and installed in production models in 1912 by Cadillac. Kettering was among many innovators of the time, from the Wright Brothers to James Cox, who were inventors, entrepreneurs, and successful businessmen all clustered in the Dayton, Ohio area.

In the meantime, General Motors Company (GM) had been founded by William C. Durant in 1908 in Flint, Michigan, and was consolidating several motorcar companies producing Buick, Oldsmobile, Cadillac, Oakland (later Pontiac), Ewing, and Marquette, among others.[19] The popularity of the electric start engine had greatly increased the demand for GM vehicles, and so in 1916 the United Motors Corporation (another Durant company that was absorbed into GM in 1918) offered to purchase DELCO from Deeds and Kettering, making Kettering a significant shareholder. On June 1, 1916, Kettering opened an unincorporated private office (precursor to his family office) in Dayton to handle his affairs. A brilliant and humble inventor, entrepreneur, and business leader, Charles F. Kettering rode the wave of the industrialization as head of the General Motors Research Corporation, accumulating 186 US patents by the end of his career in 1947.

Expansion, Diversification, and Structure

Beginning in 1925, when his first and only son Eugene was 17 years old, Kettering began to transform the management of his affairs from a private office to a constellation of formal entities. The first was C.F. Kettering Inc., in which his investment interests were brought under one umbrella for the first time. Two years later in 1927, he established The Charles F. Kettering Foundation to formalize his philanthropic activities and "sponsor and carry out scientific research for the benefit of humanity." In 1935, when his first grandchild was four years old, he established the first family trust. During the later 1930s, among other investments, he purchased a controlling stake in

Winters National Bank, which eventually became not just an investment holding but deeply involved with family administration, including the fiduciary oversight of the Kettering trusts. In 1945, Kettering, together with long-time peer, Alfred P. Sloan, GM's longtime chairman, established the Memorial Sloan-Kettering Institute for Cancer Research in New York City.[20]

The family's governance approach has remained much as Charles F. Kettering originally established it. Since 1925, the organizations have utilized a formal corporate governance process, including through written books and records and decision-making through a formal board with both family and independent directors. Grant revealed, "It's not dissimilar to how other families of a similar vintage function in terms of implementing more formalized governance for the family and the family office."[21] Grant and Charlie shared during their interviews the importance the family attaches to formal governance, documentation including meeting minutes, and consensus driven decision-making, all of which have helped the family to maintain focus, control, and organization of their investment and philanthropic activities. Grant shared, "We still have the minute books going back to the twenties, which are incredibly interesting to read nearly 100 years later."[22]

Perhaps more importantly, Kettering also established the family's foundational values, culture, and operating norms that have shaped the decorum and demeanor of the family and set high standards for business, philanthropy, privacy, modesty, and inclusivity. Grant highlighted that stewardship is perhaps the most foundational family value, saying "We were taught to look at this wealth and the family office as something we should take care of on behalf of future generations in the family and the broader community . . . not something that belongs to us individually."[23] In 2017, the family adopted a vision statement formalizing this attitude, pledging to be a "philanthropic and investment organization that benefits the family, its local communities, and the world, for future generations."

When Charles Kettering passed in 1958, his thirty-three years of planning, philanthropies, and structuring from 1925 onward made for a smooth, tax-efficient transfer of ownership and control to the next generation. And in many ways, the portfolio stayed relatively consistent for the succeeding decades. There were over the years some acquisitions and some asset dispossessions, including eventually the sale of Winters National Bank to become part of what is today J.P. Morgan Chase Bank.

After Charles's death, his son, Eugene, and his wife, Virginia, devoted much of their time and resources to philanthropy. Among other activities, they donated much of the funding to build the Kettering Memorial Hospital in Kettering, Ohio, and the development and expansion of United States

Air Force Museum in Dayton. In the 1950s and 60s Eugene and Virginia expanded their philanthropy by establishing The Kettering Family Foundation. Unfortunately, Eugene's leadership tenure was cut short when he passed in 1968 at the age of 62, leaving behind his wife, Virginia, and three children. Eugene and Virginia's only son, Charles F. Kettering II, unfortunately passed in 1971.

Beginning in the 1980s Grant's father, Charlie, came of age and assumed a leadership role. Grant recounted that "the fourth generation had a fresh and different perspective, and my father's first responsibility, so to speak, was to educate and convince the family as a whole, including especially my great grandmother Virginia, to diversify and divest some of their concentrated holdings, including General Motors."[24] This was difficult given that GM was a flagship of American industry and still regarded as part of the family, but Charlie shared that he keenly understood the risk of such concentrated holdings. The move to diversify proved prescient, as the family members were no longer shareholders of General Motors when it entered bankruptcy protection in 2009.

Kettering Family Office Governance Evolution

Beginning in the 1990s, as the family footprint began to expand rapidly and the fifth generation continued to grow in size, the family began to institute new policies and establish new organizations to prepare for a future of more scale and complexity. Charlie recalled being invited while still in grade school to observe his first family meetings at The Carlyle Hotel in New York, stating, "I remember my first meeting and there were four or five people in the room . . . but a family of this [now growing] scale cannot be run like a small family business. This has been my life's work; get this repositioned for the next generation and those after, which will include many more people."[25]

First, the family decided to pursue a policy of internal transparency in order to maintain family harmony and encourage education and participation: All adult family members are permitted to attend and observe the board or committee meeting discussions. Grant advises that the invitation and access to participate and observe is a powerful expression of the family's commitment to transparency and inclusivity. Second, the family allowed each family unit to make their own decisions about participation and the manner of bringing in the next generation. Charlie shared, "It was up to the parents to prepare, educate, and permit their children to get involved."[26] Third, the family began to increase involvement of married-in members of the family, whom it sees as highly respected, valued, and welcome to participate in the broader family governance once they have been educated and committed to become involved.

   In the mid 2000s, discussions began about the establishment of a new, formal family office entity to serve as a more efficient central governance and operating function for the growing family, which was established in 2009. The intention was to preserve the way in which the family made decisions by consensus, but also to simplify and consolidate decision-making across the family. "We had many overlapping members that were serving on many different boards and committees" shared Grant. The new structure has provided a structure for graduated participation and a centralization of information flows, while retaining the same formal approach inherited from the family's past.

Family Culture and Guiding Family Values

Family culture and values are at the core of the Kettering family. The family holds dear their shared family values that are captured in Figure 11.2 about their guiding family values and aspirational quotes from key family leaders. The family elder quotes provide keen insight to the core family values and their family culture.

FIGURE 11.2 Kettering Family Values and Principles

Kettering Family Culture

"Ten years from now, we shall be thinking thoughts and dreaming dreams not even in our conscious thought now."
—C.F. Kettering

"One has to work to produce wealth. You can't wave a wand and take it out of a hat."
—C.F. Kettering

"Leave more than you receive."
—Virginia W. Kettering

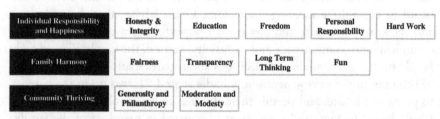

Individual Responsibility and Happiness	Honesty & Integrity	Education	Freedom	Personal Responsibility	Hard Work
Family Harmony	Fairness	Transparency	Long Term Thinking	Fun	
Community Thriving	Generosity and Philanthropy	Moderation and Modesty			

Source: Grant Kettering, 2020.

Grant attributes the family office success to its mission to support the growth of the family culture in five key areas:

1. *Role Modeling:* Elder family and advisors providing action-based guidance and mentoring to family.
2. *Trusted Advisors:* Support from independent, objective advisors who provide education and support to create the Kettering's customized plan and develop strategy to execute based on the family's goals and objectives.
3. *Family/Corporate Governance:* Committees formed within the family to create structure and consistency, increase communication, and provide guidance to decision-making process.
4. *Family Champions:* Family leaders who play a critical role, involving participation from family to preserve wealth and ensure family continuity throughout generations.
5. *Family Rituals:* The importance of regular family gatherings (virtually and in-person) to encourage community and continuity throughout the generations.

With more than twenty-five members in Grant's generation, finding opportunities and on-ramps for engagement, awareness, and to be good stewards of the wealth and ownership is paramount. The values of responsibility, accountability, and stewardship have been keenly woven in the family fabric. Grant expressed the value and power of their pooled wealth to collectively bargain and the importance to modernize and keep pace with change, coupled with the transparency, communication, and good access to information to empower the family and the family office.

Family Governance Committee Structures

The Kettering family office has instituted several smaller committees to help forward various initiatives. The committees all have specifically defined scope and operational protocols for meetings, having quorums to make resolutions, document decisions, and amend and evolve their charters as necessary. Grant further explained that there is a document that explains the authority amongst the various committees some of which include:

- Family Council
- Board of Directors
- Executive Committee

- Nominating Committee
- Compensation Committee
- Investment Committee
- Audit Committee
- Philanthropic Board of Trustees
- Eight Sub-Committees in Different Giving Interest Areas

Each committee has its own charter, defined operational procedures, and understanding of what committee membership requires. The committee's resolutions and actions all feed up to the Board's mandate. Grant explains that the investment committee, for example, provides recommendations on asset allocation, investment opportunities, tax considerations, and so forth that the appropriate Board takes under advisement to make decisions with respect to its investment policies.

Conclusion: Embracing the Future

The Kettering family has evolved their family office over almost the last thirty years from having one physical office in Ohio to now having another in Delaware and a robust virtual presence with family office advisors, consultants, and key owners spread across global geographies.

Enabled through outsourced institutional partners, consultants, experts, and advisors, the family has put in place robust virtual systems enabled by enterprise class technology to support cloud document storage, information sharing, collaboration, workflow management, cyber security, virtual communication with video conferencing, and so on. These new virtual tools have made the family's work more efficient, but the same basic processes are still being carried on in their new virtual form.

Charles F. Kettering once shared, "We should be concerned about the future because we will have to spend the rest of our lives there." The Kettering Family governs to moderate the changing family footprint and their evolving needs, embracing what is next; adaption and stewardship are central premises to the future family office and its good governance.

Conclusion and Final Thoughts

In this chapter, an overview of various facets of successful family governance, which is an integral part of an exceptional family office, was shared. From recommended practices and the benefits of a strong Board and/or advisory

Board, to the important elements of family participation, accountability, transparency, and involvement of future members of the family in the governance of the family office, this chapter illustrates the bridge between governance of the family and the family office. Next, the chapter covered succession planning and a broader discussion of decision-making in the family and how to get started with developing a governance process in your family. The chapter concluded with the Kettering Family Case Study, which detailed a seventh-generation family and its evolving governance practices. From developing a family council to a developing a family constitution, there are a number of governance structures that can increase the effectiveness of the decision-making process. Effective family governance can be an important contributing factor to sustainability, as it can help foster a sense of unity, togetherness, and cohesion in the family. Family governance can help to bridge family leadership generation to generation, build family consensus, and bring a sense of continuity in a family. Strong governance practices can be the compass that helps keep them on track, particularly as families face periods of transitions. Thank you to Charlie and Grant Kettering for sharing the wisdom and insights from the Kettering heritage in the governance case study for this chapter.

Notes

1. OECD, "OECD Principles of Corporate Governance," Paris, France, 2004, available at www.oecd.org/corporate/corporateaffairs/corporategovernanceprinciples/31557724.pdf.
2. Kirby Rosplock, Dianne H.B. Welsh, Juan Roure, and Juan Luis Segurado, "Sustaining the Family Enterprise Report of Findings," GenSpring Family Offices, 2012.
3. David Toth, "Why Family Office Boards are Indispensable," Family Office Exchange, 2018. To learn more visit, https://www.familyoffice.com/insights/why-family-office-boards-are-indispensable.
4. Ibid.
5. Campden UBS Global Family Office Report, 2019, p. 80.
6. Ibid., 79.
7. Ibid., 76.
8. Kirby Rosplock, Dianne H.B. Welsh, Juan Roure, and Juan Luis Segurado, "Sustaining the Family Enterprise Report of Findings," GenSpring Family Offices, 2012.
9. *The International Family Offices Journal*, December 2019, p. 64.
10. Campden UBS Global Family Office Report, 2019, p. 76.

11. Ibid., 76.
12. Kirby Rosplock, "Wealth Alignment Report of Findings," GenSpring Family Offices, 2008.
13. Ivan Lansberg, *Succeeding Generations: Realizing the Dream of Families in Business* (Boston, MA: Harvard Business School Press, 1999).
14. From interview with Edouard Thijssen, Founder and Commercial Director of TrustedFamily, LLC, 2012.
15. Kirby Rosplock, Dianne H.B. Welsh, Juan Roure, and Juan Luis Segurado, "Sustaining the Family Enterprise Report of Findings," GenSpring Family Offices, 2012.
16. Ibid.
17. This list of topic areas for a family constitution was assembled and informed by the following sources: Barbara Hauser, *International Family Governance* (Minneapolis, MN: Mesatop Press, 2009); Mark Haynes Daniell, *Strategy for the Wealthy Family* (Singapore: John Wiley & Sons, 2008); Dennis Jaffe, *Stewardship in Your Family Enterprise: Developing Responsible Family Leadership Across Generations* (Maui, HI: Pioneer Imprints, 2010).
18. Marc A. Shampo, Robert A. Kyle, and David P. Steensma, "Charles F. Kettering—Medical Philanthropist and Inventor," *Mayo Clinic Proceedings* 2012, May, 87(5): e35. To download the article, https://www.ncbi.nlm.nih.gov/pmc/articles/PMC3498412/.
19. To learn more about General Motor Company, visit https://www.britannica.com/topic/General-Motors-Corporation.
20. To learn more about the Sloan-Kettering Institute, visit https://www.mskcc.org/research/ski.
21. Ibid.
22. Interviews with Grant Kettering, March 2020, and Charles F. Kettering, III, April 2020.
23. Interview with Grant Kettering, March 2020.
24. Ibid.
25. Interview with Charles F. Kettering, III, April 2020.
26. Ibid.

CHAPTER 12

Family Education and the Family Office

Kirby Rosplock, PhD

> What lies behind us
> And what lies before us
> Are small matters
> Compared to what lies within us.
>
> Henry Stanley Haskins (1875–1957)

There is a sea change occurring around the globe in response to how family offices are conceiving and implementing their education programs and preparing the next generation. Family offices are faced with a new reality post-pandemic: Will the Millennial and Generation Z family members transition back to work or be called by personal passions, charitable pursuits, and/or other aspirations to take action and cultivate a different purposeful path?[1] As the largest segment of the workforce, 72 percent of Millennials are employed, but questions loom about how they will see the world and what they deem as priority to apply their passions, skills, and means.[2]

Another factor impacting the prioritization of wealth education in the family office is the increased retirement of Boomers. Pew Research released data indicating that the Millennials have overtaken the Boomers as the largest generation, as Millennials number 72.1 million whereas Boomers number 71.6 million. Generation X numbers 65.2 million and is projected to grow larger than the Boomer population by 2028.[3] The projections on wealth transfer from Boomers and the Silent generations to younger offspring over the coming few decades are staggering. One study expects $15.4 trillion to be transferred by 2030 by individuals with $5 million or more in net worth. Consider that this sum is comparable to the economy of China or 17 times the market capitalization of Amazon.[4] In North America, a total of $8.8 trillion will be passed on to heirs by 2030; in Europe, an older wealthy population, Wealth-X projects $3.2 trillion will be transferred.[5]

Meanwhile, The Pandemic of 2020 is reshaping behavioral norms. In-person classrooms have been exchanged for at-a-distance video conferencing for both companies and schools around the world. Learning, communicating, and decision-making via screens are more the norm than ever. Time will tell, but social distancing, quarantining, and sheltering measures likely will have lasting effects impacting everyone, but most acutely the Millennials and Generation Z. This will be their 9/11. For those Millennials and Generation Z members who are fortunate recipients of the wealth transfer, grooming, preparing, and educating them to be savvy beneficiaries has never been so critical.

The family office is at the heart of this matter but the old ways of approaching education, such as sending family to wealth camps, to closed door private membership organization weekend learning retreats, or even to a high-end university or Ivy League school's weeklong or weekend intensive on wealth management, are less and less attractive post-Covid-19. The "Rising Generation," as Hughes, Whittaker, and Massenzio coined, is in the cross currents of a time of incredible attention to the now, but also with the inspiration of innovation and impact. As wealth sits in trust for many of these affluent offspring, the question of stewardship has expanded but also has evolved.

A large part of family wealth sustainability is a function of the stewardship and success of ensuing generations. From mentorship, financial education, and awareness building for family members of all ages, grooming successful offspring is a function of many small steps leading to a bigger result. This chapter walks through five components: (1) meaning, (2) modeling, (3) mentoring, (4) management, and (5) mastery to prepare family members for their responsibilities of wealth, investments, finances, and the family office. The chapter shares solutions for family offices to approach learning opportunities and education for heirs and/or resources to outsource this education through practical examples and cases. It addresses the importance of financial literacy as well as the challenges that exist in most families of significant wealth when it comes to the wealth transfer discussion. The chapter addresses questions such as: How do you have this conversation? Who is the best person to facilitate this discussion? Should it be the parent, trustee, or the family office sharing the news? Through a case study, the chapter shares one family's education journey. What does it mean to prepare the next generation for the responsibilities of wealth?

Stewardship of Wealth

Famous American industrialist and philanthropist, Andrew Carnegie, who came to the US from Scotland in the late 1800s, was thought to have also brought wisdom on the topic of stewardship. In an old Lancashire proverb attributed to him, Carnegie shares, "There's nobbut three generations atween a clog and clog."[6] The expression is well known as the "shirtsleeves to shirtsleeves in three generations" proverb, which appears in countless other cultures and languages. The desire to provide children with a life better than their own is common among parents who were not born into wealth. Many parents are "immigrants" themselves to wealth, versus their children who are "natives."[7] For parents who were brought up affluent, the notion of being able to accommodate all the material wishes of a child can bring a sense of pride and accomplishment. As a family ascends the economic and social class hierarchy, access to resources and mentors as well as to work, education, and networking opportunities increase. This can provide a significant advantage to their children. That head start can help advance well-rounded, worldly offspring, but this exposure may create a false sense of security in parents that their children will be financially successful in their own right because of their pedigree and grooming.

Most affluent parents want to create a family culture of gratitude, modesty, pride, and humbleness, in addition to stewardship when it comes to preparing their heirs. One hundred percent of individuals aged 25 to 49 responded that being a good steward of wealth is of importance to them.[8] As parents, their goal is to develop independent, confident, and empowered children. Identifying opportunities for their children to exert their independence and recognizing teachable moments for mentoring youth are paramount. But understanding the gaps in their children's financial literacy and fluency is key. Another survey found that 89 percent of teenagers want to learn how to invest their money, 65 percent of them find learning about money management interesting, 60 percent said learning money management skills is a top priority, 82 percent have learned about money management from their parents, and 77 percent see their parents as money management role models.[9] As such, parents in wealthy families often teach their children about the family wealth history and the scope of that wealth. As their children get older, parents can teach them increasingly complex financial concepts such as investing, taxes, credit, budgeting, saving, finance, and philanthropy.

Psychology of Wealth and Child Development

From a psychological perspective, the period from early childhood to young adulthood is when a person develops identity, values, preferences, and core beliefs. Questions that can arise in this difficult period might include: Who am I? How do I see myself in my family and in the world? What values do I hold? Which are solely mine? Which are informed by those of my family, my peers, or from the world? What are my goals and ambitions? What are my perceived limitations, self-imposed or otherwise? How can I become self-reliant and independent? How can I achieve my own goals and passions? What kind of career, life, and family do I want?

This process of individuation can be riddled with challenges and transformation regardless of financial means. Although wealthy parents have the ability to provide their children with education, travel, and cultural experiences, enhanced by technology, this can also negatively influence them. A comfortable upbringing may lead offspring to feel a false sense of security. The blessing of wealth can become a debilitating curse that thwarts ambition and poisons the spirit.

Jessie O'Neill is the granddaughter of Charles Erwin Wilson, one-time president of General Motors. She is a licensed therapist, specializing in the psychology of wealth and money and its effect on personal and professional relationships. She is also passionate about climate change, the effect that "affluenza" has had on it, and how the wealthy can contribute to solving the global problem. Her book, *The Golden Ghetto*, is a deeply personal and vivid account of how the trappings of wealth can create a gilded cage or a golden ghetto for children. Children growing up in abject poverty may experience living in a ghetto without enough food, water, shelter, and clothing. *The Golden Ghetto*, as O'Neill describes, creates the same sense of longing and sense of loss, yet from the opposite circumstances. Instead of having no material possessions, the golden ghetto is one that is filled with every material thing, but typically lacks human connection, love, and a sense of belonging.

The American psychologist Abraham Maslow created the concept of a hierarchy of needs.[10] (See Figure 12.1.) He theorized that individuals prioritize core basic needs—food and shelter—before psychological or self-fulfillment needs. Children born into affluence may never be fully exposed to the base of Maslow's pyramid.

FIGURE 12.1 Maslow's Hierarchy of Needs

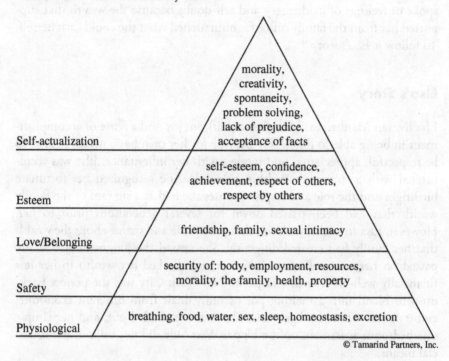

© Tamarind Partners, Inc.

Maslow believed that people focus on the level of need that is unmet, and do not progress to meeting higher levels of need until the previous level is met. Some children suffer at the most basic level, when their physical needs (e.g., food) are unmet. Other children have food, but their need for security is not met. Most would agree that children whose basic survival or security needs are unmet struggle with poverty. However, what about the children whose physical and security needs are met to excess? Are they in poverty? By economic standards, no. But what this one-dimensional view of poverty ignores is that there are other types of poverty beyond those that can be measured financially. Children living in the golden ghetto experience economic excess but may face a traumatizing lack of love, belonging, self-esteem, and opportunity for self-actualization—needs that are reflected at the higher levels of Maslow's hierarchy. O'Neill argues that these children are deeply impoverished as well. The psychological and existential trauma that results from disconnection from both their parents and their peers is very difficult to overcome; some never overcome the deep sense of isolation.

In an interview, a next-generation inheritor who was early in her career spoke of feelings of inadequacy and self-doubt because the wealth that supported her from the family office far outmatched what she could earn herself. To follow is Elsa's story.[11]

Elsa's Story

Elsa lives in Manhattan.[12] She feels significant joy and a sense of accomplishment in being able to financially provide for her own basic needs. Reared to be respectful, appreciative, and modest with her inheritance, Elsa was acculturated with a strong stewardship principle. She recognized her fortunate birthright and the role and responsibilities she had as a steward of the family wealth that had been passed down for several generations prior to her. However, Elsa struggled with simultaneous pride and shame about the wealth that her family had created diligently. She sensed the judgment that many passed on her as a well-to-do inheritor and masked her wealth to her less financially well-off friends and peers. New York City was the perfect backdrop to blend into a melting pot of individuals from different economic, cultural, and ethnic backgrounds. She was not singled out, and her simple one-bedroom apartment on the Upper West Side did not call out her financial means.

Elsa indicated that although her inheritance was significant, it did not mean as much to as her as the money she earned herself. Although her inheritance could accommodate her lifestyle and then some, she always had a sense of guilt for not being able to financially make it on her own. She felt codependent on the family office and the wealth that it doled out, which, in many respects, made her resent that she was not financially independent to make it on her own. When she finally landed a position that allowed her to stop the supplemental payments for her lifestyle, she felt freed and empowered to take care of herself.

Joanie Bronfman, an inheritor and expert in the field of wealth and psychology, has spent much of her professional life exploring the complex relationship of individuals to wealth. Her dissertation was a qualitative study in the field of sociology on the experience of the inheritor, and provided windows to some of the psychological hardship—from lack of self-worth and self-confidence to feelings of resentment and hostility—that inheritance can perpetuate.[13] Helping a child develop a healthy self-esteem and identity is the bedrock for preparing the generation to be strong stewards of wealth. So how does this stewardship ethos develop?

Parents are often the first role models when it comes to affluence. The way they perceive wealth often influences how their children see it. Some will put undue pressure on their children to excel and rise to their accomplishments. What would happen if parents went from a "child-centric" lens towards a family-centric type of approach within the family? This involves developing an understanding that children and parents may have independent interests, needs, and expectations. Young people long for opportunities and experiences that show them as separate from their parents. Parents who understand that desire can encourage their children to seek those experiences, whether they bring success or failure. The family can celebrate and emphasize opportunities to have shared experiences as well as to pursue individual passions. When parents do this in conjunction with wealth, they can move away from creating a sense of dependence on material things. They can emphasize the value of *doing* rather than *having*, and foster children's sense of independence rather than co-dependence on their parents and the wealth.

Overcoming Communication Challenges

When members of the younger generation are fully aware of their present and future wealth, they tend to be more empowered to take responsibility and be involved with the decision-making for it. Mindy Kalinowski Earley, the Chief Learning Officer at Family Office Exchange (FOX), runs FOX's Rising Gen Leadership Programs geared for children and young adults of wealthy families; she knows well how important engagement and communication are when it comes to next generation family members. The FOX program emphasizes creating a safe place to engage learners where they are, identifying their skills and strengths, finding a peer group to reflect, and discussing practical cases that apply to them. FOX notes six best practices when it comes to family learning and family offices, including designing next generation programs that are (1) expansive, (2) practical, (3) inclusive, (4) clear, (5) instructive, and (6) helpful as an example for others to follow.[14]

Chelsea Toler-Hoffmann, President of the Keep Families Giving Foundation, is a millennial philanthropist and advocate for next-generation empowerment. She knows firsthand the importance of open family communication and peer networking to learn from other millennial inheritors. This cornerstone belief is why she hosted the InterGen Family Summit. Never has there been a time so great for fruitful conversations among next-generation family members that can lead to collective action, giving, and impact. "Being together inspires us to positive possibilities for change and now Keep

Families Giving has taken the conversation virtually as we manage through the pandemic together. In a world that needs generosity, collaboration, and innovation, the time is now more than ever before," notes Toler-Hoffman.[15] During Covid-19, she also launched a global next generation coalition with peers such as NEXUS that inspired #NextGenGenerosity and #GivingTuesdayNow.[16] Together they raised more than $400,000 and completed over 700,000 next generation acts of generosity to demonstrate the importance of how the next generation is making a difference. Chelsea is actively engaged with her parents and their family foundation, inspired by philanthropy after the death of her grandmother. Finding opportunities to link means with meaning helps families appreciate their birthright for what it is, a privilege and a responsibility. Family communication breakdowns are critical potential points of dislocation in the preparation of the next generation. In fact, 60 percent of wealth transfer failures are due to lack of communication and trust within a family.[17] To avoid that fate, Ellen Perry, founder of Wealthbridge Partners and author of *A Wealth of Possibilities: Navigating Family, Money and Possibilities,* recommends that parents teach their children their values through modeling those values, meaning showing them in action.[18] Perry recommends teaching young people that their money has meaning, such as by teaching them how the family came to achieve its affluence, sharing stories about their ancestors, and talking of family memories and traditions. A third recommendation is that family members should be given a voice and be involved in decision-making, as it leads to them taking responsibility for their wealth and being committed to it. Open and honest communication that is age appropriate is thus essential. Inheritors can be well prepared for their inheritance with education about both the opportunities and the difficulties that arise in a life with wealth. Acquiring the ability to recognize attitudes and emotions related to affluence is also important.

Jamie Johnson, grandson and an heir to the Johnson & Johnson fortune, provides a window into his personal experience of growing up in a privileged life in his personal documentary film, *Born Rich.* The millennial filmmaker at the fledgling age of 23 opens the film as he primps for his twenty-first birthday party, a *Great Gatsby*–type gala, and remarks that at the stroke of midnight, he will inherit more than most will ever be able to earn in their lifetime. In addition to sharing his own personal story, Johnson interviews a series of wealthy heirs from well-known families including the Trumps, Vanderbilts, Newhouses, and Bloombergs. The consistent themes were the taboo nature of talking openly about their family's financial means, the challenges wealth presents to forging authentic friendships, and the difficulties in finding their own personal identity amidst their families' material wealth. Johnson alludes to some of his own family's scandals and conflicts stemming from the wealth and confesses to his own fears for the "voodoo inherited wealth."[19] Inherited wealth is a double-edged sword: It can provide tremendous opportunities for children to get the best educations, training, and cultural experiences, but it also can thwart the development of self-worth and pride in accomplishments of achieving success independently from the materialism of their birthright. Elders often fear the latter, and the following case study provides an anonymous account of family elders who dreaded telling a beneficiary of his inherited wealth. The case study that follows illustrates the challenges that can come with the opportunities when inheriting wealth and the customized education that is required to help beneficiaries thrive, not just survive.

Case Study: Waithram Family

Educating adult children about the responsibilities of wealth is not as simple as it may seem. The Waithram family learned this truism after the father cashed out a significant closely held business that was acquired by a larger conglomerate. He received cash and stock in the acquiring firm, which six months later had an initial public offering. His offspring, two sons and a daughter, had always lived comfortably, but had veered from their father's business and wealth creator path to pursue careers in education, charitable sector, and natural sciences. When the reality set in that their personal trusts went from $5 million to more than $50 million each, the children felt overwhelmed and afraid of failing. Likewise, the father understood that a "great way to screw up your children is to try to teach them about the wealth that *you* made, not them." Stepping back, he observed that his family office was not set up for "ride-alongs" to meet with investment managers, nor did he ascribe to the school of thought that an Ivy League school could inculcate what they practically need to know about their wealth from a PhD with advanced degrees in economics, finance, and discreet math. "My children need to know how to be shrewd, responsible stewards, not hardliner wealth creators. They need to know how to spot the fraudsters and the gaps in their stories, how to read reports and plan accordingly to always live well below or within their means."

Jim, the father, and his wife, Karen, had brought up their children modeling their values of hard work, discipline, education, integrity, and caring for others and for one's self. They involved their children in finding a family wealth education specialist to co-create a learning path that suited their busy lives, schedules, and burgeoning families. Tamarind Partners, Inc., was selected to take them through the process to create a custom, actionable education path that was geared just for them, using their bespoke fact pattern and information. The process started with a kickoff meeting over two days to co-create the learning objectives based on their goals and clarify the learning areas that were priority. Logistically, Tamarind understood that one son lived with roommates who were not aware of his family wealth situation, one son had two small children and a wife in medical school and the daughter was working part-time in a social services clinic and considering law school. Meeting in-person routinely was not going to be (1) cost effective, (2) logistically feasible as they were spread across the South, and (3) possible to schedule due to their family and work commitments. Thus, a virtual learning path was created to engage them twice a month via videoconference call, coupled with one-on-one mentoring calls to follow up on each of their specific learning agendas.

The three siblings identified nine areas (Figure 12.2) that they desired to cover over the year including:

- Budgeting
- Career Planning
- Financial Planning
- Investing
- Understanding Investment and Financial Statements
- Trust Basics
- Best Practices for Working with Advisors
- Direct Investing

FIGURE 12.2   Custom Family Learning Path

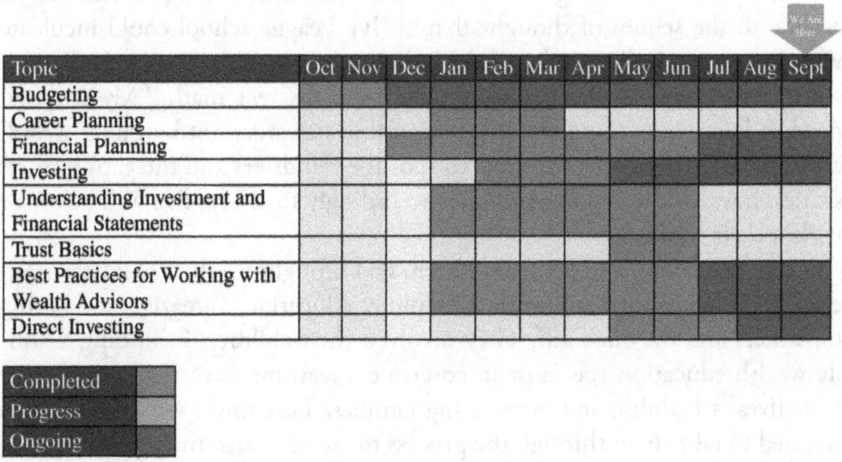

Topic	Oct	Nov	Dec	Jan	Feb	Mar	Apr	May	Jun	Jul	Aug	Sept
Budgeting												
Career Planning												
Financial Planning												
Investing												
Understanding Investment and Financial Statements												
Trust Basics												
Best Practices for Working with Wealth Advisors												
Direct Investing												

Completed	
Progress	
Ongoing	

Source: © Tamarind Partners, Inc.

Figure 12.2 provides the learning progression through the coursework that was based on the siblings, desired plans and what was timely. For example, the siblings had a shared family limited partnership with holdings that they were looking to liquidate and redeploy. Tamarind Partners, Inc., took the siblings through an exercise to consider alternative investment options (passive versus active) and/or investing into a family vacation home together. Once the brothers and sister considered the time, management, oversight, governance, insurance, and upkeep not to mention agreeing on a location, they looked at each of their investment holdings and realized they would rather rent or lease homes, come together in different geographies, and/or purchase places independently of one another. To follow in Figure 12.3 are the accomplishments after one year of disciplined education, practical application, and hard work.

FIGURE 12.3 Sibling Cohort Accomplishments

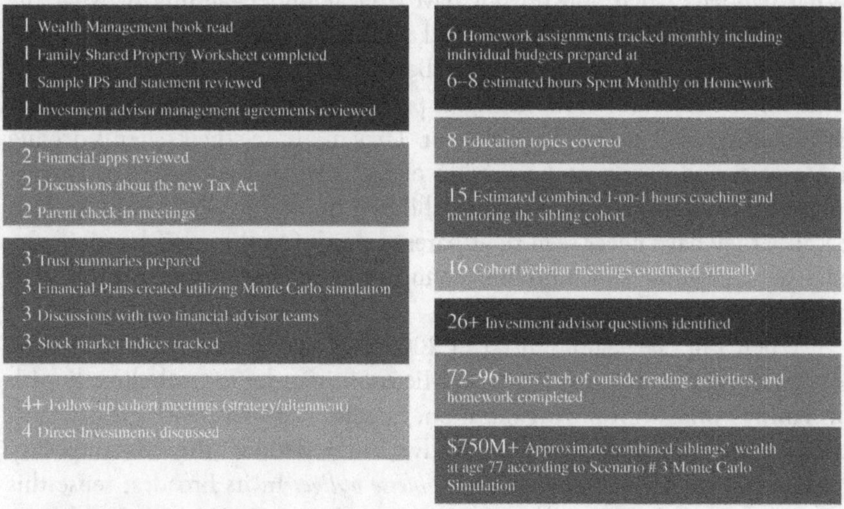

1 Wealth Management book read
1 Family Shared Property Worksheet completed
1 Sample IPS and statement reviewed
1 Investment advisor management agreements reviewed

2 Financial apps reviewed
2 Discussions about the new Tax Act
2 Parent check-in meetings

3 Trust summaries prepared
3 Financial Plans created utilizing Monte Carlo simulation
3 Discussions with two financial advisor teams
3 Stock market Indices tracked

4+ Follow-up cohort meetings (strategy/alignment)
4 Direct Investments discussed

6 Homework assignments tracked monthly including individual budgets prepared at
6–8 estimated hours Spent Monthly on Homework

8 Education topics covered

15 Estimated combined 1-on-1 hours coaching and mentoring the sibling cohort

16 Cohort webinar meetings conducted virtually

26+ Investment advisor questions identified

72–96 hours each of outside reading, activities, and homework completed

$750M+ Approximate combined siblings' wealth at age 77 according to Scenario # 3 Monte Carlo Simulation

Source: © Tamarind Partners, Inc.

The siblings completed the learning path, presented major outcomes from the virtual learning experience, and shared insights, questions, and feedback to their parents on how they had grown. One sibling shared that "a holistic approach to family wealth education was so impactful." He emphasized that, rather than sitting around a conference table quarterly, his relationship with his siblings grew with the dynamic education and mentorship."[20] Finally, a year after the engagement Tamarind received a phone call. It was Jim calling to share that he was unwinding his investments in closely held businesses. I inquired why? He shared that his children had respectfully asked him how long he hoped to work as managing director of that aspect of their investment holdings, as they admitted that (1) they really did not know how/ if they could replace him and (2) hoped to invest in lower-risk investment strategies that did not require subject matter expertise and operational day-to-day involvement. Jim and his children discussed that the portfolio had a five-to-seven-year time horizon at best, and if he continued to deploy capital in this manner, it might be longer than 10 to 15 years to exit some of the companies. Jim thanked Tamarind Partners again for helping him learn from his adult children that life is short and letting go of certain ambitions and dreams makes way for new opportunities.

Clear Expectations and the Power of Inherited Wealth

What happens when you do not have a clear understanding of what the expectations or intentions are behind wealth that is inherited? You create your own, and it may or may not be one that is realistic or attainable. Children are creatures of modeling. If parents show entitlement, chances are their children will model that behavior. They might see their parents driving a Maserati and expect to be driving one too when they turn 16. Parents might have a housekeeper, and thus children think they never have to clean because they have never seen their parents clean. On the other hand, if parents are gracious and humble, chances are children will exhibit that behavior too.

When Bill Gates announced in 2006 that two years later he would be leaving the day-to-day operations of Microsoft in order to work directly with his family's philanthropic organization, he said, "I believe with great wealth comes great responsibility." He inadvertently defined the contemporary meaning of the French expression, *noblesse oblige*. In its broadest sense this expression is used to mean that there is an understanding that those who are a bit better off should help out those who are worse off.

In an interview with Dr. Keith Whitaker and Dr. Susan Massenzio, the founders of Wise Counsel Research, a series of questions were asked, including what are new trends when it comes to educating and preparing beneficiaries and next generation stewards? What do we need to pay attention to in terms of how we are communicating and engaging the next generation of inheritors? What is so different about the issues they will face versus prior generations when it comes to wealth? How do we rear responsible beneficiaries who are stewards of the wealth and engender trustees to advise with the values, intention, and wisdom of the grantor in mind? What are your views on the opportunities/challenges of trustee/beneficiary relationship? Where do parents come into play?

Whitaker and Massenzio, co-authors with Jay Hughes of *Cycle of a Gift*, provided insights about the opportunities and challenges of both giving and receiving gifts. In an interview they shared, "Generations face many of the same difficulties over time. We have come to see that individuals go through a cycle of life with regard to giving. We all begin mainly as recipients. As we mature, we move from receiving to beginning to build our own lives and families. In older age, we turn primarily to giving back. And in extreme old age, we become recipients once more. The struggle we see is that parents who are in that 'giving back' stage tend to judge their children negatively. They sometimes expect them to take a lead in giving, perhaps through leadership of a private foundation. They then become disappointed if their children do not take up that challenge in the ways they, the parents, would wish. What some of these parents are missing is that their children are not being selfish or uncharitable: They are being young, still in that first stage of primarily receiving. Education about giving is something they can receive, but it is hard to expect someone to become a great giver when they have not had much experience in the world and, in particular, have not had the experience of making something themselves from which to give to others."[21] For parents of affluent children, the goal should be to incrementally create a path of clear expectations of what it means to be part of a family of wealth.

Warren Buffett is known to enact *noblesse oblige* through his philanthropy, and he instilled this value in his children who are carrying on the philanthropic tradition. The Buffetts set up charitable foundations that each of their children has been running in the late 1990s.[22] Howard Buffett has said of his father, whose fortune is approximately $47 billion, "I think the only pressure I feel from him is making sure we're smart about how we spend the money. He's had no influence on where we give money, but he's had a big influence on how we go about it." Susie Buffett said of her mother, "She had me in the car with her at a very early age in the housing projects and deep in the community. She was very involved personally. It was not a check-writing thing. It was her being there." About raising independent children without "entitlitis," Warren Buffett himself has said that the perfect amount of money to leave them is "enough money so that they would feel they could do anything, but not so much that they could do nothing."[23]

Joline Godfrey, SVP and MD of Family Learning at Hawthorn Family Institute for Success, is a leading financial education expert for children and families of affluence. She has been providing information and facilitating experiences for the purpose of affluent inheritor education for more than three decades. In Godfrey's book, *Raising Financially Fit Kids*, Godfrey outlines the various ages and stages of developmentally appropriate financial knowledge and money skills. Joline Godfrey's book outlines stages of financial development during the apprenticeship years, ages 5–19+. Children tend to move through the stages in sequence, although they may begin a stage at any age. If your child is 16 and has not acquired the skills from an earlier stage such as appreciating the value of money, you can help him/her do activities appropriate to an earlier stage and move along from there. It is never too late—even for adults—to become financially fit.

Instilling the importance of being financially self-sufficient and encouraging the next generation to grow their own wealth is an important value found in families who do not succumb to the shirtsleeves-to-shirtsleeves paradigm. The shirtsleeves-to-shirtsleeves concept is reflected in a comment by a highly affluent participant in a focus group discussion of the positives and negatives of great wealth.[24] She noted that having wealth can demotivate people from working hard and lead to dependence on their money. She said that this could lead them to "lose their sense of 'I can do it myself.'" She elaborated on the three-generation demise of wealth as "wonder, blunder, dunder." The wonder creates the wealth; the blunder loses it and results in the dunder of having the family wealth squandered in three generations.

Tom Rogerson, President and Chief Learning officer of GenLeg Co., Inc., describes a pattern of unsuccessful wealth transition in terms of generations.[25] In the first generation there are the wealth builders, and the second generation is made up of assimilators. They engage in stewardship of the wealth they inherited. When the wealth appears to be inevitably sustainable, they raise a third generation, the enjoyment generation, who use their family's fortune not for a better life, but for the good life. This leads to the lamentation generation, who look back at a family history of gains and then losses of wealth, with despair. (See Figure 12.4.)

All these paradigms suggest the rise and fall of wealth holders in a matter of a few generations, and if we consider the typical human life cycle of living for approximately two to three generations, we may see an interesting parallel. When the beneficiary becomes so distanced from the experience of the creation of the wealth, there is less and less identification with the wealth creators' experience, tenacity, and hard work to create the wealth. Thus, the work needed to prepare a beneficiary becomes even that much more intense when this modeled behavior is not part of their reality.

FIGURE 12.4 Wealth over Generations

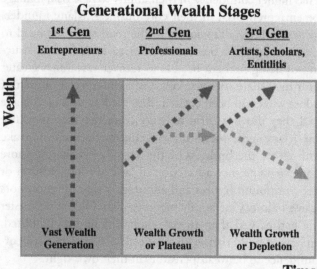

Source: © Tamarind Partners, Inc.

Inspiring Entrepreneurship and the Next Generation

Fear of the next generation having little motivation to earn their own way is often a common concern for affluent parents. Although they have peace of mind knowing they can provide for them, they often still desire to see that their children have the means to be financially independent. A past study found that older-generation parents (i.e., those over age 50) wanted their children to be involved in decisions about the family wealth while also pursuing a career. In contrast, younger-generation parents (i.e., those aged 25 to 49) tended to encourage their children to do whatever they want to do.[26] Inspiring entrepreneurism has been a concern of many affluent families when it comes to the next generation. This concept is more fully discussed along with family banks in Chapter 13. Research supports that many family members born into wealth have less risk appetites than that of the family members that created the wealth. In fact, some inheritors find that they are caught between two tidal currents so to speak, as wealth creators may ask them to be good stewards and responsible owners, and at the same time ask them to be financially independent and wealth creators in their own right. The mixed messaging can lead to a form of family wealth paralysis, as the fear of not letting down one generation can lead a generation to "reach for the brass ring" despite it being out of reach.

Anecdotal experience with wealth creators reveals that the owner or wealth creator often has higher confidence in their ability to take risk, manage financial loss, and be entrepreneurial in their core business. Many founders experience other business failures, drawdowns in the market, or the need to make major strategic shifts in their businesses prior to their financial success. Their perception of being resilient or able to recover was much greater than what an inheritor may share. Because successors often feel a burden of responsibility to not lose what had been created, they are less willing to make a mistake, risk capital they did not earn, or stray from the success course that got them this far. Many successors want to mitigate losses and not take unnecessary risks with either the business or the wealth. Finally, the more conservative successors' views are not a function of lack of sophistication or experience, but rather a profound respect and admiration that the successors have for those who came before. One family member shared that it was easier to risk the capital he had earned than to risk the assets he had inherited. Inspiring family members to build their own financial independence is a cornerstone to build confidence to be wealth creators in their own right.

Entrepreneurial spirit is founded through modeling, education, and inspiring a vision in the succeeding generations of their *own* entrepreneurial tendencies. When families utilize their wealth, education, and positive influences, they can foster empowerment in the next generation to become entrepreneurial. Where sometimes an inheritor fears filling the shoes of a successful entrepreneurial matriarch or patriarch, families can encourage and impassion inheritors to become entrepreneurs. Entrepreneurship can be supported at a very young age. Entrepreneurial beginnings can be found in a host of ways, from providing opportunities for children to set up lemonade or vegetable stands to teenagers establishing a car wash. Children, tweens, teenagers, and young adults are continually inspired by technology, medicine, health, the environment, and other areas that are ripe for innovation. Chapter 13, on the role of the family bank, provides more examples of fostering entrepreneurship through a family bank. The following case study illustrates how one family member found her passion, purpose, and financial success after facing some trying times.

Case Study: Jennifer's Story

Jennifer had struggled to find her path, dropping out of college, getting in with a bad crowd, and eventually finding herself in rehab by 23.[27] Her father was a Wall Street legend, successful, lauded, and revered; however, finance was not a path Jennifer aspired. Her mother sadly passed early in her life, when she was only 18, which may have been the root cause for her to drop out of college. Once clean, she found her passion helping others in emergency services, studying and passing the EMT test, and getting to work in an ambulance. She later started volunteering with the Coast Guard and analyzing data around suspicious watercraft patterns of suspected smuggler and drug dealers, while finishing her bachelors online. Jennifer witnessed firsthand some of the gaps in the emergency response technology, their tools, devices, gears, and vehicles as well as within the Coast Guard. She eventually approached her father to consider creating a private fund to specialize in this niche sector. Jennifer and her father approached Tamarind Partners to help Jennifer become educated on the financial, investment, and technical due diligence, and business plan for the closed fund. By turning her passion into an investment opportunity, she could demonstrate her passion and innovate and create something that brought her closer to her father while crafting an advisory board for the fund consisting of security, emergency service, and Coast Guard veterans, including a former chief of police. Together, Tamarind Partners with the advisory board helped her garner the expertise, build the business plan, and eventually to deploy the fund. Fast-forward three years later, and the initial $5 million deployed has spawned three new funds taking in outside capital of more than $250 million. Jennifer has proven that power that passion, persistence, and hard work can lead to new successful outcomes.

The Power, Influence, and Inspiration of Mentors

You only need to meet Bob Danzig and hear his personal story to marvel at the powerful role that mentors may provide. Danzig's story is the type that inspires Hollywood movies. In a nutshell, Danzig's story is of an orphan working in the mailroom who makes it to the C-suite at one of the largest media publication giants, Hearst Corporation, a multibillion dollar media corporation whose well-known publications include *Cosmopolitan*; *O, The Oprah Magazine*; *ELLE*; *Country Living*; *Harper's Bazaar*; *Redbook*; *Esquire*; and *Popular Mechanics* (and the list of iconic brands goes on).

Bob Danzig spent most of his childhood bouncing around the foster care system and struggling to find a place where he truly belonged. His first job was as an office boy at the *Albany Times Union*. The newspaper and his co-workers became his first family. Inspired and motivated by a caring boss, who remarked to him, "I believe you are full of promise," Danzig used these words like a boom to a sail.[28] Danzig mentioned it was having a developmental plan and mentorship that helped set him on a path to success.

He next went on to join the Navy for three years and then to college at night for five years. He attributes much of his success to the pivotal, transformational moments that mentors played in his life to keep him reaching farther than he thought he personally could. He was awarded a journalism fellowship to Stanford University, and nineteen years after his first job as an office boy, Danzig was promoted to publisher of the *Times Union*. Danzig took another significant promotion seven years later, when he was named president of all Hearst Newspapers nationwide. Over the following two decades, Danzig led the 6,000 employee/colleague company to a revitalization, which included inspiring company talent, devising the company's strategic purpose, and building the growth of the company 100 times. His accomplishments have earned him the respect of the media publication industry as an innovator, thinker, and transformational leader. Yet Danzig is incredibly humble and generous with his time, even though he is a professional speaker and in high demand. He still volunteers and actively helps others on their journey, knowing how profoundly different his life became as result of a few individuals whom he respected taking an active interest in his personal success. Mentoring can be a formal process, but Danzig shares that it can also happen organically and informally, as was the case with his personal situation.

As outsiders, mentors and coaches offer a unique perspective about the special, unique aspects about the client that may not be visible to him or her. Thus, coaching and mentoring can provide tremendous opportunities to build greater self-awareness and one's emotional intelligence (EQ). Professional coaches often use standard personality tests and/or 360-type evaluations to garner a better understanding of the individual before the formal coaching or mentoring begins. The benefits of formal coaching arrangements are that the mentee knows that mentoring/coaching is coming. Danzig figured out and tuned into the informal coaches that showed up in his life, but not all will see the call signs of a casual coach or mentor. Understanding what you or your next-generation family member may need is critical, and sometimes informal mentoring will suffice.

Not surprisingly, chemistry is foundational to the success of any mentor/mentee relationship. Therefore, it helps to interview coaches just as you would interview any professional advisor before signing up. Do you feel comfortable, relaxed, and excited to engage with this individual? Do they understand you and does there seems to be a click with your connection to them as a coach? Ask about their process, what you will experience, and/or what types of outcomes may be expected. Get clear on the time commitment to do the work, for you and for the coach, and how they charge. Coaching is not inexpensive if you work with certified professionals; however, the payoff can be multifold if clients are able to get out of a rut or move to the next level with their family, career, business, and/or relationships.

For next-generation family members whose situations require intervention or counseling from a licensed therapist or psychotherapist, consider identifying a psychotherapist whose practice focuses on the psychological dysfunction that stem from wealth inheritance. Thayer Cheatham Willis is an internationally known psychotherapist, specialist, educator, author, speaker, and leading authority in wealth counseling. Willis's focus is working with inheritors and their families as they cope with the psychological challenges of wealth. Born into the family who founded the multinational Georgia-Pacific Corporation, Willis had to face some of her own inner demons in her personal journey with family wealth. Depending on the symptoms and issues that are present, such as depression, addiction, anger management issues, isolation, motivation, and attachment or commitment issues, among other types of dysfunction, the next-generation family member may need to reach out to a professional psychotherapist to create sanity and freedom beyond the financial wealth in their life. Mentors, coaches, and therapists can play complementary roles to the family office advisor that may be providing the wealth education for the next generation family member. Be they family office advisors or other professional advisors who are able to professionally mentor and coach the next generation, the trusted advisors will foster family connectivity and bonds. Not all professional advisors are cut from that mentoring cloth, and partnering with a professional outside coach or mentor can sometimes be the best way to inspire, motivate, and empower the next generation to be the best they can be.

Creating a Family Education Plan

Jay Hughes reminds family office professionals that a family seeking to preserve its wealth must understand the need for all its members to be thoroughly educated on how to be owners of the shared family enterprise. Without this preparation, family members will not be competent to make risk-taking decisions as owners together.[29] Most family offices seek guidance from education or next-generation consultants, family wealth advisors at institutional, the peer family offices, or professional family office membership organizations to garner a basic family education framework. Depending on the size and complexity of the family, some of these solutions may work in part. However, the financial literacy and fiduciary responsibilities of most owners and their offspring require high-touch, hands-on, and very specific support and guidance. The struggle is coming up with a solid roadmap.

Tamarind Partners recommends that a family office first survey the current knowledge and awareness of family members, understanding their education needs by looking at what they perceive they know, what they desire to learn, and where they feel most vulnerable. Administering an intelligence test to test their knowledge can lead to more problems, as it may trigger fear, inferiority complexes, anxiety, and/or unintended conflict about the prioritization of learning. Mapping the family members' (1) needs, (2) wants, (3) current knowledge, and (4) priority to learn can provide a useful glimpse into the gaps and learning path. (See Figure 12.5.)

FIGURE 12.5 Education Plan Mapping

Topic	Needs (functional requirements)	Wants (Nice to Have, but not Required)	Current Education Level	Aspirational Level
	I need education on:	I want education on:	My current knowledge is:	My desired knowledge is:
Budgeting				
Financial Planning				
Understanding Statements				
Career Planning				
Stewardship				
Estate Planning				
Trusts				
Working with Advisors				
Investing				
Entrepreneurship				
Direct Investing				
Saving				
Lifestyle Management				
Philanthropy				
Impact Investing				
Family Governance				
Wealth Transfer				
Family Office				
Credit/Debt/Lending				
Other:				

Source: © Tamarind Partners, Inc.

Once the education topics have been mapped, a curriculum may be created that helps prioritize learning objectives that align with the family office's vision for education. A key to success is also establishing learning goals and benchmarks for achievement that may be identified for an individual's strategic learning path.[30] Often families may want to determine the educational expectations or requirements of mastery for current or future beneficiaries. By matching the family norms and expectations against the participants' skills, competencies, attitudes, and behaviors, the gaps and opportunities are revealed to customize the family curriculum.[31] Tamarind Partners has developed an online tool to gauge and assess these learning needs and wants across family generations, branches, or in-laws and heirs. Once the assessment has been completed, data may be analyzed to determine educational goals for cohorts based on age and experience. The next step is to garner buy-in of the families who are interested to participate. From this point, involving the prospective learner to help advise, co-develop, and own their learning journey is important. The content should be practical and engaging, while manageable. Understanding how the curriculum translates into measurable outcomes for the family office to monitor and manage is also important for the learners to be able to demonstrate their progress, but also for the family office to monitor. Follow-up actions to some of the curriculum, such as one-on-one coaching, distance learning, and/or pairing next-generation family with more senior family members, can be very helpful to achieve the desired results. Continuous feedback on a family's education strategy and programs is part of the process to implement a successful education plan.

Where do families and family offices go to get help preparing family members for the responsibilities of wealth? Some family offices look to the commercial peers or multi-family offices to both educate as well as inspire their clients through learning events, seminars, webinars, or experiential learning. Providing memorable, interactive learning experiences is one way to open the hearts and minds to content that can be otherwise dull and less engaging. Through living case studies and interactive working sessions to solve issues, certain multifamily offices have been leaders in providing learning experiences in a more scalable fashion for affluent families. And now more than ever, there is an appetite to learn peer-to-peer when it comes to their wealth. One example was during a large client event where a multi-family office collaborated with Shaking the Tree, a theatrical company specializing in family wealth topics and customizing interactive learning case studies. The live case study is facilitated and punctuated with pauses to allow the audience to engage and comment on the status of a family scenario that played out live on stage. Participants can be both a part of the experience, yet quietly and personally reflect on how these similar issues around the social and emotional aspects of wealth played out in their own family experiences. Other multi-family offices may outsource their education and mentoring experiences to outfits such as Tamarind Learning, a family office education platform providing custom learning for beneficiaries, family office advisors, and trustees.[32] From next-generation education, to beneficiary stewardship, to workshops on philanthropy and impact investing, Tamarind Learning provides unique learning experiences to prepare all members of the family.[33] The Accredited Beneficiary Stewardship Program (ABS) allows family members to learn asynchronously and privately. They can take the course in the comfort, safety, and convenience of their home or when on the go. The learning path covers nine areas including: (1) Stewardship and Code of Conduct, (2) Beneficiary Fundamentals, (3) Trustee Basics,

(4) Introduction to Estate Planning, (5) Personal Finance Fundamentals, (6) Trust Fundamentals, (7) Trust Administration and Working with Advisors, (8) Foundations of Tax, and (9) Fundamentals of Trust Investments. Tamarind Learning may also help family offices to create a customized learning curriculum, with their own portal access and training for family office executives to deliver to family members. One family office executive, retiring from his leadership role as chief learning officer, shared, "The most important area for a family to invest is their family capital. Without excelling stewards, what is the legacy of wealth and the future of the family office?"[34]

Conclusion and Final Thoughts

> Treat people as if they were what they ought to be and you help them become what they are capable of being.
>
> —Goethe[35]

This chapter reviews several important considerations for sustaining family wealth by building awareness, educating, and mentoring family members of all ages. The keys to preparing the next generation are oriented around five Ms. First is *meaning*. Help your children appreciate what wealth means (and what it doesn't). Based on this meaning, help them understand how to organize and prepare for the responsibilities of wealth. Second is *modeling*. Remember that children do what they are shown, not necessarily what they are told. Practice the behaviors you want to see in them. Third is *mentoring*. Your children need your guidance in addition to education, awareness, and empowerment to be able to effectively manage the family wealth. Working in lockstep with your family office to create a financial education plan for your family at the various stages of development can provide a roadmap toward financial preparedness and empowerment. Build a team of financial mentors and consider looking within and outside the family and family office for experts and mentors in different areas. Fourth is *management*. Family members need a plan and learning path to help them acquire the skills, knowledge, and competence to be responsible owners. Involving family first-hand exposes them to understand and rise to the challenges of family wealth ownership. Creating responsible owners in the next generation requires at some point passing the proverbial baton. The opportunities to gently groom offspring to assume the responsibilities of wealth can be a powerful experience that can set in motion positive modeling. The final element is *mastery*. Through understanding the meaning, observing, modeling, finding mentors in or outside the family and/or the family office, and being actively engaged in the management of wealth, the next generation can move to a place of self-empowerment and mastery. Mastery does not mean ending the learning cycle; rather it reveals the power of perpetual learning and seeking truth, knowledge, and oversight of one's financial life.

Notes

1. Generation Xers were born between 1965 and 1980, Millennials were born between 1981 and 1996, and Generation Zers were born between 1997 and the present according to the Pew Research Center. To learn more visit, https://www.pewresearch.org/topics/generations-and-age/.
2. How Millennials Compare with Prior Generations, Pew Center for Research, 2018.
3. Richard Fry, Millennials overtake Baby Boomers as America's largest generation, Pew Charitable Research Center, April 28, 2020. To read more visit https://www.pewresearch.org/fact-tank/2020/04/28/millennials-overtake-baby-boomers-as-americas-largest-generation/.
4. Wealth-X Family Wealth Transfer Report, 2019. p. 4.
5. Ibid. p. 4.
6. According to Richard M. Segal, as noted in *Goals-based Wealth Management: An Integrated and Practical Approach to Changing the Structure of Wealth Advisory Practices,* by Jean Brunel, Wiley, 2015, p. 11.
7. Dennis T. Jaffe and James A. Grubman, "Acquirers' and Inheritors' Dilemma: Discovering Life Purpose and Building Personal Identity in the Presence of Wealth," *The Journal of Wealth Management* 10.2 (2007): 20–44.
8. Mindy Rosenthal, "Next-Generation Wealth: The New Face of Affluence," Morgan Stanley Private Wealth Management/Campden Research, 2012.
9. Atlantic Trust Private Wealth Management, "The 20-Somethings: A Decade of Teachable Moments," 2011, downloaded from www.atlantictrust.com/site/at/pdf/2013-The_20-Somethings.pdf.
10. This adaption of Maslow's Hierarchy of Needs was downloaded from http://upload.wikimedia.org/wikipedia/commons/5/58/Maslow's_hierarchy_of_needs.svg.
11. Kirby Rosplock, "Women & Wealth Study Report of Findings," GenSpring Family Offices, LLC, 2006.
12. Elsa is a pseudonym.
13. Joanie Bronfman, "The Experience of Inherited Wealth: A Social-Psychological Perspective," Dissertation Abstracts International 48(4), 1033A. (AAT 8715730), 1987.
14. FOX Foresight Newsletter 2020, Engaging for Impact: Family Learning Theories and Best Practices.

15. Correspondence with Chelsea Toler-Hoffmann, May 2020.
16. To learn more visit www.nextgnenerosity.com.
17. Roy Williams and Vic Preisser, authors of *Preparing Heirs*, Robert Reed Publishers, 2010.
18. Ellen Perry, *Wealth Matters: Navigating Family, Money and Legacy* (Washington DC: Egremont Press, 2012).
19. *Born Rich* (documentary), 2003. Director, Jamie Johnson, Sheila Nevins (executive producer), Dirk Wittenborn (produced by), and Jamie Johnson (producer).
20. Anonymous feedback from a Tamarind Partner's client.
21. Interview with Dr. Keith Whitaker and Dr. Susan Massenzio, 2012.
22. Josh Funk, "Warren Buffett's Kids Follow Dad's Philanthropic Lead," HuffPost Money, www.huffingtonpost.com/2012/10/01/warren-buffett-kids_n_1928665.html.
23. Richard I. Kirkland, "Should You Leave It All to the Children?" CNNMoney, http://management.fortune.cnn.com/2012/11/21/buffett-inheiritance/.
24. To read more, reach out to the author to learn about her dissertation research. Kirby Rosplock, "Women's Interest, Attitudes and Involvement with Their Wealth," Saybrook University, 2007.
25. Joline Godfrey, *Sea-Change: Family Education for the 21st Century* (Santa Barbara, CA: Independent Means, Inc., 2009).
26. Mindy Rosenthal, "Next-Generation Wealth: The New Face of Affluence," Morgan Stanley Private Wealth Management/Camden Research, 2012.
27. Jennifer is a pseudonym.
28. Interview with Bob Danzig, 2013.
29. Personal correspondence with Jay Hughes, 2012.
30. Tamarind Partners, Inc., and Tamarind Learning. To learn more visit www.TamarindLearning.com and www.TamarindPartners.com.
31. Ibid.
32. Ibid.
33. Ibid.
34. Anonymous interview with family office executive, April 2020.
35. Source: http://appreciativeinquiry.case.edu/practice/quotesDetail.cfm?coid=1336.

CHAPTER 13

Family Entrepreneurship and the Family Bank

Warner King Babcock

Kirby Rosplock, PhD

The family bank is one approach to supporting and promoting current and future family careers, entrepreneurship, diversification, personal interests, human capital development, and wealth creators.

This chapter provides an updated view to the family bank concept, including its purpose and scope, how a family bank might reposition a family whose wealth was inherited or being generated on an ongoing basis from an operating company, pathways to a family bank, and how family banks may be used to develop entrepreneurial opportunities for ensuing generations. Throughout this chapter we discuss the broader benefits and potential disadvantages, pitfalls, and limitations of the family bank, and illustrate these with a variety of cases.

What Is a Family Bank?

Family banks can be a central approach and tool used by any family office or family with significant assets to leverage family resources to help the next generation, or they may be viewed as a means to educate, mentor, and develop family members to become business builders, responsible stewards, and wealth creators. Thomas J. Handler, J.D., P.C., Partner at Handler Thayer, LPP notes that although family banks may not be as well-known, widely adopted, and implemented, he is a "strong proponent of family banks for families that want to instill positive values in their children so that they become responsible, empowered adults that are grateful for every day of their lives. Family bank structures are a best-in-class global strategy designed to achieve these results."[1]

While there is no legal or widely accepted definition of a family bank, these special entities typically provide an organized structure and process for funding *from* family members *to* family members. If it is planned and implemented correctly with an applied governance system, it can be a powerful mechanism to put wealth to good use for the benefit and development of all participating family members and their relationships.

Historically, some of the earliest family banks were established in Europe by families such as the Rothschilds and Pictets, and these semi-informal lending operations eventually grew into larger commercial banking operations. Several of the larger US financial institutions today are a function of families such as the Mellons, Pews, Phipps, Rockefellers, and others who built broad commercial capabilities out of their family enterprises. The purpose of this chapter, however, is to focus on intra-family financing as a non-commercial, non-regulated activity or entity. Family banks are vehicles that provide intra-family financing with some form of governance and discipline by using five basic principles and structured and operated within tax guidelines and regulations.

Thus, we do not model or base the concept on the activity of providing traditional commercial bank loans, gifts, grants, or informal intra-family loans to family members. Instead, we define the family bank as a private entity, like a family business or trust, that is specifically created, funded, and supported by family members solely to provide financing to family members and/or their related entities for the benefit of all qualified and participating family members.

The following are just a few of the many potential overall benefits of a family bank:

- Leveraging family wealth to assist other family members for profitable and development purposes
- Providing intra-family funds without creating unintended family relationship, tax, or other problems
- Inspiring and supporting family entrepreneurship
- Developing accountability and fiscal responsibility
- Providing financing with more flexible criteria and terms

- Promoting the development of family members through direct experience
- Funding special family assets, business ventures, and other for-profit purposes

Since it is rare that all family members can or want to work in the family business, manage family investments, or run a family office, a family bank can also be an effective way to encourage a strong sense of creating one's own career, interests, and wealth. Seeding, rekindling, incubating, and sustaining family entrepreneurship, along with developing and experiencing good business and governance practices, as well as making decisions together that fit the rising members of the family, are all powerful tools.

By providing short-term, long-term, and more flexible loans, family banks can also provide more patient, supportive capital through loans or empower members to get back on their feet after a personal setback. Unlike typical financing from outside institutions or private equity firms, a family bank can build in a more family friendly process, support system and terms, while still promoting accountability, character development, good governance, perseverance, and business practices.

Family banks are most effective when their policies and processes are clear about the expectations and accountability with open, honest, and frank communication of both the goals of the bank and the participating family members. Therefore, participating family members will benefit most when there are clearly stated values, mission, vision, objectives, and funding criteria. While many families understand that failure is likely in the majority of early and seed-stage investment funding situations, having defined principles, processes, procedures, and guidance for recipients allows the family bank concept to succeed over time.

Unlike gifts from parents or distributions directly from trusts, a family bank is designed as a sustainable family business providing potential funding to family members or a related entity. A family bank is not a guaranteed pool of money from which any family member can withdraw at any time or for any purpose. Funding must be applied for and reviewed under criteria, policies, and processes governing the family bank. Reckless, spendthrift, or unaccountable use of family bank funds does not lead to instilling confidence, responsibility, or accountability in future generations. Don Kozusko, Partner at Kozusko Harris Duncan LLP, counsels international and domestic entrepreneurs, investors, philanthropists, and privately held businesses in the tax and legal issues relating to their investments, business activities, estate planning, and charitable endeavors. Kozusko shared that when it comes to family banks and making family bank investments, the importance of governance, oversight, and accountability cannot be overstated. He noted, "Without accountability, people don't really grow."[2]

Setting up a family bank is best executed as part of integrated, careful planning with the broader family enterprise, not in isolation. Simply making a loan to a family member or just forming a trust or corporate entity to provide financing to family members will most likely lead to many issues over time, including the potential for conflictive family dynamics, as exemplified in the next example where in one family, an affluent corporate executive financed his oldest son's effort to buy and build a business from a pool of family capital. The broader family inferred that they too were investing in this young man's future success and would one day reap the benefits. Most of the family members, who had their own small businesses, enjoyed watching the oldest son's business grow. Eventually the oldest son decided to sell the business and suddenly became very wealthy; however, the other family members never shared in the proceeds of the sale of the business. More explicit documentation showing other family members of the nature of the capital invested would have clarified the expectations from the intra-family financing. The other children felt that they were left out and cheated, causing complex conflicts that later destroyed family relationships. Because there was no formal family bank entity, explicit family or corporate governance, or proper documentation, the success of the investment was ultimately divisive to family harmony.

Two Mindsets to Your Family Bank

Philosophically, there are two different mindsets regarding how a family conceives their family bank. According to James E. Hughes Jr., well-known thought leader and advisor to families, "Loans from a family bank are usually made for two purposes: investment, to increase the family's financial and intellectual capital; or enhancement to the family's intellectual and human capital."[3] The family bank can also be more clearly defined by its application as a *hard bank* and *soft bank*.[4] A hard bank is defined as a family bank that is formed and used for purely investment reasons, with some even seeking to maximize return-on-investment. Many direct investment and investment offices may have a portfolio under their umbrella of holdings that operates as a hard bank.

A family creating a soft bank, on the other hand, has established the pool of capital for family member loans and may be willing to accept nominal returns in exchange for the opportunity to build human capital.[5] In many cases, the goals of a family who starts a soft bank encompass cultivating future entrepreneurs without a mandate that the family bank must only fund ventures that have a high probability to have positive strong returns. Some families want to inspire family entrepreneurship and are willing to fund smaller ventures or concepts to provide experience, exposure, and education for future generations, while others may seek a more balanced approach between human and financial capital development. Being clear about the focus of your family bank is critical; understanding the goals of a hard versus a soft bank, and what are its expected outcomes, is important to articulate and communicate with all parties involved.

Establishing and Funding a Family Bank

Funding for a family bank typically comes from senior generations, such as family matriarch or patriarch, trusts, or a family-owned entity that generates income or can transfer assets. Depending on the family bank's mission, the next generations may also be given the opportunity to participate by investing some of their own funds in the family bank. Thomas J. Handler, J.D., P.C. Partner, shared, "It is not uncommon for a family bank to comprise 10 to 20 percent of a family's holdings. The idea being they are investing both in their offspring to become educated and they are engaging them to be invested and interested in the portfolio and holdings of the family office via the family bank."[6]

For the next generation, having "skin in the game" creates a sense of direct interest regarding the health, governance, and sustainability of the family bank. This is critically important, as their involvement in the development of its mission, vision, objective, values, and governance provides an onramp for the "rising generation" to feel part of what is being built. Like their family office or businesses, shareholder and member agreements should be carefully planned and structured to cover the range of family ownership, reinvestment, distribution, transfer, and buy-sell issues. For example, the family bank's ownership agreements can be structured to provide co-investment rights with each funding the family bank provides. Good family and corporate governance, as well as sound legal advice, will help with this process.

Family bank funding is not intended to provide a source of informal loans or regular gifts to family members, or to engender a sense of entitlement through ongoing trust funds or their distributions. Funding a family bank is best executed when it is provided based on merits and alignment with the agreed-upon mission, objectives, criteria, and other factors under policies and processes, and with good discipline and proper documentation, controls, and reporting. Family banks are not intended to micromanage the personal assets or next-generation business activities or control the personal lives of the next generation. Family banks are meant to inspire, promote, and support the healthy independent development of the next generation. According to

Hughes, "the borrower should be encouraged to state how such a loan will increase his or her independence and how the loan will add to the family's intellectual capital."[7]

Five Principles for Family Banks

After many years of working with enterprising families on areas of wealth, entrepreneurship, and governance, these five principles have been developed to help guide family offices and families to form and build a family bank: democratize, harmonize, customize, flexibilize, and professionalize.

Democratize

Engaging all family members with a system to provide input and participate in decision-making is one of the primary ways to maintain a healthy family. A family bank should facilitate this objective by giving the next generation a chance for full participation and a sense of responsible ownership. By giving the next generation a voice in decision-making, the family bank empowers them while supporting their development. If they do not feel they are a part of a joint decision-making process, the next generation may be less interested and motivated to participate in the family bank over time. Similarly, if the terms are not relevant to them or are dictated to them, the newly formed family bank may not have any next-generation participants.

Consider the example of one very well-intended, hardworking senior member of a family who invested a significant amount of time and money with his wealth management firm and his trust and estate and tax advisors to develop a new transgenerational structure to generously provide the next generation with jointly owned assets. After careful consideration, the next generation politely declined any interest in participating in the entity or jointly owning the assets. Although grateful, the next generation did not feel the terms were what they wanted, and they felt left out of the process.

If the next generation was involved early on and throughout the process, the outcome may have been different and the senior member's efforts, time, and money could have been used better.

Harmonize

Building and maintaining healthy family relationships is paramount to preserving and growing financial and human capital across generations. Without good family relationships and a strong governance system for family members to work together harmoniously, a family bank, like any family-owned entity, is in jeopardy of developing complex conflicts and destructive family dynamics. These negative outcomes can potentially be prevented by promoting healthy family core values (such as integrity, respect, trust, and openness) and a sense of responsibility, while also creating processes and policies for open communication and conflict resolution. Harmonize does not mean that everyone in the family always must get along; rather, it means that family members understand how to manage conflict productively and to engage in healthy dissent. Some families have a consensus-driven approach, whereby they must come to a majority agreement, while others may have a process to reach a super-majority or two-thirds vote to reach a verdict. In some families, members may be owners, but non-voting, but able to participate in the forum for discussion. Conflict and disagreement, when handled professionally, can be extraordinarily productive and healthy to establishing long-lasting harmony.

Customize

Each family is unique, and each family's mission, vision, objectives, values, level of participation, time horizon, estate, appetite for risk, and resources are different. The following questions can help families clarify what is most important to them:

- Are they most interested in developing a soft bank, a hard bank, or a family bank that balances these two approaches?
- Does the family want to develop one family bank for all descendants or one for each branch of the family? Should the next generation be provided an option to invest in the family bank over time?
- What are the limits to the types and terms of loans or financing? What type of return should a family bank investor expect for their return on investment? Can spouses, stepchildren, or distant relatives qualify for loans?
- What level of governance policy and process detail is appropriate?
- Are there any unique terms or intentions that the family wants the bank to achieve?

In one family bank case, unique terms were defined by the family branches, which stipulated that the family bank must maintain a minimum amount of reserves for family members to receive distributions. For example, if the distributions to a branch exceeded a certain threshold, or if the bank does not maintain a minimum balance of $10 million, then additional distributions may not be administered to family members. Further, this family also instituted permanent life insurance policies taken out by senior family members to "rejuvenate" the bank corpus overtime as funds were diminishing. In most cases, this insurance is comprised of investment grade, non-modified endowment contract (MEC) policies that allowed borrowing from the cash value without income taxation, if capital was critically needed before the insured family member passed away. Moreover, the policy could also be sold if more capital was needed before the family member passed. Unique and creative terms, policies, and agreements can be customized to tailor how a bank is governed and administered.

Flexibilize

Family offices and families should be careful and thoughtful about creating irrevocable entities, structures, or terms that are too complicated or rigid. Because change is inevitable—such as in family membership due to birth, adoptions, deaths, marriages, and divorces—the criteria for involvement, circumstances, processes, and policies of a family bank need to be flexible and able to adapt. Each generation should consider including a process and the opportunity to periodically review and modify terms to be able to adapt and amend beyond the initial assumptions and detailed terms. A family bank that ultimately becomes irrelevant or unattractive to its members will lose interest and participation overtime. The goal should be to inspire, support, and foster family engagement while also pursuing their own passions and abilities to create their own wealth. Some entities and structures may be considered good for control, protection, and/or estate tax advantages; early consideration should be given to how they will be administered and overseen, what the unintended consequences may be over time. It is important to build in flexibility, so those responsible for fulfilling administrative, fiduciary, and other oversight roles are given the right and power to adapt, make changes, and best serve family members' interests. This includes deciding if the family bank activities would be best guided by a corporate entity under the business judgment rule or the duties and constraints of trusts and trusteeship. It is important to ensure that the family bank remains relevant, next-generation centric, and family friendly, as these will increase the chance for its own sustainability and usefulness.

Professionalize

The professionalism of a family bank can help prevent many business, legal, financial, and tax missteps. Managing the family bank as a professional, disciplined family business by taking such steps as formalizing the financing policies and process and incorporating the independent oversight of non-family board members is key. The bank also can facilitate training and mentoring of next-generation entrepreneurs by bringing in experienced outside advisors to provide unbiased expertise. Family banks that involve independent board, investment, or loan review committee members can help take the suspicion of favoritism or bias out of decisions and transactions and sidestep potentially unhealthy family dynamics.

Each of the distinct groups related to the bank (the family, the bank itself, and its board/advisors) should be well defined, with professional structures, agreements, and documents. An open flow of communications between these groups enables them to make well-informed decisions that are aligned with the best interests of all involved. It is well known that an independent board of directors, board of advisors, and committees can play a key role between a family and a family business entity.

But even with the formation of a board of directors or advisory board and strong communication, families would be best served if they developed a healthy family governance system early in conceiving a family bank. A strong family governance system will provide the rules, policies, and guidelines to address family communications, joint decision-making, values, mission, and guidance for the board. Professionalization of the family bank system and each of the subsystems influences the family bank's long-term sustainability.

Mini-Case Study: Intra-Family Financing of New Family Businesses

A successful chemical and materials industry entrepreneur provided the financing to two of his children and his wife to each start businesses of their own. An advisory board oversaw the businesses for the children. The patriarch saw his role as one of raising the children, providing them with a good education, money to help them start their own businesses, engaging a trusted board of advisors, and then getting out of the way. Each new business was formed as a corporation and funded directly by family funds, so there was no formal family bank to provide the overall governance for intra-family financing. While the business ventures are doing well, no succession or estate planning has been done yet, exposing the family to potential estate tax liabilities, future control issues, or possibly the inability to write-off bad debt.

Takeaways

- An independent board of advisors strengthens business ventures.
- Structure separate corporate entities to fit each business.
- Tax, trust, and estate plans should be addressed early to avoid potential future tax, control, and governance issues.
- Create a professionalized family bank system to include a good family governance system for long-term sustainability.

Organizing a Family Bank

Family banks are not just about financial transactions. It is important to keep in mind human behavior and development, as well as current and future family circumstances, goals, and relationships, particularly when creating an entity that will provide family funds to other family members. Therefore, boilerplate entities, structures, terms, and policies will be a challenge during implementation over time, and if the above five principles are not followed.

The purpose of the family bank and the range of its activities may change over time, as may those responsible for overseeing and managing it. Expecting the application of traditional fiduciary standards may also become problematic, given the purpose may be primarily to provide financing to assist family members versus seeking to grow the shareholder's value or maximize the ROI.

Allocate enough time and resources to set up the family bank, as it does take time. It may be worthwhile to engage the next generation early for their involvement. One should be careful, so as not to make it too complex and complicated to manage. Obtain good professional advice, compensate board and/or investment committee members for their work, and consider making advisers/mentors available. Plan for all the proper documentation, filings, monitoring, and reporting. Start with enough capital that is anticipated to fund family members for at least the near-term. The bank may allow or anticipate more capital contributions to the family bank over time if needed. Providing flexibility to add capital will assist with unanticipated and growing participation.

By identifying experienced professional accounting, legal, financial planning, and governance advice also helps to de-risk the family bank. Finally, bifurcating roles and responsibilities and being clear about their duties for each of those involved early will also help reduce problems. For some families and circumstances, it is better to start with a simple family bank and then develop an entity with more detailed terms, structures, policies, and agreements over time.

Entity Choice

Although a range of structures and entities can be considered, one option is to initiate a family bank with a simple approach, with the limited liability company (LLC) option having the most flexibility over time. Figure 13.1 provides an example of a structure whereby a family trust, private trust company, or the LLC is formed, whose purpose includes providing loans or other such financing to family members, as well as protecting other family assets. The LLC provides the most overall latitude and flexible governance over time.

FIGURE 13.1 Family Bank Established as a Private Trust Company, Trust or LLC

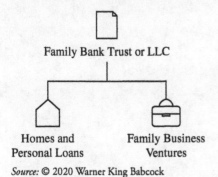

Family Bank Trust or LLC

Homes and Personal Loans

Family Business Ventures

Source: © 2020 Warner King Babcock

If a trust structure is utilized, trustees will have the fiduciary duty to administer the trust under the terms of the governing instrument and state statutes in the best interest of the beneficiaries. If the trust is irrevocable, this may not provide the needed flexibility over time. However, trusts may be more beneficial for estate and tax planning, control, and asset protection purposes.

If an LLC structure is utilized, the managing member(s) will have duties and powers, as stated in the operating agreement, and any side agreements allowed under state corporate statutes. The terms of the LLC and any agreements can be modified over time as well as allow for future contributions of capital and changes in ownership interests. The governance, oversight, and terms for the corporate entity will be simpler to start and manage, and decisions will be guided by the business judgment rule along with other corporate statutes versus more restrictive trustee duties and trust law.

Figure 13.2 is an example of how a family can set up their family bank offering with even more long-term advantages by having the family bank formed as an LLC held within a family trust. Although more complicated and costly to form, this combination of entities provides both the benefits a trust provides for estate purposes and the flexibility to adapt over time offered by the LLC, as described earlier. This more involved structure can be providing more family asset protections and still allow changes across generations, making it more attractive and relevant over time.

There are other alternatives that can be used, such as having a family holding company hold a family bank entity. Each structure should be carefully considered for its own advantages and disadvantages to determine the one that best fits the family's vision, objectives, goals, needs, and preferences over time.

FIGURE 13.2   Family Bank LLC Inside of a Family Trust

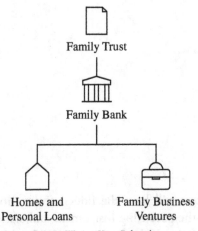

Source: © 2020 Warner King Babcock

Evolution of Family Banks: From Simple to Complex

The scope of a family bank can vary greatly, based on factors such as:

- Participating family members' interests and needs
- Their age, knowledge, and experience
- The amount of funds available to capitalize and grow the bank
- The range, types, and complexity of next-generation needs to be funded

- The family's appetite for risk
- The planned life of the bank
- Tax and estate planning issues

Family banks can range from being very simple to very complex, and each family bank can morph and evolve with the needs and specifications of the family and each generation as it matures. The bank's function is to meet the purpose and scope of funding for the needs of the next generation while considering future generations. Most families launch a family bank with a more simplistic approach, desiring to test the waters prior to establishing a very technical, complicated structure and governance system. Over time, families and their family banks can grow larger and more complex, building out the required specifications as their needs evolve.

A family bank with the mission of providing simple loans to younger family members can be easily formed with elementary governance, and the loans can be made using IRS guidelines. A transgenerational, multi-purpose family bank that has a mission of providing a wide range of more sophisticated financing to family members can involve complex tax and estate planning, multiple trusts, multiple corporate entities, and advanced independent governance systems with elaborate policies and processes. The following provides a brief overview of how the family bank can evolve throughout different stages of the family. The reader may use this guide to identify where the family is on this evolutionary scale, and what work still must be done to prepare for the creation of a family bank.

For younger and less experienced family members, the family bank may have a very simple corporate and governance structure providing a small amount of funding for simple activities and personal assets. Some examples may be when a parent wants to make funding available to the next generation to purchase their first car, equipment for a summer job, or a small residence during college. The simplest family bank is useful for introducing elementary business, financial, and governance principles and practices to the next generation. Senior and junior family members can voluntarily fund the bank, and the next generation can obtain funding based on a request that meets some general predetermined criteria and terms. While this type of entity is not complex enough to require a fully professionalized governance system with independent oversight, it should focus on democratizing and harmonizing the process of providing intra-family financing by facilitating good relationships, communications, joint decision-making, and accountability. The terms of financing should meet the requirements of the IRS for making intra-family loans and be well documented (these aspects are discussed in greater detail later in the chapter).

As next-generation family members become more knowledgeable about business and financial matters, and they desire to obtain a larger amount of bank funding for larger personal assets, such as primary or vacation homes, the family bank's objectives, succession planning, business plans, and corporate and governance structure must evolve. At this point, the family's financing needs are still relatively basic and can be accomplished under basic terms along with policies and processes to monitor and mitigate basic risks, including some general predetermined criteria and terms to qualify for funding. In addition to building strong relationships, communication, joint decision-making, process, and accountability, governance should also provide transparency and frequent reporting.

As next-generation family members become interested in entrepreneurship and want to form their own businesses, the scope of the family bank must evolve once more. If they are interested in acquiring, owning, and operating properties or companies, they should receive appropriate education and have relevant business, financial, and investment experience. Any proposal from a family member also may be accompanied by a detailed business plan. At this stage, the family bank is useful for providing funding for larger amounts of capital for longer periods at higher risk. In addition to a focus on building a democratized and harmonious entity, governance at this stage ideally incorporates a form of independent oversight, advice, and/or mentoring. This independent oversight can be accomplished with independent members on a family bank board of directors, an investment committee, or an advisory committee.

In the next stage of complexity, the family bank can be useful for providing larger amounts of capital for longer periods at higher risk. Family members may have achieved substantial business, financial, and investment experience, and they desire to utilize a significant amount of funding from the family bank, such as for investments in multiple new ventures, properties, investment funds, or acquisitions. Depending on the family bank's agreed purpose, other uses may also include funding to buy out a part or all of an existing family enterprise, buy out an employee stock ownership plan, purchase large family properties, or any combination of the above. It can also be used to transfer wealth and assets to the next generation.

To accomplish this more complex financing from family banks, a comprehensive and highly disciplined analysis, approach, and plan are needed. Proposals for funding typically include detailed business plans, considering all aspects of the use of the funding, as well as the participating family members' long-term interests and capacity to repay the funds being provided. In weighing each loan, the family bank must consider available bank capital, permissible financing criteria, terms, and the bank's appetite for risk, as well as the bank's longer-term sustainability, succession planning, and the next generation's long-term interest. The monitoring, reporting, and financial transactions of this level of bank are more complex, sophisticated, and challenging. The governance systems should be scaled and tailored to fit this more complex family bank system. Governance is focused on building long-term, sustainable shareholder value and promoting a strong, professionalized source of funds with independent oversight, while supporting healthy family relationships.

In a more complex family bank system, family members can voluntarily participate at both the family bank level, as well as co-own or co-invest in different assets depending on the charter and other agreements. Requiring or allowing the next generation to commit some of their own funds into fixed, financial, or operating assets, when they are seeking additional financing from the family bank, not only shares risk, but also provides additional motivation to the family members to be accountable and successful. The mini-case that follows provides insights to how a family may design a family bank to evolve with the needs of the next generation.

Mini-Case Study: A Family Bank Designed to Develop the Next Generation

A Midwestern family with franchises, professional services firms, and real estate provides a good example of letting children fail a little to learn without it being catastrophic. A college student family member requested a letter of credit (LOC) from their family bank for financing a real estate business with a few other college classmates including two engineers, one that worked construction and a family member that served in several capacities including as accountant, law coordinator, and even landscaper. Under the terms of this family bank, education and weddings would be fully paid, almost unconditionally, and family members were not entitled to anything other than fair consideration until after education and weddings were covered. However, family bank capital was made available under more flexible terms for purposes the family deemed positive; these circumstances included, for example, mortgages or second mortgages on primary residences, loans for business or investment purposes and equity, mezzanine debt, or convertible debt for business ventures.

One such example of flexibility included a family member who was a student who did not want an equity investment; but rather, this family member requested financing to purchase, renovate, put on additions, landscape, and flip single-family homes, as well as operate a multi-unit rental property. Ultimately, the family bank provided a letter of credit that was enough to acquire, add on, and renovate two properties at a time. This entrepreneurial, next-generation family member and his enterprising student colleagues at college took on five projects in two years, making money on the rental property and three of the four single-family homes.

A downturn in the economy worked against them, and they incurred a loss on the investment in one home, and were near break-even or achieved modest earnings on other homes. The interest rate charged by the family bank was significantly lower than the business could have obtained from a commercial bank, if they even could have secured an LOC. At the same time, the family bank was earning a higher interest rate on the LOC than it was previously earning on its cash and cash-equivalent reserves. Thus, the other members in the family bank were better off. At the conclusion of the venture, which was shortly before their graduation, all the business partners, in four years, fully repaid the LOC with interest. This turned out to be a win-win for the family, the next-generation family member, and real estate business partners. In the process, the family member learned about business organizations, contracts, accounting, debt, secured transactions and financing, liens, permits and city approvals, and dealing with contractors (on work they could not do themselves). Six years later, on the day of the family member's wedding, a long, heart-felt letter was handed to the parents, which included sincere gratitude for the "chance" the family took in trusting the family member with a significant LOC, while still a college student. The letter also stated the experience provided was perhaps the best learning experience so far. This also included learning about the strong points and shortcomings of partners, dealing with government employees, difficult clients/buyers, legal, accounting, finance lessons, and more.

Takeaways

- Flexibility is important as too rigid terms may alienate future adopters.
- Anticipate what the next generation wants or needs, and when is difficult; leaving the door open to adapt and be flexible is important.
- The entrepreneurial and business learning experience can be even more valuable than the family bank return on investment.

Good Governance: Family Bank Boards, Committees, and Trustees

All family enterprises, including family banks, benefit from good governance including objective, fresh perspectives, advice, and oversight of a board of directors or other advisory committee. Having independent input to key decisions can assist families, their investments, and entities by making careful judgments objectively and without family emotions. For larger, more complex family banks and financial transactions, governance should include a formal board of directors and/or an investment or funding review committee with independent members. These professional boards and committees should have clear charters with duties and policies clearly understood. Advisors, boards, committees, and trustees should be provided insurance for limited liability protection. Family members may also want to consider an agreement to release and indemnify each member providing oversight.

Selecting family bank advisors, board and committee members, as well as trustees, is one of the most important decisions for all stakeholders. Independent board and committee members, as well as trustees, should have the following experience, knowledge, and qualities beyond the usual fiduciary duties:

- Experience with, concern for, and commitment to assisting the next generation
- Direct experience with making special private investments, including forming new ventures
- Understanding of the unique duties, roles, and sensitive issues of boards and governance within entrepreneurial or family enterprises
- Independence, with no conflicts of interest, including not receiving compensation from family members or their entities

Difficult oversight and funding decisions by independent outsiders can reduce problems caused by family conflicts, jealousy, suspicion, emotions, and dynamics. The following mini-case demonstrates how a family entrepreneur is supported with funding from a holding company owned by family trusts for wealth planning purposes, but without family governance or corporate governance systems.

Mini-Case Study: Family Bank Without Good Governance

A successful patriarch and entrepreneur along with his spouse formed irrevocable trusts for each of their children to fund and own family businesses. All the trusts exclusively owned a holding company that in turn funded a new business based on one of their son's newly patented inventions. Each of the siblings' trusts indirectly owned a proportionate share of the son's new business venture. As the business grew, the patriarch, who was a trustee of each trust, began to become involved in management decisions and asserted influence and control over some key business decisions at various times. In later years, this began to hinder the senior management team and the growth of the business, creating many conflicts. Although the basic trust and corporate structures were in place to provide funding to family businesses, there was no healthy governance system with independent trustees or board members, policies, and processes. There was no family governance system in place to communicate with other family members, build relationships, or obtain input from the next generation. The early intention was just to form a traditional trust for tax and estate planning purposes without consideration of good governance. There was no family council, family governance, or independent board or advisors to help build and maintain a healthy family bank system and family relationships. This resulted in creating inefficiencies and business and family conflicts that limited the ability to grow the business venture. The son's new venture owned by the trusts was eventually merged into the patriarch's own business to keep it under his control, and the frustrated founding son left to start other successful businesses.

Takeaways

- Develop a good family governance system before forming a family bank to help harmonize and democratize the process.
- Use trusts to address tax and estate issues, but structure the family bank as a corporate entity.
- Coordinate and customize trust and corporate governance systems with some independent advisors, board members, and trustees.
- Clearly define duties, roles, and responsibilities for all parties.
- Develop a family bank system like a professionalized family business system.

Limitations of Trusts

As shown in the case study on a family bank without good governance, a trust can be created to be a source of capital for the family bank, particularly by carrying a family bank entity as an asset within a trust across generations. However, because of the more restrictive governance and rigid fiduciary duties of typical family trusts, family banks should be formed as a corporate entity or LLC and governed by corporate or LLC statutory laws and common law. The bylaws, shareholder agreements, operating agreements, fiduciary duties, policies, processes, and the business judgment rule afford family banks more flexibility, as compared with the more restrictive trust laws and fiduciary duties of trustees. Complex trust documents and laws, as well as a different set of fiduciary duties and their limitations, make it more difficult for a trustee to effectively support higher-risk, entrepreneurial family ventures. Trustees may also not have the type of business experience, judgment, and venture background to provide the type of oversight, business perspective, advice, and guidance needed for family bank financings. Family offices should carefully consider the best structure, entity, and governance to provide the greatest flexibility, joint decision-making, transparency, business judgment, and adaptability across generations to build family relationships and human and financial capital over the long term.

The Role of the Family Office

Although the family office typically has been viewed as a defensive vehicle for wealth preservation and to mitigate principle erosion, the family office can also be proactive in supporting, facilitating, and building a strategy for family entrepreneurship. Family banks are at the crossroads of family business systems, entrepreneurship, direct venture start-up and private investing, as well as family, investment, and corporate governance, not to mention corporate, estate, and tax planning with the possibility of trusts.

Because traditional family offices are positioned at the center of the financial, legal, investment, accounting, and wealth transfer needs of the family, they can play a key role in supporting family banks by becoming a conduit to provide these areas of expertise to the family. They can also provide education to family members about what it means to be entrepreneurial and how to gauge opportunities. However, not all family offices have the breadth, depth, experience, and expertise in all the areas necessary to create, grow, and maintain a healthy, sustainable family bank. Family banks are unique family businesses that require thoughtful consideration, planning, and work.

Often, the family office may have links into new ventures and businesses through private equity investments or direct investments, as well as involvement with one or more family businesses. These resources can provide access to entrepreneurs and exposure to how businesses are formed, operated, and grown. Some family offices with direct venture investment or family business experience can be instrumental in supporting family members as they develop a business case and plan for the venture they are considering. Ideally, the family office can assist with the selection, coordination, and oversight of the independent expert advisors, such as lawyers, tax advisors, and others.

In cases when the family office does not offer these resources, either in-house or through strategic partners, the family may need to look elsewhere for the appropriate resources and partners.

The Role of Outside Experts

Independent experts who understand the practical aspects and nuances of family banks help all parties think through all options and the proper design and formation of a custom family bank. These outside experts can provide realistic, unbiased options, plans, and advice during the formation and life of the family bank, including policies for financing entrepreneurial ventures.

There are generally two types of outside experts that a family and family office should consider when forming a family bank and making family entrepreneurial investments. The first type is the expert generalist discussed in Chapter 10. This multidisciplinary expert understands many of the benefits and limitations of the wide variety of possible family bank structures, and this person often has direct experience working with the senior- and next-generation family members, family offices, and family enterprise systems.

The second type of outside expert is one who can provide tangible experience and wisdom to the enterprise being funded. This type of expert may be a serial entrepreneur or very experienced corporate or direct venture investor who can function as an objective source of feedback and guidance about the true nature of start-up ventures, the industry, the risks, and prospects. They often have had successful business careers in related fields and can help the family member significantly shortcut how to enter the field by explaining pitfalls to avoid and opportunities to exploit. Their independent oversight, advice, and insights can increase the chances of overall positive outcomes and reduce risks and costly mistakes.

Family offices with experienced direct venture investment staff can assist with unique venture investment analysis, terms, structuring, due diligence, monitoring, and reporting; however, entrepreneurial family ventures are different than venture capital, private equity funds, or external (non-family) venture direct investments. The often-risky nature of these ventures can affect staff members' careers, reputations, and family client relationships; outside experts often are best positioned to assist with these issues. The combination of the guidance and wisdom from the family office, along with the exposure and experience of a few independent experts, will create a robust team that can foster the proper formation and development of a customized family bank.

Family offices and outside experts can work together to help educate family members about family banks and entrepreneurship. Professional advisors who are really experienced in the areas of expertise noted previously can assist the family by being very thoughtful, asking the right critical questions, and determining if a family bank and entrepreneurship is appropriate.

Tax and Legal Considerations of Family Banks

While family banks provide greater flexibility than commercial banks, all financings must be done within tax code guidelines and the interest rate must be at or above the Applicable Federal Rate (AFR). Without proper documentation, the IRS may consider the loan a gift, therefore disallowing deductions or creating future tax liabilities. The key to avoiding this situation is to operate the bank as a professional business, provide funding at arm's length, and observe all debtor–creditor formalities (such as promissory notes and collateral pledges).[8] A tax and estate planning advisor should review all family bank policies and financings. Family banks take time to create, and it is important to choose a law firm that can provide flexible legal advice with options that fit your unique circumstances. The aim is for legal advice not to create unwarranted complexity, or additional unnecessary administrative costs, while addressing the family human capital development objectives.

The Anderson Family Case Study

The Anderson Family Case study brings together a culmination of learnings from this chapter.[9] This case provides many discussion points regarding the good intentions that families may have as they embark on creating a family bank, as well as the many hurdles they may face in sustaining that bank.

The Anderson family grew a large, complex real estate enterprise in the Midwest. The father, Hank Anderson, had started a real estate development company in the 1980s and thoughtfully expanded it over the years into a half-billion-dollar enterprise. His sons, Liam and Ron, and daughter Eleanor, exhibited a keen interest in the business and, at first, would help summers on vacations. After college, Liam decided to intern with his father and learn the ropes of the family business. Ron also worked in the business while completing his graduate studies at Kellogg Business School. Eleanor, the youngest, kept up with her brothers and joined the family business in 2003. The siblings flourished and each developed different interests and expertise: Liam worked closely with the finance department structuring the terms of various deals; Ron worked closely with his father on the identification, selection, and due diligence of real estate projects; and Eleanor displayed a passion in marketing, public relations, and branding of the firm.

In 2006, the real estate business was at an all-time high in terms of growth and the values of its properties. Hank wanted to take his enterprise to the next level and had been considering how to groom his children to not only operate, but to one day run the family enterprise. He decided they had garnered the most value from their experiences of learning the business internally and working in various facets of the business. As a next step in their development, he sought counsel with his most trusted advisors on his advisory board to engage their thinking in developing a family bank. The intention of the bank was to provide more substantial leadership development opportunities for any offspring who wanted to apply for financing of ventures, which they would oversee, run, and routinely report back to Hank, his family office executives, and the advisory board. The family office would play an instrumental role in the coordination and organization of executing the family bank. Hank designated Annmarie, his lead advisor, as the liaison with his children on this front.

Hank and Annmarie sat down with Liam, Ron, and Eleanor to describe this concept and, immediately, a fruitful dialogue ensued of dreams of business ventures that might transpire. Hank was clear that he would help in an advisory capacity and that Annmarie was also available for advice. He described that the terms would be more lenient in the initial years of funding, but that the operation would have to show a return and eventually return the family capital to the bank that was loaned. These funds were by no means intended as a gift, as the children already received regular gifts from Hank and his wife, Martha. Hank was thrilled with the immediate excitement and positive response. So too were Liam, Ron, and Eleanor on the ability to build ventures. The siblings sat down to discuss whether they would prefer to do individual applications or work collectively to apply for financial from the family bank. Understanding that each of them had different entrepreneurial strengths, they decided that they felt more confident working together on their venture than separately.

In the latter part of 2006, after doing his due diligence, Ron identified four properties that would be successful. Liam developed pro forma and cash flow analysis to support the business venture and discussed the required financing to purchase these properties—two that were assisted living facilities and two that were commercial medical spaces. Eleanor, a strong business writer, drafted the applications to submit to the advisory board for consideration. In 2007, the proposal was approved, and all four properties were funded for a combined financing of $8 million. Annmarie was added with the setup, funding, and structure of the family bank in conjunction with Hank's expert outside advisors. The siblings each had a one-third stake in the success or failure of the ventures, but felt confident given the support, mentoring, and guidance of their father and the advisory board.

Then the banking and financial of crisis of 2008 occurred. Hank was consumed with keeping his primary real estate enterprise afloat. Liam, Ron, and Eleanor continued to press on; however, their optimistic projections now seemed completely unrealistic, and these ventures were going to take an additional three to five years to really start cash flowing. Annmarie attempted to keep on top of the reporting; however, Hank's children became less responsive. Further, Hank was now regretting the timing of launching the family bank and requested less and less information from his children. With his family enterprise's financial crunch from 2008, he could not devote the energy he had anticipated to helping his children and these new ventures, let alone manage his own ailing enterprise. Further, the primary lending organizations that had always backed his firm were now denying him the ability to draw on additional lines of credit and other lending instruments. Annmarie realized that the family bank was important; however, it was not the critical issue at hand for Hank and his family—saving the family business was.

Meanwhile, Eleanor took time off to have her first child, and Liam and Ron also had growing families: Each had three children under the age of 10. The new ventures took a backseat to the demands of the primary family enterprise and home life. Workdays got shorter with the demands of parenthood. Eleanor was enjoying being a stay-at-home mom during her maternity and decided that she did not want to return full-time to her prior post in marketing. Less time was devoted to these new ventures, as the slow recovery in 2009 and 2010 had Hank, Liam, and Ron more focused on the larger family enterprise.

Fast-forward to 2012 and one of Hank's board members asked Annmarie about how the family bank and the ventures were progressing. Annmarie responded that she really did not know . . . no updates had been provided by Hank's children since 2010. Hank had neglected to follow up as well regarding the expectation to re-amortize the outstanding loans, which was supposed to happen in fourth quarter 2010. Hank had dramatically reduced his expectations for the new ventures and feared causing conflict with his children by holding them accountable. Further, Eleanor had her second child and decided to stay home and be a full-time mother. Although she continued to play a minor role in these nascent ventures, her involvement was very limited. Ron and Liam had come to think of the funding for the ventures more as an informal gift and less as a loan requiring repayment, despite Annmarie's clarification regarding the expectation and intention. When asked by Annmarie about providing financials to justify why re-amortization of the loan was not possible, Liam expressed his concern that Hank did not trust his own children and how they were managing the enterprises. This caused an even deeper rift between Liam and Ron, who had increasing differences about the management of the four properties, placing Annmarie in the middle. The family bank was breaking the family apart with no good solution in sight.

Conclusion and Final Thoughts

Family offices can play a key role in helping financial and operating families consider different options and important steps to help develop and prepare the next generation to become responsible, self-sufficient, and empowered wealth creators. By starting early with a good education and a culture of entrepreneurial orientation and family entrepreneurship, along with a sense of accountability and a healthy next-generation governance system, families can help prepare the next generation for happy, productive lives.

Intra-family loans have been used for a very long time to help the next generation; however, they have not always helped families accomplish the healthy development and growth of family relationships as well as human and financial capital. Family banks can be a powerful mechanism to build this human and financial capital when they are customized, democratized, harmonized, and professionalized with good governance systems for each family.

Each family bank should be scaled appropriately for its purpose and complexity, and it should be flexible to evolve over time for each generation. Forming and developing family banks should not merely be a matter of creating traditional trust or corporate entities, but rather should be very carefully planned, tailored, and governed like a healthy family business system with the participation of the next generation and guidance from a multidisciplinary family office and independent experts.

As the Anderson case illustrates, establishing and maintaining a successful family bank can be challenging. However, properly planned family banks that are structured as professional entities that meet the needs of multiple generations are powerful vehicles to develop and support the next generation, as well as for providing new streams of capital to enhance the family's wealth.

Family banks can provide the opportunity for family members to form and build ventures with healthy cultures and leading practices to do the right things and attract the best people to set examples for the next generation and society. With education, forward thinking, and experienced experts, family offices can help families advance and prepare the next generation to achieve a great family legacy and responsible wealth and happiness.

Notes

1. Correspondence with Thomas J. Handler, J.D., P.C., Partner, Handler Thayer, LLP, February 2020.
2. Correspondence with Don Kozusko, Partner, Kozusko Harris Duncan LLP, January 2020.
3. James E. Hughes, Jr., Susan E. Massenzio, and Keith Whitaker, *Complete Family Wealth: Keeping It in the Family* (Princeton, NJ: Bloomberg Press, 2018).
4. First published by Warner K. Babcock, "Financing the Next Generation: Understanding Family Banks," Institute for Private Investors, webinar presentation, January 2013. Shared by Kirby Rosplock and Warner K. Babcock at the New York Family Firm Institute Study Group, 2018.
5. Ibid.
6. Correspondence with Thomas J. Handler, J.D., P.C., Partner, Handler Thayer, LLP, February 2020.
7. James E. Hughes, Jr. et al., *Complete Family Wealth: Keeping It in the Family* (Princeton, NJ: Bloomberg Press, 2018).
8. Warner K. Babcock, "The Power of the Family Bank," *Family Business,* September/October 2012.
9. The Anderson family is based in part on a real family story; however, their name is a pseudonym and personally identifying information has been disguised.

CHAPTER 14

Legacy, Philanthropy, and Impact Investing

Kirby Rosplock, PhD

> The mission of life: live, love, learn, and leave a legacy.
>
> —Stephen Covey

Legacy has a variety of meanings depending on how one interprets this simple word. For some families, philanthropy and making an impact is an integral part of their legacy and for others, it may have a separate connotation. This chapter discusses the role that a family office may play in supporting a family's legacy and philanthropy objectives. This chapter shares the common interpretations of legacy—financial, social, and philanthropic, and how our values and worldview may inform and shape one's perspective on legacy and philanthropy. Further, the chapter discusses impact investing and shares family office research giving, foundations, and the role of impact investing. From education, governance, and operational support to compliance and grant making, the role of the family office in administering the family foundation can be quite involved. This chapter closes with questions that family office leaders and senior family members should consider regarding the legacy of the family compared to the legacy of the family office.

Introduction to Legacy

The dictionary defines legacy as:

1. A gift of property, especially personal property, as money, by will; a bequest.
2. Anything handed down from the past, as from an ancestor or predecessor.[1]

Yet, when you ask individuals how they define their legacy, their answers vary greatly. For some, legacy may mean their ethical will that conveys important personal stories that highlight their values, principles, and beliefs. For others, legacy may be financial and about leaving actual valuables, keepsakes, or wealth. And for others, legacy may connote a philanthropic footprint that influences, impacts, and endows causes, charities, and people to make the world a better place. Legacy is a complex concept and may be described and interpreted several different ways. How does one come into focus around what is important for others to know, remember, honor, or appreciate about one's life? Legacy may be embodied through a social legacy, financial legacy, and philanthropic legacy. These concepts are more deeply explored in this chapter. But as we delve into this topic, the key is to recognize the important role that the family office can play in supporting an enduring legacy of a family and its individual family members.

A Generational Lens to Legacy

For members of the senior generation, defining one's legacy is a powerful exercise that can illuminate the character of an individual and what they have endured in their lives. Articulating one's legacy provides family members the wisdom from the most influential stories that shaped their lives. Thus, legacy may be captured through oral, written, film, or online media to share these pivotal stories and experiences. Iris Wagner, founder and film producer of Memoirs Productions, helps individuals articulate and capture their legacy to share with family members young, old, and those yet to be born. Iris reveals that preserving legacy is as much about the process of helping individuals reflect on what has given their lives most meaning as it is about the end product. "Reflecting on the stories that have shaped these individuals' lives is powerful. Often, stories are revealed that even their children have never heard. Legacy is about linking the past to the present and providing guideposts for future generations," shares Wagner.[2] These stories, woven together, are the fabric of a family's values and build a mantel of moral fibers that can bridge one generation to the next.

Fredda Herz Brown, PhD, and Fran Lotery, PhD, note in their book *Family Wealth Sustainability Toolkit* that "a legacy is at once timeless and time bound. By the time a family business has been shaped into a family enterprise, the group understands that its legacy is something different than what it owns, and a shared vision and values have been adopted. Each generation then has the important responsibility of molding its own vision and values, recommitting to the family legacy, and reshaping it for the future."[3] For Herz Brown and Lotery, legacy is a way to reconnect to the values and heritage of the family and to help recharge and reinvigorate the vision of the family. Similar to the discussion in Chapter 3 on Values, Mission, and Vision, capturing one's legacy can help anchor and ground a family's vision in addition to honoring the past.

John A. Warnick is founder of the Purposeful Planning Institute, a professional organization whose members assist clients in creating purposeful legacies. Warnick suggests the purpose and meaning of a family's wealth is too often buried beneath complicated legal and estate documents. "Lost in the sterility of the typical legalese of wills and trusts is the love parents and grandparents feel for their children and grandchildren—the faith they have in their descendants' potential to grow and develop, and the hope they hold for the future."[4] Describing himself as a recovering tax attorney, Warnick warns that families shouldn't let the "tax tail wag the rest of the legacy." He trains advisors to use visioning exercises and purposeful conversations to harness a client's positive emotional energy and skillfully interlace those expressions of love, meaning, values, and wisdom into the financial and estate planning structure. Warnick finds it sparks a much stronger appreciation for the purpose and meaning of the wealth and is a powerful antidote against entitlement. Warnick also stresses the importance of family meetings, storytelling, and meaningful conversations as additional ingredients in the purposeful transitioning of all dimensions of a family's wealth.

The legacy conversation in a family may be captured and memorialized in several different ways. In my family, my mother's father would capture lessons learned and inspiring, humorous quotes and sayings to memorialize and celebrate each milestone birthday (30, 40, 50, 60, and so forth). The 50- to 60-page small books were self-published and shared with family members and friends as a keepsake and a reminder to what he personally had witnessed or experienced in the prior decade. These were significant keepsakes that provided his daughters and future generations a glimpse into what he lived, learned, and experienced decade by decade.

The act of committing to capturing your legacy requires taking a journey to different parts of one's life, to experiences, places, and influential people who have impacted them. Many family members interviewed for this book shared that they make it a part of the educational process to engage future generations in interviewing the elders. These informal discussions sometimes are recorded and transcribed, and in other accounts, next-generation family members may present what they learned from the great aunt or grandfather at a family retreat or meeting. The power of the next generation revealing what they learned from the stories, values, and impressions of the senior generation is another enlightening exercise to inspire and motivate members of the next generation.

That legacy, to those who inherit it, may be received with appreciation and gratitude, while others may feel weight and sadness. Utilizing various conversation tools and exercises such as the Legacy Conversation developed by Dr. Carolyn Friend and Dr. James Weiner may help bridge the conversation for generations.[5] Dr. Friend shared in an interview her personal experience as a beneficiary of wealth left by her parents. Yet, the valuables left behind were mere objects, and what Friend longed for was to have many insights to unanswered questions by her deceased parents about their legacy. Today, Dr. Friend and Dr. Weiner engage not just the senior generation, but their children in a broader legacy conversation to inspire their future together. "Family dynamics in affluent families can be transformed through the process of engaging a family in a legacy dialogue that reaches across generations. The power of the conversation is not only on the senior generation, but the meaning it can bestow on the future members of the family," shares Friend and Weiner.[6] Friend and Weiner have built their advisory practice to aid affluent families to have intergenerational dialogue around legacy.

Defining Legacy

Based on past client work with affluent families and family offices, research from my dissertation, as well as secondary research, noteworthy findings emerged about the topic of legacy.[7] A great number of those with affluence desire leaving one or more of three kinds of legacy—financial, social, or philanthropic. A financial legacy may focus on the amount of financial wealth to be passed on to beneficiaries. A social legacy is the values and attitudes that are modeled for the next generation to adopt and often has a broader lens to community, regional, or national considerations. A philanthropic legacy is that which is left to a charity or causes with the purpose of providing for an individual in need or improving matters at a local, regional, national, or global level.

Financial Legacy

Financial legacy may be interpreted many ways, and when asked about how their wealth may impact their heirs upon their deaths, eight in ten women felt strongly about leaving a legacy and 95 percent of the women planned to distribute their wealth equally among all their children.[8] Similarly, when men were asked the same questions in a follow on study, 78 percent of men felt strongly about leaving a legacy and 97 percent of men would like their children to inherit their wealth equally.[9] Men and women ideally envisioned passing approximately half of their wealth on to their children and stepchildren. This data reveals the more progressive thinking to treat daughters and sons as equal when it comes to inheritance as opposed to primogeniture, the passing on of most of the wealth to the firstborn son. Endowing family as beneficiaries with financial means is a key aspect of many affluent individual's financial legacy. Nearly two-thirds (62 percent) desire their children to receive $1 to $10 million upon their death.[10] That the net worth of the women far exceeded the amount they desired to pass on to heirs suggests that their intention was to provide their children with a financial head start, but not excess. One respondent noted about passing on wealth that "only for right reasons [such as] education, support if working in a charitable environment, but not to sustain a lifestyle—let them earn it."[11] Another respondent shared, "They know that there will be some wealth, but that they need to work."[12] Although seven in ten respondents said that they are proud of their family's wealth, 81 percent of men and only 46 percent of women said that they are prouder of their financial contributions.[13] Endowing offspring is important, but a financial legacy also encompasses manifesting their own financial success for many affluent. A financial legacy has both tangible and intangible elements. Legacy planning involves transitioning wealth or valuables, with purpose and meaning, which are at their essences about the grantor's values, wealth transfer intentions, and personal beliefs. Understanding that giving, impact, and sustainable investing are about connecting the impact of valuables to areas of value, necessity, or need is a major paradigm shift. In the past wealth was often viewed as leverage used for the purpose of growing more wealth. Some still hold this value, but many affluent are connecting the dots between their valuable and their values. (See Figure 14.1.)

FIGURE 14.1 Valuables Versus Values

Values

Innate and evolve

Shapes us from the inside; guide our behaviors and choices

Can never be bought

Moderate our decisions and choices

Influenced by emotive events -
extreme joy, happiness, despair, pain, anguish

Where we find alignment

Valuables

Physical and transactional

Assets, collectibles, homes, etc. that may identify
preferences from the outside; may reflect values

Always acquired; temporary

May reflect ownership and financial value

May be a reward upon achievement, milestones, advancement

Fluid; may be intended for short- or long-term

Source: © Tamarind Partners, Inc.

A family's values, beliefs, and core principals are at the essence of its social legacy.

Social Legacy

Leaving a social legacy typically may entail an emphasis to aid family, community, the environment, social networks, and/or all humankind. For many, a social legacy connects to the concept of stewardship and providing wealth for future generations, the significance of living within one's means, and the belief that having financial wealth does not connote superiority to others. For others, a social legacy is about "teaching the next generation to be responsible in their spending, the importance of continued growth, the importance of giving back to the community," As one woman shared:

> Taking what you need and being prepared to pass on or give to others was also expressed. One woman interviewed shared that . . . money is like a stream flowing past your house. You can take some out, you can drink it, you can water your garden with it, but you may not dam it up. . . I think the other thing that very much informs my thinking [around stewardship] is that I consider that wealth is not just money; it is everything you have. I believe that I am a steward of this and that it all is actually God's money. And that I have an opportunity to help in the creating of the better world by judicious use of that money.[14]

Planning for the future and the stewarding of a family's wealth for future generations is thus of great significance. Social legacy also encompasses the belief that in order for their family and future generations to sustain their wealth, their children should value, respect, and be responsible for it. Striking the balance between enjoyment and the responsibility of wealth and its impact on others is another component of social legacy. One interviewee shared that they enjoy what wealth can do for them, but that they also have a responsibility of passing it on and being mindful of other's needs. How might this wealth help others to rise up? Another study participant shared, "Legacy is much more than just about money. It is about transferring values and morals; there is an inherent responsibility, especially when it comes to long-term wealth transfer."[15] Others shared how the value of living within one's means was a final ingredient to one's social legacy. For example, one interviewee said, "[It is important to] not live beyond your means. I've never been one to live on credit."

The final theme arising about social legacy is that with wealth comes responsibility, but wealth does not ensure one's happiness. One interviewee stated about her own mother, who "taught [her] that money doesn't mean happiness, that it doesn't mean that you are of any more importance than anyone else." Also emerging in this theme was the concept that personal happiness and fulfillment is not contingent upon having wealth. One participant stated, "If you're not happy without it, money is not going to make you happy if you have it . . . You have to have an original core value of knowing who you are, what life means to you, what your family means to you before . . . and money should just enhance it." She also warned against equating love with the lavishing of gifts. A social legacy is perhaps the most important vehicle to transpose values, beliefs, and kernels of wisdom to others. Learning from the experiences and defining moments from a relative can be transformational.

Philanthropic Legacy

One's philanthropic legacy takes shape through a desire to give back and help causes, among them underserved communities or macro-level, global issues such as social justice, the environment, political stability, and human rights. Many family offices focus on the lessons that philanthropy might teach next-generation family members about wealth. From soft skills, communication, team building, conflict management, and leadership to technical skills including sourcing, planning, budgeting, performance, and broader management skills, a philanthropic legacy can have a double bottom line—good for the recipient and good for the family members who are fortunate enough to be able to give away their wealth.

Increasingly, the Boomers, Silent, and Millennial generations who are affluent are turning their attention to giving in the now, versus deferring until their passing. Leaving a philanthropic legacy increasingly means giving while you are living and seeing the impact of the giving while alive. This often inspires others to give and may inculcate their offspring to as well. Some are motivated by their faith and actively set aside a portion of income to tithe or tzedakah. One gentleman from Eastern Europe has made it his mission to give as much as he can during his lifetime. A Russian-Armenian entrepreneur, venture philanthropist, and investor, Ruben Vardanyan has made it part of his personal mission to leave a philanthropic legacy and has given more than $300 million to causes and issues about which he is passionate. In an article in the *Financial Times,* Vardanyan shared that, "We believe philanthropy will move very fast in the next five years, but people have no culture to think about it. This will be critical for Russia. Who can they learn from?" Vardanyan reflected on legacy as it means to prepare heirs for wealth and its impact. He shared, "My main advice is whatever you have decided, it will take time to explain to your family—five years or more . . . if you don't start now, it will be dangerous. It's a long-term process that requires lots of effort and commitment. Do it as soon as you can.[16] The Covid-19 pandemic has also inspired large-scale giving, as described by Sean Davis, founder and CEO of Merton Capital Partners, a social impact advisory firm that focuses on large-scale impact investment programs. He shares that this is an unprecedented time requiring "big bets" on the best in breed charities that will go the distance to solve for universal problems. Jack Dorsey, Twitter and Square founder, must have gotten this memo, as he has recently committed nearly a third of his total wealth (28 percent) to make grants towards Covid-19 relief and to inspire others. "Why now? The needs are increasingly urgent, and I want to see the impact in my lifetime," shares Dorsey.[17] From first-generation techpreneurs and investment and finance gurus, to industrial revolution families who are four, five, or more generations old, leaving a philanthropic legacy is also increasingly becoming a function of impact investing.

Philanthropy, Impact, and Sustainable Investing

The Greek words *philos* and *anthropose* combine to create *philanthropy,* which means "the love of humanity." The contemporary understanding of the term is one of "private initiatives for public good, focusing on quality of life."[18] Philanthropy is appealing to affluent individuals and families because it can be a way for them to identify their passions and contribute to society. A family may be recognized for its philanthropic endeavors, setting it apart from other families. It creates an identity for a family—who it *is*, not just what it *does*.

Philanthropy is no longer the only way that families are actualizing their giving, rather impact investing has increasing been found to be a smart and effective way of bridging generations. Developing an ethos of philanthropy and/or impact investing across generations in a family can help the first generation of a family find alignment, common ground, and passion from their offspring. A recent interview with a financial family revealed that education through venture capital with an impact orientation has been a powerful teaching tool for their adult children. Another multigenerational family office shared that family members are permitted to observe the family's foundation meetings as soon as they come of age. They encourage active participation and involvement. Even the patriarch of the family recalled in his early twenties being a senior leader for the family's major foundation.

One example of a legacy enacted through philanthropy is that of the Joseph and Harvey Meyerhoff Family Charitable Funds.[19] Joseph Meyerhoff was a Baltimore businessperson who initiated a tradition of philanthropy that has become a legacy through his children, grandchildren, and great-grandchildren. They primarily support causes in Baltimore and in Israel. His son, Harvey M. (Bud) Meyerhoff, has followed in his father's footsteps by being an instrumental figure in the building of the United States Holocaust Memorial Museum in Washington, DC, and as a supporter of Johns Hopkins University, Johns Hopkins Hospital, and the Johns Hopkins Health System. His children and grandchildren are also active on family foundation boards. Joseph's daughter, Elizabeth Meyerhoff Katz, and her own children are active participants in family foundations and community initiatives.

Elizabeth Minkin is a descendent of Joseph Meyerhoff and directs the funds' activity in Baltimore and the local area. She clearly states how philanthropy realizes a family's legacy. "This is a business. This is our long-term legacy—to steward this money, which has been entrusted to good decisions made by the family. Our goal is to involve all generations in carrying on the family tradition of philanthropy."[20]

The new generations of investors are thinking differently on how they want their wealth to change the world, as 63 percent of Millennials and 40 percent of Generation Xers indicated interest in ESG- and impact-related investments.[21] A recent study found that over one-third of family offices are currently now engaged in sustainable investing practices and a quarter in impact investing.[22] According to the Campden UBS Global Family Office Report, sustainable investing is defined as "an investment approach that involves the consideration of environmental, social, and governance (ESG) factors in the investment process. Three distinct sub-approaches, which can be used individually or in combination, can be identified: (1) exclusion—excluding investments that are not aligned with an investor's values; (2) integration—incorporating ESG factors into traditional investment processes; and (3) impact investing—investing with the intention to generate measurable environmental or social impact, alongside providing a competitive financial return."[23] Research on the increase of sustainable investing reveals that approximately $31 trillion of assets globally are being managed under sustainable investment strategies, up 34 percent from 2016.[24] The study found that the average family office allocates approximately 19 percent to sustainable investments, but there is an increasing trend to allocate most if not all wealth towards impact according to Richard Azarnia, who directs impact and sustainable investing for his family office. As the founder of Mlinda, a nonprofit focused on renewable energy for rural communities in India, Azarnia believes there are ample opportunities to do well and do good. He is passionate about helping build environmentally sustainable businesses that are energy efficient and utilizing green technologies, helping rural villages experience positive impact to the environment, as well as social and financial outcomes including reducing CO_2 emissions and increasing household income.[25]

Many other Millennials have followed suit by pursuing vigorously the family office as their champion for impact investing and change. Rachel Gerrol, chief executive officer and co-founder of Nexus, an international network of more than 5,000 young investors, social entrepreneurs, and philanthropists, mostly aged 20–40, observes that: "At least 50 percent of the people who self-identified as philanthropists in 2011 are now self-identifying as impact investors."[26] The movement is afoot, and nonprofit organizations such as The ImPact—cofounded by Fernando Scodro, a Brazilian entrepreneur, Jean Case, CEO of the Case Foundation, and Liesel Pritzker Simmons, a beneficiary and philanthropist—aid families and their family offices when it comes to making more effective and efficient impact investments. Liesel Pritzker Simmons and her husband, Ian Simmons, started Blue Haven Initiative, a family office based in Cambridge, Massachusetts, in 2012, and their entire portfolio is committed to impact investments. But philanthropy, impact, and sustainable investing are all correlated to improving the welfare, well-being, and sustainable prospects of our planet and its people. Pritzker Simmons shared, "There's often been quite a bit of privacy or opacity around how families do business and invest. This generation is being out front and center about how they're making their investments."[27]

Opportunities and Challenges of Philanthropy, Impact, and Sustainable Investing

There are opportunities in managing philanthropy and impact investing through the family office. Benefits include the integration of key functions, such as administration, tax strategy, and governance; the alignment of the foundation with the family's values on governance, financial management, long-term planning, and family leadership development; economies of scale by operating the philanthropic initiatives along with the standard administrative matters; and efficient communication through one point of contact for family members. That single point of contact is effective in the family's control of their financial interests, because it represents a centralized structure managing all the family's concerns in a way that is aligned with the family's vision. Each family office can be customized to each family's needs and interests, in a way that is ongoing as the family itself evolves. The family office may provide critical planning, particularly with making sure that the minimum-grant allotment of 5 percent of the foundation's assets is made annually. Further, for families whose family office manages the investable wealth of the family, the assets of the foundation may be invested in accordance with socially responsible investment practices, if that is a value to the family. The Cordes Family case study provides an excellent example of the coordination of a family's giving, impact and family office in synchronicity, later in this chapter.

Family offices have proven to effectively support and, in many situations, lead the family's foundation(s). This success is a result of certain characteristics. Family office staff who are knowledgeable about the family history, can help ensure that current philanthropic practices are aligned with the original intent of the donor. Family office staff have project management skills and can thus help a family bring its vision for a foundation to life by mapping out plans and then executing them. Family office staff can act as mentors to younger family members and can train them to become foundation leaders. Being accountable is highly important to family office staff. Therefore, they will hold everyone involved in the foundation accountable, making sure all processes are followed and documentation is accurately provided.[28]

With the opportunities, there may also be certain challenges in managing philanthropy and impact investments through the family office. There is a natural tension between the family office and the family foundation, as they ultimately may have conflicting goals—one to preserve or grow wealth and the other to give it away or in the case of impact investing, to invest in opportunities that have a triple bottom line, investments that make a profit, benefit people and ultimately the planet. Traditional investing may only value financial and performance goals. In various investment circles the debate still remains: whether it is more efficient to build wealth to give away or invest with an impact or sustainable investment thesis. The two approaches ultimately come down the family and how they purse their giving or impact agenda.

In addition to receiving clear direction from the family, sharing a common language and developing mutual respect and understanding will help these two entities and organizations integrate their operations. Clear roles and boundaries can, in fact, create synergies between the family office and foundation and the impact segment of the portfolio with the traditional asset allocation. Traditionally, the family office entity focuses on investment management, foundation administration, and reporting and compliance, while the foundation entity focuses on grantmaking, philanthropic strategy, foundation administration, and governance. When a family office is involved in the family philanthropy, and impact investing is also involved in leading the development of the foundation—including creating its vision and focus, hiring foundation staff, grantmaking, and, for some study respondents, engaging in program evaluation—fruitful outcomes may be a result. More and more foundations are seeking opportunities to invest in impact or sustainable investment strategies as a way to expand the positive change and difference their philanthropic dollars may make. A hurdle continues to be the impression that impact investing means conceding investment returns. Jean Case of the Case Foundation notes that this is "one of the great myths . . . It is not necessarily concessionary, and in some cases, there is outperformance where impact is there from the start."[29] A family office and family foundation relationship works best when there is a clear and strong family governance structure, when the office and foundation have knowledge of the family and share their goals, and when there are explicit reporting relationships among staff. Finally, a crucial element is a good feedback loop of communication between the family with its staff, and between the family office and its philanthropy or impact investing professionals, and with the community or causes they are giving to and/or impact investing in. (See Figure 14.2.)

FIGURE 14.2 Relationships Among Family, Family Office, Giving, and Community

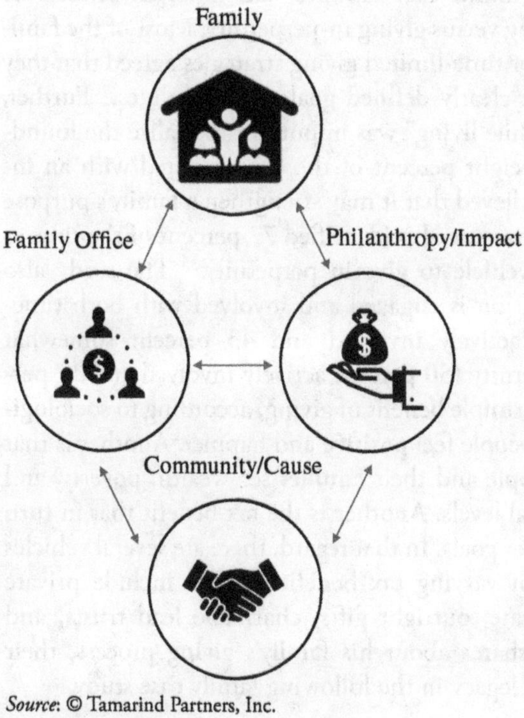

Family

Family Office

Philanthropy/Impact

Community/Cause

Source: © Tamarind Partners, Inc.

Family Philanthropy and Foundations

According to a global philanthropy study, the most popular vehicles for giving are family foundations (64 percent), followed by direct gifts or donations to charities or nonprofits (45 percent), donor advised funds (16 percent), and corporate/business foundations (15 percent).[30] The study invited families of wealth and private philanthropists from around the globe to participate, and its sample had 50 percent from the US, 25 percent from Europe, 20 percent from Asia-Pacific, and the remaining participants (5 percent) came primarily from South and Central America. The average net worth of the family/private philanthropists was $1.2 billion, and their philanthropic organizations, mostly foundations with sizes of $155 million each gave on average of $11.9

million away over the last 12 months.[31] Half of families (50 percent) reviewed their giving strategies annually, and 59 percent reviewed their time-limited giving annually. The study found that families had different schools of thought on time-limited giving versus giving in-perpetuity. Most of the families (55 percent) who opted for time-limited giving strategies agreed that they made it more likely to have "clearly defined goals and timelines." Further, they indicated that "giving while living" was important to realize the founder's giving intention.[32] Forty-eight percent of those who opted with an in-perpetuity giving approach believed that it may strengthen a family's purpose and values. Family foundations were also identified 77 percent of the time as the preferred philanthropic vehicle to give in perpetuity.[33] The study also revealed that the next generation is engaged and involved with both time-limited giving (37 percent actively involved and 43 percent somewhat involved) and giving in perpetuity (50 percent actively involved and 37 percent somewhat involved).[34] A simple benefit of giving, according to sociological research, is that it makes people feel positive and happier. Another is that giving can shape the way people and their families see wealth, poverty, and social issues at local and global levels. Another is the tax benefit that in turn assists people in achieving other goals. In that regard, there are several vehicles for philanthropic giving with varying tax benefits. These include private foundations, retained life estate, outright gifts, charitable lead trusts, and many others. Preston Root shares about his family's giving process, their foundation, and the power of legacy in the following family case study.

The Root Family Legacy and Evolving Their Philanthropy

The legacy of Root Glass, who invented the design for the original Coca-Cola bottle, plays out in the evolution of their giving. In correspondence with Preston Root, a fourth-generation owner and former president of the Root Family Board of Directors, he shared the impact of legacy and philanthropy in his family. His story follows:

My great-grandfather designed, patented, and manufactured the original 6½-ounce Coca-Cola bottle at Root Glass Company, founded in 1900. That was the first generation. The second generation was comprised of my grandfather, who was killed prematurely in 1932 at a young age in an airplane accident. My father, the only member of the third generation, was raised by his grandfather. The fourth generation consists of me and five siblings. The fifth generation consists of 14 children and there is a rapidly expanding sixth generation. I am proud of the 130-year-old, six-generation family business heritage of the Root family that stems from our early beginnings as a glass manufacturer. Originally, our glass jars were primarily used for storing food items, and then our family went on to design and create the iconic Coca-Cola bottle. Today, that bottle is a powerful symbol not only of our legacy, but of America. Our legacy is much more than Root Glass Company or the bottle design; our legacy is the people who make up our heritage.

Legacy, to our family, is who our ancestors were and all the people that make up the generations after them. Legacy is about family, and it's about commitment to community as well as the business. The reason our family maintains extensive archives and family mementos is so my daughter can look at pictures and artifacts and say, "That's what my great-grandfather looked like." There are films of Coca-Cola bottles being made at Root Glass Company. I believe those are the tangible ingredients that make up the Root Family legacy. The product that you build with those ingredients is the bridge from the past generation to all future generations. Our generation hopes that through dedication this legacy continues.

Although the physical wealth in many families may decrease over time with expanding generations, the key is to invest in the future human capital of the family in the hope that each new generation will find innovative and new opportunities for growing their personal wealth and involving them in the family's shared philanthropy. We have found innovative opportunities through our family foundation to provide chances for leadership development, family governance, and education through practical application of grantmaking and foundation management. We had a member of the fifth generation establish an online, automated grant review process whereby family members could weigh in on various grantmaking opportunities. This helped us solve family members being geographically dispersed and gave us a systematic approach to gauge individual feedback. Seeing opportunities to engage and harness the thinking of the next generations is also part of our family legacy.

We went one step further by engaging the member of the fifth generation to help the family improve the grantmaking process. They provided some wonderful insights and creativity to innovate our process. The family now has a grant that is exclusive to the fifth generation (ages 14–40). The fifth-generation family members are asked to submit a one-page grant request and to create a self-made video alongside the charity—think TED talk. The professional production quality is not being judged, rather the compelling nature of the content to answer questions like: What is the purpose of the charity? Who does it serve? How will the funds be used? What metrics to evaluate the charity's success? How does this fall in line with the philanthropic values shared by the family and foundation? The fifth-generation family members might spend three to five hours interacting with the charity to capture the video and make a compelling case for the grant. A major grant may be as much as twenty-five thousand dollars and all others may receive a five-thousand-dollar stipend for their participation. As a result of this program, the fifth generation is more involved, galvanized, and participatory than ever before. For the seven years the family has been operating this innovative program, it has led to the fifth-generation finalist being invited to the "G5 panel." (No older generation family members are allowed.) Why is this type of initiative so important? Because we are grooming members of the fifth generation to be able to lead the family foundation into a new future.

I realize that the whole point of family legacy is to illustrate for the next generations that come along that your heritage is what's important: It's not how much money you have; it is who you are. It serves as a real grounding element for those generations. It's a way of saying that who we are is not what we have; it's what we've done and what we are doing. That's that other really important component of legacy, which is community service. My great-grandparents and grandparents gave away a great deal of money, and that's a legacy that stands out for all the generations to say, "Life is about working hard and achieving results, but those results are put to higher use than self-enrichment. There's a real desire for improving the communities that we live in." We all have an opportunity and responsibility to give back.

My family's values are embedded in my family's legacy. In our archives, there are many hours of video from the early 1900s and we have distilled some of these films into vignettes about my father. He is about two or three years old. My family and I have looked at it several times and have been humbled by my father's modest beginnings. It's in their house, around their Christmas tree in 1928, and you can see how humility was such a part of my dad's upbringing. We were raised with the same kind of values. One of the most important values that my dad taught all of us and exemplified was honesty. He was always honest in his business life. Honesty is one of our core values.

Family first is another top value. Your family is the most important thing you have, and they deserve your time, your respect, and your love. My dad took six or eight weeks off in the summer while we were all out of school to travel with us. We would all pile in a car and go out West to national parks. That was a great example of being with family. You cannot replace quantity time with quality time. The first thing you need is enough of quantity time before it can ever turn into quality time, and believe me, when you're traveling from Florida to Los Angeles in a car, indeed you have plenty of time! Making quality time out of that is a huge value of ours. Time together means something. It breeds *joie de vivre*.

Work ethic is another important value. We all saw my dad work, but he didn't overwork. He was a 9-to-5 guy. He left when we left for school in the morning, and he came back after we got back from school. He wasn't working all the time. He wasn't gone on weekends very much. When we were about 14 or 15 years old, he'd ask "What kind of job are you thinking about? You have to do something with your time." It was a great lesson in the purpose of professional life. We have a family cliché: While you're working, you're not spending money and you're staying out of trouble. Being the youngest of six, I feel I really received the benefit of his work ethic. I've had a career in broadcasting for 29 years and finished up the last 15 with a company outside the family business that is an industry leader. It's not always been about the paycheck. It has been about working for a good company, developing the satisfaction of building a career, and having the professional fulfillment of excellence. All of these components allow for building capacity and contributing to a greater good. I am very proud of my family's heritage and know that it makes each generation stronger with an understanding, appreciation, and respect of the family's legacy.[35]

The Family Office Supporting Family Philanthropy

How important a role does the family office play in family legacy and philanthropic endeavors? What oversight, management, and direction come from the family offices versus a family's foundation when it comes to legacy and philanthropic pursuits? Before we tackle these topics, it may be helpful to understand more of the motivations around legacy and philanthropy.

A study of philanthropic families and philanthropists found that 75 percent give because they want to give back to society, have an interest to create social change (55 percent), want to put their values into action (50 percent), and address social inequality (47 percent).[36] More families are partnering with the family office to invest foundation assets efficiently and effectively with an eye on taxes and wealth transfer. The estate planners and tax accountants for a family may consider the tax benefits of philanthropy, the wealth creators or inheritors may see it as a part of their personal or family mission, and the next generation may see it as a learning tool and experience to better educate themselves on wealth, leadership, and governance. For most families, the decision to engage philanthropically is typically a culmination of one or more of those primary motivations.

The role a family office may play in orchestrating, organizing, governing, and in certain cases, leading the family foundation can be a powerful, positive, and generative influence. Just like the variance in family offices, no two family offices appear to have the same approach or delivery in supporting a family and its charitable intent. Generally, a family office attends to a family's philanthropic giving by supporting the family's philanthropic goals, administering family foundations, attending to family legacy and leadership by supporting the family's long-term strategic vision, and guiding and promoting governance and committee business. The following case study shares the Cordes family's foundation and family office journey.

Cordes Family Case Study

Ron and Marty Cordes started their family foundation and family office in 2006 after Ron sold his investment management business, AssetMark, which he had co-founded in 1996. The early days of the Cordes Foundation are notable for two hallmarks—tall ambitions and some hurdles they encountered along the way that started the Cordes family down the path of becoming impact investors and trailblazers among family foundations. As one of the first family foundations to transition to a 100 percent impact focus, the Cordes family's journey to impact investing is unique. There were no playbooks to follow or even advisors to direct their way. The Cordes family had to write the rules themselves.

The impact marketplace has evolved significantly since the early days of the Cordes's first forays into impact investing, but the Cordes family's experiences and institutional knowledge are instructive and inspirational for family offices active in or contemplating a pivot towards impact.

Rethinking the Foundation Model

The foundation originally envisioned making its mark by helping solve some of society's biggest problems like global poverty, the role of women and girls in the world, and economic inequality. But almost from its origin, Ron and Marty were frustrated to discover that philanthropic organizations typically only distributed a small portion of their assets annually (the minimum required distribution of 5 percent) to address the problems they cared about.

About the same time, Ron and Marty started to learn about and meet social entrepreneurs that were developing new for-profit solutions to address at scale some of the issues the foundation was focused on, but who needed different forms of capital beyond traditional grant dollars. This is well before the term "impact investing" was even coined, and social enterprise investing, as it was called then, was still very new. Their definition then and still today was investing for dual purpose to generate a financial return both market-rate and concessionary as well as a measurable impact return.

Ron and Marty realized in 2007 that if they were going to maximize the impact of their foundation, it made sense to explore how the foundation might go about investing in some of these for-profit enterprises through the corpus. They also wanted to see if they could allocate more of the corpus of the foundation's assets to their mission beyond the minimum required distribution (5 percent) into impact investments.

To Ron and Marty's further frustration, they could not find a team of advisors who could create a foundation structure that could accomplish both their grant and investment objectives at the same time. In fact, they exhausted three sets of advisors and lawyers before they found the right team. After a few years, they finally had a solid plan in place, they received board approval for their new foundation structure and by 2008 the foundation had embarked on its exciting journey into uncharted waters.

When the 2008 financial crisis hit, 20 percent of the foundation's assets were invested for dual purpose to generate returns as well as impact back to society. Those private investments ended up outperforming every other part of their traditional portfolio. At the time, they had invested mostly private debt and equity in the young microfinance sector that focused on the empowerment of women. Most of these investments were uncorrelated to the public markets, which is why they did so well through a volatile global market. Ron shared that their holdings were largely spared, and "never got the memo that the financial markets had melted down."

The Cordes's saw how their portfolio and the impact investment thesis held up despite one of the most challenging investment cycles, convincing the family that there was a lot more to this impact investing after all.

It's a Family Affair—Getting to 100 Percent

By 2014 the foundation had progressed in its grantmaking and investments in social enterprises that were now a part of what had become the burgeoning ecosystem of impact investing. By this time, the foundation was invested across all asset classes besides cash and had moved from 20 percent to 40 percent toward mission alignment.

Ron and Marty were joined at the foundation in 2014 by their only child, Stephanie (Steph), and now son-in-law, Eric. For Steph, she had a personal revelation about the impact of her current work in advertising then— she wanted to make a difference beyond just selling print advertisements. She started to engage with the various investments and grants her parents were making, often of similar size to the advertisements she was selling. Then it clicked . . . she saw the opportunity, passion, and commitment that her parents demonstrated and desired to put her skills and interests to align with her parents in driving the foundation forward.

Beyond just doubling the capacity and rounding out the skillsets of the operation, Steph and Eric brought along with them new skillsets and the kind of fresh, bright new thinking that one might expect from the NexGen. It was Steph and Eric, whose outlooks were grounded in a commitment to mission and values, who were the first to raise the idea of moving from 40 percent to 100 percent commitment to impact investing.

In the seven years since inception, the family had greatly increased its network, the sophistication with how it was approaching impact investing, and the process to source, vet, diligence, and deploy capital. Impact investing in 2014 was still not mainstream, and had not taken hold, hence Ron and Marty and their family's foundation was considered by their professional peers as a trailblazer. Needing to build out their professional infrastructure, the Cordes family set its sights on improving (1) process and (2) people, and both would be instrumental in getting to 100 percent alignment and they would have to build in order to get there.

The expanded Cordes team quickly got to work putting in place a series of processes to make their infrastructure more robust. This effort spanned enhanced deal sourcing to due diligence to determining which deals should be put before the independent board, which has always been made up of more outside professionals than family members to keep independence and objectivity.

In many ways, the family, the board, and their outside advisors were uniquely positioned to make this novel transition to 100 percent. Each came with their own highly useful skillset that could drive the effort forward. Ron had the financial services investment acumen, and together with Marty, had years of institutional knowledge about the challenges facing women and girls around the world and how to better their lives.

Over the years, Ron and Marty had done a lot of work to evolve and refocus the mandate of the foundation. Originally the foundation had a broad scope, working on education and healthcare and making grants in a wide variety of areas. But Ron and Marty increasingly felt that they were not having the kind of deep impact they were hoping for because their resources were spread too wide rather than strategically focused where they could derive the most value both from a grant perspective as well as investment. There were so many great cause-related investments that could improve the lives of women and girls, and that while the foundation's assets were significant, they were dwarfed by the scale of the problems they wanted to address.

To deepen their impact, they would have to sharpen their focus. Steph and Eric would begin developing a deeper pipeline to analyze from as well as custom metrics to look at the effectiveness of the impact without burdening the organizations.

Steph was very interested in sustainable fashion and helped open the eyes of everyone on the team to the interplay between fashion and the empowerment of women. Artisanship globally is second only to agriculture as an employer of women. So, the foundation began to find ways to support artists and networks and make investments in companies that support artisans. The foundation currently focuses on investing in economic opportunities for women, specifically in the artisan/sustainable fashion area as well as investing in opportunities to strengthen the impact ecosystem by investing in women-led companies and funds.[37]

Here are two examples of the kinds of investments in the current portfolio that meet the foundation's mission and risk/return criteria:

- *All Across Africa* brings together artisan collectives that sell home decor, primarily hand-woven baskets. They have created a multimillion global network for these artisans whose jewelry is sold through small and large retailers like IKEA, Bed Bath & Beyond, Target, and Kohl's. The investment helps provide working capital to the purchase materials needed for production.
- *Soko Jewelry* is a women-led ethical jewelry brand and manufacturing platform in Nairobi, Kenya, that sells wholesale and retail around the world and in the US through stores like Nordstrom. All the jewelry is produced by small artisans, most of whom reside in Kibera, one of the largest slums in the world. To propel its success, Soko has built a proprietary technology that relies on smartphone technology to take orders from anywhere in the world and transmit them immediately to various artisans who are triaged based on their capacity so they can create and deliver the jewelry on time. Notably, Soko was very powerful in unlocking the capital of co-investors via Align Impact to invest alongside the Cordes Foundation, earning an 8 percent return on a 12-month note which was backed by their accounts receivable. The subordinated debt the families provided resulted in unlocking a larger line of credit for Soko with Grassroots Business Fund.

The foundation maintained its own pipeline that they reviewed together monthly or quarterly. They did the analysis themselves, determined which ones they should take meetings, and ultimately which ones they should present to the foundation's independent board. And once a deal got the board signoff, they assigned a person to be the relationship lead so they could keep a hand into each of their investments and provide strategic guidance and operational support similar to how a private equity firm may interact with their portfolio companies.

To date, they have approximately 30 active investments and sit on about 15 different boards (i.e., boards of directors, boards of trustees, boards of advisors) in a variety of capacities helping the companies they are invested in and other impact organizations set their strategy and benefit from the family's decade plus in the field. They continue to be big believers in community and co-invest along with a handful of other families via the foundations impact advisor, Align Impact, finding great value in experiencing the journey alongside other families.

Lessons Learned from the Cordes Family's Impact Investment Journey

For the family office that has yet to begin their own impact investing journey or for the family office that does not have all of the skillsets they need to make a transition themselves like the Cordes family did, the Cordes family has lots of insights from their experience.

Figure out what gets you excited

A family foundation is an opportunity for a family to make its mark on the world. Rather than starting with figuring out how to go about the nuts and bolts of moving towards impact, the Cordes family strongly advocates starting with what motivates them. As Marty says, the most important priority is to arrive at an understanding of "what gets you up in the morning—what gets you excited."[38] Ron adds that the foundation's impact advisor, Jenn Kenning of Align Impact, often formulates this issue for clients as they are figuring out their "why" and a plan for how best to execute.[39]

Anticipate that change and adaption is part of the process

Another important lesson learned is that where you start is likely not where you will end up in three to five years. The Cordes family cites their own evolution of their foundation's broad mandate to their current focus as an example of the kind of trajectory that needs to happen authentically for every family so that they can embrace their "why" and it can evolve over time.

Eric points out that once a family office knows what excites them, they need to come up with a strategy before they can truly dive in. Each family office needs to evaluate what they like doing and what they want to do, and this comes from developing a better understanding of the impact marketplace and how other family offices have approached their impact investing. Everyone on the Cordes team wears multiple hats, but as Eric puts it, "You don't know what you don't know until you undertake this process."[40]

Learn from the best expert advisors to avoid pitfalls

It is not easy for many family offices to find out the answers to these questions themselves or to find the time to familiarize themselves sufficiently with the impact marketplace to get comfortable as an investor. In Eric's experience this process often involves a lot of soul searching. What is more, as Ron points out, philanthropy is relatively straightforward but translating your mission into an investment strategy is more complex.

Many family offices turn to outside experts for help, and in the years since the Cordes Foundation charted their own course towards 100 percent impact, an entire sub-specialty of impact advisors has emerged. Impact advisors can help family offices get started on their own impact journey in a number of ways including (1) helping hone in on their passion; (2) developing an investment and grant strategy; (3) providing access to deal flow; (4) providing back-end services like diligence, monitoring, and reporting; and (5) providing valuable introductions and contacts to others in the industry.

Even for foundations that are optimized for impact, like the Cordes's, it may still make sense to use an outside consultant. The Cordes family started working with Align Impact in 2017 to help them with due diligence on deals, gaining access to co-investment opportunities, monitoring, and reporting and generally staying up to speed on deal flow and marketplace activities as the impact marketplace quickly grew up.

Prepare for the difficult conversations

The Cordes family has amassed tremendous institutional knowledge and passion for impact investing; their journey to impact is well known to many at this point and their affection for one another so palpable that one might walk away from a conversation thinking that this all came easy. However, anyone who presses them as to whether there were any challenges along the way between them will be greeted with spontaneous giggling from them, as it was not easy but now in hindsight very much worth it.

Every member of the Cordes family acknowledged that feathers did and still do get ruffled from time to time. Someone might have a particular point of view that the others might not share or be the only one to feel very strongly about a particular investment, for example. Each pointed out the importance of creating an environment where every person felt comfortable sharing their thoughts *and* their feelings. And because they each maintain a great respect for the different skillsets and perspectives that each member of the family brings to the endeavor, there are possibilities for cross-generational learning.

Impact investing can achieve attractive risk-adjusted returns, not concessions

Similarly, the Cordes family is quick to point out that those that are new to impact investing may bring their own biases about what it means to be an impact investor, and one of the most common is to conflate impact investing with concessionary returns. The Cordes family looks to achieve risk-adjusted returns in their impact portfolio that match their appetite for risk across the different asset classes—debt, equity, later stage, and so on. With respect to debt, for example, they seek out high single-digit returns that also maximize the impact they can have.

Balance the impact and investment outcomes by taking consideration for one's emotions

Ron cautioned that one of the biggest challenges in making the transition from grantmaking to impact is avoiding the mistake of leading with the heart on the investment side and focusing on the mission of the investment at perhaps the exclusion of the financial viability. He pointed out that a good impact advisor who has an objective, critical eye can help an impact investor create a diversified portfolio that is structured with a risk/reward profile that suits them just as an investor would demand for their traditional investments.[41]

Eric warns that family offices also need to be prepared for the emotional dimensions that come with some of the conversations with potential investees. Turning down an enterprise whose mission you believe in but just is not a good fit from an investment perspective can be very difficult on a personal and family level.

Impact investing is more than the financial investment

One of the prevailing themes that emerges from conversations with the Cordes family about impact investing is what they refer to as being "helpful beyond the dollar."[42] They always ask themselves: How can we be more helpful in supporting others in the community do their work and achieve better outcomes with this impact investment? Unlike the traditional investing space, collaboration is a huge component of the success in the impact arena since we are taking on the world's biggest problems.

But in the end, conversations with the Cordes family about impact investing almost always end up in the same place—the impact. They are very sure of their "why." It's authentic, front and center in everything they do including how they live their lives. The scaling of the sector, the relationships they have made, the positive influence they have on others—all of that matters to the Cordes family, but what matters most is the end result: catalyzing impact that advances their mission while not sacrificing returns. There is much that remains to be done and the impact investing sector needs more families to discover their own motivations, transition their dollars towards impact, measure the effectiveness, so the investing world pivots where impact investing just becomes the universal standard thanks to pioneering families such as the Cordes.

Conclusion and Final Thoughts

> No one has ever become poor by giving.
>
> —Anne Frank

A family's legacy is often defined uniquely through how they bring meaning to their wealth. This chapter focuses on the opportunities that philanthropy, impact, and sustainable investing may provide a family when it comes to their legacy. More families are focusing on time-limited giving strategies to enact their giving, and research found that family foundations are increasingly the preferred vehicle by which to give. The two case studies shared in this chapter by the Root family and the Cordes family demonstrate the important legacy that giving imparts on the next generation. Both cases illuminate how involvement from one generation to the next can be a powerful means to build shared values and feel positive on the impact that giving may have to others and to important causes in the future. For many families, the quote from Winston Churchill rings true: "We make a living by what we get, but we make a life by what we give." I am grateful to Preston Root for sharing insights of his family giving and to the Cordes family and Jennifer Kenning for sharing their power impact investing and family office story.

Notes

1. http://dictionary.reference.com/browse/legacy.
2. Correspondence with Iris Wagner, CEO of Memoirs Productions, 2012.
3. Fredda Herz Brown and Fran Lotery, *Family Wealth Sustainability Toolkit* (Hoboken, NJ: John Wiley & Sons, 2012), p. 4.
4. John A. Warnick, Purposeful Trust Workshop, Westminster, CO, August 1, 2012. To learn more about Purposeful Planning Institute, visit https://purposefulplanninginstitute.com/.
5. Various conversation tools and activities are available. Consider visiting the websites of 21/64 at https://2164.net/, Dr. Dennis Jaffe at https://dennisjaffe.com/, and Inheriting Wisdom at https://inheritingwisdom.com/.
6. Interview with Dr. James Weiner and Dr. Carolyn Friend, 2012.
7. To learn more about the author's dissertation, please contact me at Kirby@rosplock.net. Kirby Rosplock, "Women's Interest, Attitudes and Involvement with Their Wealth," Saybrook Graduate School and Research Center, 2007.
8. Kirby Rosplock, "Women's Interest, Attitudes, and Involvement with Their Wealth," 2007.
9. Kirby Rosplock, "Men and Wealth Study. Report of Findings," GenSpring Suntrust Private Wealth, 2008.
10. Ibid.
11. Kirby Rosplock, "Women's Interest, Attitudes, and Involvement with Their Wealth," 2007.
12. Ibid.
13. Ibid.
14. Ibid.
15. Kirby Rosplock, "Men and Wealth Study Report of Findings," GenSpring Suntrust Private Wealth, 2008.
16. Andrew Jack, "Ruben Vardanyan: the Russian-Armenian Businessman Focusing on Giving Wealth Away" *Financial Times,* October 19, 2018.
17. To read more visit, https://www.nytimes.com/2020/04/07/technology/jack-dorsey-donate-1-billion-coronavirus.html
18. Family Office Exchange, Legacy Planning: It's Not About the Money (Chicago, IL: Family Office Exchange, 2011).
19. Joseph and Harvey Meyerhoff Family Charitable Funds.
20. Ibid.
21. Goldman Sachs The ESG and Impact Investing Landscape.
22. Campden UBS Global Family Office Report, 2019, p. 3.
23. Ibid., p. 31.
24. According to Global Sustainable Investment Alliance, 2019 as mentioned in Campden UBS Global Family Office Report, 2019, p. 31.
25. To learn more about Mlinda, visit www.mlinda.org.

26. Sarah Murray, "Rich Millennials Push to Put Family Wealth into Impact Investments," *Financial Times*, October 16, 2019.

27. Ibid.

28. National Center for Family Philanthropy, "Working Together for Common Purpose: The First National Study of Family Philanthropy Through the Family Office," Washington, DC, 2012.

29. Sarah Murray, "Rich Millennials Push to Put Family Wealth into Impact Investments," *Financial Times*, October 16, 2019.

30. Global Trends and Strategic Time Horizons in Family Philanthropy 2020, Campden Wealth and Rockefeller Philanthropy Advisors, p. 6.

31. Ibid., p. 9.

32. Ibid., p. 21.

33. Ibid., p. 23.

34. Ibid., p. 25.

35. Correspondence with Preston Root, Chairman, Root Board of Directors, Root Glass Co., 2020.

36. Global Trends and Strategic Time Horizons in Family Philanthropy 2020, Campden Wealth and Rockefeller Philanthropy Advisors, p. 6.

37. Correspondence with Stephanie Cordes Stephenson, Cordes Family Foundation, March 2020.

38. Correspondence with Marty Cordes, Cordes Family Foundation, March 2020.

39. Eric Stephenson joined Align Impact in 2018 and is currently Director of Client Services.

40. Correspondence with Eric Stephenson, Cordes Family Foundation, March 2020.

41. Correspondence with Ron Cordes, Cordes Family Foundation, March 2020.

42. Ibid.

CHAPTER 15

Private Trust Companies: Creating the Ideal Trustee

Miles Padgett

Partner, Kozusko Harris Duncan

Don Kozusko

Partner, Kozusko Harris Duncan

This chapter focuses on the role of the private trust company (PTC) as the key fiduciary for wealthy families. We begin by providing a basic understanding of PTCs: what is a private trust company, and why would a family consider establishing one? We then address how a private trust company works by exploring the "nuts and bolts" of creating a PTC. The latter portion of this chapter shifts gear and delves into the standards, goals, and intangibles that a PTC must achieve for success by using a parable and analyzing lessons learned from experienced PTC executives.

The Broader View

What Is a Private Trust Company?

A private trust company (PTC) is an entity customarily owned by one family and created specifically to serve as the trustee for trusts created by that family, and to serve as the family's fiduciary in certain other contexts, such as an executor of a family member's probate estate or as the guardian for an incompetent family member. A PTC is typically structured to look like, and function as, a state law corporation, even though in most cases in the US, a PTC is chartered as a state law limited liability company.

A PTC is typically organized to function as if it were a commercial trust institution, governed by a board of directors and managed by them through the use of board committees such as a trust committee, audit committee, and investment committee, and through delegation to officers, such as a president, vice president, senior trust officer, compliance officer, etc. Graphically, this resembles the following (see Figure 15.1):

FIGURE 15.1   Example of Private Trust Company Governance Structure

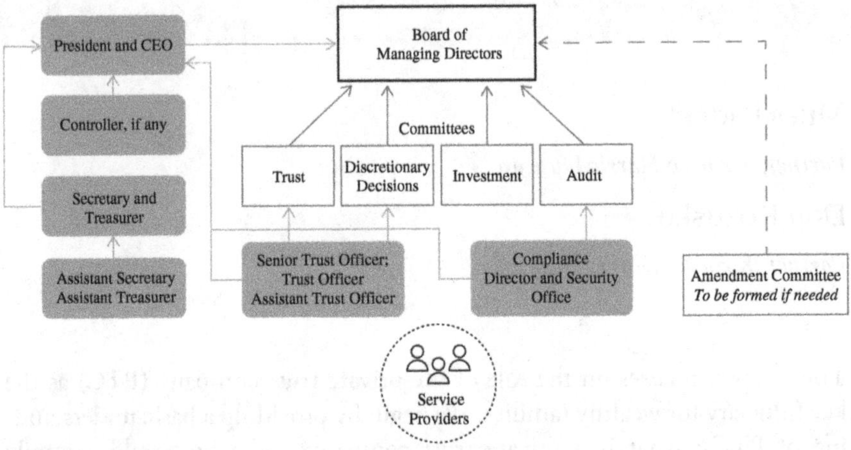

Source: © 2016 Kozusko Harris Duncan

What Are the Differences Between a Private Trust Company and a Commercial Trust Company?

Readers may be fairly familiar with commercial trust companies: financial institutions that are (i) licensed, or "chartered," by either a state or the Office of the Comptroller of the Currency, (ii) subject to regulation by state or various federal agencies, or both, and (iii) authorized to conduct trust business with the general public. In contrast, a PTC is legally authorized to conduct trust business generally with only one family.

As a practical matter, a commercial trust institution and PTC operate similarly. Both entities' operations involve:

- An Audit Committee that is responsible for annual audits of the trust company's financials and ensuring compliance with the company's expressed fiduciary processes;
- An Investment Committee that sets investment strategy for the trust company's trust clients and vets investment solutions to implement that strategy;
- A Trust Committee that oversees trust company operations to ensure that they are occurring in proper fashion and that the details of trust client matters are accomplished appropriately and timely (e.g., ensuring the preparation and timely filing of tax returns for trust clients);
- Company officers to execute routine activities, vet prospective clients and client transactions for regulatory compliance, etc.; and
- A Board of Directors to oversee all of the company's operations and set strategy for the trust company.

The primary operational difference consists of the use of a committee in a PTC that makes certain tax-sensitive decisions, such as over discretionary distributions.[1] As implied, that committee is designed to insulate family members from adverse transfer tax results described in guidance from the Internal Revenue Service,[2] but more importantly, that committee provides structure and discipline, as well as flexibility, for the process of making distribution decisions for trust beneficiaries. This function is discussed later in this chapter.

Another difference between a PTC and a commercial trust company is that, while both types of trust institutions make strategic-level investment decisions for their clients' trusts (primarily long-term asset allocation) through an Investment Committee, a PTC family's family office is customarily tasked with execution of that investment strategy, either itself or as a manager of managers, again pursuant to a written agreement (either with the PTC or a trust client itself). Furthermore, back-office functions of a PTC can be performed through a combination of a part-time PTC officer being assigned such tasks in conjunction with delegation (by contract) to a service provider, either the family's family office or a third-party professional firm. In a commercial trust company, most if not all operational functions are performed in-house. In summary, while both PTCs and commercial trust companies make important fiduciary decisions for their trust clients related to distributions, investment strategy, and so on, unlike a commercial trust company, a PTC looks primarily to others to do the majority of the work required to execute those decisions.

Why Do Families Consider Creating a PTC?

Being responsible for the management and operations of a family-owned financial institution is usually the last thing that senior family members would volunteer to undertake. They correctly suspect that forming a PTC, and managing its operations, requires substantial resources in time and capital, as well as effort. Despite such misgivings, families create PTCs because senior family members and their advisers recognize that there is usually a need to do several of the following:

- Maintain family's control over the family's business in either private (resisting sale) or public contexts
- Attract, retain, and provide for the succession of capable individuals and advisors, particularly liability protection
- Take command of services provided to the family's trusts and their beneficiaries
- Change state fiduciary income tax situs of trusts (for US families)
- Change administrative or substantive law, or both, that govern family trusts
- Maintain family's control over the family's wealth by consciously and systematically addressing the causes of long-term decline, namely minimizing family dissension and avoiding fragmentation of asset management
- Implement coordinated risk management by the family concerning both fiduciary and investment decisions, in part to maintain higher concentrations of illiquid (higher risk/return) assets

Of those, the best reasons to create a PTC are the final two points: (1) maintaining family control of assets and (2) implementing coordinated risk management. Those two items overlap, and both depend upon the family's ability to create and maintain a system for family decision-making that is supported by the family and increases family member engagement and facilitates family member development.

What Are the Key Considerations to Be Addressed Prior to Pursuing a PTC?

Before addressing certain practical aspects of creating a PTC, we should identify two criteria that will indicate whether a PTC will be a suitable choice for the family trusts: (1) cost and (2) commitment to the process required to operate what is technically a financial institution (albeit family controlled).

What Are the Costs?

While the expense of creating a PTC and the cost of its operations, as described below, may seem prohibitive for many families, the required asset base is not as high as one might imagine. While much depends of course upon the circumstances of a particular family and its trusts in question, our rule of thumb concerning the asset base required to justify a PTC is the following:

- Between $100 and $250 million of collective family assets is enough for an exceptionally motivated and unified family that sees a PTC as the only possible way to achieve adequate control over management of trust assets or to obtain one or more other primary benefits of a PTC.
- $500 million is more typical and generally sufficient to justify a PTC's expense for a family seeking to obtain the benefits of a PTC with a more customary level of commitment to family-wide goals.
- $1 billion (or more) makes the costs of properly operating a PTC a rounding error on the family's P&L for each year, and is, as some have said, a "no-brainer" as to the cost issue.

More specifically, the soft-dollar costs of doing the internal work necessary to vet the concept and to participate with external counsel and other advisers in the creation process varies greatly and is not quantifiable (with confidence), given current available data. Nevertheless, anyone who has ever been involved in this process can attest to the fact that those costs are significant. However, while this is not a marketing piece for the legal community, it should be noted that engaging experienced legal counsel early in the vetting process can materially reduce the soft-dollar costs of many families. Experienced counsel can help families conclude that they are not suited for a PTC far earlier than they would reach that conclusion themselves, and for those families that are suitable, can narrow the range of issues for them to consider in the vetting process to those that are most important. Accordingly, applying resources to engage outside counsel early in the process is money wisely spent.

As for hard-dollar costs, our experience has been that the out-of-pocket expense to create a PTC varies widely, between $100,000 and $500,000 for the entire process, and depends among other things upon:

- Whether the PTC will be licensed and regulated by a state;
- The efficiency with which the family and its close advisors participate in the creation process;

- How complex the family's current trust and investment situation is; and
- Most importantly, whether the family's governance system will be designed and implemented at the same time as the PTC, and the complexity of that system.

Fortunately, those costs are materially within the control of the family.

As for operating a PTC business, to do so properly requires between $75,000 and $125,000 annually for most families. This figure consists primarily of insurance, office space, travel, regulatory fees, proper audits, and a required local, part-time employee. However, that figure excludes other personnel costs and the costs of investing, but those excluded costs are of course present regardless of whether a PTC is used and depend on the family's exact situation and needs.

Is There Commitment to Process?

More important than costs and the required asset base, however, is the required commitment to conduct operations properly and to prioritize the *process* of decision-making *over* the decisions themselves. It is axiomatic in the trust legal world that trustees are not liable for bad results; they are liable for failures of process. This concept is particularly acute in a PTC.

Whether a family will be sufficiently dedicated to proper process requires some soul-searching by a family and its trusted advisors prior to embarking on the journey. Unlike investing, there is nothing interesting and engaging about following proper fiduciary process. "Proper process" seems like a euphemism for what is bureaucratic and boring. Most fear process, believing that it will be overly restrictive and constraining; the reality, however, is that process gives order, sets boundaries and expectations, and can help when precedents are achieved. Truth be told, successfully pursuing proper process will likely result in non-events. In other words, the voyage will not be notable for including memorable bad events; if the sailboat avoids the reef, the passengers do not notice.

Accordingly, PTC management and the family must be prepared, at the outset, to perform the hard work and to allocate the necessary resources (not only financial but also intellectual and especially emotional) to prioritizing process, and without expecting to receive much recognition for doing so. However, despite the fact that process is hard and that there is little glamour in doing it well, many families come to realize that when approached as a series of small tasks and steps, the challenge of the required commitment to process becomes quite doable.

What Are the Alternatives?

For those families for whom cost and required commitment for a PTC are problematic, they are left with few alternatives. In brief, those consist of:

- *Commercial Trust Companies:* For some families, this is an acceptable solution, but for most legacy families, the reason they are considering a PTC is dissatisfaction with their current commercial trust company. The advantages (e.g., professionalism, logical decision-making, good compliance, and administrative hygiene, etc.), and disadvantages (risk intolerance, poor service, oriented towards profit for the institution, bureaucratic, etc.) of utilizing a commercial trust company are well known, and so will not be explored here.
- *Individual Trustees:* Individuals have historically been the solution for wealth creators, and for those members of legacy families who were of the Baby Boom generation and older. Those persons utilized their trusted advisors, employees, and family members to serve as fiduciaries for family trusts. Of course, the most significant challenge to this approach is obvious: mortality. The need for a successor to a deceased or retiring individual inevitably arises, but in today's environment, knowledgeable and capable individuals who in the past would have agreed to be successors are now highly reluctant to accept such roles due to potential liability and other drawbacks.

  Less obvious is the challenge presented by an individual who is declining slowly due to age; that person poses an underappreciated yet significant risk to trusts because, in our experience, they become disinterested and less than capable as time progresses but fail to recognize the need to retire from the position until a material mistake has been made.

  Finally and with greater frequency these days, the younger generations typically are dissatisfied with the individuals chosen by the prior generations, either because of an inherent distrust of "dad's trustee" or a demonstrable lack of rapport (and often respect) between the trustees and the younger generation beneficiaries. All of this is not to say that using individual trustees is doomed to failure; there are many instances when that structure works perfectly well, but our experience over the past 40 plus years tells us that such positive outcomes, in the long run, are becoming rare.

• *Directed Trusts:* In short, certain states allow the trustee's role to be divided by the trust agreement. In such agreements, the trust's fiduciary functions are allocated among multiple fiduciaries so that the responsibility for each such function is allocated exclusively to one (or more) rather than all of the fiduciaries. For example, an Investment Director (the labels are not important) can be empowered to give instructions to an Administrative Trustee as to investment decisions, and the Administrative Trustee is required to execute those instructions, all the while being absolved of responsibility for failures of the investments; that responsibility lies solely with the Investment Director. Similarly, a Distribution Director can direct an Administrative Trustee as to distributions, with the same effect.

For certain situations, the directed trust structure is a good solution. For example, the directed trust structure works well for a family that has only a handful of trusts, rather than scores of them. Or, it fits if a family wants to control only one aspect of a trust, such as investments, but is otherwise satisfied with their corporate trustee as to administrative matters and distributions. In those cases, the structure works well.

However, we have observed that the risks and challenges of such multi-participant trust structures are often underappreciated or not recognized whatsoever. For those families that have a material number of trusts, the process of managing a multi-participant structure for each of those trusts is not simpler than using a private trust company. While there are different labels to the participants ("Investment Directors" rather than "Investment Committee," "Distribution Directors" rather than "Discretionary Distribution Committees," etc.), the same volume and types of information are required to be collected, processed, disseminated, and recorded, and the same work and hard decisions have to be made to do it well. In reality, the process may be more complicated when:

• No one knows where the various fiduciaries (e.g., the Distribution Director) of a directed trust are located sufficiently for a state to assess an income tax. If there are three members of the Distribution Director, for example, situs for state income tax purposes could be any of the states of residence of those three individuals or it could be the state where those three individuals meet to make decisions (if indeed they always meet together in the same state). Contrast that with a distribution committee that is a creature of a state-law entity. There are decades of legal precedents where a committee of a corporate board is located, and it is not per se the state of residence of any one or more of the board members.

- Except for lawyers who draft multi-participant trust structures well, few people appreciate the difficulty of getting the internal governance of a directed trust correct, until a problem becomes apparent. A simple example would be: If the Distribution Director wishes to make a distribution for a beneficiary but the Investment Director refuses to raise the cash needed because doing so would necessitate selling assets during a market decline . . . whose determination trumps? Matters such as this are not an issue in a PTC because the committee structure of a PTC is able to rely on customs built over the last 170 years for state law corporations, as well as state statutes, regarding internal governance procedures and authority. In other words, the PTC, inherently, imposes structure on internal activities and governance due to its entity nature, applicable laws, and the customs present in the commercial trustee industry, whereas in directed trusts that structure has to be imposed by each and every trust document with the result that consistency over time is often difficult to achieve.
- With a PTC, there is an entity wrapped around the fiduciary activities being conducted by the individuals involved in trust administration. In the case of litigation against an individual involved in such administration, this creates two advantages over a multi-participant (directed) trust. First, the wrapper itself provides a liability shield. Secondly, a trust might procure insurance for a trustee to protect the trustee from claims of breach of fiduciary duty, but that is different than the wrapper *itself* providing a liability shield. In the context of a PTC as compared to insurance, there is no dispute as to whether something is a "covered claim" or whether the deductible has been met. Moreover, we are unaware of any litigation that has tested, and approved, the use of trust assets to pay for insurance against the trustee's negligence. We do know, however, that an entity (the PTC) serving as trustee can use its own assets to buy insurance for itself.

Thus, as a general rule, directed trusts can be a good solution for a limited number of families who have a small handful of large trusts, but are not the optimal solution for families with dozens or scores of trusts. More importantly, even in those cases where a directed trust is appropriate, there are still drawbacks that should be appreciated fully and that are not present in the context of PTC entity.

Steps to Creating a PTC

Once a family has determined that its needs and resources justify the creation of a PTC, and that the alternatives are not feasible or palatable, then the family is immediately faced with an overarching, practical question: In which jurisdiction should the PTC be located? The choice will affect how efficiently and effectively the trust company performs important trust company activities, conducts actual operations in some circumstances, manages risk, and addresses the inevitable challenges. Those factors can be organized into the following areas:

- *Regulatory Regime:* Whether the PTC must be primarily concerned with being regulated by the US Securities and Exchange Commission (SEC) or a state banking agency, or what is required not to be regulated by those agencies?
- *Geographic Convenience:* How much travel will be required and how much travel is palatable to senior management?
- *Substantive Trust Laws:* What are the laws governing the administration of trusts for which the PTC serves as trustee and the interpretation of those trusts, as well as the determination of the property interests of the beneficiaries?
- *Substantive Trust Company Laws:* How demanding are the banking laws governing the PTC itself and its operations?
- *Public Policy Milieu:* How responsive and robust is the judicial and legislative systems in the jurisdiction of the PTC?
- *Tax Laws Impacting the Entity and Trusts It Administers:* How costly is the tax drag to operate the PTC in a jurisdiction and for a trust to be tax resident in that jurisdiction?

Choice of Regulatory Regime

Almost all PTCs provide investment advice as defined by the US Securities and Exchange Commission (SEC), whether in the basic form of making recommendations to the PTC's clients regarding where to park cash temporarily or in the form of full-blown investment advisory services to trusts and family members, such as asset allocation, stock selection, and manager due diligence. Because most families determine that they wish to have as little regulation as possible, the family's proposed PTC must conform to the requirements of the SEC's "single-family office rule" (SFO Rule).[3] If the proposed PTC's activities can conform to that rule and thus the PTC does not need a license issued by a state banking regulator, this will narrow the selection of the possible jurisdictions for the PTC because only a handful of states permit unlicensed PTCs.[4]

If, however, the proposed PTC's activities cannot conform to the SFO Rule (e.g., because the intended clients of the PTC exceed those permitted under the SFO Rule), then a family must abandon pursuing an unlicensed PTC and must choose between having the PTC's investment advisory activities, either regulated directly by the SEC (or the applicable state securities regulator) as a registered investment adviser or regulated by a state banking regulator as a licensed trust company.[5] Being regulated by a state banking authority is a way to avoid direct oversight by the SEC (or applicable state securities agency), because there is an exclusion from being considered an investment adviser under the US Investment Adviser Act of 1940 for "banks" (including trust companies) that are licensed by a state banking authority and in fact examined by it.[6] Thus, if a PTC cannot meet the requirements of the SFO Rule, then the PTC can be licensed by a state banking authority as a state trust company. In those situations, where the PTC would otherwise be forced to register as an investment adviser (either with the SEC or the applicable state securities agency), being a licensed state trust company allows the PTC to avoid registration as an investment advisor in exchange for regulation and examination by state banking authorities.

At this stage, there is a single logical question for a family contemplating a PTC that will not meet the requirements of the SFO Rule: *Will regulation by the SEC (or state securities agency) be equally (or less) burdensome as regulation by a state banking authority?* The simple answer is "no, it will not." The SEC does not care about the success or financial health of registered investment advisers; instead the SEC only cares about whether it is "protecting investors" based on the SEC's view of what is in investors' best interests. In contrast, bank regulators must care about the safety and soundness, which includes financial well-being of regulated entities not only as their mission but also as a practical matter: If a regulated state trust company fails, the state banking regulator has full responsibility for dealing with the failure. This leads to state banking regulators seeking to be helpful to their regulated institutions as long as they have confidence in management. Most regulated PTCs find that the banking regulators are in fact helpful to them in understanding how to operate a trust company and the applicable standards and practices of trustees. After advice, families in this situation almost always prefer to be regulated by a state banking authority.

Accordingly, when seeking a license from a state banking agency, selection of the jurisdiction becomes even more important because the family is really choosing the regulatory team that will oversee the operations of the proposed PTC, that is, the team that will "examine" the PTC's operations. As one can imagine, there is significant disparity between regulatory teams of the various US states whose laws permit PTCs; in other words, some state banking authorities are more helpful and less demanding than others:

- For example, at least one US state specifically examines a licensed PTC not for safety and soundness, but only for qualification as a "family trust company" under that state's statute; thus, even though a PTC would hold a license to conduct a trust company business from that state's banking agency, that PTC by definition cannot avail itself of the above described exclusion from securities regulation as an investment advisor.[7]
- Other states are quite interested in assisting PTC management in running a better trust company business for the family and so try to be helpful whenever possible with advice and forgiveness of the occasional straying from standard commercial trust company operating procedures.

Accordingly, selection of the jurisdiction from which to seek a license is important in part because it is essentially the choice of the PTC's regulatory partner.

Geographical Convenience

Inherent in the choice of jurisdiction is the practical consideration of how much the family and its advisors are willing to travel. At a minimum, they will be required to travel to the jurisdiction of choice at least once, and in some cases, sometimes multiple times per year, to conduct the business of managing a PTC.[8] We advise our clients that all true fiduciary actions (e.g., board and committee meetings in which decisions about trust distributions, investment policy, etc. are made) must occur in the situs jurisdiction.[9] Also permitted are such activities when conducted from a trust office not in the situs jurisdiction but in a jurisdiction that has approved specifically the opening of a trust office by the PTC at issue. We strongly advise our clients not to conduct material fiduciary activities outside of those two locations, because doing so runs the risk of the jurisdiction where such activities in fact take place viewing the PTC as conducting a trust business in that jurisdiction without legal authority and contrary to that state's law. Indeed, conducting such activities without legal authority oftentimes carries a substantial civil penalty and sometimes a criminal one.[10] Suffice it to say that being physically in the proper jurisdiction to execute certain activities and the related willingness to travel are real, practical issues to be considered by a family.

Substantive Trust Laws

Another important element of the choice of jurisdiction for a PTC is whether a state's substantive trust laws provide the necessary tools to manage a trust institution and various client situations over the long term. By "substantive trust laws," we are referring to those laws of a state governing administering a trust as well as determining and interpreting the beneficial interests in a trust. For example, administrative laws would (i) dictate the type and frequency of information to be provided to beneficiaries of a trust, (ii) provide rules concerning the liability of trustees, and (iii) determine what receipts constitute trust accounting "income" compared to trust accounting "principal," etc.[11] Likewise, determining and interpreting the beneficial interests in a trust would include matters such as (i) whether adopted persons are included in the terms "children" or "descendants," (ii) how long property can remain in trust and who receives the property at the end of the trust, and (iii) whether the language of a trust entitles a person to distributions or creates a mere expectancy that is subject to the trustee's discretion, etc.

We advise clients to seek a jurisdiction that has a demonstrable commitment to the maintaining top-notch laws for each of the following:

- *Flexibility for Settlors Creating Trusts:* Includes providing statutory support for the supremacy of settlors' choices as articulated in their trust documents, especially when those choices diverge from common law or statutory defaults; adopting a robust Prudent Investor Rule[12] and a progressive trust statute (as in the Uniform Trust Code) that impose few mandatory default rules for trust documents and disengaging from the prior common law of the enacting state; explicit authority for directed/multi-fiduciary trusts and rules governing the relationships between the various fiduciaries of such trusts; and allowing specialized trusts that are used frequently in modern trust practice, such as Dynasty Trusts (can last forever or nearly forever), Purpose Trusts (need not have identifiable beneficiaries but instead can be for a particular purpose such as owning the stock of a closely held business as an end unto itself), Quiet Trusts (limits duty to inform beneficiaries of the existence of a trust) and Asset Protection trusts (trust assets protected against beneficiary or settlor creditors).
- *Flexibility for Beneficiaries:* Includes providing strong and efficient downstream course correction ability, such as decanting authority and trust reformations, modifications, and terminations (both judicial and non-judicial); and strong virtual representation that allows older family members or similar situation beneficiaries (and certain others) to represent the legal interests of younger or absent beneficiaries.

- *Reasonable Protections for Trustees:* Includes a shortened statute of limitations on legal actions against the trustee, strong authority to delegate prudently and protection to fiduciaries for doing so, and explicit characterization of fiduciary standards as "administrative law" and therefore applicable to every trust administered in the state unless a trust specifies otherwise. Reasonable protections allow trustees to make the kinds of difficult decisions which are required by today's world (and often by a family's circumstances) and which they otherwise would avoid making if the risks of liability are too great under the average applicable law, and yet would not provide so much protection that a trustee could feel as if it could act with impunity and without accountability.

These issues are usually the most relevant to choosing a jurisdiction. Each US state has unique trust laws, and currently no one state's trust laws are ideal for all trust issues. How each of the leading states addresses each of these issues changes frequently, and the test of what is "ideal" is also a bit of a moving target. Given this constant evolution, including of the issues most important to a set of family trusts at any given time, it would be misleading to identify here the "ideal" choice of jurisdiction for a family's PTC. Fortunately, each of the leading states come close, and more importantly, each of those states is committed to maintaining its reputation as a leading candidate.

Trust Company Laws

Another important element of the choice of jurisdiction for a PTC is consideration of a state's trust company laws. As noted earlier in the chapter, only certain states provide the authority for a PTC to conduct a trust business, and some of the states permitting PTCs allow only licensed PTCs. Moreover, each of the states allowing PTCs has variations regarding those to whom a PTC may provide fiduciary services (i.e., who can be a PTC client), regulatory capital requirements, notice filings, and so on. Each state's requirements must be carefully compared when determining the location from which a family would be best situated to conduct a trust business. Again, a detailed, state-by-state analysis of the various nuances is beyond the scope of this chapter (yet should be done prior to embarking on the creation of a PTC), but when we assist clients in examining jurisdictions as potential situs candidates for their PTCs, we look to the following issues:

- *Regulated vs. Unregulated:* We generally prefer states that offer both unregulated and regulated PTCs. Even if an unregulated PTC is not desirable for the long run, we often encounter clients who begin operations as an unregulated PTC, usually due to a short time frame within which to begin operations and which does not allow for the licensing process. For those clients, circumstances arise later that require a regulated PTC (e.g., an out-of-state trust office becomes necessary that was not contemplated at the time of formation), and thus, starting in a state that allows both enables an easy conversion without having to move to a new jurisdiction.
- *Directors (Number, Number of Meetings and Residency):* The most attractive states typically require only a modest number of directors for the board of directors of a trust company (sometimes only one) and require only a modest number of board meetings each year. Jurisdictions that require at least one resident director are typically seen as marginally less desirable.[13] In practice, however, such a requirement is merely an annoyance because, where the client lacks such a person among the client's cast of characters, there are third-party service providers whose business offering is to provide such an individual.[14]
- *Application Process; Public Notice and Hearing:* In the event a license is sought, we prefer states whose license application process is not onerous— that is, among other things, does not require public notice of the application or a hearing before a special board, proceeds with modest alacrity, and does not require voluminous and time consuming disclosures.
- *Express Authority to Use Affiliated Advisors and Investments:* We insist upon states that allow a PTC to employ related companies, including affiliated investment advisors and related funds, and to pay them for their services; a self-executing ability to do so is preferred (i.e., no notice required to trust participants or other parties).
- *Capital and Insurance Requirements:* Shareholders' equity capital requirements range from $200,000 to $500,000, and most states require a fidelity bond against theft, whether by a PTC employee or outside party. Moreover, certain states require that shareholders' equity capital be invested in low risk investments. Such requirements, however, typically apply only in the context of a licensed PTC, but in all events, we advise clients with licensed and unlicensed PTCs (i) to capitalize the PTC sufficiently to ensure that it is respected as a business entity by all parties, (ii) to maintain errors and omissions, and directors' and officers' liability insurance policy(ies), in each case appropriate for the level of business and risks of the PTC, and (iii) to maintain sufficient working capital to run the trust business properly.

- *Interstate Offices-Regulated PTCs:* Many states allow an out-of-state, licensed PTC to establish a full-service trust office in their state on a reciprocal basis.[15] This not only can provide convenience for the PTC and its clients but also allows a PTC chartered in one state to take advantage of a special trust law or client need (e.g., estate administration; holding real estate outright in trust) in another state. Equally important, it provides the PTC a hedge against the risk of adverse changes in the laws or policies in its home state, and it should be noted that, when a licensed PTC establishes an out-of-state office, its home state regulator continues to exercise primary regulatory authority, thereby limiting exposure to duplicative or inconsistent regulation.

Public Policy Environment

Our experience teaches us that the top PTC states provide public policy environments conducive to forming and operating a PTC, whether unregulated or licensed. In advising clients on the selection of situs jurisdiction for their PTC, we look for the following:

- *Responsive State Legislature:* Showing a willingness to consider and enact legislation to make and keep its trusts and trust company laws attractive and to adapt to advances in other states in a timely fashion (all of course due in part to their trust companies' lobbies and state trust bars being actively involved and for the most part committed to keeping their trust laws among the best).
- *Responsive State Banking Regulator:* Ideally encouraged by the legislative and executive branches to only impose regulatory burdens on PTCs proportionate to the more limited risk they pose to the public; this aspect applies almost exclusively to licensed PTCs. For example, we customarily wish to see an expedited time frame for approval of a license for a PTC, and less frequent and less burdensome examinations.
- *Quality Judicial System:* Assuring that knowledgeable jurists and court administrators, without anti-wealth biases, will hear trust disputes and otherwise address trust issues requiring court participation, and which assures that matters brought before a court can be promptly addressed. For example, the best states have sizable, specialized legal bars that remain focused on trust and trust company issues.[16] Moreover, some states have a specialized probate or district court system where judges, experienced in trust and probate matters, supported by experienced administrative staff (that local counsel advise are in most cases also knowledgeable), and not prejudiced against wealthy clients, hear trust cases exclusively.[17]

- *Avenues for Properly Informing the Law and Rule-Making Process:* Including private-public working group and/or other public-private cooperation between executive and legislative branches of the state and bar groups, banking associations, trust institutions, and wealthy families, dedicated to ensuring that state laws, regulations, and the PTC environment remain current with that of other leading states, the needs of wealthy families, and the requirements for PTCs to be successful.
- *Robust Supporting Business Infrastructure:* Clients starting trust companies at a distance from their primary locations require support in the PTC situs jurisdiction; they require local resources that can provide an adequate office, receptionist, and assistant trust officer and possibly additional back-office and/or compliance services, all at a reasonable price.

While it may appear less relevant at the time of formation, over time, a jurisdiction's public policy environment takes on greater importance because it directly affects how the PTC conducts its business and ongoing operations.

Trust and Trust Company Taxes

Finally, taxation at the state level must be addressed in selecting the jurisdiction for the PTC since the location of the PTC often determines whether undistributed trust income will be taxed. Accordingly, the selection process targets states where there are:

- Low or no state and local income taxes on trust income;[18] and
- Reasonable trust company taxes, regardless of form (e.g., business corporation, non-corporate franchise taxes, or profits tax, etc.).

There are few jurisdictions that permit PTCs and that also impose no taxes on either the PTC or its trust clients.[19] However, other choices are available where the tax burden is modest enough to be tolerated as the cost of doing business.

Achieving Success in a PTC: Setting Priorities

So far, we have explored the following: what a PTC is, how it is structured and generally how it operates, why a family would pursue a PTC, when a family is not suited to a PTC, and certain fundamental topics through the lens of jurisdiction selection. We have deliberately not addressed the details of PTC operations at length. A detailed discussion of most operational issues (such as proxy voting, anti-money laundering compliance, board meeting mechanics, etc.) would not be interesting to the reader.

Instead, we will emphasize here a much more important question about how to run a PTC: what operating principles and practices will contribute to the long-term success of the trust company? The recommendations we will offer here are, generally speaking, not legally prescribed by any trust or tax law, but we believe that the success of the trust company enterprise will be put at risk if these principles and practices are disregarded as optional and therefore unnecessary. The previous discussion has been task-oriented; this discussion now goes beyond the task level and considers how to tap the full potential of the PTC as a strategic, long-term structure for managing a family's wealth.

Fostering Beneficiary Development Should Be the Primary Objective of the PTC

Whether expressly stated or not, the overriding goal of every trust is to make the lives of its beneficiaries better. Virtually every wealthy family wants to use its resources to support the development of individual family members. Successful support for individuals also helps the family as a whole. Fortunately, the PTC can provide a near-perfect environment for achieving that success because it can naturally use the family's substantial resources in the thoughtful pursuit of that objective.

Pursuing that objective requires a reorientation in the way trusts are ordinarily managed. Success in investing and tax planning, and proper accounting and compliance, should no longer define success for the trust and the trustee. Creating and preserving financial resources provide the pre-conditions for success but do not stand for its full measure. Since the major objective of the PTC should be to support beneficiary development, its operations should focus on the third function of a trustee—the use of the trust funds through distributions.

This increased attention to distributions will require creativity, patience, continuity, and caring. Making distributions to serve this primary purpose will not be as easy as it seems. The trust company in its operations must make a deliberate effort to know, and sometimes determine, the needs, desires, and resources of a trust's beneficiaries, and doing that properly requires building a working, trusting relationship with those beneficiaries. This effort will involve repeated opportunities to help beneficiaries to develop or refine their individual needs, wants, and aspirations and to lead them in a non-patronizing way to develop the ability to deepen their personal relationships and their understanding of their family's values and their own.

This process requires gathering, creating, and keeping relevant information current and creating a strong relationship between those representing the PTC and the trust beneficiaries. Those bonds will help family member beneficiaries become kinder, more resilient, and more "individualized" humans, and also facilitate meaningful engagement between a beneficiary and the family at large (through the family's avatar, the PTC). In this way, family resources would be used to better the lives of beneficiaries; and this effort will indirectly improve how different generations understand each other.

This effort will be the responsibility of the PTC's Discretionary Decisions Committee, or the committee will help the beneficiaries find others who can serve that role to the extent that the members themselves lack the personal skills or time to serve that enhanced role. One would think this orientation would come naturally to trust managers. Not so, for these reasons:

- The trust distribution process tends to be mechanical because quantitative steps are much more easily tracked and reviewed than making qualitative progress in how the distributions can support the personal development of the beneficiaries. Hear the beneficiary's request, read the document, write the check or not. The default in this process is "keep it simple" and "measure it."[20]
- Financial assets require regular care and feeding of some degree. Beneficiaries do not customarily attract the same attention. They are regarded as either an undifferentiated class of individuals responsible for their own welfare, or the responsibilities of their parents.
- A proactive distribution practice is also time consuming. Unlike asset management, it cannot be scaled up by applying technology and systems.

Hartley Goldstone, who has chronicled several positive trust histories, recounts the experience of a young woman who sought his help in understanding her role as a trust beneficiary. She was one of eight beneficiaries in her generation in a trust managed by "quite elderly" gentlemen trustees. After preparation, here is how she presented herself at the next meeting with the trustees: "She asked the trustees at the beginning of the meeting, 'Will you receive me as myself? Will you listen to me as myself? Will you suspend your likely thought that I am simply one of eight to be treated the same way?'"[21]

Keep in mind that in many circumstances the beneficiary does not pick the trustee. As Ellen Perry described it, "He or she may be quite unhappy that there even is a trustee. . . . The marriage, so to speak, has been arranged. The question is: how can it best be managed?"[22] Given that starting point, it takes work. This new orientation to develop an interactive relationship between the trustee and the beneficiary will not be a simple casual adjustment in how trust management usually works.

Principles and Practices for a Successful Private Trust Company

The success of the trust company depends upon thoughtfully managing the relationship with the trust beneficiaries, and that requires a different orientation than managing assets and taxes. Success will depend on looking at the intangible drivers of success. Accepting the need for this distinct orientation is critical. Think of it this way: When investing in a new venture, the decision depends on much more than quantifiable factors such as the business model and deal structure. The decision depends on intangibles such as: Who's in leadership? What is their vision, knowledge, and expertise? Their energy . . . resilience . . . creativity . . . network . . . advisors . . . governance . . . oversight?? These are all questions a prospective investor wants answered because they are all factors in a successful venture.

Intangibles of a different sort are factors too in the success of a private trust company, and the difference in the intangibles must be understood and valued in managing trust company operations:

- A private trust company for family trusts is not a business in the ordinary sense; its function is more akin to a nonprofit corporation; the distribution function is the nonprofit function—the benefit function. It addresses "health, support, and education" (or "best interests"), but all of these are in the broad sense "helping."
- There is no market in the sense of customers choosing to buy goods.
- Beneficiaries are stakeholders rather than customers, although even that term does not capture the point; there is no "us versus them" and no classic separation between buyer and seller.
- If the above are not understood, then the distribution function becomes boring and routine, especially as compared to the dynamic process of making investments and building wealth, and beneficiaries become merely debits to cash.
- Success is not easily measured by metrics; the trustee organization must be financially self-sustaining but maximizing financial returns is not the goal.
- Success is not determined on a quarterly or even annual scale; indeed, one may never notice success because, in a sense, a successful trust relationship is one where nothing goes seriously wrong.

As a result, special skillsets are required that resemble those in a profession more than a business, especially when considering trust functions other than investments and administration. A parable can help illustrate this "intangibles" issue and some ways to address it.[23]

The Parable Family

The Parable family is working on a plan to manage the transition to a private trust company from relying on a close-knit group of advisors who have served the family for decades, including as individual trustees.

The advisor group is still intact but plans staggered retirements over the next few years. The family is seeking input from the advisors, and the advisor group is actively committed to helping the transition succeed. That's a blessing. The Parable family knows of several family offices where the incumbent advisors resisted change and were unwilling to give up their positions as individual trustees, looking to their trustee fees to supplement their income in retirement. In one case the litigating attorney told the family trustees she was representing: "I can defend you on the tax issue you missed. It really wasn't your fault. But you must resign. The judge has signaled to me that he will find a way to remove you if you don't resign. He sees you as trustees holding on in semi-retirement who were close to the settlor but have no relationship with the beneficiary. No emotional connection at all."

So who in the Parable family will take the lead in this effort? Enter Elizabeth, the family member in the middle generation who has been asked to lead the transition with help from her brother, John. Effectively, those two will control how the new trustee plan is constructed. Both subscribe wholeheartedly to the introduction of the family private trust company. It was an easy choice. The family's highly regarded new legal counsel explained the limitations of the leading alternative (a directed trust with multiple fiduciary roles), and it proved difficult to recruit candidates to fill those roles due to concerns of personal liability. Elizabeth also concluded that the trust company structure would make it over time much easier to manage and adjust the relationship between investment and distribution decisions. Also, the overall trust governance structure will need adjustments from time to time, either because of oversights and miscues in the prior version or because of changes in the family's dynamics. The PTC's legal "space" to house decision-making is much more easily remodeled than a collection of directed trusts.

Elizabeth and John are working through the varying recommendations of the existing advisors on how to organize the functions of the trust company. John has sorted those into two competing management concepts: the traditional trustee role as applied in the past by many, if not most, families, and the "reformist" approach that seeks to shift priorities in trust management and apply new methods. He presents Elizabeth with a deliberately polarized version of the competing approaches, in order to highlight the differences. John has labeled the proponents of the traditional approach as the Traditionalists and those proposing the new ways as the Radicals. Here is his write-up.

Selection of Individuals to Serve as the Key Executives for the Trust Company

The Radicals see the trust company as a way to avoid the limitations of the tradition of using individuals as trustees. In that "system," there is little or no specialization of roles. A trustee must be trusted to make all the right decisions across the board, and thus the grantor chooses trustees from among his or her contemporaries and peers, though usually these individuals have little or no experience or training in the trustee function or no natural rapport with the younger beneficiaries.

The Radicals contend instead, with acknowledged irony, that in choosing trusted decision-makers one must trust people one does not know (or know well). The trust company needs to be run by a team of experienced trained specialists. The same people who make highly effective investment or business decisions (the grantor's peers) do not tend to have the particular experience, motivation, and mind-set that is needed to make highly effective distribution plans and decisions for and with trust beneficiaries, or to plan strategically for how the trust funds can help the family and how the generational transitions will play out. Nor are they much interested in (or see the importance of) the more mundane administrative decisions or process.

The Radicals believe that the trust company can help the family only if its executives know and care deeply about trusts and benefiting people rather than building net asset values. As they put it: "We need decision-makers who can confidently challenge the natural instinct to grow accumulations in trust rather than focus on how the assets can be used. Their motivations must go beyond fear—fear of loss from taxes, improvident beneficiaries, divorce, creditors . . . bad things happening."

The Traditionalists have a simple response: "Accomplished, smart individuals can do more than one thing at a time, even if one of the things is not their strong suit. We need to rely on people we know, peers and contemporaries who have been tested and succeeded, people who know us well and our past struggles, our values and our ambitions for the future. Besides the distribution function of a trust company is just not that difficult—not 'rocket science'—and can be managed by the staff. Legacies are not built by the Discretionary Decisions Committee."

Dealing with a Naturally Dissolving Community

The Radicals challenge the spoken or unspoken assumptions in family succession. It is all simply mythology. The future will not replicate past experiences.

- By definition "extraordinary" financial success as an entrepreneur or astute investor is indeed extraordinary, not likely to be repeated in each member of each succeeding generation or perhaps in any member of any succeeding generation.
- Many of the potential successors for filling the trustee positions are otherwise engaged in their own endeavors, interests, and lives.
- Unlike the initial building of wealth, the husbanding of inherited money is not a naturally all-consuming activity. Therefore, the generations that follow "the Founder" will not be fully occupied by wealth management alone. They will seek their own opportunities and face different challenges.

The Radicals are not claiming that the wealth does not matter. Most members of succeeding generations will naturally desire independence, and yet the extraordinary success that created the wealth provides a bond of financial security that tends to keep the family connected. The geographic mobility of the family and the mobility and liquidity of its asset base can promote, or dampen, the desire for independence. Cultural and social factors can also influence the desire for independence, but that centrifugal force won't disappear. Accordingly, the Radicals point out that, for better or worse, trust company executives will need to anticipate and accommodate these competing forces and not be taken by surprise or see it as threatening if some family members want to break away, or somehow gain more control, without adverse consequences of course.

That possibility leads to more questions concerning whether to build in some independence (or even an exit ramp):

- Must the trust company therefore allocate decision-making along branch lines (or otherwise) in order to disperse control over distributions and therefore investments?
- Does this require multiple committees, comprised of different individuals whose portfolios of responsibility are the same as to subject matter just with different stakeholders, or even more than one trust company?
- Is there a balance to be struck, and adjusted from time to time, between centralization and independence depending on how many beneficiaries have other outlets for independence such as control over assets not under the trust company umbrella?

The Traditionalists believe, however, that decentralized control is inefficient; and, even by its own standards, a plan to decentralize to accommodate a degree of independence is not practical because there is no suitable substitute for centralization. For example, if the trust company were to disperse control over distributions, it is unrealistic to assume that control can always be divided along family branch lines in order to accomplish that objective. Decision-making along branch lines can be tainted, for example, by poor parent-child relationships within a given branch in ways that affects even the outside advisors who serve on committees. According to the Traditionalists, it is far better to have a centralized distribution and investment committee for all covered trusts, and if necessary, to manage the issue by choosing not to take all assets and all trusts under the trust company umbrella and by providing different choices on the level of service provided to the trusts covered by the trust company, to the extent that trustee services can be modulated.

How the Parable Family Trust Company Was Then Organized, and the Results 20 Years Later

- Because a substantial part of the Parable trust assets consisted of a controlling position in an established family business, the new trust company included a distinct *strategic-planning committee* at the outset that focused exclusively on the future, in order to deal, for example, with potential disruptions to the business and the effect on the trust and beneficiaries. This committee consisted of trust company executives who specialized in strategic business planning. A non-voting observer position was created and filled on a rotating cycle by members of the younger generations, so the trust company wasn't just "my parents' idea." Their mission was to see and plan for possible outcomes that the family business executives could overlook.

- Change did come to the door. Over the next 20 years the business evolved from a traditional manufacturing company producing commodity fasteners for commercial products in the auto industry into a highly technical and specialized manufacturer of customized connections and parts for applications in robotics. While this transformation saved the company, it tended to displace family involvement (because of the need for outside capital and specialized executive talent). The headquarters moved from its historical roots in a single community where the family had substantial social standing to a more suitable location disconnected from the family. At the same time the younger generations dispersed in order to follow their own new career opportunities, and not coincidentally, they enjoyed the greater financial freedom provided by the substantial increase in the cash dividends received by their trusts from the reorganized business.

- The strategic planning committee had anticipated this dissolution of some of the family "glue" and had caused the trust company to create certain committees years ago to keep the trust company relevant to the younger beneficiaries. In particular, the trust company now has a set of small committees that focus on what the beneficiaries need and think they need. Distribution decisions are still centralized in a single committee, but that committee relies heavily on input from the different "beneficiary relationship committees" and is grateful for that resource.
- The beneficiary relationship committees try hard to avoid being paternalistic and controlling, which is especially difficult when there is a breakdown due to neglect in parenting or to beneficiary substance abuse. *The theme is "help and mentoring" but it is a work in process.* The committees are generally comprised of a parent of the beneficiary, as well as a counselor and investment team that serves several committees. The extra expense of bringing in more outside professionals has been offset by reducing the portion of assets for which active manager fees are paid.
- The trust company structure is not only dynamic and proactive in these ways but is *protective of its executives and staff.* While the liability insurance coverage is substantial, the trust company also maintains significant liquid equity capital as a backup. The general plan is to curb unwarranted claims by providing for graduated deterrents (in the trust documents and beneficiary agreements) to discourage baseless claims (rather than just blunt all-or-nothing "no contest clauses" that tend to be waived in negotiations). The beneficiary relationship committees noted above also inhibit the development of frictional relationships between beneficiaries and the trust company.
- Education has become a key operating practice on several levels and in the broadest sense. *The Chief Learning Officer makes sure the trust company educates its executives, not just its trust beneficiaries.* Most importantly the company engages in a *peer review* process every five years to compare its practices with other trust companies, focusing on certain functions each time. Beneficiaries are encouraged to pursue, and indeed are financially supported in pursuing, life-long learning, both for their personal careers and for better understanding wealth management. This has been particularly useful when a beneficiary has been forced to make an entire career change due to industry disruptions.
  - As to wealth management, the goal of trust company management (and the beneficiaries themselves) is to help the beneficiaries of long-term trusts to acquire the skills necessary to manage the trust assets *as if the trusts were going to terminate in their lifetime, in, say, a 10-year horizon.* In that way, the beneficiaries' participation in the ongoing trust is more meaningful, and there is a sense of urgency around beneficiary development.

- Beneficiaries are exposed to the thinking that created the trust company and how adjustments may be made over time. For example, they are encouraged to learn more about the *methods the trust company has used to plan for the future*, a point driven home by the reorganization of the family business

Insights from the Parable Family Trust Company

We trust that our parable has helped to illustrate the benefits of forward planning, engaging new advisors, and adopting a new orientation so that the PTC and the family trusts can be successful in their primary objective of supporting beneficiary development.

This new orientation will also encourage and enable the family to address the larger issue that's always a challenge—how to manage transitions from one generation to the next—because it will promote a culture of forward planning, communication and empathy.

- The "forward" modifier is used here to emphasize that the planning horizon has to be more than a few years, not 100 but maybe a dozen years. The planning skills and acumen that build wealth are not the same as needed for planning on how to pass it on. But creating wealth and passing it on have two things in common: You cannot dictate the result, but you can improve the results by planning. (As Yogi Berra could have put it, "The future is coming. Pick more than one.") Fortunately, there are many resources and methods available today to help the leaders project ahead and be prepared to deal with more than one outcome.[24]
- In this new orientation, the need to develop and apply communication skills becomes a priority, supported by empathy, because of the need to bridge the information and experience gaps between trustee and beneficiary, and thus between generations.[25] Similarly the finance and investment quants in the family need to engage with the artists and other creatives. This is particularly productive when the trusts have a stake in active businesses, either family-controlled or through private equity.[26] It also forces the recognition that not everyone in the family needs to work together. There is a widespread assumption that holding the family together in as many ways as possible is the hallmark of success. If instead you plan for a more realistic result of blending togetherness and independence, that can be achieved and heralded as a success.

- In this process, it is helpful to remember that, as the family moves through time, it is influenced by the larger communities around it, both local and global and in between. Senior generation family members must acknowledge the reality that societal norms change, causing younger family members to develop different values on topics such as climate change or "humane" H.R. policies. More fundamentally, the differences in how people learn, as influenced today by ubiquitous media and technology, can influence how they work together.

The resources and commitment applied to creating and operating a PTC provides the ideal environment for the family to address in this way the full potential of the family trusts by creating and maintaining the best trust management culture. That's not a burden. That's an advantage that will reward the effort with an enduring and productive trustee-beneficiary experience. Time and effort devoted to family governance in this way is well spent. As Patricia Angus explains, "Whether they realize it or not, families already have a way of governing themselves. There are psychological ways of making decisions that are ingrained in the family. And, for the lawyers in the group, it's obvious that they already have governance responsibilities—corporate boards, owners, trustees, beneficiaries, and co-owned assets. The question is whether they want to be intentional—and successful—at it, or not."[27]

Conclusion and Final Thoughts

Deciding whether and how to create and operate a PTC involves a lot of choices. Some of these choices provide the opportunity to the family to address their specific needs, while others are more of a burden than a benefit. In weighing the choices, and in deciding the more fundamental question of whether to create a PTC, it is important to acknowledge that none of the choices for managing and transitioning family wealth are simple, unless the family is prepared to give up substantial control and flexibility (and likely create a structure that has a shorter life before it or will need to be fixed).

In its operating principles and practices, we recommend that the family take advantage of the power of a PTC to encourage their trustee's active engagement with the beneficiaries to help them assess their needs and to support their dreams, rather than be a passive adjudicator. The PTC offers the best environment for re-orienting the family trusts to fulfill this primary purpose, that is, benefiting the beneficiaries.

This recommendation also grows out of observations that the most enduring structures in wealth management follow principles and practices that positively embrace the transition to the next generation rather than follow a negative culture that dwells on fear of loss. Creating a culture based on shared knowledge and values will become even more important in the future as the pace of change accelerates and nothing seems permanent. Every generation is naturally inclined to challenge inherited decisions, and the increasing pace of change in almost every aspect of society will accentuate that instinct. Trusts used to be immune from change, but those days are past. The success in wealth management can only continue over time in a culture that naturally engages the next generation to "buy in" so that the younger family members have had a meaningful voice in where the family and its trusts are headed.

Notes

1. Often called the "Discretionary Decisions Committee" or "Beneficiary Relations Committee."
2. See IRS Notice 2008-63, 2008-2 CB 261.
3. See 17 CFR Section 275.202(a)(11)(G)-1 (2015).
4. Permitted at this time only in Missouri, Nevada, New Hampshire, Ohio, Wyoming, Pennsylvania, and Florida.
5. Federal banking regulators are specifically not mentioned as an alternative regulator because, currently, procuring a national banking association license with related trust powers is very difficult and extremely expensive (e.g., in terms of required regulatory capital, etc.). Accordingly, a national charter is not a practical option for even the most affluent families in the United States and will continue not to be an option until major change occurs at the respective federal agencies.
6. A "bank" is exempt from the requirement to register as an investment adviser with the SEC under the Advisers Act of 1940. For this purpose, a "bank" includes a trust company that is *licensed and examined* by a federal or state regulator. Investment Advisers Act of 1940, 15 USCS Section 80b-2(a)(2) & (11) (2020).
7. Fla. Stat. Section 662.141 (2020).
8. For example, South Dakota requires quarterly meetings in that state for a private trust company created in that state. S.D. Codified Laws Section 51A-6A-15 (2020).
9. That is, the jurisdiction that provides the entity with the legal authority to conduct a PTC trust business.
10. For example, South Dakota treats the unauthorized conduct of a trust business (that is, unauthority provision of fiduciary services) as an unclassified criminal misdemeanor, punishable by fine. S.D. Codified Laws Section 51A-6A-11 (2020).

11. In the context of a marital trust, this distinction between "income" and "principal" is important because often a person's surviving spouse is entitled to all trust accounting "income" but may not be entitled to any principal.

12. The Prudent Investor Rule creates the parameters within which a trustee generally can invest trust assets, for example, can a trustee employ modern portfolio theory and look at the risk and return profile of a portfolio as a whole when investing in particular assets, or must the trustee make a determination on an asset-by-asset basis without regard to the overall portfolio?

13. For example, Florida and South Dakota require one state-resident director: Fla. Stat. 662.125 (2020) and S.D. Codified Laws Section 51A-6A-13 (2020).

14. For example, South Dakota Trust Company.

15. Wyoming historically did not allow reciprocity for trust companies but in recent legislation allows reciprocity for regulated PTCs but interestingly not commercial trust companies. Wyo. Stat. §13-5-219 (2020).

16. For example, New Hampshire, Nevada, Tennessee, and South Dakota.

17. For example, New Hampshire and Tennessee.

18. We also seek states that permit elective community property asset trusts, resulting in 100 percent step up in basis for federal income tax purposes at time of first to die of a married couple, but such laws are currently found only in Alaska and Tennessee.

19. For example, Wyoming.

20. As Mary Duke has commented from her wide experience, "A trust would not exist but for the existence of the beneficiary, and yet so much of the work of trustees has been focused on administration and investing. . . . Many trustees treat distributions as a mechanical, "tick-box" exercise. . . . the work of fiduciaries has become a business. . . . This focus on numbers—by both regulators and business heads—has reinforced the tendency of trustees to focus on things that are easily measured." Correspondence with Mary K. Duke, independent advisor to families, and Founder, High Road Advisors, February 2020.

21. Hartley Goldstone and Kathy Wiseman, *Trustworthy: New Angles on Trusts from Beneficiaries and Trustees* (Denver: Trustscape, LLC, 2012), 45.

22. Ellen Miley Perry, *A Wealth of Possibilities: Navigating, Family, Money, and Legacy*, (Washington, DC: Egremont Press, 2012).

23. This is a composite fictional set of facts and issues that represents the views and experiences of several different families and advisers.

24. We can manage for future risks if we admit our level of ignorance and adjust accordingly. "The core of the illusion is that we believe we understand the past, which implies that the future also should be knowable, but in fact we understand the past less than we believe we do." Daniel Kahneman, *Thinking, Fast and Slow* (Macmillan, 2011). Rafael Ramírez and Angela Wilkinson, *Strategic Reframing: The Oxford Scenario Planning Approach* (Oxford University Press, 2016). Thomas J. Chermack, *Scenario Planning in Organizations: How to Create, Use and Assess Scenarios* (Berrett-Koehler Publishers, 2011).

25. Ellen Miley Perry *A Wealth of Possibilities: Navigating, Family, Money, and Legacy*, (Washington, DC: Egremont Press. 2012), points out: "A common and complicating factor for G2 and G3 is that inheritors hardly ever learn fabulous communication skills from their parents. Why? Because highly successful entrepreneurs are often poor listeners. They are rarely patient, curious about the other's perspective, or sensitive about ensuring that the other person feels heard. (Should I say this more gently, dear reader?)"

26. As a board member of an international PTC put it: "When a family business is an asset of one or more trusts of which the PTC is trustee, the PTC must address the fact that the beneficiaries (i) will have differing levels of knowledge of and interest in the business, financial sophistication, and business acumen; (ii) may not all have had an identical relationship with members of the senior generation, which can affect how members of the younger generation value the retention of the business; and, (iii) may ascribe different weight to the idea of "legacy" or "lineage." Consider having a person whose primary job responsibility is to act as a liaison between the business and the family members. Family members who work "in" the business need to similarly be thoughtful about those who do not."

27. Patricia M. Angus, "Governance for Business-Owning Families: Part II," March 2018, *Trusts & Estates*, p. 47.

Appendix A: Family Office Complexity Assessment

Family Complexity	Complexity Questions	Response
Households Served	How many generations does the family have?	
	How many family branches does the family have?	
	How many households are in the family?	
	How many members are in the family?	
	How many family members does the family office?	
	How many family members have health concerns, disabilities, or major illnesses?	
	How many beneficiaries are there of family trusts?	
Location of Domicile of Households Served	How many countries does the family reside in?	
	How many family members DO NOT have USA citizenship?	
Frequency of Changes within the Family	How frequently are there family changes (i.e., births, deaths, marriages, divorces) (within a three-year timeframe)?	
Professional Services	How many law firms the family use?	
	How many tax or accounting firms are utilized by the family?	
	How many trustees and other independent advisors are utilized by the family?	
Asset Complexity	How many residences does the family own?	
	How many valuable collectibles does the family own?	
	How many watercrafts, planes, cars, etc. does the family own?	
Household Staff	How many full-time staff are hired to manage family property (e.g., real estate, plane, yacht)?	
	How many service providers are utilized to manage family property?	
Education Complexity	How many family members do not have a degree in a business-related field?	
	How many family members require wealth education?	
	Total Family Complexity	

© Tamarind Partners, Inc.

419

Technology Complexity	Complexity Questions	Response
Reporting	How many reports are required monthly?	
	How many reports are required daily?	
	How many reports are required quarterly?	
	How many reports are custom and not system generated?	
	How many different types of reports are required?	
Analytics	Is automated consolidated reports and data required?	
	Is automated aggregation of reports and data required?	
	Is net worth reporting required?	
Data Management	Is eSignature required?	
	Is document sharing required?	
	Is a CRM solution required?	
	Is document archiving required?	
	Is personal asset document management required?	
	Will board meeting minutes need to be captured?	
Accounting	Is operations accounting required vs. investment accounting?	
	Is foundation and grant accounting required?	
	Is payroll accounting required?	
	Is trust accounting required?	
	Is partnership accounting required?	
	Is asset allocation rebalancing automation required?	
	Is BillPay required?	
Automation	Are ticklers and approval solutions required?	
	Is task management required?	
	Are business process workflows required?	
Communication	Is a family calendar required?	
	Is a family message board required?	
	Is a family newsletter required?	
	Is a family online portal required?	
	Is a family email solution required?	

Total Technology Complexity

Wealth Management Complexity	Complexity Questions	Response
Investment Complexity	How many asset classes are within the family investment portfolio?	
	How many assets are within those asset classes?	
	How many alternative assets are within the portfolio?	
	What is the number of internal funds?	
	What is the number of external funds?	
	How many derivatives are there?	
	How many securities transactions occur every month?	
	How many alternatives transactions occur every month?	
	How many direct investment transactions occur every year?	
	How many investment advisors are utilized by the family?	
	How many investment transactions occur in one month?	
	Are financial planning solutions required?	
	Are estate planning solutions required?	
	Are insurance planning solutions required?	
Finance/Accounting/ Tax Complexity	How many bank/custodian accounts does the family have?	
	How many bank/custodian accounts reconcile monthly?	
	How many cash transactions occur in one month?	
	How many distributions occur in one month?	
	How many accounts have distributions?	
	How many tax returns are filed for the family?	
	How many tax jurisdictions are filed for the family?	
	How many employees are dedicated to accounting, tax, finance, compliance, and related administration?	
	How many K-1's does the family create?	
	How many K-1's does the family receive?	

Total Wealth Management Complexity

© Tamarind Partners, Inc.

Operations Complexity	Complexity Questions	Response
Entity Complexity	How many legal entities have been established?	
	How many entities require active management (i.e., Business Partnerships, Trusts that have annual distributions)?	
	How many non-investment or trust entities have been established (i.e., Operating or Private Foundations, Farming Operations)?	
	How many entities include employees?	
	How many entities include family?	
	How many entitles include non-family members who have ownership?	
	How many entitles are passive pass-through?	
	How many locations are the entities located?	
	How many entities do not have an operating budget?	
	How many entities do not have a multi-year business plan?	
Family Office Services	How many services will be required by the family?	
	How many service providers are utilized by the family office?	
	How many services will be outsourced or performed by a family business?	
	What is the number of full-time family office staff?	
Lifestyle Management Complexity	How many family members require concierge services?	
	How many family members require travel services including using private aviation?	
	Total Operations Complexity	
	Total Family Office Complexity Score	

© Tamarind Partners, Inc.

Appendix B: Family Office Technology Segments

Accounting

- General ledger
- Operational accounting
- Trusts
- Philanthropy
- Accounts payables and receivables
- Partnership accounting
- Bill pay and eCheck
- Payroll
- Investment accounting
- Illiquid assets
- Capital calls and cash disbursements

Reporting

- Illiquid assets
- Analytics
- Graphical
- Aggregation by family member, business, and family
- Ad-hoc and templates
- Net worth
- Liquidity
- Financials

Data Management

- Where is the data hosted
- CRM
- Version control
- Personal assets
- Document linking to assets and entity
- User data to be stored
- Integrate with other 3rd party software - CRM, accounting, email, etc.
- Type of server used
- File types that can be uploaded
- Document storage
- How is the data stored
- Data audit logs
- Integrations with financial institutions
  - Manual and automated feeds
  - Timing of automatic feeds (daily, monthly, real time)

Analytics

- Financial projections
- Budgeting
- Portfolio allocation monitoring
- Investment management fees monitoring
- Financial planning
- Estate planning
- Financial data consolidation
- Provide capital gains/losses
- Operational planning

(Continued)

Security

- Access to the data
- Single sign-on
- Are employees required to sign confidentiality agreements

- Security policy
- Two-factor sign-on
- Security protocols and certifications
- Encryption

System Operations

- Systems redundancy and backup
- Alerts and ticklers
- Investment types system can manage
- Administrative system audits
- eSignature
- List of approved 3rd party add-ons
- Disaster recovery plan

- Type of entities system can manage
- Workflows
- Trading platform for investments
- Email, calendar, and/or message board
- Tax preparation
- Technologies used within the software

Concierge

- Travel planning
- Household employee management
- Art and collectibles

- Property management
- Aircraft and yacht management

User Interface

- Dashboards
- Drill-down capabilities

- Mobile device access

© Tamarind Partners, Inc.

About the Author

Kirby Rosplock is a founder of consulting firm Tamarind Partners, Inc., an innovator, an advisor, an author, and a speaker in the family business and family office domains. As evidenced by Tamarind Partners' two high honors, named 2019 Best Family Office Management Consultancy and Best Family Wealth Counseling by the Family Wealth Report, the firm provides leading-edge insights, knowledge, and solutions through its research and multidisciplinary consulting approach to families, advisors, and institutions connected to the family office market.

Kirby and her husband, John, founded Tamarind Learning, Inc., a family wealth education and online learning firm that provides foundational applied knowledge for beneficiaries, wealth inheritors, family members, their advisors, and executives. Tamarind Learning prepares the next generation with engaging, expert family wealth education and provides options from customizable programs for individuals and families to cohort learning, self-paced online learning, and more. To learn more, visit TamarindLearning.com.

Born into a complex enterprising family, Kirby understands firsthand what it is to be a beneficial owner, inheritor, fiduciary, and family operator. For more than 20 years, she has worked in the world of investing, finance, family wealth, and family business. Given her experiences on both sides of the table, Kirby is passionate about helping families of wealth find the right solutions for their bespoke needs. In doing so, she has instilled unbiased, research-based methods into the firm's advisory approach and fee-based compensation model.

Kirby's ability to combine her practical life experiences with her passions for research and client advisory and her love of writing has culminated in many articles, research studies, and books. She was the editor of the private-label book, *A Family's Guide to Wealth: Insights from Thought Leaders and Pioneers,* and author of the first edition of *The Complete Family Office Handbook* and *The Complete Direct Investing Handbook.* The first edition of *The Complete Family Office Handbook* was translated into Chinese in 2016.

In 2018, she contributed chapters to *Family Offices: The STEP Handbook for Advisers, Second Edition,* and *Wealth of Wisdom: Top 50 Questions Wealthy Families Ask.* She has also contributed book chapters to *Handbook of Research on Entrepreneurs' Engagement in Philanthropy, Perspectives,* and *The Landscape of Family Business.* In addition to books, Kirby has written numerous articles, bylines, and blogs. To read her blog, visit https://tamarindpartners.com/thought-leadership/blog/.

Kirby has received many honors including the prestigious Family Wealth Industry Thought Leadership award in 2018 from the Family Wealth Alliance, which has been awarded only two times in the last decade. In 2018, she also received the Family Firm Institute's (FFI) Richard Beckhard Practice award for lifetime achievement and outstanding contributions to the field of family business. Earlier honors include her recognition as one of twenty-five "Stars" of Family Dynamics by RayLign Advisors, a Family Owned Business Institute (FOBI) Research Grant Award in 2011, and second place at the Family Enterprise Research Conference in 2010.

She earned her undergraduate degree with honors from Middlebury College, an MBA from Marquette University, and a PhD in Organizational Systems from Saybrook University. Her prior experiences range from living and working abroad for an international bipartisan American nonprofit, to working in the securities industry for a broker-dealer, to working for more than a decade in a prominent multi-family office as the head of Research and Development in its Innovation and Learning Center. She and her husband have also owned, operated, and invested in several businesses and partnerships and are active philanthropically in their local community.

Kirby is Dean of Family Office at the Purposeful Planning Institute, a Fellow and Family Governance Faculty of the FFI GEN Program; co-trustee of the Harbeck Family Foundation; and board member of her family's business. She currently serves on the advisory board of Merton Venture Philanthropy and board of directors of Hope Trust. She is married with two daughters and enjoys the symphony, traveling, playing golf and tennis.

About the Contributors

Warner King Babcock is the CEO and founder of the NYC Family Enterprise Center. Previously he advised family enterprises, family members, and family offices through AM Private Enterprises, AM Private Investments, and AM Corporate Strategy and Development beginning in 1987. He has been an industry thought leader on family banks, as well as advising family members on creating new ventures and making direct private investments, all based on their personal interests and preferences. Earlier in his career, he was the CEO of a family business, board member, member of a family council, and trustee controlling family businesses.

David S. Guin, leader of Withers Bergman LLP's commercial practice group, is a nationally recognized thought leader on regulatory and compliance issues for family enterprises and family offices. He advises high net worth domestic and international individuals, families, family offices and their advisers about their obligations under US securities laws, including the acquisition and disposition of public and private securities, beneficial ownership reporting obligations, and the applicability of the Investment Advisers Act, Investment Company Act and Commodity Exchange Act to their investment activities. David also advises investment advisers, fund managers, and family offices on governance, structuring, commercial, and compliance issues.

Barbara R Hauser, with more than 30 years of experience with wealthy families, is sought after for creating flexible family offices; leading families through a tailored governance process; organizing their global assets; and bringing in the next generation. With clients in the United States, Europe, Asia, and the Gulf Region, she is a frequent speaker and published author. She is the Editor-in-Chief of *The International Family Offices Journal* and is on the Advisory Board of the Family Office Association, ValueWorks (Switzerland), and the Family Wealth Library, and is a Director Emeritus of the Pitcairn family office. She is the author of *International Estate Planning, International Family*

Governance, Mommy Are We Rich?, Never Ask Where You Are and *Saudi-Girl Barbara,* and is a co-author of *Setting Up Your Family Office* and advisory editor of Trusts in Prime Jurisdictions and Advising the Wealthy Client. A graduate of Wellesley College and Penn Law School, she had the honor of clerking at the US Supreme Court. See www.brhauser.com.

Rob Kaufold is the President and Chief Risk Officer of Cauldera, LLC, a single-family office located in Boulder, Colorado. As part of this role, Rob also serves as the Executive Director of the Hemera Foundation, the family's private foundation. Since 2006 Rob has helped family offices and family philanthropies implement efficient strategies that promote the family's values, protect their members, and simplify data management so to enhance communication and decision-making within the family system. Rob is a New York CPA, holds a BS in Accounting from Providence College, and will complete his Master's in Philanthropic Studies from the Lilly School of Philanthropy at IUPUI in December 2020. He lives in Broomfield, Colorado, with his wife, Erin, and his two daughters, Emily and Molly.

William J. Kambas, a partner in Withers Bergman LLP's Private Client and Tax Group, advises family and business-owning clients worldwide on the development of integrated tax planning, governance, and business succession strategies. An integral part of Bill's practice involves working with families and family enterprises and/or their family offices on the formation, management, and periodic evaluation of multinational, multigenerational centralized control structures, which often include the use of corporations, partnerships, limited liability companies, and/or trusts as well as on the application of tax treaties. He regularly speaks and writes on topics relating to business and investment ownership structures.

Don Kozusko is a partner at Kozusko Harris Duncan, where he counsels international and domestic entrepreneurs, investors, philanthropists, and privately-held businesses in the tax and legal issues relating to their investments, business activities, estate planning, and charitable endeavors. He has also served as a mediator and an advocate in disputes involving the control of privately-owned businesses, investment ventures, and family trusts. He has recently focused his practice on helping families resolve major disputes or minimize future conflicts, drawing on not only his litigation experience but his interest in studying how to deal with difficult personalities and how to employ scenario planning.

Miles C. Padgett, JD and is a partner at Kozusko Harris Duncan in the firm's Washington, D.C., office. Miles focuses on tax, business, and regulatory planning for family offices and their family member clients, tax planning for managers of private equity and other investment funds, and the chartering and management of private and retail trust companies for highly successful, strategic families and domestic and international financial institutions. Miles routinely writes and speaks on the topics of family governance, wealth management, and structuring and regulatory matters. In addition to being a lawyer, Miles spent over five years as an investment consultant focusing on asset allocation and manager search and selection.

John Rosplock is the COO and CFO for Tamarind Partners, Inc. and co-founder of Tamarind Learning. He manages the operations and finances for both companies. An experienced business leader, visionary, and entrepreneur, John's background is multifaceted, with expertise in real estate, finance, accounting, tax, IT, and project management. John's career started at a third-generation family business working more than a decade as operations manager. John worked for Florida Power and Light and Northwestern Mutual, leading and supporting multimillion-dollar projects. John earned his undergraduate business degree from the University of Wisconsinat Milwaukee and an MBA from Florida Atlantic University. John served in the Marine Corps and enjoys playing golf, soccer, and tennis with his family. See www.TamarindPartners.com and www.TamarindLearning.com.

Ivan A. Sacks, a Partner of Withers Bergman LLP, provides clients with innovative domestic and international tax, trust, and estate planning solutions, recognizing that comprehensive planning is a highly personal process, with individual circumstances demanding flexible, tailored solutions. He counsels leading families, fiduciaries, and entrepreneurs worldwide on a wide range of international private client matters relating to closely held business interests, family offices, foundations, trusts, and estates as well as developing comprehensive risk management, governance, and succession solutions. He is an active member of several bar and professional associations and speaks frequently on topics related to international wealth planning.

Index

Page references followed by f indicate an illustrated figure; followed by t indicate a table.